SHELLEY'S RELIGION

SHELLEY'S RELIGION

ELLSWORTH BARNARD

NEW YORK
RUSSELL & RUSSELL · INC
1964

COPYRIGHT, 1937, BY THE UNIVERSITY OF MINNESOTA
COPYRIGHT, 1964, BY ELLSWORTH BARNARD
REISSUED, 1964, BY RUSSELL & RUSSELL, INC.
BY ARRANGEMENT WITH THE UNIVERSITY OF MINNESOTA PRESS
L. C. CATALOG CARD NO: 64—18594

PRINTED IN THE UNITED STATES OF AMERICA

To those of my former students at Massachusetts State College who will understand the wish that in their hearts, as in Shelley's, the flame of rebellion against the world of *things* may never die.

Alas! for Liberty!
If numbers, wealth, or unfulfilling years,
    Or fate, can quell the free!
        Alas! for Virtue, when
Torments, or contumely, or the sneers
        Of erring judging men
    Can break the heart where it abides.
Alas! if Love, whose smile makes this obscure
        world splendid,
    Can change with its false times and tides,
        Like hope and terror,—
            Alas for Love!
And Truth, who wanderest lone and unbefriended,
If thou canst veil thy lie-consuming mirror
    Before the dazzled eyes of Error,
    Alas for thee! Image of the Above.

                                        Hellas

ACKNOWLEDGMENTS

The present study was written as a doctoral dissertation at the University of Minnesota, and I should like to express here my gratitude, first, to the group committee for allowing me to choose so perilous a subject, and second, to my particular thesis committee for permitting me to treat it essentially in my own way. Especially to Professor Joseph Warren Beach, who supervised the thesis, and to Professors Douglas Bush and Alburey Castell I am grateful not only for a number of suggestions as to matter and manner, which I have followed in giving the work its final form, but even more for their tolerance of opinions and attitudes which were in many cases widely different from theirs. It would be an ill return not to attempt to free them from responsibility for whatever in this work may be judged by the reader to be deserving of blame.

I wish also to acknowledge my real indebtedness to those critics who are so often referred to hereafter as "Shelley's detractors"; first, for providing a contrast which cannot but add definiteness and lucidity to the presentation of my own opinions; and again, for inciting me on some occasions to what I hope will not be regarded as an excessive animation of style, which the mere conviction of my own rightness would not (though perhaps it ought to) have been able to inspire. And I should like to soften as far as may be the asperities of literary controversy by adding that among my closest friends there are those whose opinions concerning Shelley differ violently and irreconcilably from mine, and that I hope the severity of my strictures upon what seem to me unjust estimates of Shelley's work and character will not be taken in general as reflecting personally on the critics by whom they have been voiced.

Deeper, of course, is my debt to Shelley's true admirers. I cannot here name them all, but I cannot refrain from mentioning two, both of the generation just passed away: one an American critic and man of letters, the other a British philosopher. The writings of George Edward Woodberry and Francis Herbert Bradley (although the latter wrote no formal criticism of Shelley's work) have beyond all others illuminated for me the meaning which always lies beneath the music of the poet's words, and, more than this, have confirmed my conviction that that meaning has profound significance for religion and the spiritual life.

Still one more obligation I must record, deeper than any of these: to Ray E. Torrey, Professor of Botany at Massachusetts State College. Whatever real value this study may have springs from its devotion, however wavering, to that Research Magnificent whose glory he first unveiled to my young eyes and to which his own life has been so passionately dedicated.

Not less real, though on a different level, is my indebtedness to the editors of the University of Minnesota Press. With whatever distaste an author may regard the vast number of routine details incident to the publication of his work, still the drudgery of attending to them (especially burdensome in the case of such a work as this) must fall upon some one; and my sincerest thanks are due to the editors for their infinitely painstaking efforts to bring the work as near as possible to formal perfection and to eliminate all but the irreducible minimum of error.

CONTENTS

SHELLEY'S RELIGION

ERRATA

p. 7, *l.* 13 *for* withdrawn *read* undrawn

p. 48, *l.* 20 *for* nine *read* seven

p. 92, *l.* 31 *for* received *read* receive

p. 120, *l.* 6 *for* tryants *read* tyrants

p. 124, *n.* 82 for Cf. note 74 *read* Cf. note 75

p. 131, *n.* 7, *l.* 10 *for* make *read* makes

p. 192, *l.* 2 *for* of patronizing *read* in patronizing

p. 204, *l.* 37 *add punctuation to read* fill . . .

p. 266, *l.* 14 *for* the going out *read* a going out

p. 275, *l.* 2 of *n.* 7 *for* Letters, I *read* Letters, II

p. 290, *n.* 43 *for Humanism and read Humanism in*

p. 310, Sec. III, item 1 under Marjory A. Bald
   for Contemporary Review, CXXI *read* CXXXI

p. 312, entry following Archibald T. Strong (date)
   for 1927 *read* 1921

p. 313, first item in Sec. IV *for* Beaven *read* Beavan

CHAPTER I

INTRODUCTION

IN A NOTE to his first long poem, *Queen Mab*, Shelley defines religion as "the perception of the relation in which we stand to the principle of the universe." [1] In *A Defence of Poetry*, written in 1821, a year before his death, he speaks of "that partial apprehension of the agencies of the invisible world which is called religion." [2] In *Julian and Maddalo*, written in 1818, there is an implicit definition in the statement that

> those who suffer with their suffering kind
> Yet feel their faith, religion. [3]

According to these utterances, religion is thought of as concerned with man's relation to the universe, as recognizing that the material world is subject to the influence of spiritual powers, and as arising from man's experience of suffering, which implies the existence in his universe of some discordant element or force. Its chief aim is therefore the removal or resolution of this discord; and in its attempt to realize this aim, it is led to seek knowledge of the two worlds, the visible and the invisible, in which man lives — hoping from this knowledge to learn the source of his suffering, the state of being (the realization of which is assumed to be the final end or purpose of his life) in which that suffering shall cease to exist,

[1] Note on VI, l. 198. *Complete Poetical Works of Percy Bysshe Shelley*, edited by Thomas Hutchinson with introduction and notes by Benjamin P. Kurtz (Oxford University Press, 1933), p. 811. All quotations from Shelley's poems or prefaces follow the text of this edition unless otherwise noted. It will be referred to hereafter as "Hutchinson." Shelley's aim in this note, of course, is to *attack* religion. He continues, "But if the principle of the universe be not an organic being, the model and prototype of man, the relation between it and human beings is absolutely none." *Queen Mab* itself, however, refutes this extravagant statement, and Shelley soon repudiated it completely.

[2] *Shelley's Literary and Philosophical Criticism*, edited with an introduction by John Shawcross (London, 1909), p. 124. This work will hereafter be referred to as "Shawcross."

[3] Ll. 190–91.

and the means by which that state of being is attainable. The
purpose of this study is to present the final position of Shelley's
mind in regard to each of these problems, and to indicate in some
degree the course of its development.

This view of religion evidently limits it very nearly to theology.
Religion as a historical fact Shelley regarded as largely a series of
perversions and abuses, in which the orthodox faith had always
either engaged in persecution and terrorism on its own account, or
been a willing instrument in the hands of political oppression; and
had always been, in any case, the most powerful factor in the preservation of social injustice of every kind. As for ritual and dogma,
they had no place whatever in Shelley's scheme of things. He was
intensely individualistic — no less than Blake "born into the church
of rebels"—and he repudiated formalism and authoritarianism of
every kind. For him religion was a question solely of the relation
between the individual and whatever "agencies of the invisible
world" he might believe in and worship. "Where two or three
are gathered together, the devil is among them";[4] thus he wrote
to his wife not long before his death; and the statement is far
from being intended as a jest. It is elaborated with almost fierce
earnestness in a late fragment *On the Doctrines of Christ.*

Let us beware, if we love liberty and truth, if we loathe tyranny and
imposture, if, imperfect ourselves, we still aspire to that freedom of
internal purity, and cherish the elevated hope that mankind may not be
everlastingly condemned to the bondage of their own passions and the
passions of their fellow beings, let us beware. An established religion
returns to death-like apathy the sublimest ebullitions of most exalted
genius, and the spirit-stirring truths of a mind inflamed with a desire
to benefit mankind.[5]

In his youthful crusade to free the Irish he fervently asks: "Can
there be worse slavery than the depending for the safety of your
soul on the will of another man?"[6] And this attitude he never

[4] *Letters of Percy Bysshe Shelley*, edited by Roger Ingpen (2 vols., London,
1914), II, 905. This work will be referred to hereafter as *Letters.*
[5] *Shelley's Complete Works*, Julian Edition, edited by Roger Ingpen and Walter
E. Peck (10 vols., London, 1926–30), VII, 145–46. This edition will hereafter
be referred to as *Complete Works.*
[6] "Address to the Irish People," *Shelley's Prose Works*, edited by Richard Herne
Shepherd (2 vols., London, 1888), I, 228. This edition will hereafter be referred
to as *Prose Works.*

abandons. He is the essential Protestant; and he follows the Protestant principle of individualism to its logical end in the denial of the need, in religion, of any organization whatever.

Saying no more at present as to what constitutes religion, I pass to a justification of "Shelley's Religion" as the subject of a study that is supposed to make an original contribution to knowledge. I do not mean, of course, that the topic *in itself* needs to be defended. Everyone who knows Shelley's work knows that he had a religion — unless religion is to be limited to some kind of religious *orthodoxy*. I mean that the topic may be thought to have been adequately treated already. In view of the vast amount of criticism, much of it controversial, of which Shelley and his writings have been the nominal subjects, it would at first glance seem unlikely, in regard to Shelley's thought, that anything worth saying should yet remain unsaid. It is of course true that, even among educated people, misconceptions of his beliefs and teachings are still prevalent; but this state of affairs may be attributed to the uncritical acceptance of venerable myths, in ignorance of the fact that these, for the most part, have been long since exploded. There are, in fact, already in existence a number of admirable expositions of Shelley's philosophical and religious beliefs, some of which aim at covering nearly the same ground as the present study; and that these have not yet secured for him general recognition as one of the keenest and soundest thinkers among English poets only bears witness to the extraordinary vigor with which error always flourishes amid unregenerate humanity.

Let me say at once, then, that the present work claims to advance no great number of important ideas that are absolutely new. It records no striking discovery, it expounds no startling theory, it pretends to render accessible no yet unscaled intellectual vantage point. But, on the other hand, there are certain grounds for hoping that it may not be altogether without value. And, first, I believe that it is the most thorough treatment which Shelley's religious ideas have ever received. It is not exhaustive, but it comes nearer to being so than any other work with which I am familiar. In this respect, indeed, there are doubtless many critics who will consider it only too successful; and I am myself aware that thorough-

ness is in itself no virtue, and that what is not worth doing at all
is only the more justly damnable for being done thoroughly. But
Shelley criticism can as yet scarcely be said to have suffered from
an excess of conscientiousness in the use of the poet's words to
support the critics' theories. Too often, as in Arnold's notorious
essay, a mere nebulous sentiment, supported by a few seemingly
apt quotations, has been received as a reasoned and intelligent judgment. I do not suppose that this study will change the opinion of
any anti-Shelleyan who may happen to read it. But a serious refutation of its main contentions will demand a more solid knowledge
of Shelley's work and a higher degree of ingenuity than is usually
to be met with among the poet's detractors.[7] And still, it might

[7] A case in point is the most recent expression, by any notable critic, of an active
antipathy toward Shelley and his poetry. Mr. T. S. Eliot, in an essay on "Shelley
and Keats" contained in his recent book *The Use of Poetry and the Use of
Criticism*, writes as follows: "But good lines among bad can never give more
than a regretful pleasure. In reading *Epipsychidion* I am thoroughly gravelled by
lines like:

> True love in this differs from dross or clay,
> That to divide is not to take away . . .
> I never was attached to that great sect
> Whose doctrine is, that each one should select
> Out of the crowd, a mistress or a friend
> And all the rest, though fair and wise, commend
> To cold oblivion . . .

so that when I come, a few lines later, upon a lovely image like:

> A vision like incarnate April, warning
> With smiles and tears, Frost the anatomy
> Into his summer grave,

I am as much shocked by finding it in such indifferent company as pleased by finding it at all." (Pages 83–84.) Anyone who has respect for accuracy in critical
writing, whether he admires Shelley's poetry or not, will be as much shocked as
Mr. Eliot by the version which is here given of *Epipsychidion*. Who would guess
that the last five lines of the first quotation actually *precede* the first two by some
ten lines? Or that the "lovely image" which follows "a few lines later" does in
fact precede by thirty lines the first of the previous quotations? Or that the first line
which the critic quotes ends, as written by Shelley, with the words "gold and
clay" — a change which makes a vast difference both in meaning and music?
Perhaps the errors do not invalidate Mr. Eliot's contention (assuming that it has
any validity, even as it stands). But surely there is something wrong in this complete mangling of one of Shelley's most famous poems. Surely such reckless misquo-
tation indicates a degree of unfamiliarity with the poet's work which must render
worthless the critic's verdict. One may even suspect Mr. Eliot's pronouncements
that Shelley was "humorless, pedantic, self-centered, and sometimes almost a blackguard," and that "his letters are insufferably dull" (page 80), to be based on
something other than knowledge. Mr. Eliot is entitled to his prejudice and is to be
admired for his frankness; but prejudice based upon ignorance ought hardly to

easily have been made much more detailed. There are many relevant passages in Shelley's writings which it would have been a pleasure to dwell on, but which I have been forced to pass over entirely or touch upon only lightly, lest the discussion should end by being far too cumbrous. And, after all, it is simply impossible to exhaust the store of ideas which a poet of Shelley's insight inevitably puts into his work. Shelley's splendid words in reference to Dante may be applied to his own best poetry:

His very words are instinct with spirit; each is as a spark, a burning atom of inextinguishable thought; and many yet lie covered in the ashes of their birth, and pregnant with a lightning which has yet found no conductor. All high poetry is infinite; it is as the first acorn, which contained all oaks potentially. Veil after veil may be withdrawn, and the inmost naked beauty of the meaning never exposed. A great poem is a fountain for ever overflowing with the waters of wisdom and delight; and after one person and one age has exhausted all its divine effluence which their peculiar relations enable them to share, another and yet another succeeds, and new relations are ever developed, the source of an unforeseen and an unconceived delight.[8]

Again, the present study aims at bringing known facts and recognized opinions into new relations with each other, and thereby giving them fresh significance. Scattered fragments of thought, when united in an ordered and more or less harmonious whole, often appear far other than in their separate state. A single vital principle of control may animate inert and seemingly incoherent materials, and like Amphion's lyre, cause them to take their places in a structure of harmony and beauty, standing where most men had hitherto seen only a jumble of ruins. I do not undertake to say, of course, how far I have been successful. Similar syntheses

be condoned in a professional critic. If he had really *studied* Shelley's life and writings, he would perhaps have refrained from passing so harsh a judgment. He might even have come to see (though this is doubtful) that to no man more justly than to Shelley could his fine words concerning Charles Eliot Norton be applied: "To do the useful thing, to say the courageous thing, to contemplate the beautiful thing: that is enough for one man's life." (Page 3.) There may be some value, it seems, in thoroughness.

[8] *A Defence of Poetry*, in Shawcross, pp. 147–48. The thought of this passage is very close to Newman's theory of development in Christian doctrine; and this is not surprising, since (as will appear in the final chapter of this study) no Christian ever believed more literally in the divine inspiration of Scripture than Shelley in the divine origin of great poetry.

have been attempted before; never, I feel, with complete success. Moreover, there is always the danger that only a specious unity will be achieved, at the cost of slighting some important element or aspect of the poet's work. Critical history shows the utter folly of trying to fit the life and the thought of any great man into a perfectly consistent pattern or system. It cannot be done; and a thesis, by the fact of its being a thesis, confesses to being partial. In Shelley's case, however, many of the apparent contradictions can be removed by a study of the *development* of his ideas. It has been too much the habit of critics carelessly to assume that the poet's views always remained essentially the same as they were at the time he wrote *Queen Mab* — a supposition that is absurd on the face of it. Shelley lived thirty years; and we are asked to believe that during the last ten of those years he learned nothing and changed his views on no important subject. As a matter of fact, his writings give evidence, to the very end, of constant growth in intellectual no less than artistic power, and in moral and religious insight. The course of this growth, in regard to each of his important religious ideas, is indicated in the present study.[9] But even if the attempt to apply to an author's work some unifying principle fails to be altogether successful, nevertheless, if done with sincerity by a person of some intelligence, it can scarcely fail to shed new light upon the subject, and contribute to a more accurate critical estimate.

In the third place, so detailed an examination of Shelley's work as is here undertaken will inevitably call attention to some significant passages that have been previously overlooked, and offer helpful interpretations of others, of which the meaning has hitherto remained obscure. In the case of some poets, it is true, this result would hardly be worth while; but I am quite certain that Shelley's verse is thronged with lines which, passed over by the casual reader as "mere poetry," would be discovered, by a sharp enough scrutiny, to contain profound ideas. And whoever has pondered upon the

[9] Two recent works, *The Pursuit of Death*, by Benjamin P. Kurtz (Oxford University Press, 1933), and *Desire and Restraint in Shelley* (Duke University Press, 1931), by Floyd Stovall, which I shall have occasion to refer to below, seek to establish a principle of development in Shelley's life and work. But each, in my opinion, concerns itself with a development which is simply not there. Both works, however, contain valuable incidental criticism.

inordinate expenditure of labor upon the text of Shakespeare, where often nothing of importance is at stake, will hardly begrudge the careful study of the work of a poet who was something more than a master of words and meter and dramatic artifice.

The present study is also to some extent original in being, avowedly, not only an exposition of Shelley's religious beliefs, but also a defense of them — implicit where not explicit. The views which I here present, I for the most part share. I believe that they have intrinsic value, and deserve the serious attention of any person who cares for the aims and ideals of the spiritual life. If I thought otherwise, I should consider Shelley a poet of the second rank, and my present task not worth doing. Nor do I feel that this attitude, although doubtless rare in the writers of doctoral dissertations, calls for any apology. If Shelley had been the fool that many critics still think him, I do not see why anybody should care what his beliefs were.

Nor am I willing to admit — and here, perhaps, is the crux of the matter — that when the fact is once stated, its value automatically becomes clear: that when Shelley's ideas have been reduced to a number of intelligible propositions, their truth or falsity, their worth or worthlessness, is immediately evident. Perhaps I lack the true scholar's faith in the power of truth. I may be rebuked, as Shelley was by Godwin, for not being willing to stand aside and let truth and reason triumph in their own good time. But for myself, a truth worth finding is a truth worth fighting for; as Arnold said that the aim of "culture" was not merely to *know* reason and the will of God, but to make reason and the will of God *prevail*. And if anyone retorts that Arnold or Shelley or I may fall into the error of identifying reason and the will of God with our conception of what they ought to be, I am willing to give him my cloak along with my coat, and go with him not one mile, but twain; answering that not only Arnold and Shelley and I may, but everybody in reality does and must fall into the same error, if an error it be — everybody, that is, who ventures upon any kind of judgment. This inevitable risk of error is the price a man must pay for being an autonomous and responsible individual.

And not only do all judgments of value necessarily involve such a risk, but so — in the interpretation of poetry, at least — do most judgments of fact. The controversy concerning Shelley's philosophical ideas rests not only on disagreement as to what value those ideas have, but also on disparity of opinion as to what those ideas are. The truth of this statement will be made abundantly clear in the following chapters. And I must add that I do not see how these disagreements can ever be resolved. Neither this study nor any other does or can prove beyond all doubt that Shelley believed one thing rather than its opposite.

Perhaps this sounds like intellectual nihilism: perhaps it is. But I cannot help it. Every conclusion is based upon premises; and although these may be themselves the conclusions of other premises, yet at last we come to certain first principles, which must be assumed, and which cannot be argued about. As Newman says, "Without assumptions, nobody can prove anything about anything." [10] Now, the premises upon which the conclusions of this or any similar study must rest are the meanings which are to be attached to certain passages in Shelley's writings. But these meanings are often far from self-evident. They are themselves matters of argument, and to demonstrate that any particular meaning of a passage is *the* meaning seems in many cases to be quite impossible. In the interpretation of one passage, we must refer to others, which are themselves of doubtful meaning. And presently we are driven outside the writings themselves, to see if the life of the writer will afford us any clue. But here the situation is still worse. We do not know, and I suppose cannot know, the really important facts about a person's life. As Shelley himself asks, "Who can know them but the actors?" [11] In his own life, the "facts" concerning his unhappy separation from Harriet are not and never will be known. And if we turn from the "facts" of a person's life to the comments of his contemporaries, the "evidence" is still more precarious. Even the accounts of Shelley written by some of his professed friends are nearly as full of untruths (for it is much easier to detect falsehood than to discover truth) as the notoriously unscrupulous attacks of

[10] *A Grammar of Assent*, p. 410.
[11] *Letters*, II, 648.

the writers in the reviews. And so we have to turn back to his writings to seek the key to his life and character and beliefs, and move in a circle from which there is no escape. When we know all the "facts" that it is possible to know, we can still never be sure that we are absolutely correct in the opinions we form as to what a man's character was, and what his writings mean.

I therefore assert, without apology, that before this thesis can be fairly judged, I must be granted certain assumptions. If what follows is consistent with these, nothing more can be reasonably demanded. And the chief assumption upon which this study is based is that Shelley possessed a brilliant intellect and a noble character. Begin with the assumption that Shelley was shallow and selfish, a weakling or a profligate, "pedantic, self-centered, and sometimes almost a blackguard," and nothing is easier than to "prove" — by judicious selection and interpretation — that his views are exactly what one would expect from a person of such character. And I know of no author who has ever lived of whom the same might not be said.[12]

Nor is this situation really surprising. We may say that language is our only means of communication, but this does not alter the fact that it is an imperfect and inadequate one, especially in the expression of emotion and of abstract ideas, and more especially still in the expression of emotions and ideas such as are connected with those ultimate problems of life that religion involves. Anyone who has tried to express his views concerning these subjects must sympathize to some extent with Shelley's despairing exclamation in a footnote to his essay *On Love:* "These words are ineffectual and metaphorical. Most words are so — No help!"[13] Any statement that will not admit of more than one interpretation — at least

[12] It may be objected by those who think the scientific method can be applied to the study of literature that the question of Shelley's character is irrelevant. But to me it seems self-evident that our interpretation of what Shelley said depends necessarily upon our conception of what he was. Moreover, as I have already intimated, I am not interested merely in what Shelley's beliefs were, but in what value those beliefs have — for me and for others; and this is a question which cannot be answered without reference to his character. For if a man's religious beliefs have no influence upon his life and character, then I deny that they ought to be called religious. In regard to questions of religion, at least, it can be truly said of a man that "as he thinketh in his heart, so is he." (Proverbs 23 : 7.)

[13] Shawcross, p. 44.

in the field of experience with which we are here concerned — must be so nearly self-evident that there is no need to state it at all. How can we be sure of what anyone else believes? Nay, is it not often difficult to make clear to ourselves what our own beliefs on ultimate questions are, to say nothing of giving them a verbal expression that can be understood and cannot be mistaken by other persons — who have perhaps never even known the experience in which those beliefs had their origin?

It will be protested that all this makes impossible any standards of judgment in a study of this kind. Precisely. And if anyone can show that such standards have ever in fact existed, or that the interpretation and evaluation of literature has ever been anything more than the expression of individual likes and dislikes, I shall be willing to retract. But experience forces me to the conclusion that all literary comment or criticism, whether it be a matter of judgment or interpretation, must answer to F. H. Bradley's description of metaphysics: "The finding of bad reasons for what we believe on instinct." But the same philosopher adds that "to find those reasons is no less an instinct." And so literary studies continue to be written by many persons who naïvely assume that their particular prejudices are universal truths, and can be proved to be so; as well as by a few who are rational enough to see that their judgments necessarily contain an irrational element, and who are honest enough to say: "Here is what I believe; it makes no pretensions to absolute truth; take it or leave it."

There is, to be sure, much talk about "impartial" interpretation. But impartiality evidently means one of two things — either indifference or honesty. If it means indifference, I suppose there are few criticisms which are impartial — else why should they be written at all? And if there really are such, they obviously can be of but little value. If, on the other hand, impartiality means honesty — that is, the refusal deliberately to suppress or distort any evidence that seems to weaken one's own argument — then, certainly, it is the cardinal virtue of criticism. But this is essentially a moral virtue, involving a way of living and not merely a rule of writing; and I do not see any particular use in talking about it. As a matter of fact, the strongest professions of impartiality are usually followed by what seem to me the most flagrant perversions of an author's meaning. Probably most of these critics do not intentionally falsify the evidence (although one wonders); and perhaps they do not falsify it at all, and it is I who am deceiving myself. But it would be more honest, in any case, not to try to impose on the reader by a pretense of infallibility.

The point of this whole discussion is that I am willing to admit that my own interpretation and evaluation of Shelley's religious thought are liable to error, for the sake of demonstrating that the same is true of those interpretations and evaluations by which my own are opposed or contradicted; so that the reader will not be awed by the baseless claims of omniscience so often made or implied by Shelley's critics, but will remain free to form his own opinion. It is very difficult to overcome the feeling that whatever has got into print must contain some truth; but the resolute suppression of this feeling, together with the determination to rely on one's own best judgment, is indispensable to spiritual freedom. To paraphrase Shelley's question: "Can there be worse slavery than the depending for the safety of your soul on the opinions of another man?" The duties of the scholar, as Emerson says in that great essay of which the spirit is exactly the opposite of what is now called scholarship, "may all be comprised in self-trust." And were we really to take this principle to heart, and meditate upon it and its implications, we should be more conscientious in forming our opinions, and less hasty either to try to force our beliefs upon the world, or to take unthinkingly the world's beliefs for our own; and the labors of the bibliographer would be immensely lightened.

And now, having put myself already beyond the pale, I will venture upon another treasonable utterance by saying that this study is concerned only incidentally with the "sources" of Shelley's thought; that my purpose is to state what I think Shelley's religious ideas were, and not where I think they came from; that these two topics seem to me to be in general quite distinct; and that I consider the second of them to have no particular bearing upon the first. I have, indeed, been forced to investigate the relation of Shelley's opinions to those of Godwin, in order to show the falsity of the popular belief, fathered by a former generation of source-hunters, that the poet derived all his important principles from his

philosophically inclined father-in-law. It has been said that Shelley
cannot be understood without a knowledge of Godwin;[14] it is much
more accurate to say that Shelley cannot be understood until Godwin has been forgotten. His work would have been much more
correctly interpreted, and far more fairly judged, if no one had
ever heard of William Godwin and *Political Justice*. We might
indeed be at a loss to explain the contrast between *Queen Mab* and
Prometheus Unbound; but we should never have been guilty of
the egregious error of reading specifically Godwinian doctrines into
works written at a time when those doctrines had been in large
measure repudiated. Even in the comparatively few cases where
Shelley adheres to the letter of Godwin's teaching, he changes the
spirit utterly.[15]

It seems to me, indeed, that the contemporary world of letters
attaches an altogether exaggerated value to the study of "sources"
and "influences." Usually this amounts to nothing more than the
grubbing up of particular details of fact, which are of value only
as satisfying a more or less idle curiosity. Frequently, however, it
is more pernicious in its tendency, affecting to explain *why* an
author wrote what he did write; and thereby implying that the
creation of literature is a purely mechanical process — that is, not
creative at all; and that literature itself is not the living record of
living minds, but a dead, inert mass, like the ink and paper by
which it is preserved — and equally capable of being tested and
measured and analyzed. But whether source-hunting be a mere
game, or a kind of literary chemistry, it leads in either case to the
neglect of what I take to be the real value of a work of literature:

[14] I believe that the indiscriminate application of the scientific method to the
study of literature has produced (among other abuses) a practical perversion of
language, so that "to understand" is usually taken as synonymous with "to know
the sources of." The result is a confusion of thought. Surely we can understand the
meaning of what Shelley says in *Queen Mab* about "Necessity" without knowing
that Godwin had said the same thing before.

[15] The truth of these generalizations will become apparent during the course of
this study. It is perhaps true that Godwin's masterpiece did more than any other
single work to turn Shelley's interest from Gothic romance to philosophy. It is also
true that to the end of his life Shelley spoke with respect of Godwin's intellectual
powers. But this must be attributed to his natural reverence and loyalty toward any
person to whom he considered himself indebted in any way. He was always inclined
to overestimate the abilities and achievements of his friends.

that is, what it *means*, in terms of pleasure, or knowledge, or moral strength, or religious insight, to those who read it by and for itself.

There is, indeed, one sort of study of sources which is of the highest value: that which is a means to the discovery of some vital principle of continuity, some persistent thought or feeling which forms a part of the mental and spiritual life of an individual or a nation or a race, and which endures and changes as does that life itself. And such a discovery certainly has meaning and value in the terms I have just mentioned. But study of this kind is what few attempt and fewer still achieve. In general, as I have said, the search for sources and influences has no value except for the private amusement of the searcher, while it ignores or obscures those values that are enduring and universal. And I, for one, must ask to be excused for not wishing to be numbered among those who can find no better intellectual employment than heaping academic dust upon the corpse of literature.

It may seem that I am here imitating Shelley's own perhaps admirable, but undeniably imprudent, candor, when, to his father's ill-advised attempt to bully him into a recantation of his principles, he responded with a letter containing the statement: "I confess I write this more to discharge a duty of telling you what I think, than hoping that my representations will be effectual." [16] Still, I suppose no one writes a book without some faint hope that his representations will be to some slight degree effectual; and I therefore offer a brief comment concerning the trend of the "representations" in regard to Shelley's religious views which this study contains. The table of contents offers a more or less detailed summary of the ideas here set forth; but one or two general remarks may here be added. The one great development in the poet's thought is the change from Godwinian rationalism to an avowed mysticism, in which Platonic, neo-Platonic, and Christian elements are fused. Thus Shelley passes from an optimistic humanitarianism, which looks forward to almost perfect happiness for man on earth, to a denial of the reality or value of the whole realm of physical existence in space and time, except as it gives birth to the beauty and

[16] Roger Ingpen, *Shelley in England* (London, 1917), p. 330.

goodness by which it is transcended, and which alone have eternal reality. Between these two views of life the distance is immeasurable; and although in Shelley's early writings are to be found many foreshadowings of his final position, his latest works contain scarcely a trace of those doctrines which in his youth he had been most eager to flaunt in the face of the world. His moral ideal — unselfishness, forgiveness of injuries, unwavering opposition to what he believed to be evil — alone remains unchanged.

And, finally, I should like to say that Shelley's works were intended to be *read* — to serve as the source of enjoyment and knowledge and inspiration, and not as the object of erudite dissertations. I do not think that there is any important belief of Shelley's stated in this study which Shelley himself has not stated better. The real success of such a work as this must lie not in convincing its readers that Shelley's views were in fact as they are here represented but in influencing those readers to return to Shelley's own writings, to study — perhaps with new sympathy and at least with greater care — his words themselves; by which, in the end, and not by the words of his commentators, he must stand or fall.

CHAPTER II

SHELLEY'S GOD

LORD BYRON once objected to having his daughter Allegra brought up by the Shelleys, on the ground that he did not wish *his* child to "be taught to believe that there is no Deity." [1] It is not difficult to understand his speaking in such a manner, or to show that his words ought not to be taken too seriously; just as it is easy to explain the *Quarterly* reviewer's reference to Shelley as one of a "miserable crew of atheists and pantheists," [2] and the horror of a writer in the *Literary Gazette* at the "hideous blasphemy," "impious profanation," and "pages of raving atheism" in *Queen Mab*.[3] Nor is it surprising that such criticism should have resulted in making Shelley's name a byword among the majority of middle-class readers for nearly three decades after his death; not the less so because *Queen Mab* (in pirated editions) had become a sort of Bible among the Owenites and other radicals. The mother of Dante Gabriel Rossetti was so terrified at her son's youthful desire to read Shelley — though only for the "poetry" and not for the ideas — that filial affection led him to postpone the adventure for several years![4] And even today, when dogmatic religion seems, in intel-

---

[1] *The Works of Lord Byron. Letters and Journals,* edited by R. E. Prothero (6 vols., New York, 1898–1901), V, 15. This, from the author of *Manfred, Cain,* and *Don Juan,* is very funny, but it is significant of Byron's fundamental conventionality. Thomas Moore (another pillar of orthodoxy!) was constantly worrying lest Byron himself should be corrupted by associating with Shelley; and the latter asked Horace Smith to allay Moore's fears, declaring that he had no power over Byron's opinions, but adding, "if I had, I certainly should employ it to eradicate from his great mind the delusions of Christianity." *Letters,* II, 959. On another occasion Byron himself, despite the remark quoted above, undertook to soothe the misgivings of his future biographer by defending Shelley against the charge of infidelity. *Letters and Journals,* VI, 35.

[2] *Quarterly Review,* XXI, 461 (April, 1819). Shelley attributed the article to Southey, and an interesting correspondence ensued. The author was John Taylor Coleridge, Shelley's former school-fellow at Eton.

[3] May 19, 1821 (p. 307).

[4] Rossetti's mother was a sister of the Dr. Polidori who was Byron's companion during the months that Byron and Shelley spent together in Switzerland in 1816.

lectual circles, to be definitely on the defensive, when the impenetrable mists of sectarianism no longer cloud the mental horizons of most educated persons, and when it is the fashion to be amused rather than shocked at the poet's iconoclastic outbursts, there are not a few critics to whom the assertion that Shelley believed in a God would seem to be merely trifling with words, and who find in his work only the expression, at most, of a vague belief in some "impersonal," "abstract" "force" or "power" which rules the universe.[5] This view also I can understand; but I cannot admit that it is either adequate or accurate. It is true that Shelley always rejected — in youth, violently — the notion of an anthropomorphic God possessed of the baser as well as the nobler (he would have said, to the *exclusion* of the nobler) attributes of human nature, such as he conceived to be the center of the Christian system. It is *not* true that he was ever consistently an atheist or even a pantheist. On the contrary, he believed — at least in his mature years, when his native genius asserted itself, shattered to bits the various realms of thought that had been the resting places of his spiritual pilgrimage, and from the fragments built "a brighter Hellas" nearer to his heart's desire — in a creative and personal God, who "comprehends within himself all that constitutes human perfection." [6]

I

It is difficult to discover the exact time at which Shelley's skepticism concerning Christianity and its God began. There is no evidence of it in the Gothic romances of his Eton days, *Zastrozzi* and *St. Irvyne,* which were published in June, 1810, and January, 1811,

    [5] Cf. S. F. Gingerich, "Beauty in Shelley, Keats, and Poe," University of Michigan Publications: Language and Literature, VIII, 175, where it is stated that the ideas in Shelley's long poems "run toward an impersonal determinism"; also Newman White, *The Best of Shelley* (New York, 1932), p. xi: "At no time did he believe in a personal deity"; he "did believe in an impersonal force governing the universe." Cf. also the essays on Shelley by Walter Bagehot, *Estimations in Criticism* (London, 1908), Vol. I; Paul Elmer More, *Shelburne Essays, Seventh Series* (New York, 1910); George R. Elliott, *The Cycle of Modern Poetry* (Princeton University Press, 1929); and other critics *passim.*

    [6] Shelley's *Essay on Christianity,* in Shawcross, p. 100. Shelley actually wrote, according to Koszul's edition of *Shelley's Prose in the Bodleian Manuscript* (London, 1910), "within itself." I do not think that this is important, though others may. See note 86, p. 70 below. The terms "creative" and "personal," of course, need definition, and will be defined in the course of this discussion.

respectively, though it is probable that each was written some months before publication.[7] On the contrary, they contain a number of passages which seem to indicate that the author's views were perfectly orthodox. "Convinced of the folly of hope, he addressed a prayer to his Creator — to Him who hears a suppliant from the bowels of the earth."[8] "Thus sophistically argued Zastrozzi [in defense of revenge and atheism]. His soul, deadened by crime, could only entertain confused ideas of immortal happiness; for in proportion as human nature departs from virtue, so far are they [sic] from being able to contemplate the wonderful operations, the mysterious ways of Providence."[9] "Mathilda knew not how to pray; but God, who from the height of heaven penetrates the inmost thoughts of terrestrial hearts, heard the outcast sinner, as in tears of true and agonizing repentance, she knelt before him."[10]

There is one paragraph of this sort in *St. Irvyne*, which is rendered very amusing by later events. The heroine has allowed herself to be seduced by one of the villains, and the future disciple of Godwin exclaims dramatically: " 'Tis done; and amid the vows of a transitory delirium of pleasure, regret, horror, and misery, arise! they shake their Gorgon locks at Eloise! appalled she shudders with affright, and shrinks from the contemplation of the horrors of her imprudence. Beware, Eloise! — a precipice, a frightful precipice yawns at thy feet! advance yet a step further and thou perishest! No, give not up thy religion — it is that alone which can support thee under the miseries, with which imprudence has so darkly marked the progress of thine existence."[11] This moving exhortation is followed almost immediately by a discourse no less remarkable, in which Ginotti (one of the principal characters, who has sold his soul to the Devil, and at the end of the story is borne away by his Master, amid thunder and lightning, "on the pinions of hell's sulphurous whirlwind" to "a dateless and hopeless eternity of horror") relates the story of his intellectual and moral development: his early and lasting interest in natural science and "meta-

[7] See Shelley's letter to Edward Graham, dated April 1, 1810 (*Letters*, I, 4), where he speaks of "my new Romance," apparently *St. Irvyne*. It was printed before December 10, although not advertised by Stockdale until January 26, 1811.
[8] *Zastrozzi*, in *Prose Works*, I, 6.
[9] *Ibid.*, I, 50.   [10] *Ibid.*, I, 104.   [11] *Ibid.*, I, 197.

physical calculations," his contempt for priestcraft and superstition, his "sophistical arguments" to prove "the non-existence of a First Cause," his thoughts of suicide, and an apparently miraculous revelation of "the existence of a superior and beneficent *Spirit*, in whose image is made the soul of man" — notwithstanding which, he deliberately gives himself up to Satan.[12]

Mr. Walter E. Peck thinks that this account, "supplemented by the much-quoted letter to Godwin, will afford us a fairly comprehensive notion of the growth" of Shelley's mind,[13] and believes that it was not until January, 1811, that Shelley, "who had upheld the idea of God or an over-ruling Providence, in his novels, but who had been dipping into Locke, Hume, Sir William Drummond, Dugald Stewart, and Spinoza, felt himself slipping from orthodoxy into belief in a First Cause which he devoutly wished might be 'the soul of the Universe, the spirit of universal, imperishable love!' "[14] The last statement may contain some truth, but the literal application to Shelley of Ginotti's account of himself in *St. Irvyne* is utterly fantastic.[15] All that can be legitimately inferred is that Shelley at the time of writing was to some degree acquainted with skeptical thought. It seems unwise to take too seriously any statements of doctrine contained in these extravagant romances, which were written before the age of eighteen, with no other purpose than to catch the eye of the public and cater to the taste of the time.[16]

[12] *Ibid.*, I, 198–201 (Chapter X).

[13] Walter E. Peck, *Shelley: His Life and Work* (2 vols., New York, 1927), I, 96. The letter to Godwin is that of January 10, 1812.

[14] *Ibid.*, I, 102.

[15] Not only would it involve an incredibly facile succession of changes between orthodoxy and unbelief, but the passage quite obviously expresses nothing more than the belief of pious people of all ages concerning the lives of those who become the Devil's disciples. Even belief in the true God is a necessary step, so that the final choice may be without excuse. In the same speech, Ginotti tells of poisoning a schoolmate by way of experiment, and a consistent interpretation would attribute this deed also to Shelley. However, it is not known that any of the poet's companions at Eton "expired in agonies the most terrific" as the result of his experiments. This is one example of a great weakness in Mr. Peck's work: an unrestrained indulgence in the perilous practice of reading imaginative works as records of actual fact. There is no broader way to the limbo of critical irresponsibility.

[16] In a letter to Godwin dated March 8, 1812, Shelley speaks of "the state of intellectual sickliness and lethargy into which I was plunged two years ago, and of which 'St. Irvyne' and 'Zastrozzi' were the distempered, although unoriginal visions." *Letters*, I, 271.

Probably Shelley had not yet begun really to think for himself, or to question the truth of the religious beliefs amid which he had been brought up. But he was soon to arrive at the age when a person of alert mind often begins to ponder upon ultimate questions and to resent the complacent indifference always manifested, by the vast majority of human beings, to the doubts that seem to him so unanswerable and so inescapable.

Shelley's awakening, like many another, was hastened and embittered by a disappointment in love. He had been engaged to his beautiful cousin, Harriet Grove, for whom he appears to have had a deep, if boyish, affection. But during the autumn of 1810, according to her brother's account, "she became uneasy at the tone of his letters on speculative subjects," [17] her parents shared her feelings, and the match was broken off.

There could have been no surer way of strengthening Shelley's skepticism. Having to suffer for his way of thinking only made him the more determined to persist in it. All his life he was animated by a rare devotion to the things of the mind; he was ready at any time to face martyrdom for the sake of an abstract idea; he was the last person in the world to surrender his principles for fear of persecution or the destruction of any selfish hopes. There is little doubt that this first Harriet (like few of the women who came into the poet's life) acted wisely for her own and Shelley's happiness. But a boy of eighteen could not be expected to see that. On December 20, 1810, at the beginning of his first Oxford vacation, in a letter to his friend Thomas Jefferson Hogg, he swears "on the altar of perjured Love to revenge" himself on intolerance. [18] It never occurred to him to abandon his heterodox opinions; rather he would have tried to convert Harriet to them. "What offence to reason, to virtue, was there in desiring the communication of a lengthened correspondence, in order that both, she and myself, might see, if by coincidence of intellect we were willing to enter into a closer, an eternal union? No, it is no offence to reason, or virtue; it is obeying its most imperious dictates, it is complying

[17] Thomas Jefferson Hogg, *The Life of Percy Bysshe Shelley*, edited by Edward Dowden (London, New York, 1906), p. 575.
[18] *Letters*, I, 19.

with the designs of the Author of our nature . . ." [19] This was about seven weeks before the appearance of *The Necessity of Atheism*.

In the meantime other clouds were gathering. The publisher of some of Shelley's early literary ventures, one Stockdale, took it upon himself to inform Timothy Shelley, the poet's father, that his son was developing "predispositions against revealed religion." [20] The elder Shelley seems to have been as well-meaning and kind-hearted as was consistent with his being vain, pompous, apparently mindless, and an abject worshipper of convention, resembling his son chiefly in his deep-rooted stubbornness. The result of Stockdale's action may be gathered from the letter to Hogg already quoted:

My father called on S. in London, who converted him to Christianity. He mentioned my name, as a supporter of deistical principles. My father wrote me, and I am now surrounded, environed by dangers, to which compared the devils, who besieged St. Anthony, were all inefficient. They attack me for my detestable principles; I am reckoned an outcast; yet I defy them, and laugh at their ineffectual efforts. . . . My father wished to withdraw me from college: I would not consent to it. There lowers a terrific tempest, but I stand, as it were, on a pharos, and smile exultingly at the vain beating of the billows below. So much for egotism! [21]

So young Ajax, intoxicated by the wine of new ideas, stands confidently upon the rock of reason, and almost gaily defies the lightning. Years later, still unsubmissive, though sadly aware of the devastating power of Jupiter's thunderbolts, he told Trelawny, "Everybody saying a thing does not make it right." The only arbiter in which Shelley ever trusted was his own conscience; and

[19] *Ibid.*, I, 23.

[20] *Letters*, I, 18n. On September 28 he had written to Stockdale concerning *The Wandering Jew*, a poem somewhat in the style of Scott, apparently the joint composition of Shelley and his cousin Thomas Medwin: "As to its containing Atheistical principles, I assure you I was wholly unaware of the fact hinted at." *Letters*, I, 12. On November 11, however, he had asked his publisher to obtain for him a certain "Hebrew essay, demonstrating that the Christian religion is false." *Loc. cit.*

[21] *Ibid.*, I, 18–19. Ingpen, following Hogg, prints *sanctity* for *Christianity* in the first sentence and *sceptical* for *deistical* in the second. He makes the correction in the Julian Edition. Hogg was perhaps the most deliberately unscrupulous of Shelley's early biographers — which is saying much.

that never became trained to the service of the deities either of Hebraism or Philistinism.

Accordingly, his conscience failed to tell him that it was not right to publish a tract on *The Necessity of Atheism;* or that to send copies of it to all the bishops of the Church of England and all the heads of colleges at Oxford was very wrong indeed. Without this latter proceeding, in fact, it is probable that no untoward consequences would have followed, for the sale of the little pamphlet was stopped almost as soon as begun, and all available copies burned.[22] But even the intellectual stagnation of Oxford was rippled by Shelley's explosive missile; protests were made, and, the author's identity being an open secret, the offender was called before the Master and Fellows of University College, and upon refusing either to deny or affirm his authorship of the tract, was expelled. His friend Hogg chose to share his fate. Thus once more was Shelley made aware of the extent and power of intolerance, and once more the effect was only to intensify his hatred against orthodoxy of every sort.

The argument of the pamphlet is very simple. It opens with an assertion which Shelley often repeated, although in his later life he had less to say about it, and probably modified his views: that belief is involuntary, and therefore can be under no circumstances either moral or immoral.[23] The grounds of belief are then stated to be three: namely, the evidence of the senses, the decision of reason (which depends upon the senses), and the testimony of other persons. But none of these, it is argued, affords any basis whatever for belief in the existence of a Deity: the first because "the God of

---

[22] Through the prudent advice of the Reverend John Walker, Fellow of New College, who happened to see it in the shop of the Oxford booksellers, Munday and Slatter, and called their attention to its dangerous tendency. The proprietors agreed with him, and even offered some private admonition to the wayward author, but without effect. All this occurred about February 15, 1811.

[23] This is an idea which frequently occurs in Godwin's *Political Justice,* with which Shelley had become familiar some time during 1810, but there would be nothing remarkable in Shelley's having developed it himself: it is the natural outcome of youthful skepticism in conflict with dogmatism. A more accurate view would doubtless distinguish (as Shelley does not) between belief as mere assent to a mathematical proposition, and the much more complicated belief involved in religious faith. Shelley had not yet learned that life cannot be reduced to a mathematical or logical proposition. He concluded *The Necessity of Atheism* with Q. E. D.!

Theologians is incapable of local visibility";[24] the second because "it is easier to suppose that the universe has existed from all eternity than to conceive a being beyond its limits capable of creating it," such being the two alternatives between which reason forces us to choose; and the third because it is intrinsically more probable that the witnesses "should have been deceived than that the Deity should have appeared to them." [25] Two years later, in reprinting the essay (with a few changes) as a note to *Queen Mab* on the line "There is no God," Shelley prefixed the statement: "This negation must be understood solely to affect a creative Deity. The hypothesis of a pervading Spirit coeternal with the Universe remains unshaken." Probably this indicates no modification of the writer's opinion, but is added merely for the sake of clarity.

Shelley's aim in publishing the tract was not to overthrow orthodoxy or to convert the world to atheism. He wrote to his father shortly after his expulsion:

The case was this: — You well know that a train of reasoning and not any great profligacy has induced me to disbelieve the scriptures:—this train myself and my friend pursued, we found to our surprise that (strange as it may appear) the proofs of an existing Deity were as far as we had observed defective.

We therefore embodied our doubts on the subject and arranged them methodically in the form of "The Necessity of Atheism," thinking thereby to obtain a satisfactory or an unsatisfactory answer from men who had made Divinity the study of their lives.[26]

There is no reason to doubt the essential accuracy of this account. It is borne out by the "Advertisement" prefixed to the tract: "Advertisement. As a love of truth is the only motive which actuates the

---

[24] This statement was not in *The Necessity*, where it is merely said: "If the Deity should appear to us, if he should convince our senses of his existence; this revelation would necessarily command belief; — Those to whom the Deity has thus appeared, have the strongest possible conviction of his existence." This leaves the whole-question open, and so Shelley adds what he had meant to imply, that the Deity neither has appeared nor can appear to man.

[25] Note on *Queen Mab*, VII, l. 13. With the exception noted, the quotations are exactly the same as in the original pamphlet. The underlying premiss that all knowledge originates in sensations may be traced to Locke's *Essay on the Human Understanding*; the final argument is essentially that of Hume's *Essay on Miracles*; both of these works Shelley and Hogg had read together at Oxford. Hogg, *Life*, p. 163.

[26] Ingpen, *Shelley in England*, pp. 214–15.

Author of this little tract, he earnestly entreats that those of his readers who may discover any deficiency in his reasoning, or may be in possession of proofs which his mind could never obtain, would offer them, together with their objections to the Public as briefly, as methodically, as plainly as he has taken the liberty of doing. Thro' deficiency of proof.—AN ATHEIST." [27]   Hogg, it is true, rather makes light of the whole affair. He tells in a characteristically facetious manner of Shelley's delight in argument for argument's sake and his habit of addressing to strangers pseudonymous letters on the subject of religion, in the hope of engaging them in controversy. He intended to use *The Necessity* in this manner, professing himself to be entirely disinterested and to have discovered the pamphlet by chance, and asking if the person addressed could refute the arguments that were advanced. To the worldly Hogg all this must have been very amusing; and no doubt Shelley, too, saw the humorous side of his course of action, and pursued it with a certain amount of boyish exuberance. It is clear, also, that unbelief was never to him a tragic matter, as to young persons it so often is. For one thing, he had never known anyone to whom religious faith was more than an empty formula, not worth keeping. In the second place, the skeptical views which appealed to him so strongly often went hand in hand with that unbounded optimism and fantastic faith in perfectibility which accompanied the French Revolution, and which he met first in Godwin's *Political Justice* and later in such French writers as Condorcet.

But if there is no reason to suppose that Shelley's rejection of orthodox Christianity cost him any particular pain, there are likewise no grounds for saying that he was not deeply in earnest in his religious thinking. His letters to Hogg during January, 1811, show that his mind was in a ferment. He had begun to reason about the first principles of religious belief, and to ask himself questions to which he was not yet ready to give definite answers. But against bigotry, intolerance, and superstition he was more than ready to hurl eternal defiance. He had at last become convinced that all was at an end between him and Harriet Grove, and the realization led him to hysterical condemnation of what he believed to be the

---

[27] Quoted by Ingpen, in *Shelley in England*, p. 216n.

cause. Concerning the abstract principles of religious belief he could talk calmly, if not coherently. But when he thought of the actual effects of what people called their religion, his emotions carried him away completely. On January 3, he wrote:

Before we deny or believe the existence of anything, it is necessary that we should have a tolerably clear idea of what it is. The word "God," a vague word, has been, and will continue to be, the source of numberless errors, until it is erased from the nomenclature of philosophy. Does it not imply "the soul of the universe, the intelligent and *necessarily* benefi- cent, actuating principle." This it is impossible not to believe in; I may not be able to adduce proofs, but I think that the leaf of a tree, the meanest insect on which we trample, are, in themselves, arguments more conclusive than any which can be advanced, that some vast intellect animates infinity. If we disbelieve *this*, the strongest argument in support of the existence of a future state instantly becomes annihilated. I confess that I think Pope's

All are but parts of one stupendous whole,

something more than poetry. It has ever been my favorite theory, for the immoral soul, "never to be able to die, never to escape from some shrine as chilling as the clay-formed dungeon, which now it inhabits"; it is the future punishment which I can most easily believe in . . . yet here, I swear — and as I break my oaths, may Infinity, Eternity blast me — here I swear that never will I forgive intolerance! . . . You shall see — you shall hear — how it has injured me. She is no longer mine! she abhors me as a sceptic, as what *she* was before! Oh, bigotry! When I pardon this last, this severest of thy persecutions, may Heaven (if there be wrath in Heaven) blast me! [28]

A similar communication followed nine days later.

To *you* I dare represent myself as I am: wretched to the last de- gree . . . I never, never can feel peace again. What necessity is there for continuing in existence? But Heaven! Eternity! Love! My dear friend, I am yet a sceptic on these subjects; would that I could believe them to be, as they are represented; would that I could totally disbelieve them! But no! That would be selfish. I still have firmness enough to resist this last, this most horrible of errors. Is my despair the result of the hot, sickly love which inflames the admirers of Sterne or Moore? [29]

[28] *Letters*, I, 29–30.
[29] "Dr. John Moore (1729–1802) physician, and the author of some books of travel and three novels: — 'Zeluco' (1786), 'Edward' (1796) and 'Mordaunt' (1800)." Ingpen's note.

It is the conviction of unmerited unkindness, the conviction that, should a future world exist, the object of my attachment would be as miserable as myself, is the cause of it.

I here take God (and a God exists) to witness, that I wish torments, which beggar the futile description of a fancied hell, would fall upon me; provided I could obtain thereby that happiness for *what* I love, which, I fear, can never be. The question is, what do I love? It is almost unnecessary to answer. Do I love the person, the embodied identity, if I may be allowed the expression? No! I love what is superior, what is excellent, or what I conceive to be so; and I wish, ardently wish, to be profoundly convinced of the existence of a Deity, that so superior a spirit might derive some degree of happiness from my feeble exertions; for love is heaven, and heaven is love. You think so, too, and you disbelieve not the existence of an eternal, omnipresent Spirit. Am I not mad? Alas! I am, but I pour out my ravings into the ear of a friend who will pardon them. Stay! I have an idea. I think I can prove the existence of a Deity — A First Cause. I will ask a materialist, how came this universe at first? He will answer, By chance. What chance? I will answer in the words of Spinoza: "An infinite number of atoms had been floating from all eternity in space, till at last one of them fortuitously diverged from its track, which, dragging with it another, formed the principle of gravitation, and in consequence the universe." What cause produced this change, this chance? For where do we know that causes arise without their corresponding effects; at least we must here, on so abstract a subject, reason analogically. Was not this then a *cause*, was it not a *first* cause? Was not this first cause a Deity? Now nothing remains but to prove that this Deity has a care, or rather that its only employment consists in regulating the present and future happiness of its creation. Our ideas of infinite space, etc., are scarcely to be called ideas, for we cannot either comprehend or explain them; therefore the Deity must be judged by us from attributes analogical to our situation. Oh, that this Deity were the soul of the universe, the spirit of universal, imperishable love! Indeed, I believe it is . . . Adieu! Excuse my mad arguments; they are none at all, for I am rather confused, and fear, in consequence of a fever, they will not allow me to come on the 26th, but I will. Adieu! [30]

No comment can bring order out of the chaos of this extraordinary letter, which from another person might be judged to be mere affectation. But whatever faults Shelley may have had, insincerity

[30] *Letters*, I, 40–43. The idea here attributed to Spinoza is not to be found in his works, and is even in opposition to his view. See Helene Richter, "Zu Shelley's philosophischer Weltanschauung," *Englische Studien*, XXX, 232–33.

was not among them; and in his letters to those whom he believed to be his friends, he recorded his thoughts and emotions exactly as they came to him. Hence, it is easy to find examples of illogical and incoherent thinking, of hasty and sometimes even unkind judgment; but there are few who, were they as honest with themselves as Shelley was with all the world, would not hesitate to cast the first stone. In the letter quoted, the poet is writing from his heart, and his words seem inadequate and unimpressive only because it is impossible that a boy of eighteen should have learned, by *living,* the real significance of the ideas he presents. But whatever may be one's judgment upon this effusion, it certainly does not indicate any hasty or arrogant assumption of atheism. It is worth noting, too, that Shelley here states the argument for the existence of a First Cause, which in *The Necessity of Atheism,* probably already written, is specifically rejected. The truth evidently is that he knew not what to believe, and was honestly trying to find out; that beyond a determination to "crush intolerance" he had as yet no plan or intention to reform the world.

What Shelley *was* determined on was the assertion and preservation of his intellectual integrity, of the right to follow the dictates of his own reason, and to hold the conclusions to which his thinking led him. When his father urged upon him the advantages of orthodoxy, he replied, in a letter written early in February, 1811, that as for "those who do not think at all, a species which contains by far the major part of even civilized society," "it is best that they should follow the religion of their fathers whatever it may be"; [31] but that when a person has once begun to reason, "you cannot deny him *that* which is, or ought to be the essence of his being . . ."; [32] and that "Religion fetters a reasoning mind with the very bonds which restrain the unthinking one from mischief." [33] Shelley felt that his very existence as a truly human being depended upon freedom of thought; he was prepared to make any sacrifice rather than surrender his ideal. After his expulsion from Oxford he chose to

---

[31] Ingpen, *Shelley in England,* p. 168. The distrust of the mass of humanity which is here expressed grew stronger throughout Shelley's life, and should be considered by those who attribute to the poet an easy and unqualified faith in the benevolence and wisdom of human nature.

[32] *Ibid.,* p. 169.   [33] *Ibid.,* p. 170.

live in poverty and loneliness rather than accept a reconciliation with his father, which could only be gained by renouncing his opinions. He and Hogg were willing to agree, in order to regain the favor of their parents, that they would "not obtrude Atheistical opinions upon any one whatever," and that they would "refrain from publishing Atheistical Doctrines or even speculations." [34] But this failed to satisfy Shelley's father: his erring son must give up his opinions altogether, and return to the fold of orthodoxy. And such a demand Shelley rejected with indignation and contempt. Two years later, still estranged from his father, he wrote to the Duke of Norfolk, who had offered his services as peacemaker: "I was prepared to make my father every reasonable concession, but I am not so degraded and miserable a slave as publicly to disavow an opinion which I believe to be true." [35] One might build a religion and a life upon a worse foundation.

Evidence of his general attitude may also be found in his Irish pamphlets, which appeared in the early days of 1812. It must be remembered, of course, that he was addressing a public of relatively uneducated Roman Catholics. On the other hand, such passages as the following seem rather hard to reconcile with the "raving atheism" which some critics would still attribute to Shelley at this period; although it is true that the writer insists again on the right of the individual to think for himself. "Can there be worse slavery than the depending for the safety of your soul on the will of another man? Is one man more favored than another by God? No, certainly, they are favored according to the good they do, and not according to the rank or position that they hold." [36] "Does a God rule this illimitable universe? Are you thankful for his beneficence — do you adore his wisdom — do you hang upon his altar the garland of your devotion? Curse not your brother, though he hath enwreathed with his [,] flowers of a different hue; the purest religion is that of charity." [37]

[34] Ibid., p. 232. Some nine months later, Shelley wrote to Godwin, in the same temperate vein: "I will not again crudely obtrude the question of atheism on the world." Letters, I, 223.

[35] Letters, I, 403.

[36] Address to the Irish People, in Prose Works, I, 228.

[37] Proposals for an Association of Philanthropists, in Prose Works, I, 267.

In the meantime, reason led him farther and farther from the beaten paths of religious thought; and the "necessarily beneficent" Deity, the "spirit of universal, imperishable love," faded away into a shadowy Unknowable, concerning which he discoursed as follows to Elizabeth Hitchener, his too willing disciple:

To a belief in Deity I have no objection on the score of feeling: I would as gladly, perhaps with greater pleasure, admit than doubt his existence. . . . I now do neither, I have not the shadow of a doubt. . . . What then is a "God"? It is a name which expresses the unknown cause, the suppositious origin of all existence. . . . The word God then, in the sense which you take it analogises with the universe, as the soul of man to his body, as the vegetative power to vegetables, the stony power to stones. Yet, were each of these adjuncts taken away, what would be the remainder? What is man without his soul? he is not man . . . What are vegetables without their vegetative power? stones without their stony? Each of these as much constitutes the essence of men, stones, etc., as much make it to be what it is, as your "God" does the universe. In this sense I acknowledge a God, but merely as a synonime [*sic*] for *the existing power of existence.* . . . I do not in *this* (nor can you do, I think) recognize a being which has created that to which it is confessedly annexed as an essence, as that without which the universe would not be what it is. It is therefore the essence of the universe, the universe is the essence of it. It is another *word for* the essence of the universe. You recognize not in this an identical being to whom are attributable the properties of virtue, mercy, loveliness — imagination delights in personification; were it not for this embodying quality of eccentric fancy, we should be to this day without a God. . . .[38]

This passage seems to point in the direction of a thoroughgoing materialism; for although it is true that a verbal distinction is made between "the universe" and its "essence," yet no real content seems assignable to the second term; and hence the distinction has little significance.[39]

On the other hand, to say that God and the universe are identical is not necessarily to accept a naturalistic philosophy. Absolute idealists sometimes say much the same thing. The difference lies in the answer to the question, "What *is* the universe?" Naturalism reduces it to physical ("natural") processes, idealism to mind, or intelli-

[38] *Letters,* I, 91–93 (June 11, 1811).
[39] Cf. *A Refutation of Deism:* "in the language of reason, the words God and Universe are synonymous." *Prose Works,* I, 328.

gence. It cannot be denied that Shelley sometimes inclines toward
the former, but only in his early writings; and even here idealism
is usually dominant. There can be no doubt that Shelley's final view
was that the physical universe is dependent upon mind; and not
vice versa. But his idealism was never absolute, for in his mature
thought he did not identify God either with the universe or with
mind. His earlier views, however (say, from 1811 to 1814), seem to
be fairly stated in this passage from a letter to Miss Hitchener.

> I have lately had some conversation with Southey which has elicited
> my true opinions of God. He says I ought not to call myself an atheist,
> since in reality I believe that the universe is God. I tell him I believe
> that God is another signification for the Universe. I then explain: — I
> think reason and analogy seem to countenance the opinion that life is
> infinite; that, as the soul which now animates this frame was once the
> vivifying principle of the *infinitely* lowest link in the Chain of existence,
> so is it ultimately destined to attain the highest . . . that everything is
> animation . . . and in consequence being infinite we can never arrive
> at its termination. How, on this hypothesis, are we to arrive at a First
> Cause? — Southey admits and believes this. — Can he be a Christian?
> Can God be Three? Southey agrees in my idea of Deity, the mass of
> infinite intelligence . . . I, you, and he, are constituent parts of this
> immeasurable whole.[40]

I do not think that Shelley ever came much nearer to atheism.
Even in this creed there is nothing gross or vulgar, no blind acceptance of the seemingly obvious, no surrender of reason and
benevolence to the temptings of selfishness and sensuality. Yet the
ten years of life that remained to him witnessed an immeasurable
refinement of thought and feeling: the discipline of suffering,
physical and spiritual, of constant thought and unremitting study,
of continual struggle against human folly and selfishness, of strenuous poetical creation — all these strengthened his intellect and
widened and deepened his sympathies, and prepared him to approach with reverence the great philosophical and religious traditions of Europe, which as a boy he had overlooked or thrust aside,
and in great part to make his own the thought and spirit of Plato
and Dante and the New Testament. But this did not destroy his

---

[40] *Letters*, I, 205 (January 2, 1812). The theory of an evolution of the soul
which is here suggested, Shelley never abandoned, and it will be considered below.

hatred of what he chose to call Christianity; and before studying the development and final form of his conception of God, it will be enlightening to consider his attitude toward the anthropomorphic God which he believed to be worshipped by all orthodox Christians.[41]

II

Both the rationalist and the moralist in Shelley cried out in protest against the idea of God which most professed Christians seemed to him to hold. What folly that man should believe the infinite universe to have been created and to be governed by a God created in his own small image by his own weak fancy! How degrading that human beings should first attribute to this God their own imperfections — revengefulness, jealousy, irrationality — and then appeal to this monstrous phantasm for authority to indulge these same brutal passions! How vicious the superstition that virtue depends on the capricious will of such a Being, and that the only sanction of righteousness is the contemptible, because selfish, desire of reward, and the more contemptible, because slavish, fear of punishment! And finally, how irreconcilable the belief in an all-powerful and all-good deity with the all-pervading evil—the falsehood, the lust, the cruelty — which seems to stain and weaken every fiber in the fabric of human society!

Shelley's objections on the score of irrationality have appeared in some of the quotations given above. Perhaps the most explicit statement is in the *Letter to Lord Ellenborough*, a brief but forceful plea on behalf of the bookseller Daniel Eaton, who in 1812 was sentenced to be pilloried and imprisoned for publishing the third part of Thomas Paine's *The Age of Reason*. Going straight to first principles, Shelley protested (as he had done before and as he continued to do all his life) against the stupidity and injustice of punishing a man for his opinions, and went on to declare that

the supposition that any revelation from an unknown power avails to palliate a persecution so senseless, unprovoked, and indefensible, is at once to destroy the barrier which reason places between vice and virtue,

[41] This topic is also treated by Sophie Bernthsen, *Der Spinozismus in Shelley's Weltanschauung*, pp. 137–45, and Arthur C. Hicks, "The Place of Christianity in Shelley's Thought" (Ph. D. thesis, Stanford University, 1932), pp. 33–82.

and leave to unprincipled fanaticism a plea whereby it may excuse every act of frenzy which its own wild passions, and the inspirations of the Deity, have engendered.

Moral qualities are such as only a human being can possess. To attribute them to the Spirit of the Universe, or to suppose that it is capable of altering them, is to degrade God into man, and to annex to this incomprehensible Being qualities incompatible with any *possible definition of its nature*. It may be here objected: — Ought not the Creator to possess the perfections of the creature? No.[42] To attribute to God the moral qualities of man, is to suppose him susceptible of passions, which, arising out of corporeal organisation, it is plain that a pure Spirit cannot possess. A bear is not perfect except he is rough, a tiger is not perfect if he be not voracious, an elephant is not perfect if otherwise than docile. How *deep* an argument must not that be which proves that the Deity is as rough as a bear, as voracious as a tiger, and as docile as an elephant.[43]

This position Shelley greatly modified, as will appear in the following chapter; but he always held that the nature of the Deity could never be wholly comprehended by the human mind. In the *Essay on Christianity,* probably written in 1817,[44] he declares that Christ had considered the name of God "as having been profanely perverted to the sanctioning of the most enormous and abominable crimes. We can distinctly trace, in the tissue of his doctrines, the persuasion that God is some universal Being, differing from man and the mind of man." [45] Elsewhere he says: "The universal Being can only be described or defined by negatives which deny his subjection to the laws of all inferior existences. Where indefiniteness ends, idolatry and anthropomorphism begin." [46] Again, in *Prometheus Unbound* we find Jupiter, the God whom man has created in his own image, and endowed with his own passions, contrasted with Demogorgon, the supreme "principle of the universe," who can only be described as "a mighty darkness . . . Ungazed upon and shapeless; neither limb, Nor form, nor outline . . ." [47] And in *Hellas,* the last of the long poems to be completed, the poet speaks twice of "the unknown God" and makes Ahasuerus refer to "the Fathomless." [48]

[42] Considering the date at which this was written, the apparent acceptance of a *Creator* must be a mere oversight.

[43] *Letters*, I, 330.

[44] See A. Koszul, *Shelley's Prose in the Bodleian Manuscript*, pp. 9–12.

[45] Shawcross, p. 88. [46] *Ibid.*, p. 91. [47] II, iv, ll. 2, 5–6. [48] Ll. 211, 735, 763.

Shelley would not have objected, however, had man been content to ascribe to God only the *excellencies* of human nature. But that men should worship a God who was, if not admittedly, yet actually, the personification of their basest passions was an intolerable evil, which must be swept from the face of the earth. Two long passages, one in *Queen Mab* and the other in *The Revolt of Islam*, describe the origin and development of this degrading superstition; while the hateful effects of it are a constant theme for condemnation throughout both poems. The indictment addressed to religion in *Queen Mab* is characteristic of Shelley's mental and emotional attitude during his early years of manhood.[49]

> "Thou taintest all thou look'st upon! — the stars,
> Which on thy cradle beamed so brightly sweet,
> Were gods to the distempered playfulness
> Of thy untutored infancy: the trees,
> The grass, the clouds, the mountains, and the sea,
> All living things that walk, swim, creep, or fly,
> Were gods: the sun had homage, and the moon
> Her worshipper. Then thou becam'st, a boy,
> More daring in thy frenzies: every shape,
> Monstrous or vast, or beautifully wild,
> Which, from sensation's relics, fancy culls;
> The spirits of the air, the shuddering ghost,
> The genii of the elements, the powers
> That give a shape to Nature's varied works,
> Had life and place in the corrupt belief
> Of thy blind heart: yet still thy youthful hands
> Were pure of human blood. Then manhood gave
> Its strength and ardour to thy frenzied brain;
> Thine eager gaze scanned the stupendous scene,
> Whose wonders mocked the knowledge of thy pride:
> Their everlasting and unchanging laws
> Reproached thine ignorance. Awhile thou stoodst
> Baffled and gloomy; then thou didst sum up
> The elements of all that thou didst know;
> The changing seasons, winter's leafless reign,
> The budding of the Heaven-breathing trees,
> The eternal orbs that beautify the night,

[49] The poem seems to have been written during the year 1812, Shelley's twentieth birthday falling upon August 4 of that year. The declaration, made in 1821, that it was written at the age of eighteen (*Letters*, II, 881) must be disregarded. Shelley's memory was often at fault in such matters.

The sunrise, and the setting of the moon,
Earthquakes and wars, and poisons and disease,
And all their causes, to an abstract point
Converging, thou didst bend and called it God!
The self-sufficing, the omnipotent,
The merciful, and the avenging God!
Who, prototype of human misrule, sits
High in Heaven's realm, upon a golden throne,
Even like an earthly king; and whose dread work,
Hell, gapes forever for the unhappy slaves
Of fate, whom He created, in his sport,
To triumph in their torments when they fell!" [50]

This is by no means mere rhetoric, and is worth careful reading. It corresponds very closely to the account later given by August Comte in his formulation of the "law of the three stages" in the progress of human thought, of the first, or "theological" stage, which in turn passed through three phases: animism, polytheism, and monotheism. A less systematic and more poetic exposition of the same theme is given in *The Revolt of Islam*. In the five years intervening between the composition of the earlier poem and of the later, Shelley's genius had developed remarkably and many of his ideas and attitudes had changed. But there is no change in his attitude toward what he called the Christian God — except that he has additional reasons for rejecting such a Being.

" 'Ye feel and think—has some immortal power
Such purposes? or in a human mood,
Dream ye some Power thus builds for man in solitude?

" 'What is that Power? Ye mock yourselves, and give
A human heart to what ye cannot know;
As if the cause of life could think and live!
'Twere as if man's own works should feel, and show
The hopes, and fears, and thoughts from which they flow,
And he be like to them! Lo! Plague is free
To waste, Blight, Poison, Earthquake, Hail, and Snow,
Disease, and Want, and worse Necessity
Of hate and ill, and Pride, and Fear, and Tyranny!

" 'What is that Power? Some moon-struck sophist stood
Watching the shade from his own soul upthrown

[50] *Queen Mab*, VI, ll. 72–110.

Fill Heaven and darken Earth, and in such mood
 The Form he saw and worshipped was his own,
 His likeness in the world's vast mirror shown;
And 'twere an innocent dream, but that a faith
 Nursed by fear's dew of poison, grows thereon,
And that men say, that Power has chosen Death
On all who scorn its laws, to wreak immortal wrath. . . .

 " 'And it is said, this Power will punish wrong;
 Yes, add despair to crime, and pain to pain!
And deepest hell, and deathless snakes among,
 Will bind the wretch on whom is fixed a stain,
 Which, like a plague, a burden, and a bane,
Clung to him while he lived; — for love and hate,
 Virtue and vice, they say are difference vain —
The will of strength is right . . .' " [51]

The burning condemnation which occurs in both these passages, of the Christian belief in Hell, carrying with it, as Shelley felt, the implication that God can be actuated by the basest of all human passions, a desire for revenge, sprang from the depths of the poet's nature. For him, virtue must be its own reward and vice its own punishment.[52] "The rod and the sweetmeat" theory of morality, which the eighteenth-century opponents of orthodoxy had attacked so vigorously, as being inconsistent with the dignity of man, never met with a bitterer enemy than Shelley. Virtue, he held, is in its very nature disinterested: to act from fear of punishment or hope of reward is never virtuous and often vicious. In an early letter to Elizabeth Hitchener he protests: "Paley's 'Moral Philosophy' begins: 'Why am I *obliged* to keep my word? Because I desire Heaven and hate Hell.' *Obligation* and duty, therefore, are words of no value as the criterion of excellence." [53] Later, in the fragmentary *Speculations on Morals*, he declares: "All the theories which have refined and exalted humanity, or those which have been

---

[51] *The Revolt of Islam*, VIII, iv–vi, viii. In *Laon and Cythna*, the first version of the poem, Shelley wrote *God* instead of *Power*. This was one of a number of similar changes which he was persuaded by his publishers to make.

[52] On the punishment of evil, see below, Chapter VI.

[53] *Letters*, I, 190 (December 11, 1811). Paley was the theologian whose works Timothy Shelley had urged upon his son as a cure for his skepticism, and whose view is summed up by John Stuart Mill as follows: "God is stronger than we are, and is able to damn us if we do not do good." Quoted by Peck, I, 116.

devised as alleviations of its mistakes and evils, have been based on the elementary emotions of disinterestedness, which we feel to constitute the majesty of our nature." [54] And he returns to the charge in the *Essay on Christianity:* "The doctrine of what some fanatics have termed 'a peculiar Providence' — that is, of some power beyond and superior to that which ordinarily guides the operations of the Universe, interfering to punish the vicious and reward the virtuous — is explicitly denied by Jesus Christ. The absurd and execrable doctrine of vengeance seems to have been contemplated in all its shapes by this great moralist with the profoundest disapprobation. Nor would he permit the most venerable of names to be perverted into a sanction for the meanest and most contemptible propensities incident to the nature of man." [55]

But that a God should set up an arbitrary system of rewards and punishments was not the worst of the matter. For this God was likewise presumed to be all-powerful, and therefore responsible for the actions and the fate of his creatures; and *therefore,* argued Shelley, the only reason for the existence of Hell must be that the Creator derives a malicious pleasure from torturing the beings whom he has made. "God made man such as he is, and then damned him for being so; for to say that God was the author of all good, and man the author of all evil, is to say that one man made a straight line and a crooked one, and another man made the incongruity." [56] Could the founder of Christianity have believed, as so many of his professed followers seem to do, in "a Being who shall deliberately scheme to inflict on a large portion of the human race tortures indescribably intense and indefinitely protracted"? [57] Against such a conception as this, Shelley never ceased to hurl the bitterest invective. In the last of his prose works, *A Defence of Poetry,* he indignantly characterizes the Almighty in Milton's *Paradise Lost* as "one who in the cold security of undoubted triumph inflicts the most horrible revenge upon his enemy, not from any

[54] Shawcross, p. 78.
[55] *Ibid.,* pp. 91–92. I have corrected some details of the text by reference to the text of the manuscript, as given by Koszul in *Shelley's Prose in the Bodleian Manuscript.*
[56] Note on *Queen Mab,* VI, l. 198.
[57] *Essay on Christianity,* in Shawcross, p. 93.

mistaken notion of inducing him to repent of a perseverance in enmity, but with the alleged design of exasperating him to deserve new torments." [58]

I suppose there are few civilized persons in the present age to whom Shelley's denunciation of such a God stands in need of any defense. But there are many, doubtless, who will be unwilling to admit that his belief that such was the God of the Christian religion had any reasonable foundation. Yet it is obvious that, from a purely logical point of view, the indictment is unanswerable. If an omnipotent Being created and peopled Hell, that Being must be malignant. It is interesting to find an eminent Catholic layman, Mr. G. K. Chesterton, speaking of a certain Protestant sect in the same terms that Shelley applied to Christianity in general, and referring casually to "that quiet street in Hell, where dwell the children of that unique dispensation which theologians call Calvinism, and Christians devil-worship." [59] Calvinism, perhaps the most rigorously logical of Christian creeds, felt itself faced with the choice between an all-powerful and an all-good God, and chose the former. But Catholicism itself avoids the difficulty only by dodging the issue, and Shelley was not acting unreasonably in lumping all the Christian sects together. Thus, we find him asserting in the *Essay on Christianity:*

. . . it is the character of an evil Daemon to consign the beings whom he has endowed with sensation to unprofitable anguish. The peculiar circumstances attendant on the conception of God casting sinners to burn in Hell forever, combine to render that conception the most perfect specimen of the greatest imaginable crime. Jesus Christ represented God as the principle of all good, the source of all happiness, the wise and benevolent Creator and Preserver of all living things. But the interpreters of his doctrines have confounded the good and the evil principle. They observed the emanations of their universal natures to be inextricably entangled in the world, and, trembling before the power of the cause of all things, addressed to it such flattery as is acceptable to the ministers of human tyranny, attributing love and wisdom to those ener-

[58] *Ibid.*, p. 146. Cf. also *A Refutation of Deism:* "God is here represented as creating man with certain passions and powers, surrounding him with certain circumstances, and then condemning him to everlasting torments because he acted as omniscience had foreseen, and was such as omnipotence had made him." *Prose Works*, I, 300.

[59] *Charles Dickens*, p. 171.

gies which they felt to be exerted indifferently for the purposes of benefit and calamity.

Jesus Christ expressly asserts that distinction between the good and evil principle which it has been the practice of all theologians to confound. How far his doctrines, or their interpretation, may be true, it would scarcely have been worth while to inquire, if the one did not afford an example and an incentive to the attainment of true virtue, while the other holds out a sanction and apology for every species of mean and cruel vice.[60]

It is clear from this passage that Shelley's great objection to such a God as some Christian theologians had set up was made on the score of morality rather than metaphysics. It cannot be too strongly emphasized that before all else Shelley was a moralist. If one great passion of his life was to penetrate the mysteries of being, the other was to make men better. It is worth remarking, too, that the passage just quoted, even leaving aside the particular doctrines of Hell and eternal punishment, hints at a more fundamental difficulty in believing in the existence of the Christian God. If a benevolent and omnipotent Person rules the world, why does evil exist? — for that it does exist and is deeply rooted in the nature of things, the poet never denied, except in one or two enthusiastic outbursts in *Queen Mab*,[61] and in an argumentative assertion in *A Refutation of Deism* that good and evil are merely relative terms, significant only with respect to human feelings.[62]

I shall undertake in a later chapter to clear up the widespread (and I am tempted to add *wilful*) misunderstanding of Shelley's views upon the problem of evil; here I shall only say that it was a subject that constantly occupied his thoughts, and one to which he never found a solution. Indeed, he came to believe at last that the problem was insoluble by human reason. But whatever his theories about the subject, it is clear that his whole life, both as a man and as a poet, was a crusade against the evil in human existence. He might be temporarily carried away by the doctrine of Necessity, and expound the subject in a long note to *Queen Mab*, arguing that "we are taught, by the doctrine of Necessity, that there is neither good nor evil in the universe, otherwise than as the events

[60] Shawcross, pp. 100–01.
[61] E.g., VI, ll. 197–219.   [62] *Prose Works*, I, 324.

to which we apply these epithets have relation to our own peculiar mode of being"; [63] but his motive in writing the note was nothing except the destruction of the evils that have arisen because men have failed to recognize the truth of a doctrine which teaches that evil cannot exist, and that "in no case could any event have happened otherwise than it did happen"! The paradox is made more striking when we find the young reformer speaking in the same note of "the few fanatics who are engaged in the Herculean task of reconciling the justice of their God with the misery of man," and arguing that "if God is the author of good, He is also the author of evil; that, if He is entitled to our gratitude for the one, He is entitled to our hatred for the other." It is true, of course, that this use of the words "good," "evil," and "misery" is not necessarily incompatible with the assertion that these things have no absolute existence, and that Shelley may have been using them only in a relative sense. But in spirit, if not in matter, there is a genuine inconsistency here; and the writer's true belief clearly is that evil has absolute existence, however logic may lead him to different conclusions.

Such a belief, of course, is incompatible not merely with the Christian conception of God but with belief that *any* wholly benevolent Power completely rules the universe; and perhaps in the last analysis it is unintelligible. As I have said, Shelley was eventually obliged to give up the problem altogether. But the complacent attitude of many Christian apologists, and their refusal to admit any inconsistency between belief in the omnipotence and benevolence of the Creator on the one hand, and the utter depravity of His creatures on the other, outraged both the poet's youthful worship of reason and his lifelong sensitiveness to the sufferings of men.

It does not come within the scope of this discussion to consider Shelley's attitude toward historical Christianity and toward the Church (or churches), to record his disgust at many of the stories and doctrines contained in the Old Testament, to present in detail his contention that the teachings and the life of Christ had become

---

[63] Note on VI, l. 198. Sophie Bernthsen argues (*op. cit.*, pp. 110–12) that this quotation is characteristic of Shelley's thought, and that throughout his life he held, with Spinoza, that good and evil are merely relative. Her position cannot be defended. See below. Cf. also H. Richter, *op. cit.*

overlaid and almost obscured by a mass of superstition, or to illustrate his abhorrence of the wars and persecutions that have been instigated in the name of Christ; although it is to be remembered that it is to these things, as well as to dogmatic doctrines, that Shelley regularly applies the term *Christianity*. I have been concerned only with his views in regard to Christian theology.[64]

But it may not be out of place, in closing this chapter, to remind the reader of the actual state of the Christian religion in England at the beginning of the nineteenth century. Never, perhaps, has it touched a lower level. The Established Church seemed spiritually extinct; men took orders in it as they take up advertising or "education" today: as an easy means of getting a living, in which neither industry nor intellect is particularly essential. To the great majority it never occurred even to think about the doctrines of the religion which they professed to serve, to say nothing of trying to live up to its moral code. They were perfectly willing that the Church should be made the tool of a political party, and that its name should be used to sanction every kind of social and political oppression. The excesses of the French Revolution were attributed to reason and free thought, which were held up as painted devils to frighten the mob into a frenzy of reaction. To protest against the established order was treason; to offer a rational defense of such a protest was blasphemy. The rope and the pillory were the answer to those who had the courage to assert their right to seek and speak the truth. Under such conditions, the latent tendency

[64] The fullest statement of Shelley's objections to Christianity is to be found in *A Refutation of Deism*, a dialogue between a Christian (Eusebes) and a Deist (Theosophus), in which Shelley aims to make each speaker destroy the grounds of the other's belief. Despite the title, Christianity is much more bitterly attacked than Deism, as one might expect; for the latter has no place for the doctrines of original sin, the atonement, and eternal punishment. Shelley's attitude toward both systems appears in a letter written in May, 1811. "As you mention Religion, I will say, that my rejection of *revealed* proceeds from my perfect conviction of its insufficiency to the happiness of man — to this source *I* can trace murder, war, intolerance — my rejection of *natural* arises wholly from *reason*. I *once* was an enthusiastic Deist, but never a Christian." See *Letters*, I, 81. Eventually, he developed a sort of natural religion of his own; but he did not base it upon reason, and he never accepted the "argument from design," i.e., the inference from the order of nature to the existence of a benevolent and intelligent Deity, which is the fundamental principle of Deism. — An excellent summary of the content of *A Refutation of Deism* is given by Mr. Peck, *op. cit.*, I, 352–57.

of Christianity toward a fatalistic acquiescence in things as they
are and a belief that "Whatever is, is right" was sure to come to
the surface, and there were few of the clergy who were not willing
to kiss the rod with which a near-sighted and ruthless government
was too ready to scourge every person who showed the desire to
be a man instead of a slave. One line of Shelley's own verse describes
the situation with perfect justice: "Religion Christless, Godless, a
book sealed." [65]

What more was needed to convince Shelley that Christianity
was as unsound in practice as in theory, and that a religion which
ignored alike the dictates of reason and humanity deserved to be
destroyed? It is easy for modern critics, a century removed from
the age in which Shelley lived, to indulge in wholesale condemnation of the French Revolution; to point with scorn to the disparity between the bright Utopian dreams of liberty, equality, and
fraternity by which it was ushered in, and the dark reality of blood
and terror and moral anarchy which ensued; and to view with
amused or irritable amazement the person who could still cherish a
faith in the potential dignity and benevolence of human nature, who
was still willing to confess to "a passion for reforming the world,"
and who dared publicly to denounce as rotten the political, religious,
and social life of the time. But it ought to be evident to these same
critics that Shelley's steadfastness in holding to his chosen course
could not be the outcome of mere wilfulness, of an entirely destructive or negative creed, of either skepticism or credulity; but
could only be the outward expression of an intense and vital inward
faith. What that faith was, and how it developed, the following
chapters will attempt to show.

[65] *Sonnet: England in 1819.*

CHAPTER III

SHELLEY'S GOD (Continued)

I

IT HAS BEEN seen that Shelley was at one time inclined to deny the existence of God, except as "another signification for the Universe." This was not his final position. Nevertheless, a study of his ideas about the nature of the universe will help toward an understanding of the conception of God which he ultimately came to hold.

It is difficult, however, to determine exactly what those ideas were. Not only did Shelley's views change, but at no time did he give them complete or systematic expression. One statement, however, may be made at once: he was not a materialist. In the last year of his life he declared that "the doctrines of the French, and Material Philosophy, are as false as they are pernicious,"[1] reiterating a view which he had already expressed in the fragment *On Life*,[2] where he states:

It is a decision against which all our persuasions struggle, and we must be long convicted before we can be convinced that the solid universe of external things is "such stuff as dreams are made of." The shocking absurdities of the popular philosophy of mind and matter, its fatal consequences in morals, and their violent dogmatism concerning the source of all things, had early conducted me to materialism. This materialism is a seducing system to young and superficial minds. It allows its disciples to talk, and dispenses them from thinking. But I was discontented with

---

[1] *Letters*, II, 959–60 (April 11, 1822). He continues: "But still they are better than Christianity, inasmuch as anarchy is better than despotism; for this reason, that the former is for a season, and the latter is eternal."

[2] This fragment, like much of Shelley's prose, is of uncertain date. Mrs. Shelley first printed it as belonging to 1815; although it is hard to see why, since, according to Dowden, the MS. is contained in the same notebook as *A Philosophical View of Reform*, written in 1820, and "would hardly have had a place in this Italian notebook if it were of earlier origin than 1818 or 1819." Edward Dowden, *Transcripts and Studies* (London, 1888), p. 42. A similar date (I should say) is indicated by the style and content.

such a view of things as it afforded; man is a being of high aspirations . . . there is a spirit within him at enmity with nothingness and dissolution.[3]

It is hard to find in his writings any evidence that he was ever consistently a materialist in the extreme sense; certainly he could not long have remained so. There are, it is true, passages in his work which show him apparently inclining to materialism. In a letter to Godwin dated July 29, 1812, he writes: "Immateriality seems to me nothing but a simple denial of the presence of matter, of the presence of all the forms of being with which our senses are acquainted, and it surely is somewhat inconsistent to assign real existence to what is a mere negation of all that actual world to which our senses introduce us." [4] In *Queen Mab*, however, which was being written at this time, he puts forward the theory that matter is ultimately reducible to "soul." [5] On the other side, again, he states unequivocally in *A Refutation of Deism*, which appeared about the beginning of 1814: "The system of the Universe then is upheld solely by physical powers. The necessity of matter is the ruler of the world." [6] Yet in a letter to Hogg dated November 26, 1813, he says: "I have examined Hume's reasonings with respect to the non-existence of external things, and, I confess, they appear to me to follow from the doctrines of Locke." [7] He adds, however, as if not wholly convinced: "What am I to think of a philosophy which conducts to such a conclusion?" [8]

It was not alone the study of Berkeley and Hume, however, that led him away from materialism; but, as appears from the close of the passage quoted above from the essay *On Life*, an intuition, a feeling, deep and unconquerable, of the transience and unreality of the external world of matter, coupled with an unreasoning con-

---

[3] Shawcross, p. 54.

[4] *Letters*, I, 347. In the next sentence, he seems to speak rather disparagingly of Berkeley.

[5] IV, ll. 139–50. The passage is quoted below.

[6] *Prose Works*, I, 319–20.

[7] Locke's view that all knowledge originates in sensations, which is so evident in *The Necessity of Atheism*, was a fundamental principle in Shelley's metaphysics for some years thereafter. It is interesting, however, that in the passages in *Hellas* and *Prometheus* in which Shelley lists the elements of thought, or mind, sensation is not included. See below.

[8] *Letters*, I, 415.

viction that that realm of illusion could be transcended. More and
more in his last years, on the occasions when he surrendered himself to feeling and imagination — for in another mood he hoped and
strove to the end to elevate and purify the earthly lives of men —
the visible world seemed to slip away from him, and as though
from "far in the Unapparent," he looked back upon "the dream of
life," where human beings

> lost in stormy visions, keep
> With phantoms an unprofitable strife; [9]

where death and life are

> still arraying
> In liveries ever new, the rapid, blind
> And fleeting generations of mankind; [10]

where

> faiths and empires gleam,
> Like wrecks of a dissolving dream,

and

> Worlds on worlds are rolling ever
>   From creation to decay,
> Like the bubbles on a river
>   Sparkling, bursting, borne away . . ."[11]

In a disillusioned mood, he might urge:

> Lift not the painted veil which those who live
> Call Life: though unreal shapes be pictured there,
> And it but mimic all we would believe
> With colours idly spread . . .[12]

But he was never able to take his own advice; willingly or unwill-
ingly, he must give himself up to "thoughts that wander through
eternity." Even in *Queen Mab* he had visioned a realm where

> matter, space and time
> In those aërial mansions cease to act,[13]

whence the soul of Ianthe might view the universe and the comings

[9] *Adonais*, xxxix.
[10] *The Witch of Atlas*, lxxi.
[11] *Hellas*, ll. 1064–65, 197–200.
[12] *Sonnet* (1818). Cf. *Prometheus Unbound*, III, iv, ll. 190–93.
[13] II, ll. 91–92.

and goings of men upon the tiny sphere of earth. And in his last long poem, *The Triumph of Life,* he stands aside once more and watches the mysterious pageant of life roll past — a pitiful and dreadful vision, almost insupportable were it not for the brooding half-awareness that here all is illusion

> Where nothing is, but all things seem,
> And we the shadows of the dream.[14]

In the very last lines of the poem, the last, perhaps, that he wrote, the old question rises to his lips once more, and he cries: "Then what is life?" How he would have answered, or whether he would have answered at all, must remain unknown. But we can imagine him calmly wondering, in the last instant before the tumult of waters overwhelmed his consciousness, whether the Great Mystery was now to be solved.

It is this quality in Shelley's character and poetry — his indifference to the shows of things, his impatient disregard of the merely human and narrowly personal passions and preoccupations of the mass of mankind, his desire to rise above "that Storm Which with the shattered present chokes the past,"[15] and by which the weak are content to be driven aimlessly, while the strong take pride in vain contention with it — it is this quality that is responsible for much of the adverse criticism that has been passed upon his life and work. Matthew Arnold, engaged in a cheerful battle with the Philistines, said that neither Shelley nor his poetry was entirely sane, and many other critics of unquestioned ability and integrity have likewise felt that the appeal of his work is greatly lessened by a "lack of reality." Such criticisms have an entirely legitimate basis; what is not legitimate is the assumption which is frequently implicit in them, that this trait is an absolute poetic defect, since the function of poetry is assumed to be merely the representation of the more obvious aspects of experience. But this is a matter of opinion, and to Shelley at least the mere mirroring of the externals of life seemed rather futile. It was not that he was afraid to face what certain persons complacently call "the facts of life," or that he could not understand and master, to a far greater degree than most men, the conditions of actual earthly

[14] *The Sensitive Plant,* III, ll. 124–25..   [15] *Epipsychidion,* ll. 211–12.

existence.[16] It was simply that that existence, in and for itself, seemed utterly worthless, literally unreal. Shelley did not *retreat* from the realm of appearance: he was led away from it in his passionate search for reality. "Perhaps all discontent with the *less* (to use a Platonic sophism) supposes the sense of a just claim to the *greater*, and that we admirers of 'Faust' are on the right road to Paradise."[17] That the *greater* existed he never doubted, except in those moments of despair to which even the most religious natures — they indeed more than others — are sometimes subject.

II

But if the universe only appears to be material, what is it in reality? There are many passages in Shelley's writings which seem to indicate a belief that the only reality is mind. In the essay *On Life* he declares:

The view of life presented by the most refined deductions of the intellectual philosophy, is that of unity. Nothing exists but as it is perceived. The difference is merely nominal between those two classes of thought, which are vulgarly distinguished by the names of ideas and of external objects. Pursuing the same thread of reasoning, the existence of individual minds, similar to that which is employed in now questioning its own nature, is likewise found to be a delusion. The words *I, you, they*, are not signs of any actual difference subsisting between the assemblage of thoughts thus indicated, but are merely marks employed to denote the different modifications of the one mind.

He is careful, however, to avoid the implication of solipsism.

Let it not be supposed that this doctrine conducts to the monstrous presumption that I, the person who now write and think, am that one mind. I am but a portion of it.

Furthermore, he insists:

The relations of *things* remain unchanged, by whatever system. By the word *things* is to be understood any object of thought, that is any thought upon which any other thought is employed, with an apprehension of dis-

---

[16] Cf. John Drinkwater, *The Pilgrim of Eternity* (New York, 1925), p. 299: "The inspired idiot view of Shelley is itself idiotic. Essentially he was a master of life, because he was a master of practical logic, in the profoundest sense a seer . . ."

[17] *Letters*, II, 953 (April 10, 1822).

tinction. The relations of these remain unchanged; and such is the material of our knowledge.[18]

This unqualified idealism appears again in the *Speculations on Metaphysics*, where the writer says: "Thoughts, or ideas, or notions, call them what you will, differ from each other, not in kind, but in force"; and goes on to deny, what "has commonly been supposed," "that those distinct thoughts which affect a number of persons, at regular intervals, during the passage of a multitude of other thoughts, which are called *real* or *external objects*, are totally different in kind from those which affect only a few persons, and which recur only at irregular intervals, and are usually more obscure and indistinct, such as hallucinations, dreams, and the ideas of madness." [19]

Obviously, when Shelley wrote these passages, he was fresh from the study of Bishop Berkeley and Sir William Drummond;[20] and so far there is nothing that is not wholly in harmony with their views. But in a copy of Berkeley which he had borrowed from Charles Lloyd in 1812, he had come upon a note penciled by the latter, which impressed him quite as much as Berkeley's own doctrines, and which, as he wrote nine years later, struck him "as being the assertion of a doctrine, of which even then I had long been persuaded, and on which I had founded much of my persuasions, regarding the imagined cause of the Universe — 'Mind cannot create, it can only perceive.' " [21] How this fits in with the Berkeleian

[18] Shawcross, pp. 56–57. In regard to this essay, Mary Shelley comments: "Shelley was a disciple of the Immaterial Philosophy of Berkeley. This theory gave unity and grandeur to his ideas, while it opened a wide field for his imagination. The creation — such as it was perceived by his mind — a unit in immensity, was slight and narrow compared with the interminable forms of thought that might exist beyond, to be perhaps perceived hereafter by his own mind; or which are perceptible to other minds that fill the universe, not of space in the material sense, but of infinity in the immaterial one." Preface to *Essays, Letters from Abroad*, etc., in *Complete Works*, V, ix.

[19] *Ibid.*, p. 65.

[20] Cf. George S. Brett, "Shelley's Relation to Berkeley and Drummond," *Studies in English by Members of the University College, Toronto* (University of Toronto Press, 1931).

[21] *Letters*, II, 722 (September 27, 1819). Mr. Kurtz seems to overlook this statement when he argues (*The Pursuit of Death*, pp. 279–81) that Shelley did not understand Berkeley; since Shelley's idealism is "subjective," i.e., holding the external world to be pure illusion, while Berkeley's idealism is "objective" in that

principle that "nothing exists but as it is perceived" is not immediately clear; yet Shelley quotes it in the essay *On Life* immediately following the passages given above. Apparently he means that the perceiving mind does not create the universe, which is independent of any particular finite mind, but is itself of the nature of mind. In the individual consciousness, then, we have mind contemplating Mind. In harmony with this view is a passage in *The Daemon of the World* (a rehandling of portions of *Queen Mab*), in which the poet says, speaking of the problem of immortality:

> For birth but wakes the universal mind
> Whose mighty streams might else in silence flow
> Thro' the vast world, to individual sense
> Of outward shows, whose unexperienced shape
> New modes of passion to its frame may lend;
> Life is its state of action, and the store
> Of all events is aggregated there
> That variegate the eternal universe . . .[22]

This problem of the relation of the individual to the universal mind is, of course, one of the great stumbling-blocks in the path of the idealist, and other passages can be quoted which indicate that,

the objects of sensation have a real existence as ideas in the mind of God. The acceptance of the principle that "mind cannot create, it can only perceive" seems incompatible with "subjective" idealism.

[22] Ll. 539–46. It is interesting to compare this passage, probably written in 1815 or 1816 (a portion of this revision was published in 1816 with *Alastor*; another section, from which the lines above are quoted, remained unpublished until H. Buxton Forman's edition of Shelley's poetry in 1876), with the *Queen Mab* version (IX, ll. 155–56): "For birth but wakes the spirit to the sense Of outward shows," etc. The relation between the individual mind and the universe is a dominant theme in *Mont Blanc*, also written in 1816; but the poem is extremely obscure, and I shall offer no detailed comment. Mr. C. D. Locock, in his excellent edition of Shelley's poems, has attempted at some length to make clear the poet's meaning — not, perhaps, with entire success. His note on the opening lines is as follows: "In the first section, Shelley compares three physical phenomena with three metaphysical conceptions: (1) The Ravine, corresponding with the *universal* mind; (2) The Arve, corresponding with the everlasting Universe of Things; (3) The feeble brook, corresponding with *individual human* mind, which borrows its inspiration from the everlasting Universe. This last is the idea developed in the next section." Charles Dealtry Locock, *The Poems of Percy Bysshe Shelley* (2 vols., London, 1911), II, 489. I am inclined to question whether the "Universe of Things" is to be distinguished from "the universal mind," to which "the individual human mind" is tributary. Shelley described the poem as an "undisciplined overflowing of the soul." See Mary Shelley's "Note on Poems Written in 1816," Hutchinson, p. 536. Cf. also Peck, *op. cit.*, I, 474.

after all, Shelley's idealism in metaphysics was not absolute, and that the poet was never free from certain "ultimate doubts," from a deep and ineradicable skepticism.[23] "It is probable that what we call thought is not an actual being, but no more than the relation between certain parts of that infinitely varied mass, of which the rest of the universe is composed, and which ceases to exist as soon as those parts change their position with regard to each other."[24] The same view is stated in the *Speculations on Metaphysics.*

We see trees, houses, fields, living beings in our own shape, and in shapes more or less analogous to our own. These are perpetually changing the mode of their existence relatively to us. . . . These diversities are events or objects, and are essential, considered relatively to human identity, for the existence of the human mind. For if the inequalities, produced by what has been termed the operations of the external universe, were leveled by the perception of our being, uniting and filling up their interstices, motion and mensuration, and time, and space; the elements of the human mind being thus abstracted, sensation and imagination cease. Mind cannot be considered pure.[25]

That is, mind as we know it is only one element in ultimate reality, and not the whole. For what is this principle of change upon which the human mind depends? Why does the "universal mind" need to be "waked," and what is it that does the waking? Whence springs the "Mutability" that is named so often in Shelley's verse, and from which the poet so passionately yearns to escape, while oppressed by the knowledge that escape is unimaginable? Clearly this arises from some source other than mind. Indeed, Shelley seems sometimes to lean toward complete skepticism, as when he says, in the same *Speculations:* "It is said that mind produces motion; and it might as well have been said, that motion produces mind."[26] And farther on he remarks that it makes little difference whether we say "that when speaking of the objects of thought, we indeed only describe

---

[23] *Skepticism* is used here in a more or less technical sense, as inability to believe that "the real is the rational," that ultimate reality is of the nature of mind, and that the universe is therefore rational and intelligible throughout. This, of course, is almost the opposite of the popular sense, according to which the word is practically synonymous with *rationalism.*

[24] *On a Future State,* in Shawcross, p. 61. The second *which,* I take it, refers to *thought* and not to *mass.*

[25] Shawcross, p. 67.

[26] *Ibid.,* p. 68.

one of the forms of thought — or that, speaking of thought, we only apprehend one of the operations of the universal system of things." [27]

It must be remembered, however, that these extremely skeptical utterances occur in what was intended to be a scientific discussion — and one dealing not, as the title indicates, with metaphysics but with psychology. Indeed, Shelley says: "Metaphysics may be defined as an inquiry concerning those things belonging to, or connected with, the internal nature of man." [28] His aim seems to be simply to describe the operations of the mind, without theorizing as to their ultimate origin and significance.

In his poetry, however, Shelley places upon himself no such limitations, and from *Queen Mab* to *Hellas* we find him constantly preoccupied with the task of framing some conception of ultimate reality that will afford to his imagination some shelter, however precarious, from the oppressiveness of infinity. In *Queen Mab* he presents a theory that may best be characterized, as Santayana says, by the term "panpsychism."

> "Throughout this varied and eternal world
> Soul is the only element: the block
> That for uncounted ages has remained
> The moveless pillar of a mountain's weight
> Is active, living spirit. Every grain
> Is sentient both in unity and part,
> And the minutest atom comprehends
> A world of loves and hatreds; these beget
> Evil and good: hence truth and falsehood spring;
> Hence will and thought and action, all the germs
> Of pain or pleasure, sympathy or hate,
> That variegate the eternal universe." [29]

The poet soon abandoned the rather naïve idea upon which he lets his fancy dwell in the concluding lines, namely, that such a meta-

[27] *Ibid.*, p. 69.   [28] *Ibid.*, p. 68.
[29] IV, ll. 139–50. Brett, after attributing the source of this passage to Sir William Drummond, comments: "Soul is therefore really light, or atoms of light, and these atoms combine in various ways to form plant, animal, or human souls. Shelley goes one step further: even stones have souls." *Op. cit.*, p. 195. This emphasis upon the purely scientific aspect of Shelley's thought, which also dominates Mr. Carl H. Grabo's recent work *A Newton among Poets* (University of North

physical theory as this can really *explain* any of the conditions of human existence; but the belief that the stuff of the universe is "active, living spirit . . . sentient both in unity and part" was one that long held an attraction for him. So in the great world-chorus that closes *Prometheus Unbound*, in which Demogorgon addresses in turn the various spiritual powers of the universe, he speaks to the

> elemental Genii, who have homes
> From man's high mind even to the central stone
> Of sullen lead; from heaven's star-fretted domes
> To the dull weed some sea-worm battens on:

and "a confused Voice" replies:

> We hear: thy words waken Oblivion.[30]

If these passages from Shelley's verse are to be reconciled with his utterances in the *Speculations on Metaphysics*, it must be by assuming that the word *mind* is used in the latter in a much wider sense than is usually attached to it in philosophical writings. And

Carolina Press, 1930), and which attempts to show that the poet held recondite theories reducing matter (and everything else) to some form of energy, such as light or electricity, somewhat after the manner of modern physics, seems to me to be quite beside the point. It is true that such theories may lead to a mystical view of the universe somewhat similar to that which, as I think, Shelley ultimately came to hold. But to approach Shelley from this angle is to read the story backwards. His conception of the universe is, as I believe this chapter and those following will indicate, first of all emotional and moral — in a word (which may Heaven and Humanism pardon me for using), humanistic, and not scientific. His world is the world of Plato and Dante, not that of Newton. He does not arrive at a theory that ultimate reality is energy, and then call this energy God; he begins with "the internal nature of man," thence infers the existence of some Power governing the universe, and finally, in the endeavor to achieve a complete philosophy, enters upon speculations concerning the workings of that Power in the external world. All this, to be sure, is true in much less degree of the early than of the mature work. And Mr. Grabo, of course, says frankly that his work is limited to a consideration of the scientific side of Shelley's thought. With the passage quoted from *Queen Mab* compare the letter to Miss Hitchener dated November 24, 1811. *Letters*, I, 174.

[30] IV, ll. 539–43. Mr. Grabo suggests that in this passage Shelley is merely giving metaphorical expression to the fact, then recently discovered, that all substances are composed of a limited number of elements, in various combinations. *Op. cit.*, p. 181. No doubt Shelley had this discovery in mind; but that is not the point. The point is that even to these elementary substances he attributes life and sentience, by virtue of which, presumably, each element possesses its peculiar properties. Mr. Grabo also mentions the suggestion of Mr. C. A. Brown that the "dull weed some sea-worm battens on" is an allusion to the recently discovered element iodine. It may be so; but one is tempted to ask, "Who cares?"

indeed I think that a careful reading of Shelley's work as a whole will show that he regularly means by *mind* or *thought* not merely reason, the ratiocinative faculty, the discursive intellect, but all other forms of psychic experience as well: sensation, emotion, imagination, will — in a word, consciousness.[31]

The poet's last utterance upon the subject is put into the mouth of Ahasuerus in *Hellas*, which is in some respects the finest and most profound of his works. One has but to compare these lines with those quoted above from *Queen Mab* to perceive the measure of Shelley's growth in artistic, imaginative, and intellectual power. The same boldness of speculation is present, the same rejection of the realm of appearance, the same seeking for some deeper reality. But the one is a doctrinaire exposition of a merely intellectual theory; while in the other is a depth of thought and a power of expression that mark the inspired utterance of a great mind and a noble character self-disciplined to the service of a Power greater than they. I, at least, find in the inevitable sweep and surge, the passionate rush and rhythm of these verses, the stamp of finality.

> Sultan! talk no more
> Of thee and me, the Future and the Past;
> But look on that which cannot change — the One,
> The unborn and the undying. Earth and ocean,
> Space, and the isles of life or light that gem
> The sapphire floods of interstellar air,
> This firmament pavilioned upon chaos,
> With all its cressets of immortal fire,
> Whose outwall, bastioned impregnably
> Against the escape of boldest thoughts, repels them
> As Calpe the Atlantic clouds — this Whole
> Of suns, and worlds, and men, and beasts, and flowers,
> With all the silent or tempestuous workings
> By which they have been, are, or cease to be,
> Is but a vision; — all that it inherits
> Are motes of a sick eye, bubbles and dreams;
> Thought is its cradle and its grave, nor less
> The Future and the Past are idle shadows

[31] It is interesting to note, in this connection, that one of the few positive statements that F. H. Bradley, in *Appearance and Reality*, is willing to make concerning Ultimate Reality is that it must be of the nature of experience.

Of thought's eternal flight — they have no being:
Nought is but that which feels itself to be.[32]

Mahmud's answer shows that Shelley was quite aware of how strongly most men would be repelled by the seeming insubstantiality of such a universe as is here envisioned; of how they would shrink back into the shelter of the obvious and the commonplace, exclaiming that these words

cast on all things surest, brightest, best,
Doubt, insecurity, astonishment.[33]

Nevertheless, he reiterates his view.

Thought
Alone, and its quick elements, Will, Passion,
Reason, Imagination, cannot die;
They are, what that which they regard appears,
The stuff whence mutability can weave
All that it hath dominion o'er, worlds, worms,
Empires, and superstitions.[34]

This is great poetry, but it is not the kind which he who runs may read; and well may Mahmud describe these oracular words as "the wise mad talk of the old Jew." At first glance, Shelley seems to be setting forth the doctrine of absolute idealism; for he asserts in the strongest terms that the world we experience has no existence except as mind — and, in fact, as a Mind. All the varied forms of the universe are but ideas in this One Mind. Yet the skepticism that we have already noticed in Shelley (a kind of skepticism which, by a change of emphasis, passes into mysticism) is still present; for although thought may be the cradle and the grave of the universe,[35] yet it cannot pass beyond, and therefore is limited. Moreover, the firmament (that is, the universe — that is, the One Mind) is pavilioned upon chaos; and we must conclude that chaos, as its very name indicates, is not and cannot be comprehended within the One Mind. Yet this very chaos, if it is, as would seem, the stuff from which the universe is made, must after all, according to the final lines, be of the nature of thought or mind. And finally, the

---

[32] Ll. 766–85.   [33] Ll. 790–91.   [34] Ll. 795–801.
[35] Thought is here said to be the grave of the universe, I suppose, in the sense that if thought should cease the universe would pass out of existence.

universe is apparently said to be the creation not of mind but of
Mutability.

III

Upon these dark difficulties I hope at the end of the chapter to
be able to shed a little light.[36] What I wish to emphasize here is the
fact that, for all his apparent asseverations to the contrary, what
Shelley sees and feels in the world is not a unity but an opposition.
All idealism affects in two opposite ways man's attitude toward the
external world: it both degrades that world as being something less
than it appears, and ennobles it as being something more. In the
idealist both these tendencies are present, but one or the other
usually becomes dominant, according to the individual temperament. Hegel's idealism, for instance, is optimistic and leads, according to Santayana, to "a hearty worship of things as they are."
In Schopenhauer, on the other hand, who was a born pessimist,
idealism leads to a desire to escape from the external world as from
a realm of illusion. Shelley, of course, belongs with Schopenhauer.
In his thinking, or at least in his feeling, the external world is illusion.[37] And yet, paradoxically, it is more than illusion: he desires
to assert its unreality, but he cannot escape the feeling that there is
after all some principle by which mind — or rather, as will appear,

[36] Mr. Kurtz — who has a low opinion of *Hellas* because it does not fit into his
theory that Shelley's life and writings show a general advance "from the dream
of Plato to the greater vision of Aristotle, from a retrospective dream of appearances as declensions of reality to a forward vision of becoming" (*The Pursuit of
Death*, p. 207) — dwells at some length upon these difficulties, urging that "in
the poem no adjustment is made between 'the One, the unborn, and the undying'
and the illusory phenomena of 'matter,' " and that "the doctrine of illusion destroys
the significance of the Greek struggle for freedom by making both the struggle
and its object and its failure and its success so many illusions; and also renders
nugatory the antithesis of good and evil out of which is built the antiphonal, lyric
construction of the poem." *Ibid.*, p. 322. This seems to me to be overstating the
case; but his criticism of the line "They are what that which they regard appears"
seems just, for Shelley says, first, that the elements of thought are the only reality,
and then, that there is something which they regard.

[37] This notwithstanding the fact that he speaks of himself on one occasion as one
"whose chief pleasure in life is the contemplation of nature" (*Letters*, II, 601);
that he attributes the greatness of Greek art to the fact that the Greeks "lived in a
perpetual commerce with external nature, and nourished themselves upon the spirit
of its forms" (*ibid.*, p. 666); and that he was himself abnormally sensitive to
natural beauty. "The wind, the light, the air, the smell of a flower affects me with
violent emotions." *Ibid.*, p. 843.

the Spirit which works in mind, and attempts to impress upon it beautiful, harmonious, and permanent forms — is limited and opposed.[38]

For *thought,* or *mind,* be it noted, is only the stuff out of which the universe is made. Some Power not mind, and greater than mind, must fashion and give form to "thought's stagnant chaos," [39] and then sustain and govern the cosmos it has shaped. This Power is Shelley's God; and it is clear that in his mature thinking Shelley did not identify God with the universe, and that the tendency toward pantheism that sometimes manifests itself in his early writings was soon replaced by a fundamental dualism.

This dualism, latent even in parts of *Queen Mab,* is a dominant theme in all the later poems. That anyone who has seriously studied Shelley's work should call him a pantheist is a mystery to which I can offer no solution. But it is at any rate not difficult to show how baseless such an opinion is. And let us begin with the note to *Queen Mab* on the line "There is no God": "This negation must be understood solely to affect a creative Deity. The hypothesis of a pervading Spirit coeternal with the universe remains unshaken." There is here a clear distinction between the universe and the Spirit by which it is informed: a distinction that is maintained throughout the poem. The ruling Power of the universe, it is true, is sometimes addressed as "Nature," but more often as the "Spirit of Nature." The following passages are characteristic.

> "Spirit of Nature! thou
> Life of interminable multitudes;
> Soul of those mighty spheres
> Whose changeless paths through Heaven's deep silence lie;
> Soul of that smallest being,
> The dwelling of whose life
> Is one faint April sun-gleam . . ." [40]

> "Throughout these infinite orbs of mingling light,
> Of which yon earth is one, is wide diffused
> A Spirit of activity and life . . ." [41]

---

[38] I am not sure that the "mutability" of the lines from *Hellas* is not very similar to what Schopenhauer means by "Will"; the more so because in *The Triumph of Life* what appears to be the same principle is clearly to be identified with *desire.*

[39] *Prometheus Unbound,* IV, l. 380.

[40] III, ll. 226–32.   [41] VI, ll. 146–48.

> ". . . infinity within,
> Infinity without, belie creation;
> The exterminable spirit it contains
> Is Nature's only God . . ." [42]

Now, it is evident that whatever is "diffused" or "contained" must be diffused through, or contained in, *something*. I do not say that Shelley had this distinction clearly in mind, and I do not know how he would have reconciled it with the statement that "soul is the only element"; but I am convinced that these passages and many like them are based upon the tacit assumption of an underlying dualism. Elsewhere the poet speaks of

> Nature's soul,
> That formed this world so beautiful, that spread
> Earth's lap with plenty, and life's smallest chord
> Strung to unchanging unison . . . [43]

One might almost infer from these lines belief in a creative God; but "Nature's soul" is creative only in the sense that it (apparently) works in some primordial, unorganized stuff, gives it form and harmony, and brings a cosmos out of chaos. Such a conception, as will presently appear, is constantly recurrent in Shelley's work; and in the later writings it is repeatedly given definite and deliberate expression. Nor is there to be found in his work any explicit attempt to resolve this dualism into a higher monism, as in Spinoza's philosophy "thought" and "extension" are resolved into "Substance." Probably at first he was not aware that such a tendency existed in his thinking, or that it conflicted with "the view of life presented by . . . the intellectual philosophy," which is "that of unity"; while in his last years he cared little to try to satisfy the demands of reason, which he felt to be wholly inadequate to the solution of life's ultimate problems.

It may be argued not unreasonably, of course, that in the passages quoted from *Queen Mab* the dualism is nominal rather than real, since the informing Spirit apparently meets no resistance from the element in which it works, but finds there (or will eventually find there) perfect expression. So the poet declares, addressing the "Spirit of Nature," that the time "will swiftly, surely come" when

[42] VII, ll. 21–24.   [43] IV, ll. 89–92.

> "the unbounded frame, which thou pervadest,
>   Will be without a flaw
>   Marring its perfect symmetry." [44]

It was not many years, however, before this boyish optimism was cast aside forever. Shelley did not cease to believe (for very long, at any rate) that some benevolent Power governed the universe;[45] but he came to see that the world of human life, at least, was sadly out of joint, and that "the visitations of the divinity in man"[46] were rare and fleeting. Such is the theme and spirit of the *Hymn to Intellectual Beauty*, written in 1816.

> The awful shadow of some unseen Power
>   Floats though unseen among us, — visiting
>   This various world with as inconstant wing
>   As summer winds that creep from flower to flower . . .
>
> Spirit of BEAUTY, that dost consecrate
>   With thine own hues all thou dost shine upon
>   Of human thought or form, — where art thou gone?
>   Why dost thou pass away and leave our state,
>   This dim vast vale of tears, vacant and desolate? [47]

The "Intellectual Beauty" which Shelley here addresses is not Beauty alone but also Goodness, and may perhaps be partially identified with the Spirit of Nature in *Queen Mab*, which by its presence imparts to the external world and to human nature whatever of order and harmony they possess. But in the early poem that harmony was universal, except for the temporary imperfection of man; while now the poet is haunted, as he was to be all the rest of his life, by the frailty and transience of all things beautiful and good, whether in external nature or in human existence, and by the apparently inescapable subjection of these things to "doubt, chance, and mutability." There seems to him to be present in the world

[44] III, ll. 238–40.
[45] It must be confessed that *A Refutation of Deism* seems to be inspired by an unmitigated and militant materialism. Yet an acquaintance who was with Shelley during his last visit to his parents' home in the spring of 1814 testifies that "he spoke of the Supreme Being as of infinite mercy and benevolence"; and adds, again in striking contrast to the positive and rationalistic tone of the *Refutation*: "He disclosed no fixed views of spiritual things; all seemed wild and fanciful." Ingpen, *Shelley in England*, p. 417.
[46] *A Defence of Poetry*, in Shawcross, p. 155.
[47] Ll. 1–4, 13–17.

some principle that resists the influence of the divine Spirit of Good.[48]

The same thought is even more definitely expressed in the *Essay on Christianity*.

God is represented by Jesus Christ as the Power from which, and through which, the streams of all that is excellent and delightful flow; the Power which models, as they pass, all the elements of this mixed universe to the purest and most perfect shape which it belongs to their nature to assume . . . According to Jesus Christ, *and according to the indisputable facts of the case,* some evil spirit has dominion in this imperfect world. But there will come a time when the human mind shall be visited exclusively by the influences of the benignant Power.[49]

The last sentence, of course, makes it clear that Shelley hoped that somehow the Spirit of Good might triumph; and this hope he never abandoned, although he came to doubt whether it could ever be realized in the world of Time.[50] But in the world of common life, the conflict always goes on. It is described again in a great stanza of *Adonais*.

> He is a portion of the loveliness
> Which once he made more lovely: he doth bear
> His part, while the one Spirit's plastic stress
> Sweeps through the dull dense world, compelling there,
> All new successions to the forms they wear;
> Torturing th' unwilling dross that checks its flight
> To its own likeness, as each mass may bear;
> And bursting in its beauty and its might
> From trees and beasts and men into the Heaven's light.[51]

[48] Mr. Kurtz speaks of the "sulky Platonic dualism" of the opening stanzas of the *Hymn*. *Op. cit.*, p. 100. He is certainly correct as to the dualism, and also, I think, as to the Platonism; but I cannot help feeling that "sulky," like so many of Mr. Kurtz's adjectives, achieves picturesqueness at the expense of accuracy.

[49] Shawcross, pp. 94–95. Italics mine. The discussion of the ethical dualism of Shelley's thought is reserved, as far as possible, for the next chapter. But in Shelley, as in Plato, ethical and metaphysical dualism are closely connected. At any rate, the passage makes untenable the frequent contention that Shelley believed evil to be an easily dispelled illusion. It is also, I should say, irreconcilable with pantheism, however that word may be defined.

[50] See below, Chapter V.

[51] Stanza xliii. Mr. Kurtz thinks that the doctrine of this stanza is Aristotelian rather than Platonic, because it contains the idea of "becoming" (*op. cit.*, p. 284); and, contrasting *Hellas*, he speaks of "the more advanced monism in which *Adonais* culminates." *Ibid.*, p. 322. But we have an *unwilling* dross, which must be *tortured*

Nothing could be clearer than the tendency of the passages that I have quoted. They show beyond the possibility of doubt that Shelley believed in a cosmic dualism, in a Spirit or Power which is opposed by some recalcitrant principle, so that its government of the visible world is only partial and imperfect, and its efforts to impose upon that world harmony and order are doomed, as far as the human mind can perceive, to at least some measure of frustration.

IV

This Power, as I have said, is Shelley's God; and a clear understanding of the manner in which this Deity is conceived, and of the nature and attributes which are ascribed to it in Shelley's thinking, is obviously essential to a comprehension of his religion as a whole.

The one dominant attribute of Shelley's God is *goodness,* and goodness in a human sense. It will be remembered that the poet's strongest objection to what he regarded as the Christian conception of God was that such a Deity must be (even though Christian apologists might not admit it) the source of evil as well as of good; and such a God he would not accept. He describes with amazement, in an early letter to Hogg, his meeting with a person who frankly attributed to God, as to man, a limited and mixed nature. Exclaiming, "Now here is a new kind of God for you!" he continues: "In practice, such a Deist as this is, as they told him, an Atheist; for he believes that the Creator is by no means perfect, but composed of good and evil, like man, and producing that mixture of these principles which is evident everywhere." [52] Years later he was struck by Plato's comment on the same subject, for he translated the following fragment from the *Republic.* "God then, since he is good, cannot be, as is vulgarly supposed, the cause of all things; he is the cause, indeed, of very few things. Among the great varieties of events, which happen in the course of human affairs, evil prodigiously overbalances good in everything which regards men. Of all that is good, there can be no other cause than God; but some

into beauty; and it is not the process, but the end — the bursting into Heaven's light — which Shelley glorifies.

[52] *Letters,* I, 70 (May 8, 1811).

other cause ought to be discovered for evil, which should never be
imputed as an effect to God."[53]

Not only, however, would Shelley not admit that God could
be imperfect, but he was equally unwilling to admit that his own
perceptions of good and evil might be mistaken or illusory. He
wrote in one of his Irish pamphlets of 1812, discoursing characteristically concerning the nature of man: "The laws of his moral as
of his physical nature are immutable, as is everything of nature . . .
Any law is bad which attempts to make it criminal to do what the
plain dictates within the breast of every man tell him that he ought
to do. . . . Conscience is a government before which all others
sink into nothingness; it surpasses, and where it can act, supersedes
all other, as nature surpasses art, as God surpasses man."[54] Seven
years later, expressing to Leigh Hunt a characteristic mistrust of
his literary powers, he added: "I have confidence in my moral
sense alone."[55] He would bow to no law except that of his own
conscience. His position is perfectly expressed in Newman's statement that "no religion is from God which contradicts our sense of
right and wrong."[56] His attitude on this question, as on so many
others, was determined by his intense individualism, a trait so distinctive that it is indeed frequently declared to be the source of all
his alleged moral shortcomings. Mr. Paul Elmer More calls it "an
overweening self-trust," which "in the final test left him almost
inhuman."[57] It was also a sore point with Charles Kingsley, who
says that it was only Shelley's "intense self-opinion" which kept

[53] *The Republic*, Book II, 379, in *Complete Works*, VII, 259.
[54] *Proposals for an Association*, in *Prose Works*, I, 276–77.
[55] *Letters*, II, 755.
[56] *A Grammar of Assent*, p. 419. Newman, of course, adds some qualifications,
but none, I think, that Shelley would have been unwilling to accept. It is true that
he says that "a religion which simply commanded us to lie, or to have a community
of wives, would *ipso facto* forfeit all claim to a divine origin"; and some of
Shelley's detractors would doubtless say that the second of these commandments
would have been no obstacle to Shelley. Such folk should remember, however, that
it was once the fashion, among people of a certain sort, to call Newman himself a
liar. Newman adds: "I should in like manner repudiate a theology which taught
that men were created in order to be wicked and wretched." This is exactly what
Shelley believed Christian theology to teach.
[57] *Shelburne Essays, Seventh Series*, pp. 8–9. Cf. also Mr. More's introduction to
the Cambridge Edition of *Byron's Poetical Works*.

him from ending "in Rome as an Oratorian or a Passionist" [58] (Oh! what a weak and depraved wretch he must have been!) and declares that Shelley's "whole life through was a denial of external law, and a substitution of internal sentiment." [59] Statements such as these, however, seem in the last analysis to have little meaning. If a man cannot trust himself, whom or what can he trust? How can there be in the moral realm any "external law"? Is it moral to conform to human conventions, when one's own belief is that to do so is wrong? Is it moral to obey the commandments laid down in a book, even though it be supposed to be divinely inspired, if those commandments conflict with one's own deepest sentiments? "Everybody saying a thing does not make it right." From the moral standpoint nothing is right or wrong except what the individual believes to be so. As Santayana says, with reference to Shelley, "All moral life and all moral judgment have this deeply romantic character; they venture to assert a private ideal in the face of an intractable and omnipotent world." [60] Shelley would kneel neither to a God in whose nature, as in that of man, both good and evil are mingled, nor to a pantheistic God whose nature is neither good nor evil in any human sense. "He did not subordinate morally the individual to the cosmos. He did not surrender the authority of moral ideals in the face of physical necessity, which is properly the essence of pantheism." [61]

Now, what is the significance of Shelley's insistence on the right and the necessity of private judgment? Simply this: that if Shelley says (as he does) that there is some spiritual Power at work in the universe, and if he attributes to that Power (as he does) goodness and beauty and love, then it can be fairly asserted that he believes in a personal God; for he would never have used these words in

---

[58] *Literary and General Essays*, p. 43. It is true that Shelley's love of Dante and Calderón shows that certain aspects of Catholicism had a strong attraction for him. But perhaps neither to feel such an attraction, nor to resist it, is so heinous a sin as Kingsley would make out.

[59] *Ibid.*, p. 45. Kingsley's essay is probably the most stupid and wrongheaded criticism ever written on Shelley, and shows the presence in himself of all the faults which he unjustly charges against his victim: irrationality, uncharitableness, spiritual pride above all.

[60] George Santayana, *Winds of Doctrine* (London, 1913), p. 160.

[61] *Ibid.*, p. 184.

any except a limited and human sense, or applied them to any object which he did not feel to have a community with his own nature. He was not one to call an abstract force good or loving simply because it was powerful, but only because it had some analogy to what he believed to be good and loving in human life, was in its nature akin to human goodness and love.

This, of course, is an unorthodox view: the great majority of critics have held that Shelley's God (admitting that he believed in one) is not personal. The following statements by Mr. S. F. Gingerich fairly represent the general trend of criticism in regard to this aspect of Shelley's thought. "To conceive of power in terms of personality was instinctively difficult for him." [62] "But, governed by Necessity, the animating Spirit of this supersensuous world is devoid of will and personality, and as such is unethical, wherein Shelley was unlike Plato." [63] "The two most fundamental characteristics of the 'one mind, one power, one all-pervasive spirit' of Shelley, are, first, that it is self-creating, not in a mechanical, but in a spiritually operative sense, whereby it necessitates all life, and, secondly, that it is impersonal. . . . All Being, including the mind of man, was to him impersonal." [64] "Love, like the words Necessity and Power already noted, is a word almost interchangeable with Wisdom, or Nature, or God, and though it has a human side, it is chiefly a cosmic force as impersonal and impalpable as Time, or Nature, or any other of Shelley's abstractions, which live and work in a necessitarian spirit almost exclusively independent of the human consciousness." [65] In the same vein, Walter Bagehot declared some three-quarters of a century earlier that in Shelley the spirit of the universe "has no will and no virtue: it is animated, but unholy; alive, but unmoral: it is an object of intense admiration; it is not an object of worship." [66]

The last of these quotations can be shown to be a flat contradiction of what Shelley himself says; but the refutation of the state-

[62] Solomon F. Gingerich, *Essays in the Romantic Poets* (New York, 1929), p. 203.

[63] *Ibid.*, pp. 205–06.   [64] *Ibid.*, p. 218.

[65] *Ibid.*, p. 222. The question of Necessitarianism I reserve for the following chapter.

[66] *Estimations in Criticisms*, I, 130.

ments previously quoted is more difficult, because the writer (like most of those who criticize Shelley on this score) fails to make clear just what he means by the word *personal*. Is the reader supposed to infer that a personal God must be "a venerable old man, seated on a throne of clouds, his breast the theatre of various passions analogous to those of humanity, his will changeable and uncertain as that of an earthly king"?[67] Surely no intelligent person holds such a childish fancy, or insists that a personal God must be anthropomorphic; and yet it is difficult to understand how any other conception of personality can be denied to Shelley's God. Nobody denies that the Christian God is personal, yet how much can be inferred from the New Testament as to the personality of God the Father? We are told that "God is a spirit" and that "God is love" and that he is the "Father" of Christ. Yet the last is apparently only a figure of speech; it implies a relation far different, I should say, from the human relation of father to son. Even orthodox theologians, I believe, hold that the relation between the "Persons" of the Trinity is humanly incomprehensible. The only personal attribute consistently ascribed to the God of the New Testament is that of love.[68] As to the question of will, of which Mr. Gingerich and others make so much, we may let Shelley himself speak.

Jesus Christ attributes to this Power the faculty of Will. How far such a doctrine, in its ordinary sense, may be philosophically true, or how far Jesus Christ intentionally availed himself of a metaphor easily understood, is foreign to the subject to consider. This much is certain, that Jesus Christ represents God as the fountain of all goodness, the eternal enemy of pain and evil, the uniform and unchanging motive of the salutary operations of the material world. The supposition that this cause is excited to action by some principle analogous to the human will,

[67] *Letter to Lord Ellenborough*, in *Letters*, I, 331.

[68] In this connection it is interesting and enlightening to note that Milton, whose theology has been so long deplored as the great defect of *Paradise Lost*, has recently been presented to us as not believing in a personal God at all, his Almighty being in reality some sort of impersonal and incomprehensible Absolute. See Denis Saurat, *Milton: Man and Thinker*. If such a thesis can be argued with some plausibility in the case of Milton, why not of Dante? Or of any other Christian poet? Or of the Old Testament itself, to say nothing of the New, which is far less definite in its theology than is *Paradise Lost*? There is nothing that cannot be "proved" if one really sets one's mind to it — a remark which of course applies to my own argument as well as to those of M. Saurat, Mr. Gingerich, and others.

adds weight to the persuasion that it is foreign to its nature to inflict the slightest pain.[69]

Mr. Gingerich's statements seem hardly applicable to this passage. If Shelley is not quite willing to assert the presence in the Divine Nature of a will like that of man, yet neither does he deny it. And indeed, it may be argued that any activity which is neither mechanical nor chaotic, but purposive, working toward some end (as is the activity of Shelley's God), implies the existence of a will.

v

So much in general upon the subject of personality. It remains to see how far a further examination of Shelley's works will bear out my contention that the Spirit or Power of which he speaks so often may be fairly described as a personal God. I begin with a quotation from *Queen Mab* which flatly contradicts my thesis.

> "Spirit of Nature! all-sufficing Power,
> Necessity! Thou mother of the world!
> Unlike the God of human error, thou
> Requir'st no prayers or praises; the caprice
> Of man's weak will belongs no more to thee
> Than do the changeful passions of his breast
> To thy unvarying harmony: the slave
> Whose horrible lusts spread misery o'er the world,
> And the good man, who lifts, with virtuous pride,
> His being, in the sight of happiness,
> That springs from his own works; the poison-tree
> Beneath whose shade all life is withered up,
> And the fair oak, whose leafy dome affords
> A temple where the vows of happy love
> Are registered, are equal in thy sight:
> No love, no hate thou cherishest; revenge
> And favouritism, and worst desire of fame
> Thou know'st not: all that the wide world contains
> Are but thy passive instruments, and thou
> Regard'st them all with an impartial eye,
> Whose joy or pain thy nature cannot feel,

[69] *Essay on Christianity*, in Shawcross, p. 95. I may note, in anticipation of the next chapter, that Shelley here assumes, as a matter of course, that the human will is real, and that human beings are *not* the puppets of "Necessity."

Because thou hast not human sense,
Because thou art not human mind." [70]

There can be no argument about the meaning of these lines. If it were true, and the statement is often made,[71] that Shelley never modified the essential principles of the philosophy he set forth in *Queen Mab*, then it would be impossible not to admit that Shelley did not believe in a personal God, that his view of life is deterministic and unethical, and that at best he can be called a pantheist. The passage reads like an extremely crude statement of some of the more obvious doctrines of Spinoza,[72] without any of the depth and refinement of thought and feeling which gained for that philosopher the epithet "God-intoxicated."

But this was not Shelley's mature view, as even some of the passages quoted already will show. It belongs to the time when he was talking about God as "another signification for the universe," refuting Deism, and worshipping at the shrine of Godwin.[73] Possibly it lasted until 1815, for in the essay *On the Punishment of Death*, probably written in that year, the author speaks of "the vast sum of action and of thought which disposes and animates the universe, and is called God." [74] In the opening of *Alastor*, however, written also in 1815, although the poet addresses an invocation to the "Mother of this unfathomable world," yet this "Great Parent" is far other than the "Spirit of Nature" of *Queen Mab. That* re-

[70] VI, ll. 197–219.

[71] See Peck, *op. cit.*, I, 337–38; More, *op. cit.*, p. 14; etc., etc.

[72] A few lines farther on Shelley says that "a shrine is raised" to the Spirit of Nature, namely, "the sensitive extension of the world" (l. 231), which sounds like an echo of Spinoza's terminology. Spinoza is quoted in the note on the line "There is no God!" some twenty lines farther along.

[73] Not, perhaps, with such completely blind devotion as some critics would have us think, or even as some of his own utterances indicate. In a letter to Hogg written in 1811, he questions Godwin's authority as follows: "What constitutes real virtue? . . . Shall we take Godwin's criterion: Expediency? Oh! Surely not." See *Letters*, I, 75. Moreover, even in the first flush of his enthusiastic correspondence with his chosen counselor, he goes to Ireland against Godwin's advice; and when the philosopher condemns the proposed "Association of Philanthropists," urging that reason must be allowed to triumph peacefully by itself, Shelley bluntly asks him whether *Political Justice* has made the world any better in the twenty years since its first appearance. See *Letters*, I, 271. Shelley's mature works contain nothing of Godwin that is not common to the teachings of Plato and Christ as well.

[74] Shawcross, p. 47. Note again the distinction between God and the universe.

quired no prayer nor praise; yet the first fifty lines of *Alastor* are nothing else than a hymn of prayer and praise to the Power that rules over nature [75] — a Power that is assumed to be capable of being moved by love, since Shelley pleads:

> Favour my solemn song, for I have loved
> Thee ever, and thee only . . .

Moreover, the "Mother of the world" in *Queen Mab* looks with impartial eye upon "the good man" and the slave of "horrible lusts," upon "the poison-tree" and "the fair oak"; whereas in *Alastor* Shelley expresses the hope that the "Great Mother" will bless his efforts, inasmuch as

> no bright bird, insect, or gentle beast
> I consciously have injured . . .

It may be held, I suppose, that the whole invocation is merely a grand figure of speech, which need not be taken at all literally; and I do not know how to combat such a view except by saying that my own feeling is entirely different. I do not think that Shelley ever made a practice of indulging in figures of speech for the sake of mere poetic adornment. It seems to me quite clear that the poet is here moving toward the view expressed in the *Hymn to Intellectual Beauty* in 1816, which in turn stands close to the *Essay on Christianity*. This essay contains Shelley's latest reasoned statements concerning the nature of God: statements which sweep into the discard a large number of the arguments that are flaunted so defiantly in *Queen Mab* and *A Refutation of Deism*. To my mind, they fully establish Shelley's belief in a God that may legitimately be called personal.

It seems, however, that there are other opinions. A recent critic, and one whose aim is to show the closeness of Shelley's affinity with Christianity, maintains that Shelley in this essay "represents Christ as a believer in a benevolent Deity, invested with personality only in order to give force to the conception," [76] and that "to the end he

---

[75] Cf. Melvin T. Solve, *Shelley: His Theory of Poetry* (University of Chicago Press, 1927), p. 176, where it is said that in both *Alastor* and the *Hymn to Intellectual Beauty* "the poet's attitude is one of religious veneration and devotion."

[76] Arthur C. Hicks, "The Place of Christianity in Shelley's Thought," p. 24.

maintained his opposition to the idea of a personal God." [77] One might ask whether a "benevolent Deity," if the adjective means anything, must not be to some degree personal. The writer removes the objection, however, by saying elsewhere that Shelley's God is altogether unreal, since it "has no existence independent of Man and Nature";[78] and, again, he speaks of "Shelley's devotion to a mere abstraction — that is, the spirit of Good which does not exist apart from the beings in which it resides." [79] I am not quite sure what some of these statements mean, but I am sure that they do not give an accurate account of Shelley's conception of God.

They are not, perhaps, altogether without foundation. I have already quoted Shelley's assertion in this essay that "the Universal Being can only be described or defined by negatives which deny his subjection to the laws of all inferior existences." [80] The same idea seems to be aimed at when Shelley says with reference to Christ's teaching:

We can distinctly trace, in the tissue of his doctrines, the persuasion that God is some universal Being, differing from man and the mind of man. . . . the interfused and overruling Spirit of all the energy and wisdom included within the circle of existing things. It is important to observe that the author of the Christian system had a conception widely differing from the gross imaginations of the vulgar relatively to the ruling Power of the universe. He everywhere represents this Power as something mysteriously and illimitably pervading the frame of things.[81]

And again:

God . . . was contemplated by Jesus Christ as every poet and philosopher must have contemplated that mysterious principle. He considered that venerable word to express the overruling Spirit of the collective energy of the moral and material world.[82]

So far there is little ground for saying that Shelley's God is personal, though it can scarcely be regarded as an abstraction. But almost immediately these statements are qualified. Commenting on Christ's words "Blessed are the pure in heart, for they shall see God," Shelley says:

[77] *Ibid.*, p. 50.　　[78] *Ibid.*, p. 182.　　[79] *Ibid.*, p. 283.　　[80] Shawcross, p. 91.
[81] *Ibid.*, p. 88. I follow Koszul's edition of the MS. in reading *interfused* for *interpoint*, given by Shawcross.
[82] *Ibid.*, p. 89.

He affirms that a being of pure and gentle habits will not fail, in every thought, in every object of every thought, to be aware of benignant visitings from the invisible energies by which he is surrounded.[83]

If these visitings are truly benignant, must not the source of them have some kinship with human nature? This question seems to find an affirmative answer in what follows:

We live and move and think. But we are not the creators of our own origin and existence. We are not the arbiters of every motion of our own complicated existence; we are not the masters of our own imaginations and moods of mental being. There is a Power by which we are surrounded, like the atmosphere in which some motionless lyre is suspended, which visits with its breath our silent chords at will.

Our most imperial and stupendous qualities — those on which the majesty and the power of humanity is erected — are, relatively to the inferior portion of its mechanism, active and imperial; but they are the passive slaves of some higher and more omnipresent Power. This Power is God; and those who have seen God have, in the period of their purer and more perfect nature, been harmonized by their own will to so exquisite [a] consentaneity of power as to give forth divinest melody, when the breath of universal being sweeps over their frame.[84]

Now, either this is mere verbiage or it means that man, according to the purity and perfection of his character, participates in the nature of the Being which is here called God. Surely all this eloquence does not say merely that those who are pure in heart are pure in heart; but that they have communion with a Nature not their own and yet like their own, which is the source from which all purity and goodness flow. Still a little farther along Shelley speaks in a similar strain of

that merciful and benignant Power who scatters equally upon the beautiful earth all the elements of security and happiness — whose influencings are distributed to all whose natures admit of a participation in them — who sends to the weak and vicious creatures of his will all the benefits which they are capable of sharing . . .[85]

If this Deity, benignant, merciful, bestowing upon his creatures all the happiness which the measure of their obedience to his will

[83] *Ibid.*, p. 90.
[84] *Ibid.*, pp. 90–91. Shawcross reads *omnipotent* for the *omnipresent* of the MS. The phrase "harmonized by their own will" is significant for a later discussion.
[85] *Ibid.*, p. 92. The ethical implications of this passage will be discussed in the following chapter.

enables them to receive, if such a God is to be called impersonal (to say nothing of being labeled a mere abstraction), then those who do so ought at least to define their terms. But even yet we have not seen the most definite of Shelley's statements. He becomes more specific as he continues:

Mankind, transmitting from generation to generation the horrible legacy of accumulated vengeances, and pursuing with the feelings of duty the misery of their fellow beings, have not failed to attribute to the Universal Cause a character analogous with their own. The image of this invisible, mysterious Being is more or less excellent and perfect — resembles more or less its *original and object* — in proportion to the perfectness of the mind on which it is impressed.[86]

The perfection of the human and the divine character is thus asserted to be the same. Man, by resembling God, fulfils most accurately the tendencies of his nature; and God comprehends within itself all that constitutes human perfection. Thus God is a model through which the excellence of man is to be estimated, while the *abstract* perfection of the human character is the type of the *actual* perfection of the divine.[87]

I do not know that I can make Shelley's meaning any clearer than he makes it himself. It is only the God of Christianity (Shelley's Christianity) that is an abstraction, created by man in his own image. Man's idea of God is relative to his own nature; but the true God has an existence independent of man, whereas man is dependent upon God for whatever of good his life contains; so that man, in so far as he is good and pure, and is able to subdue his will to harmony with the "benignant visitings" of the Divine, may be truly said to be created in the image of God.[88]

Any other interpretation of Shelley's words is impossible, unless one is ready to take the position that the writer does not mean what he says, in which case, of course, all discussion or argument be-

---

[86] *Ibid.*, p. 99. Italics mine. The important words "and object" are not in most published texts, having been added by M. Koszul from the MS.

[87] *Ibid.*, p. 100. Italics Shelley's. The use of the pronoun *itself* seems to show a lingering hesitancy to speak of God as a person. But the mere form counts for little in such a context.

[88] And yet a critic can speak of "the pantheistic *Essay on Christianity*"! A. M. D. Hughes, ed., *Shelley: Poems Published in 1820* (Oxford, 1910), p. xix. However, I have no wish to quarrel about mere words, like "pantheism" and "personal." If I have made clear my conception of what Shelley's belief was, the reader may describe it in any terms that he likes.

comes futile.[89] But now what of the "illimitable" and "mysterious" God who can be described only by negatives? Does not Shelley plainly contradict himself? This is a difficult question; but it is only fair to point out that the same difficulty arises in Christian the-

[89] A third alternative may be, by some critics, considered possible: namely, that Shelley is expounding what he conceives to be the genuine teachings of Christ without reference to his own personal opinion. Thus Stopford Brooke, after quoting the passage given above, beginning "We live and move and think," continues: "But we have no business to assume that Shelley expresses in it — as I should like to assume — his settled thought. He is either saying what he thought Jesus thought about God, or he is carried away by the splendour of the speculation into emotional poetry." Stopford Brooke, *Naturalism in English Poetry* (New York, 1920), p. 222. But such a view seems to me to be untenable. In the first place, it is hard to understand why he wrote the essay at all if he was interested in Christ's doctrines only from an objective and impersonal standpoint. All that we know of Shelley's character makes it extremely improbable that he should have written so elaborate an essay on a subject in which he had no personal interest. Second, the sympathy, the eloquence, the enthusiasm, with which the poet writes seem to show unmistakably that at the time of writing, at least, he was powerfully attracted by the doctrines which he was expounding. Moreover, we know that during all his mature life Shelley had an almost unbounded admiration for the character of Christ; and before his death, he had come to consider Christ as the best and wisest man who had ever lived. (Christ is usually mentioned along with Socrates, but the place assigned to the former in *Hellas*, both in the Prologue and certain of the choruses, seems to indicate that he held the higher place in Shelley's regard.) Third, there are a number of passages in which Shelley takes pains to make clear that certain ideas which seem to be implied in the words of Christ are not in accordance with his personal views. In such cases, he follows several methods of procedure. (1) He sometimes interprets the passage so as to bring it into harmony with views which we know from other sources that he held. He declares, for example, that the words "Blessed are the pure in heart, for they shall see God" mean "no more than the most excellent philosophers have felt and expressed — that virtue is its own reward." See Shawcross, p. 89. (It is true that he goes on to interpret these words in rather a transcendental sense; but why not, since he had already written the *Hymn to Intellectual Beauty?*) In the same way, he interprets the command "Take no thought for the morrow" in the following manner: "that it is impossible at once to be highminded and just and wise, and to . . . seek honor, wealth, or empire, either from the idolatry of habit, or as the direct instruments of sensual gratification." *Ibid.*, p. 111. (2) He declares that Christ's teachings have been corrupted by his professed followers. "How monstrous a calumny have not impostors dared to advance . . . against the whole tenor of his doctrines and his life," in promulgating the dogma of eternal punishment. *Ibid.*, p. 92. Cf. pp. 101–02. (3) He insists that "Jesus Christ did what every other reformer who has produced any considerable effect upon the world has done. He accommodated his doctrines to the prepossessions of those whom he addressed." *Ibid.*, p. 104. And he adds, with almost amusing earnestness: "Let not this practice be considered as an unworthy artifice." *Ibid.*, p. 105. (4) He leaves the question open, as in the passage quoted above (page 64) on the attribution to God of will; or when he says of Christ's teaching in regard to immortality: "How delightful a picture, even if it be not true." *Ibid.*, p. 96. (5) He admits that Christ may at times have been led by

ology [90] — and is wisely dismissed as a mystery. One or two suggestions, however, may be offered. Shelley's God is a God of goodness, and his view, although he probably did not formulate it to
himself in these terms, seems to have been that to be good is not
really to be limited (although logically, of course, it is), and certainly not to be in subjection; rather it is through goodness that
escape from limitation and slavery is alone possible. Moreover,
Shelley does not say that the Divine Nature is limited by human
nature, but only that the human is limited by the Divine. God's
whole being may include elements far beyond man's comprehension or imagination; it does include what man calls good. In other
words, Shelley's God is not impersonal, but suprapersonal; that is,
personal and more than personal at the same time. And so, of
course, is the God of orthodox Christian theology.[91]

This, I take it, is the true construction to be put upon the passages referred to, and upon the account given by Shelley's friend
Horace Smith, of the poet's religious views in the year 1817. "Any
attempt at an impersonation of the Deity, or any conception of
Him otherwise than as the pervading spirit of the whole illimitable
universe, he declared to be presumptuous; for the finite cannot
grasp the infinite." [92] The thought itself is not far from that expressed in *Queen Mab,* but the difference in spirit is immeasurable.
There it was the offspring of an unquestioning, almost arrogant
faith in the power of reason; here it springs from a humble recognition of reason's limitations. After all, Shelley's objections to an an-

emotion into saying more than he meant. Cf. note 36, page 86 below. Now, it
is to me perfectly inconceivable that Shelley should have taken the trouble to make
all these fine distinctions unless he aimed at a general identification of Christ's
teachings with his own beliefs. Shelley is not merely *explaining* the doctrines: he
is unmistakably *defending* them. But after all, if one does not *feel* the truth of my
contention to be self-evident, I do not see how he can be convinced by argument.

[90] Cf. Newman, *The Idea of a University,* Discourse III, Sec. 7.

[91] This, of course, is not a rational concept. And I should perhaps state here that
in Chapter VI I shall have to withdraw most of the claims that I have just made
for the personality of Shelley's God. For I shall argue there that personality and
perfection are incompatible, and, in fact, that personality is ultimately an illusion;
so that if God is perfect, He cannot be a person. But this is a difficulty which must
be faced in every religion.

[92] Quoted by Arthur H. Beavan in *James and Horace Smith* (London, 1909),
p. 173.

thropomorphic God are only the old protest of Paul against those who "changed the glory of the uncorruptible God into an image made like to corruptible man." [93]

VI

All of Shelley's later poetry is in complete harmony with the thought and spirit of the *Essay on Christianity*. In the Preface to *The Revolt of Islam* the poet says:

I trust that the reader will carefully distinguish between those opinions which have a dramatic propriety in reference to the characters which they are designed to elucidate, and such as are properly my own. The erroneous and degrading idea which men have conceived of a Supreme Being, for instance, is spoken against, but not the Supreme Being itself. The belief which some superstitious persons whom I have brought upon the stage entertain of the Deity, as injurious to the character of his benevolence, is widely different from my own.

Moreover, this Supreme Being, at least in his government of the world of men, is far from supreme: for He is the Spirit of Good, and on earth Evil is triumphant, as it has been from the beginning of human existence. In this poem, indeed, Shelley goes so far as to represent the Spirit of Good involved in a cosmic conflict with an active Spirit of Evil; and although Good shall at last triumph, yet in every previous struggle Evil has been victorious. Their warfare is described in the magnificent first canto.

> "Know then, that from the depth of ages old,
>   Two Powers o'er mortal things dominion hold
> Ruling the world with a divided lot,
>   Immortal, all-pervading, manifold,
>   Twin Genii, equal Gods — when life and thought
> Sprang forth, they burst the womb of inessential Nought.

> "The earliest dweller of the world, alone,
>   Stood on the verge of chaos. Lo! afar
> O'er the wide wild abyss two meteors shone,
>   Sprung from the depth of its tempestuous jar:
>   A blood-red Comet and the Morning Star
> Mingling their beams in combat — as ·he stood,
>   All thoughts within his mind waged mutual war,

---

[93] Romans 1 : 23.

> In dreadful sympathy — when to the flood
> That fair Star fell, he turned and shed his brother's blood." [94]

Then the Morning Star was changed by his victorious adversary into "a dire Snake,"

> "And the great Spirit of Good did creep among
> The nations of mankind, and every tongue
> Cursed and blasphemed him as he passed . . ." [95]

At intervals the strife is renewed, and in a vision the poet has beheld the latest conflict between "the Snake and Eagle" (a symbol of the French Revolution), in which Evil once more has triumphed.

Nothing could be farther from the crude optimism of *Queen Mab*. How great is the difference between the suffering Spirit of Good, though it be immortal and all-pervading, and the irresistible Spirit of Nature and Necessity which in the earlier poem was so soon to sweep humanity, with careless indifference, into the lap of the millennium![96] Necessity is no longer the "mother of the

[94] I, xxv–xxvi.

[95] I, xxviii. This reversal of traditional symbolism is characteristic of Shelley, and is by no means due to mere perversity. He simply took the world at its word; for the world, he felt (not without reason), had chosen to worship evil, and to despise good.

[96] Perhaps some mention of Shelley's own later opinion of *Queen Mab* is apposite at this point. In 1817, sending a copy to a Mr. Waller, he described it as full of artistic defects, but added that "it was a sincere and [*sic*] overflowing of the heart and mind and that at a period when they are most uncorrupted and pure. It is the Author's boast that it constitutes no small portion of his happiness that, after six years of added experience and reflection the doctrines of equality and liberty and disinterestedness, and entire unbelief in religion of any sort, to which the Poem is devoted, have gained rather than lost that beauty and that grandeur which first determined him to devote his life to the inculcation of them." See *Complete Works*, VII, 310. In March, 1816, on the other hand, he had described *Alastor*, in sending a copy to Southey, as "my first serious attempt to interpret the best feelings of the human heart." See *Letters*, I, 471. When in 1821 Shelley heard that a pirated edition had been issued, he wrote to his publisher, Charles Ollier: "I have not seen it for some years, but inasmuch as I recollect it is villainous trash; and I dare say much better fitted to injure than to serve the cause which it advocates." *Ibid.*, II, 875–76. In a letter to John Gisborne he referred to the publication as a "droll circumstance," and described the poem as being "written in the most furious style, with long notes against Jesus Christ, and God the Father, and the King, and bishops, and marriage, and the devil knows what." "For the sake of a dignified appearance," and by way of "protest against all the bad poetry in it" (*ibid.*, p. 878), he tried—unsuccessfully—to secure an injunction against the publisher, and wrote a formal protest for Leigh Hunt's *Examiner*, in which he said: "I have not seen this production for several years; I doubt not but that

world"; it is simply another name for law, in the scientific sense (that is, "the statement of a process in nature not known to vary"), merely a word standing for the way things work in the world — the moral world, here, as well as the physical. So the poet says:

> "One comes behind,
> Who aye the future to the past will bind —
> Necessity, whose sightless strength forever
> Evil with evil, good with good must wind
> In bands of union, which no power may sever:
> They must bring forth their kind, and be divided never!" [97]

At the end of the first canto, in one of the most splendid passages of the poem, the Spirit of Good is described as reassuming his rightful shape in his Temple built in the eternal world, beyond the realm of time and space where the Spirit of Evil holds sway.

> It was a Temple, such as mortal hand
> Has never built, nor ecstasy, nor dream
> Reared in the cities of enchanted land . . .

Within the Temple sat "a mighty Senate" of the spirits of the departed Great.

> One seat was vacant in the midst, a throne,
> Reared on a pyramid like sculptured flame,
> Distinct with circling steps which rested on
> Their own deep fire . . .

it is perfectly worthless in point of literary composition; and that in all that concerns moral and political speculation, as well as in the subtler discriminations of metaphysical and religious doctrine, it is still more crude and immature." *Ibid.*, p. 881. He went on to affirm that he was still the enemy of every kind of oppression. There are in *Queen Mab*, however, as I shall later have occasion to point out, some undercurrents of thought and feeling which are opposed to its dominant theme of Necessarianism and optimism, and which look toward the later works.

[97] IX, xxvii. The "One" here is to be distinguished from "the One" of *Adonais* and *Hellas*, although the two conceptions have something in common, as they have with Demogorgon in *Prometheus Unbound*. My interpretation of the meaning of "Necessity" in *The Revolt of Islam* is substantiated by the fact that Shelley in one place (VIII, v) speaks of "worse Necessity Of hate and ill"; that is, hate and ill that have been inevitably produced by their like. (In VIII, xiii, the "one Power" which "rules both high and low" is neither Necessity nor the Spirit of Good, but the Spirit of Evil.) I take the close of the quotation — "and be divided never" — to mean not that evil and good are inseparably united to each other, and therefore relative, but that evil always springs from evil, and good from good. The idea seems to be similar to the Hindu doctrine of Karma. Shelley never uses the word "Necessity," with a capital letter, after *The Revolt of Islam*.

Presently was seen

> One clear and mighty planet hanging o'er
> A cloud of deepest shadow, which was thrown
> Athwart the glowing steps and the crystalline throne.

> The cloud which rested on that cone of flame
> Was cloven; beneath the planet sate a Form,
> Fairer than tongue can speak or thought may frame,
>> The radiance of whose limbs rose-like and warm
>> Flowed forth, and did with softest light inform
> The shadowy dome, the sculptures, and the state
>> Of those assembled shapes . . .[98]

Now, no one supposes that this is intended as a literal picture of what actually exists in some other world, any more than Milton's descriptions of Heaven are intended to be literal.[99] But granting that the Snake and the Eagle and their combat, and the Temple and the Senate and their ruling Spirit, are only symbols, still they must symbolize *something*. And that something, I will venture to assert, is not an "abstraction," unless everything is to be called so that does not have a physical existence. Such poetry as this is not written about abstractions. Shelley is writing from his heart about something that is more real to him than anything in the material world could possibly be.[1] And again, in the fifth canto, in the great hymn which Laone, or Cythna, addresses to the Spirit of Good, as it is manifested in Wisdom, Love, and Equality, the same depth of feeling appears, and imparts to the tone and movement of the poem the same intensity and grandeur. The opening of the stanza addressed to Love, especially, is in the grand style.

> "O Spirit vast and deep as Night and Heaven!
> Mother and soul of all to which is given
> The light of life, the loveliness of being,
>> Lo! thou dost re-ascend the human heart,
>> Thy throne of power . . .[2]

[98] I, xlix, lv, lvi–lvii.   [99] Cf. *Paradise Lost*, Book V, ll. 563–76.

[1] Mr. Kurtz, among others, belittles the significance of these scenes, which he describes as "part of the fairy-machinery of the poem, floating lightly in the romantic and sentimental atmosphere." *Op. cit.*, p. 131. But, like the rest of us, he tends to depreciate the significance of whatever does not go to prove his special thesis.

[2] It is to be noted that this Spirit is the mother only of light and loveliness, not of darkness and ugliness.

The great Spirit of Good which is the real protagonist of *The Revolt of Islam,* the inspiration of Laon's and Cythna's heroic deeds, hovers also above the action of *Prometheus Unbound.* But here its powers and attributes are divided among three of the actors, who, curiously enough, seem more or less to represent the Wisdom, Love, and Equality of Laone's hymn. Prometheus, suffering at the hands of Jupiter, holds the place which in *Islam* is assigned to the Spirit of Good, there degraded into the form of a serpent, yet ever resisting the seemingly omnipotent power of Evil, symbolized by the Eagle; which of course corresponds to Jupiter in the later poem. Prometheus is also described on one occasion [3] as invested with the intense yet softly glowing radiance of the Spirit in *Islam* when he assumes his proper shape. And the Titan is, besides, Divine Wisdom,[4] who first "gave wisdom, which is strength, to Jupiter," and then bestowed a measure of it upon Jupiter's human victims, giving them, besides Hope and Love, speech, and thought, "which is the measure of the universe"; and also Science, and the knowledge of arts, and the inspiration to art.[5] But Prometheus' beloved, Asia, shares also in the Divine Goodness, for she is clearly the spirit of Universal Love, the source of all beauty and harmony both in nature and in human life, "the being in whom love kindles and through whom creation becomes beautiful."[6] To her is addressed the incomparable lyric "Life of Life," the most mystical of Shelley's utterances.[7] Demogorgon, too, seems to have something in common with the Spirit of Good, although he also represents something more: he is "a living Spirit," and he seems to be on the side of good; in his elemental character he is akin to the vague "Eldest of things, divine Equality" of Laone's hymn.[8]

[3] II, i, ll. 62–78.   [4] Cf. Floyd Stovall, *Desire and Restraint in Shelley,* p. 242.
[5] II, iv, ll. 43–97.   [6] Woodberry's note, *Poetical Works* (Cambridge Ed.),
                                                                              p. 623.
[7] II, v, ll. 48–71. For a fine prose statement of the thought of this lyric see Woodberry's note. Mrs. Campbell describes this song to Asia as "celebrating in her Shelley's true God — the Spirit of Love, of Intellectual Beauty, of Life, of Nature." Olwen Ward Campbell, *Shelley and the Unromantics* (London, 1924), p. 218.
[8] It is not to my purpose to discuss in detail the allegory of *Prometheus Unbound.* On that subject volumes might be written — and, indeed, have been. Among the more detailed studies may be mentioned W. M. Rossetti's "A Study of Shelley's

Besides such general inferences as may be drawn from the characters and action of the drama, there is one passage in which the poet directly expresses his theological views. Here Asia asks Demogorgon the questions concerning the ultimate nature of things which Shelley had long been asking himself.

> *Asia.* Who made the living world?
> *Demogorgon.*   God.
> *Asia.*   Who made all
> That it contains? thought, passion, reason, will,
> Imagination? [9]
> *Demogorgon.*   God: Almighty God.
> *Asia.* Who made that sense which, when the winds of Spring
> In rarest visitation, or the voice
> Of one belovèd heard in youth alone,
> Fills the faint eyes with falling tears which dim
> The radiant looks of unbewailing flowers,
> And leaves this peopled earth a solitude
> When it returns no more?
> *Demogorgon.*   Merciful God. [10]

The last lines take us back to the *Hymn to Intellectual Beauty:* clearly the Spirit of Beauty in that poem is identical with the Power which Demogorgon here calls God. But now Asia asks who made evil; and concerning this dark problem — which was to Shelley the most perplexing mystery of life — Demogorgon can return only an obscure and oracular answer; upon which Asia asks another question.

> *Asia.* Whom called'st thou God?
> *Demogorgon.*   I spoke but as ye speak,

Prometheus Unbound, Its Meaning and Personages," *Shelley Society Papers,* Part I (1888); John Todhunter's *A Study of Shelley* (London, 1880); Vida D. Scudder's *Shelley's "Prometheus Unbound"* (Boston, 1892); Carl H. Grabo's *Prometheus Unbound: An Interpretation* (University of North Carolina Press, 1935); and G. E. Woodberry's excellent notes in the Cambridge Edition of Shelley's *Poetical Works.* Many of these interpretations are in my opinion more definite and detailed than is either safe or needful. There is considerable justification for the strictures of Newman I. White in his article "Shelley's *Prometheus Unbound,* or Every Man His Own Allegorist," *Publications of the Modern Language Association,* XL (1925), pp. 172 ff.

[9] Shelley repeats these same five nouns in *Hellas,* in a passage already quoted, declaring that they alone constitute reality. I should say that "contains" is used in the sense of "includes" or "consists of."

[10] II, iv, ll. 9–18. Cf. one of Shelley's last poems, *The Zucca,* stanzas iii–v.

For Jove is the supreme of living things.
Asia. Who is the master of the slave?
Demogorgon.   If the abysm
Could vomit forth its secrets. . . . But a voice
Is wanting, the deep truth is imageless;
For what would it avail to bid thee gaze
On the revolving world? What to bid speak
Fate, Time, Occasion, Chance, and Change? To these
All things are subject but eternal Love.[11]

Shelley believes in an eternal Love, a Spirit of Good, which in its own nature is not subject to any other power, although its workings in the manifested world *are.* This Spirit he calls God,[12] and it stands above "the supreme of living things"; yet it is itself not supreme: above it, or at least on a level with it, is some inscrutable principle, whence arise "Fate, Time, Occasion, Chance, and Change," the conditions of life as we know it, which at the same time make possible and oppose the activity of the Spirit of Good. It is enough, says Shelley, to worship this Spirit, which we know through our own experience, without trying to understand what is in its nature incomprehensible to us.

Many of Shelley's greatest poems are, or contain, hymns to this Spirit of Good. It is this Spirit which, in *The Sensitive Plant,* sheds the light of beauty and love over the garden of earthly life, remaining itself ever unchanged, though the shadow of change falls over the forms which it once inhabited, so that it becomes veiled to human sense.[13] It is this "fierce Spirit" which, in the *Ode to the West Wind,* Shelley asks to speak through his lips "to unawakened

[11] II, iv, ll. 112–20.
[12] Cf. the excellent note on this scene by A. M. D. Hughes in *Poems Published in 1820,* p. 195, in which he says, "Love we may take to be identical with God." This seems to me obvious. I do not think that when Demogorgon says, "I spoke but as ye speak," he means that *God* in his previous speech was a mere word empty of content — else why speak of *"Merciful* God"? He is merely denying that he referred to an anthropomorphic God. The God of which he speaks is evidently to be identified with the Spirit of Good in *The Revolt of Islam* and with the God of the *Essay on Christianity.* It is to be noted that Asia's question is as to who made the *"living* world"; and also that Demogorgon refuses to admit that God made evil. — The symbolic significance of Demogorgon and Asia seems to be forgotten in this scene. Shelley apparently uses them only to expound his own theology.
[13] I do not know that anyone has commented on the close parallelism between the story of *The Sensitive Plant* and that told by Rousseau in *The Triumph of Life.*

earth." It is this "Sweet Spirit" (and no mortal woman) which is the inspiration of *Epipsychidion,* a poem of which Emilia Viviani was only the occasion and not the cause, and in which she is little more than a symbol of that Beauty "Which penetrates and clasps and fills the world";[14] of

> a Power, a Love, a Joy, a God
> Which makes in mortal hearts its brief abode . . .
> Not to be touched but to be felt alone,
> It fills the world with glory — and is gone.[15]

It is this Spirit which Shelley hymns in the *Ode to Naples,* as making sacred by its presence the cause of liberty, the struggle to establish human freedom in place of inhuman bondage:

> Great Spirit, deepest Love!
> Which rulest and dost move
> All things which live and are, within the Italian shore . . .
> Oh . . . raise thy sons, as o'er the prone horizon

[14] L. 103.

[15] *Lines Connected with Epipsychidion,* ll. 134–35, 148–49. There are many critics — in fact, their name is almost legion — who think that the poem is merely a glorification of sexual love, or who, unwilling to give Shelley credit even for being able to feel a genuine passion, find in it merely the expression of "an erotic congeniality, diluted with priggish theorizing." See G. R. Elliott, *The Cycle of Modern Poetry,* p. 4. This point I decline to argue. Those who, like Mr. Peck, to say nothing of M. Maurois and his like, think it worth while to weigh the "evidence" in regard to the "Hoppner scandal" (Peck, *Shelley,* II, 234), who believe that Shelley actually wanted to run off with Emilia (*ibid.,* p. 207), and who are willing to believe — on the strength of an "unpublished letter to Byron," allegedly written at a time when Shelley had come to have anything but a high opinion of the latter — that Jane Williams was Shelley's mistress (*ibid.,* p. 199) — such folk are welcome to think what they like. Of course, when one publishes a poem like Shelley's, one must, as he himself realized, run the risk of its encountering "the malignity of those who turn sweet food into poison" (*Letters,* II, 849), and of being himself approximated "to the circle of a servant girl and her sweetheart" (*ibid.,* p. 920); and there is not the slightest use in trying to refute such a view. The whole course of Shelley's life and poetry, as I read it, makes such an attitude simply incomprehensible. But the interpretation of the poem must depend altogether on the personal opinions of the critic concerning human nature in general and Shelley's nature in particular. Even Mr. Kurtz, who yields to no one in the fervor of his praise of Shelley, says that *Epipsychidion* describes the "physical transports of Emilia and the poet," and thinks that these are not incompatible with Shelley's idealism, since "the humane life consists of nothing so much as the intellectualization of the passions — not their ascetic renunciation" (*The Pursuit of Death,* p. 262); while at the same time he declares that *The Triumph of Life* teaches the necessity of overcoming desire, and compares its ethical teaching with that of Buddhism and Hinduism. Without claiming to be an authority on the subject, I will venture to assert that neither of these religions, any more than Christi-

Thy lamp feeds every twilight wave with fire —
Be man's high hope and unextinct desire
The instrument to work thy will divine! [16]

It is this Spirit which is glorified in *Adonais* as the source of Keats's poetic genius, and as the Power by which and in which he is secure of immortality; it is the "burning fountain" whence his "pure spirit" came, and back to which it shall return when the body returns to dust; it is the Power

> Which wields the world with never-wearied love,
> Sustains it from beneath, and kindles it above; [17]

it is

> That Light whose smile kindles the Universe,
> That Beauty in which all things work and move,
> That Benediction which the eclipsing Curse
> Of birth can quench not, that sustaining Love
> Which through the web of being blindly wove
> By man and beast and earth and air and sea,
> Burns bright or dim, as each are mirrors of
> The fire for which all thirst . . . [18]

VII

That Shelley does not always call this Spirit by the name God is of little significance. That name, as he himself pointed out, may have an almost infinite number of meanings; and in his early years he connected it — not unreasonably, under the circumstances — with all that is most detestable in human nature and society. Leigh

anity, commends the "intellectualization of the passions." Nor does Shelley himself advocate so dubious a doctrine. "So much" — as he once wrote on the same general subject — "for nothing."

[16] Ll. 149–69.   [17] Stanza xlii.

[18] Stanza liv. Alfred Noyes says of Shelley: "He annunciated the most vital belief in God that had been held by any of the masters of our literature, with the sole exception, perhaps, of Milton." Alfred Noyes, *Some Aspects of Modern Poetry* (New York, 1924), pp. 15–16. If the statement is limited to poetry, at least, I do not think it can be fairly controverted. The statement of James Thomson concerning the passage just quoted is also worth considering, especially since Thomson was the last man in the world to wish to make Shelley appear orthodox: "Such a doctrine as is expressed and implied in these lines differs little from pure Theism. It simply dwells so continually on the Infinity of God as to overlook, or slightly regard His Personality: it is Spiritualism and Theism, but of the Greeks rather than the Hebrews." James Thomson, *Biographical and Critical Studies* (London, 1896), pp. 287–88.

Hunt says: "He did himself an injustice with the public, in using the popular name of the Supreme Being inconsiderately. He identified it solely with the most vulgar and tyrannical notions of a God made after the worst human fashion; and did not sufficiently reflect, that it was used by a juster devotion to express a sense of the great Mover of the Universe. . . . there was in reality no belief to which he clung with more fondness than that of some great, pervading 'Spirit of Intellectual Beauty.' " [19] But this apology applies only to the poet's youth and early manhood. In the poetry written during the last three years of his life, he repeatedly — almost habitually — applies the name God not to the anthropomorphic conception of the Deity which he persisted in attributing to Christianity but to the Spirit of Good which he himself believed in and worshipped. He uses the name, too, without apology or qualification, as if confident that his own conception of God is the same as that of other intelligent and cultured persons. The constant study of Dante and Calderón, two of the greatest of Christian poets, had taught him that Christian theology did not necessarily preclude belief in God as a pure and loving Spirit; and in his late poems he uses the name almost always with reverence, and with a frequency which will perhaps be surprising to those who are in the habit of depreciating the religious element in his poetry. One of the first instances occurs in *The Mask of Anarchy*, written in the autumn of 1819, where he bids the English people

> "Declare with measured words that ye
> Are, as God has made ye, free — " [20]

In a famous couplet in *Epipsychidion* he declares:

> The spirit of the worm beneath the sod
> In love and worship, blends itself with God.[21]

Again, in the *Lines Connected with Epipsychidion* (which were evidently originally intended to be part of the poem, and were afterwards rejected, probably on artistic grounds), occurs an apposite passage; the poet, defending his doctrine of love (which criti-

---

[19] Leigh Hunt, *Lord Byron and Some of His Contemporaries* (Philadelphia, 1828), p. 155.
[20] Stanza lxxiii.
[21] Ll. 128–29.

cal stupidity still insists upon interpreting as "free love" in the vulgar sense), offers to quote authorities

> In commendation of this kind of love: —
> Why there is first the God in heaven above,
> Who wrote a book called Nature . . .[22]

In *The Sensitive Plant* the Spirit of the garden is described as

> a ruling Grace
> Which to the flowers, did they waken or dream,
> Was as God is to the starry scheme.[23]

In the *Ode to Naples* Shelley addresses the city as

> Last of the Intercessors!
> Who 'gainst the Crowned Transgressors
> Pleadest before God's love![24]

and he bids it to "let sail" "wingèd words"

> Freighted with truth even from the throne of God . . .[25]

Even more theistic in their apparent implications are two lines from *The Boat on the Serchio:* at the dawn of day, says the poet,

> All rose to do the task He set to each,
> Who shaped us to His ends and not our own . . .[26]

In the same strain is the *Sonnet to Byron,* whose poetical creations are said to

> rise as fast and fair
> As perfect worlds at the Creator's will,

and the same comparison is expressed in a letter to John Gisborne: "Space wondered less at the swift and fair creations of God, when he grew weary of vacancy, than I at this spirit of an angel in the

[22] Ll. 29–31. The other authorities are "Socrates, the Jesus Christ of Greece" and "Jesus Christ Himself": whose names Shelley constantly links together, as the two men whose lives and teachings he reverences most.

[23] ii, ll. 2–4.   [24] Ll. 69–71.   [25] L. 99.

[26] Ll. 30–31. Browning, in his *Essay on Shelley,* quotes these lines as evidence to support his belief that "had Shelley lived, he would finally have ranged himself with the Christians." Robert Browning, *Complete Poetic and Dramatic Works,* Cambridge Ed., p. 1013. W. M. Rossetti, however, thinks that the pronoun merely refers to the *sun,* and compares a passage in *The Triumph of Life.* See R. S. Garnett, ed., *Letters about Shelley Interchanged by Three Friends* (New York, 1917), pp. 245–46. His interpretation seems to me not to make much sense. Probably the distinction is of little importance, in any case. Many religions and many poets have made the sun a symbol of God. Christ himself says, "I am the light of the world."

mortal paradise of a decaying body." [27] The same thought animates
the great figure of speech (which I hold to be far more than a
figure of speech) in *Adonais*, where Shelley speaks of

> the great morning of the world when first
> God dawned on Chaos . . .[28]

and the figure is repeated in *Hellas:*

> In the great morning of the world,
> The Spirit of God with might unfurled
> The flag of Freedom over Chaos . . .[29]

Finally, in *The Triumph of Life* Shelley twice uses the word God
in the same manner as that in which an avowedly Christian poet
might use it: once in speaking of the corruption of the original
teachings of Christ through the growth of superstition, and of

> Gregory and John, and men divine,
> Who rose like shadows between man and God . . .[30]

and again when he wonders

> why God made irreconcilable
> Good and the means of good . . .[31]

---

[27] *Letters*, II, 931 (January, 1822). There is a passage in *A Defence of Poetry*
which, as it has usually been printed, would also be important evidence. Shelley
speaks of "the mind of the Creator, which is itself the image of all other minds."
See Shawcross, p. 128. Rossetti, however, thought that in the context "Creator"
could only mean the poet, and not God. His view seems to be substantiated by the
Bodleian MS. as edited by M. Koszul, where the word is not capitalized. This has
apparently been overlooked by Mr. Melvin T. Solve, in his recent excellent study
of *Shelley: His Theory of Poetry* (page 21), where he takes "Creator" to mean
"the Creator of the Universe." I may perhaps quote here, not as being important
to the argument, but as giving a glimpse of that gayer side of Shelley's nature of
which we see too little, a passage from a letter to Henry Reveley concerning the
construction of the engine for their proposed steamboat. "Your volcanic description
of the birth of the cylinder is very characteristic of you, and of it. One might
imagine God, when he made the earth, and saw the granite mountains and flinty
promontories flow into their craggy forms, and the splendour of their fusion filling
millions of miles of the void space, like the tail of a comet, so looking, so de-
lighting in his work. God sees his machine spinning round the sun, and delights
in its success, and has taken out patents to supply all the suns in space with the
same manufacture." *Letters*, II, 751–52.
[28] Stanza xix.
[29] Ll. 46–48. Cf. *Ode to Liberty*, ll. 88–90: "one Spirit vast With life and love
makes chaos ever new . . . "
[30] Ll. 288–89.
[31] Ll. 230–31. Newman White, who denies, with most critics, that Shelley's
deity is anything more than an "impersonal force," remarks that "there are occa-

VIII

The last quotation, indeed, seems more Christian than Shelleyan, for God is here assumed to be omnipotent, whereas Shelley's God is the limited Spirit of Good. Before commenting on this seeming inconsistency, however, it may be worth while to make a few obvious remarks on the relation between Shelley's conception of God and that of Christianity, so far as I understand it. It is easy to go too far in identifying them. Shelley's Deity is altogether benevolent; it has nothing of the sternness which is traditionally attributed to the Christian God, and which leads even so gentle a person as Newman to say that the primary aspect under which God is presented to us by our conscience is that of a Judge. This attitude Shelley repudiated as due to the influence of Judaism; one of the few Godwinian principles he held to the end of his life was that justice and benevolence are identical. Whether or not this belief is in harmony with the doctrines of the New Testament, it is certainly opposed irreconcilably to traditional Christian theology.

On the other hand, Shelley's Spirit of Good seems to be closely akin — perhaps through a common Platonic influence, although Shelley knew the Bible thoroughly — to the Second Person of the Christian Trinity: the Word, or Logos, of the Gospel of John. "In the beginning was the Word, and the Word was with God, and the Word was God. The same was in the beginning with God. All things were made by him, and without him was not anything made that was made. In him was life: and the life was the light of men."[32] Shelley's God is also a creative Power, in so far as it works upon some primordial chaos, which is "without form and void," and gives to it form and harmony and beauty. I will even go so far as to say that, in *Hellas*, Shelley stands on the verge of believing his Spirit of Good to have been incarnate in Jesus Christ.

sions on which he uses the word God in the conventional way in which it was used around him by regular Christians, but these are palpable slips." See Introduction to *The Best of Shelley*, p. xl. I think, however, that the impartial reader (that myth of literary criticism) will agree with me that it is the critic who is here guilty of a "palpable slip." Aside from the frequency of these "slips," it is significant that they are confined entirely to the later poems. I believe there is no instance in any poem written before 1819 of any use of the word God except as the name of the cruel Demon which Shelley believed to be the object of worship of organized Christianity.

[32] John 1: 1–4.

A Power from the unknown God,
A Promethean conquerer, came;
Like a triumphal path he trod
The thorns of death and shame.
A mortal shape to him
Was like the vapour dim
Which the orient planet animates with light;
Hell, Sin, and Slavery came,
Like bloodhounds mild and tame,
Nor preyed, until their Lord had taken flight;
The moon of Mahomet
Arose, and it shall set:
While blazoned as on Heaven's immortal noon
The cross leads generations on.[33]

The passage is often quoted to show the poet's reverence for "the sublime human character of Jesus Christ." [34] But it has other implications. What is the opening of this magnificent stanza except a paraphrase of the Gospel account of how "the Word was made flesh, and dwelt among us"? [35] The poet clearly presents Christ, not merely as a morally perfect human being, free from sin and from the human passions that Shelley found so reprehensible in the Jehovah of the Jewish histories, with whom, as he maintained, Christ had been mistakenly identified, but as a purely spiritual being, who assumed for a time a mortal form, in order to redeem mankind from "Hell, Sin, and Slavery." [36] Such an interpretation will seem extravagant only to those who are insensible to the pervading spirit of Shelley's mature work. The analogy between Christ and Prometheus, for instance, both in their sufferings and in the motive that leads them to undergo those sufferings, is too obvious to need comment; and it cannot be doubted that Shelley was fully conscious of the parallelism. How natural it had become for him to think in terms of Christian belief is evident from a sentence in the Preface to *The Cenci.* "Imagination is as the

---

[33] Ll. 211–24.   [34] Shelley's note on line 1090.   [35] John 1:14.

[36] In the *Essay on Christianity* there is no question of Christ's being more than a man. Shelley says, for example: "It is not asserted that no degree of human indignation ever hurried him, beyond the limits which his calmer mood had placed, to disapprobation against vice and folly." See Shawcross, p. 103. I think he would hardly have spoken thus in 1822, but would have attributed all inconsistencies in the New Testament to the misunderstanding of Christ's teachings by his disciples. But this, of course, is merely an opinion — or rather, a feeling.

immortal God which should assume flesh for the redemption of mortal passion."

I do not say, of course, that Shelley would ever have been willing to accept all the implications of the Christian doctrine of the Incarnation, or to admit that Christ was "the only begotten son" of God. Every great teacher, he would doubtless have said, is in a very real sense an incarnation of the Divine; and although in the later works Christ is placed above all other men, it can hardly be asserted that he is set altogether apart from them, as in Christianity he is.[37] It should be mentioned also that Shelley says in a note on the chorus in *Hellas* of which a part has just been quoted: "The popular notions of Christianity are represented in this chorus as true in relation to the worship they superseded . . . without considering their merits in a relation more universal." But he is speaking only of "the popular notions of Christianity," and not necessarily of what he regarded as the complete and genuine teachings of Christ. Nor in the final chorus, where the poet sings:

> Saturn and Love their long repose
> Shall burst, more bright and good
> Than all who fell, than One who rose,
> Than many unsubdued . . .[38]

need we find any imputation to Christ and his teachings of human error and limitation; new Gods and new religions will not in themselves be necessarily "more bright and good" (or even different), but only so in relation to the clearer apprehension of a more nearly perfect humanity.[39]

[37] Of course, Unitarians and certain other sects deny the divinity of Christ and still consider themselves Christians. But such a denial evidently destroys every distinctive article of the Christian creed.

[38] Ll. 1090–93. "*All* those *who fell*, or the Gods of Greece, Asia, and Egypt; the *One who rose*, or Jesus Christ . . . ; and *the many unsubdued*, or the monstrous objects of the idolatry of China, India, the Antarctic Islands, and the native tribes of America . . ." (Shelley's note). Does Shelley here mean the expression "One who rose" to be taken literally? Is the reader to infer — incredible as it may seem — that Shelley believed in the resurrection of Christ?

[39] How completely Shelley had come to be dominated by his reverence for Christ may be seen from the fact that in the Preface to *Hellas* he forgets himself so far as actually to speak of *Christianity* as something good! The Turks are referred to as "the enemies of domestic happiness, of Christianity and of civilization."

IX

But regardless of Shelley's views concerning Christ, which are more or less incidental to the main purpose of this study, there is one aspect of his conception of God which remains (and to some extent must remain) obscure. His God, or the Spirit of Good, is not omnipotent or all-comprehending; and the questions immediately arise: "What, then, is Ultimate Reality? What is the God who has made irreconcilable good and the means of good? What is the unknown God of which Christ, in *Hellas,* is said to be the prophet? What does it mean to say that God dawned on Chaos? And what *is* Chaos? Is there some principle standing above and uniting in itself both the Spirit of Good and the Power which opposes the workings of that Spirit?"

No one who is not intellectually irresponsible will undertake to answer these questions dogmatically, or even, perhaps, very definitely. These or similar difficulties arise in regard to every philosophy or religion; and for myself, I should say that the human mind is by its nature incapable of finding any satisfying solution of them. Certainly there is none to be found in Shelley's writings. At the same time, he was quite aware that such problems exist, and his speculations concerning them are by no means devoid of interest; so that it is not out of place to offer a few suggestions as to the general trend which these speculations show.

To begin, then, with the relation between God and Chaos — for Shelley's God does not create the element it works in — it will be recalled that Shelley considers the primordial stuff of the universe to be of the nature of mind — "thought, passion, reason, will, imagination" — rather than matter; although this distinction is perhaps more nominal than real, and significant chiefly as showing the poet's natural tendency toward idealism. But it is mind in a chaotic, unorganized, and un-self-conscious condition. From this aimless, infinite flux the creative Spirit, which seems to comprehend within itself both the patterns or Ideas according to which it manifests itself, and the energy by which it impresses these upon the stuff in which it works, brings forth the universe which man knows. Or (to describe the same process in another way) Spirit and "matter," meeting, limit each other, and produce self-consciousness. This, at least, I take to be the meaning of Shelley's words about God unfurling "the flag of Freedom over Chaos." Without self-consciousness, freedom is obviously impossible. The same thought seems to underlie the rather cryptic line in *Hellas*, "Nought is but that which feels itself to be." Also apposite is a note on the chorus in *Hellas*, of which the second stanza has already been quoted with reference to the poet's conception of Christ. Shelley says: "The first stanza contrasts the immortality of the living and thinking beings who inhabit the planets, and to use a common and inadequate phrase, *clothe themselves in matter*, with the transience of the noblest manifestations of the external world." Why this distinction should be made is perhaps not altogether clear, since the external world also, so far as it is harmonious and beautiful (and Shelley seems usually to think that there is far less discord and ugliness in external nature than in human nature), is the creation of the divine Spirit of Good. Shelley's view, as has already been indicated, seems very close to Berkeley's: that external objects as well as "living and thinking beings" are ideas or thoughts in the mind of the Deity. But Shelley seems to hold that such of these ideas as have become self-conscious, that is, aware of their own identity, possess a higher degree of reality than the others; and eventually (although the discussion of this question belongs to another chapter) will become one with the consciousness of God.

It must be made clear, however, with reference to Shelley's Berkeleian leanings, that his God — the Spirit of Good — although it has consciousness, that is, a mind (which seems to be the cosmos), is itself not mind; for it is active, and mind is always passive. In the essay *On Life* Shelley declares: "that the basis of all things cannot be, as the popular philosophy alleges, mind, is sufficiently evident. Mind, as far as we have any experience of its properties, and beyond that experience how vain is argument! cannot create, it can only perceive. . . . It is infinitely improbable that the cause of mind, that is, of existence, is similar to mind." [40] So in *Mont Blanc* he speaks of the "secret Strength of things Which

[40] Shawcross, p. 57.

governs thought." [41] As Mr. Yeats says, Shelley "looked upon thought as a condition of life in generation and believed that the reality beyond was something other than thought." [42] Moreover, if "chaos" is of the nature of mind, it also must be passive, and therefore unable, of itself, to resist "the one Spirit's plastic stress." And yet clearly, as we have found Shelley stating over and over again, the activity of the Spirit of Good *is* resisted. I will venture to suggest that the solution of the difficulty is that, according to Shelley's conception, the world as we know it has, not one or two, but *three* fundamental principles: a neutral, passive matrix or flux of the unorganized elements of thought or mind, and, contending for the mastery of this, two active spirits or powers in constant conflict — one good, and the other, as far as man's experience goes, evil. So in a stanza already quoted from *The Revolt of Islam* "the earliest dweller of the world" stands "on the verge of chaos" and beholds "o'er the wide wild abyss" the Morning Star and the blood-red Comet, "sprung from the depths of its tempestuous jar." [43] In the later poems the evil principle shows a tendency to become less malignant, and appears to be nearly identified with "Mutability," which, however, still opposes and frustrates the efforts toward harmony and perfection of the Spirit of Good, or God. [44]

And now the other problem presents itself: whether, according to Shelley, these three principles are absolutely distinct, or whether they are ultimately resolved in some higher principle, standing alone above God and Mutability and the element in which they contend. It seems clear to me that the second alternative is the

[41] Ll. 139–40. On the other hand, there are rare passages in which mind appears to be considered as an active power, as in the following quotation from the fragmentary essay *On the Revival of Literature:* "But mind seems to govern the world without visible or substantial means. Its birth is unknown; its action and influence unperceived; and its being seems eternal." See Shawcross, p. 118.

[42] William Butler Yeats, *Essays* (London, 1924), p. 103.

[43] I, xxvi.

[44] With the general thought of this paragraph, cf. the last lines of *The Triumph of Life,* where the minds of men are said to send forth "shadows" from which the "creative ray" of the car of Life forms the "busy phantoms" which blot out the Vision of Beauty and surround humanity with delusion. I do not mean to argue, of course, that Shelley ever definitely formulated these ideas to himself. I am merely suggesting a theory which seems to me, in most cases, to give coherence to Shelley's utterances.

one that must be accepted, although Shelley apparently feels that speculation concerning these matters is for the most part futile: "the deep truth is imageless," and although "thought . . . is the measure of the universe," yet it can measure only the universe, and not what lies beyond. And Shelley seems certain that something must lie beyond; he is not willing to stop with the world of the senses and the reason, with an imperfect order where an evil Spirit has at least partial dominion.[45] So he cries out in *The Revolt of Islam* against the judgment of Sense and Reason that death is the end of all.

> "These are blind fancies — reason cannot know
>   What sense can neither feel, nor thought conceive;
> There is delusion in the world — and woe,
>   And fear, and pain — we know not whence we live,
>   Or why, or how, or what mute Power may give
> Their being to each plant, and star, and beast,
>   Or even these thoughts . . ." [46]

This utterance is perhaps not altogether consistent with the faith in the Spirit of Good which is affirmed elsewhere in the poem. But even such a faith is not enough, can answer no ultimate questions. There is, there must be, delusion in the world. The nightmare visions of *The Triumph of Life* — the blindly destructive car, the brain-born phantoms clouding the air and blotting out all beauty, the ever-changing figures which human achievement vainly paints on the world's "false and fragile glass" — this cannot be the Ultimate Reality. To accept it, and seek nothing beyond, is an act not of courage but of folly and despair. Out of the heart of hopelessness, and out of the experienced fact that the Spirit of Good, though always defeated, ever strives, one may pluck a faith in an eternal and absolute Reality which is "more than reason, more than dreams,"

[45] And, according to Shelley's final view (ninety-nine critics out of every hundred notwithstanding), will always have, from the very nature of things. See the following chapter.

[46] IX, xxxiii. This is the old sensationalism of Locke, but what a different purpose it serves now from what it had been made to serve in the poet's boyhood! Then it was part of his argument for the necessity of atheism. Now (and this was only in 1817) it becomes the basis of faith in some Power beyond the world of sense. This is characteristic of the way in which Shelley, while keeping a certain belief, turns it to different uses as his sense of human needs and values deepens.

"wherein all contradiction is solved." So Shelley himself says, with reference to the Manichean philosophy: "The supposition that the good spirit is, or hereafter will be, superior, is a personification of the principle of hope, and that thirst for improvement without which, present evil would be intolerable." [47]

This supposition of an ultimate, unifying principle will perhaps cast some light on such passages as that in the *Essay on Christianity* in which Shelley says that "the universal Being can only be described or defined by negatives," and those elsewhere in which he objects to the assumption that God can possess any of the attributes of human nature. Possibly at such times he has in mind the notion of Ultimate Reality, rather than the Spirit of Good, which is altogether another conception; whereas it must be to the latter that he refers in the essay just mentioned as "the original and object" of man's idea of God, and as the divine nature whose *"actual* perfection" is the same as the *"abstract* perfection" of human nature.

Moreover, besides permitting this confusion of terms, Shelley is not always consistent in his view that it is useless to speculate concerning Ultimate Reality. (And indeed, who ever has been or can be?) The result is that he sometimes seems to confuse it with the Spirit of Good, and not only in name but in nature. Demogorgon, in *Prometheus Unbound,* appears to represent this ultimate principle: he is "a mighty darkness," his voice can only be described as "a universal sound like words," he dwells in a cave beyond

> . . . the cloudy strife
> Of Death and of Life;
> . . . the veil and the bar
> Of things which seem and are . . . [48]

and he can only describe himself as "Eternity." Yet in a certain sense he is on the side of good, for it is through him that Prometheus' sacrifice and Jupiter's tyranny received their just recompense, exemplifying the law that "Whatsoever a man soweth, that shall he also reap." He is the principle that redeems the moral world from chaos. Mr. Brailsford comments finely: "It is the

---

[47] *On the Devil and Devils,* in *Complete Works,* VII, 87.
[48] II, iii, ll. 57–60. Woodberry comments that the Cave of Demogorgon is described as "the place of increate eternity or absolute being."

eternal x which the human spirit always assumes when it is at a
loss to balance its equations. Demogorgon is, because if It were not,
our strivings would be a battle in the mist, with no clear trumpet
note that promised triumph." [49] The same mingling of two conceptions appears to be present also in the great fifty-second stanza
of *Adonais:*

> The One remains, the many change and pass;
> Heaven's light forever shines, Earth's shadows fly;
> Life, like a dome of many-coloured glass,
> Stains the white radiance of Eternity,
> Until Death tramples it to fragments. . . .

The One here is named Eternity, as is Demogorgon, but here it is
"a white radiance" instead of "a tremendous gloom." Shelley seems
to have allowed his conception of Ultimate Reality to be assimilated
to that of "the one Spirit" of the forty-third stanza, and the
"Light . . . Beauty . . . Love" of the fifty-fourth stanza, which
clearly refer to the limited and, in a sense, personal Spirit of Good.
Again, in *Hellas,* one does not know to which conception "the
Fathomless" and "the One" are intended to refer. The "unknown
God" from which Christ is sent, however, seems to be Ultimate
Reality, or the Absolute, as is the God of *The Triumph of Life,*
who is assumed to permit the existence of evil.

This underlying assumption, in Shelley's mature thought, of
an ultimate, unifying principle, is doubtless partly responsible, along
with the Spirit of Nature in *Queen Mab,* for the widespread
acceptance of Shelley's "pantheism." But to any except the most
superficial or prejudiced student of the poet's work, it must be

[49] H. N. Brailsford, *Shelley, Godwin, and Their Circle* (New York, [1913]), p.
229. Demogorgon, like the other characters in the poem, has been the subject of
much comment. I quote two examples that more or less agree with my own view:
"Demogorgon is thus elemental in the highest degree, lying in a region back even
of the great poetic conceptions of Love and Beauty, as well as of apparently
Omnipotent Power, in the world of celestial time." He is "the ultimate of being conceivable by man's imagination." See Woodberry, *op. cit.,* p. 623. "Demogorgon is
apparently a fusion of three ideas: the inscrutable Mystery at the background of
existence, Eternity, and the Destiny which pushes the Tyrant from his throne. We
may understand him as Shelley's conception of Fate . . ." J. F. C. Gutteling,
"Demogorgon in Shelley's *Prometheus Unbound,*" *Neophilologus,* 9:285. Cf. also
Kurtz, *op. cit.,* p. 176. Those who are interested in such things will find the probable source of Shelley's conception in Peacock's note to his poem *Rhododaphne,*
VI, l. 159. It is reprinted in Hughes, *Shelley: Poems Published in 1820,* p. 175.

evident that the "Necessity! thou mother of the world!" of the youthful poem is far different from Demogorgon in *Prometheus Unbound* or "the One" of *Adonais* and *Hellas*. It is true that they are described in somewhat similar terms as being different from, and not wholly conceivable to, the human mind. But the first is arrived at through a cold-blooded process of reason, and is confidently presented as furnishing the solution to all human problems, practical or speculative; whereas the last is a mystery, born not of reason's desire for final satisfaction but of an emotional, a moral, a spiritual need for something to trust in and hold to amid the chaotic flux of earthly existence. It is, as has been said, the x in the equation of life, to which no definite value can be ascribed: yet upon the assumption of its existence all values depend. Even faith in the Spirit of Good is not enough; for that Spirit is limited and relative, and its operations must receive their sanction from some higher power; their value, if they are to have value, must carry an absolute guarantee. So Christ declares: "My doctrine is not mine but his that sent me"; [50] and in that claim lies the power of the Christian religion, for it answers a need, not of reason merely but of the whole nature of man. Those who deny the truth of Christ's assertion deny everything in his teaching that makes it a religion. I believe that it is Shelley's implicit recognition of this fact of religious experience which leads him to appeal to an absolute authority.[51]

We may indeed say that the Spirit of Good — for the poet's own words in *Hellas* suggest it — stands in Shelley's thought as Christ does in the Christian system, as the mediator between man and the Absolute.[52] And as in the Christian doctrine of the Trinity, Christ

---

[50] John 7 : 16.

[51] I presume it can be argued that this leads logically to necessarianism, pantheism, optimism, and almost anything else which Shelley's detractors would like to fasten on him as a heinous sin, in order to hold him up to scorn as a fool, a dreamer, and a moral weakling. But there is nothing of the sort in Shelley that is not inevitably present in all religious thought.

[52] Cf. Floyd Stovall, *Desire and Restraint in Shelley* (page 217). "In any case, the Spirit of Love or Beauty was the immediate object of Shelley's worship, standing to him in some such relation as Christ stands for the orthodox Christian." "The Daemon of the World, or the Spirit of Love, becomes in a sense the interpreter of inscrutable Necessity, and stands to Shelley in the same relation that Christ stands to the Christian." See page 145; also page 160. Mr. Stovall thinks, not only that this Spirit is to be regarded as "the mediator between man and the unknown,

is asserted to be at the same time identical with, and yet other than, God the Father; so in Shelley the mediating Spirit of Good, which may perhaps be said to represent the Absolute in its human aspect, is sometimes identified with that Absolute, and sometimes distinguished from it. Thus Christ, in the Prologue to *Hellas*, speaks to the Power above him, "the unknown God," as to a person (and who can doubt that the words spring from Shelley's own deepest being?) concerning the fate of Greece.

> She shall arise
> Victorious as the world arose from Chaos!
> And as the Heavens and the Earth arrayed
> Their presence in the beauty and the light
> Of Thy first smile, O Father, — as they gather
> The spirit of Thy love which paves for them
> Their path o'er the abyss, till every sphere
> Shall be one living Spirit, — so shall Greece —[53]

So, after all, even Ultimate Reality, even the Absolute, though beyond the reach of sense and reason, must be, from the religious standpoint, on the side of what man calls good. And Shelley can hardly be blamed for sometimes confusing it with the Spirit of Good, or Love, or Beauty, to which he ascribes the attributes which religious persons generally ascribe to God. A more serious consequence of his acceptance of the principle is that it leads to the conclusion (so disturbing to many critics of Shelley, and to himself before he learned to substitute faith for reason) that evil must be in some way or other unreal; and from a purely logical standpoint, of course, to make evil illusory is also to make good illusory; and human endeavor is thus deprived of meaning and value. But this paradox is inseparable from the religious view of life.

x

Let me now gather up the threads (I hope not too badly tangled) of this long and complicated discussion, reiterating a few of the

unchangeable laws of the universe," but also that "Shelley thought of love as the power that animates and controls" these laws, and perhaps as "the creator of thought, passion, imagination, and so on, which Demogorgon had said were the work of God." See pages 216–17. That is, I take it, Shelley sometimes, as I have said, identifies or confuses the Spirit of Good with the Absolute.

[53] Ll. 112–19.

more significant ideas which I have tried to establish (so far as such ideas ever *can* be established) in regard to Shelley's conception of God. In the first place, it ought now to be evident that, although Shelley at no period of his life remained for long a materialist or an atheist in any crude sense, yet between his earlier and his later thought there is a break, an opposition, a contradiction — in the spirit, perhaps, more than in the letter — which it is hardly possible to exaggerate. "The real Shelley" did not come into existence intellectually until about 1815, and as a thinker he can be fairly judged only by his later work. In the second place, I have suggested that the central religious idea of Shelley's mature thought is the conception of an active Spirit of Good, unchanging and all-pervading, which works in a passive, chaotic flux of the unorganized elements of mind, and from this flux creates a world of harmonious and beautiful forms; but the efforts of this Spirit are opposed and partially frustrated by a recalcitrant Spirit of Evil, and hence arise the discord, the ugliness, the suffering that are ever present in human life. Now, somewhere in this process there are created self-conscious beings, which partake of the nature of the Spirit of Good to which they owe their existence, and are capable of recognizing their community with it; knowing, from its operations in themselves and in the external world, that it is intelligent (although essentially other than mind), benevolent, and even "possessed of a will respecting their actions." This Spirit, I have contended, may legitimately be called a personal God. Finally, Shelley assumes (as does every religious thinker) that above and beyond the contradictions that are everywhere present in the manifested world, there stands a unifying principle, "a supra-rational Absolute," which the human mind cannot comprehend, but the existence of which man's whole nature demands that he assume.

It is possible that I have made Shelley's thought appear more consistent than in reality it is — and that, even so, it may seem far from coherent. I do not deny that it contains contradictions and inconsistencies, and that it is often obscurely expressed: that the poet's works contain many dark sayings, in the interpretation of which "each to itself must be the oracle." But of what thinker may not the same be said — even among professional philosophers, whose lifelong endeavor it is to achieve clarity and consistency? And how much less ought to be demanded of poets, who are, according to Shelley's own view, "the words which express what they understand not"! [54] "Not but that" (as Shelley himself wrote in the Advertisement to *Epipsychidion*) " 'it would be a great disgrace to him who should rhyme anything under the garb of a figure or of rhetorical coloring, if afterward, being asked, he should not be able to denude his words of this garb, in such wise that they should have a true meaning.' " [55] And I am perfectly certain that such a true meaning Shelley's words always have.

[54] *A Defence of Poetry*, in Shawcross, p. 159.

[55] Shelley quotes this passage in Italian, not quite accurately, from Dante's *Vita Nuova*. The translation is Norton's; it is given by Woodberry, p. 632.

CHAPTER IV

PROMETHEUS BOUND

I

YET HOWEVER strongly Shelley may have trusted in the ultimate triumph of good, he felt not less strongly that on earth evil prevails. The dominant force behind the life and writings of the poet is an intense perception of the overwhelming preponderance of evil in all that pertains to human life. The prevailing mood of his last years is exactly the same as that to which Newman has given unsurpassable expression at the beginning of the final chapter of his *Apologia;* to both the condition of the world is "a vision to dizzy and appall," "a profound mystery," a "heart-piercing, reason-bewildering fact." The myth that Shelley was a shallow optimist — that he believed the great mass of human beings to be naturally good; that he held all human sufferings to be the result of political, social, and religious institutions; and that he considered the destruction of these to be the one thing needful for the immediate establishment of an all-satisfying heaven-on-earth — this, as the present chapter aims to show, is perhaps the most monstrous fiction that critical perversity has ever foisted upon an unsuspecting public. Mary Shelley's own note on *Prometheus Unbound* is partly responsible.[1] "The prominent feature of Shelley's theory of the destiny of the human species was that evil is not inherent in the system of the creation, but an accident that might be expelled. . . .

[1] Mrs. Shelley's notes are often helpful, but it is almost never safe to take them at their face value. It ought to be obvious to the student of Shelley's life that Mary Shelley, for all her merits, was quite incapable, both morally and intellectually, of understanding her husband's opinions, to say nothing of sharing them. For evidence in support of so unconventional a view, the reader is referred to Francis Gribble, *The Romantic Life of Shelley and the Sequel* (London, 1911), especially *The Sequel*, and H. J. Massingham, *The Friend of Shelley* (London, 1930), a biography of Edward John Trelawny. Trelawny himself gives enough evidence, in his *Records of Shelley, Byron, and the Author* (London, 1887), but it is usual to discount his statements, on the ground that he was piqued by Mary's refusal to marry him after Shelley's death. However, as Mr. Gribble says, "the evidence that Mary declined the proposal is stronger than the evidence that Trelawny made it" (page 361).

Shelley believed that man had only to will that there should be no evil, and there would be none." Even in what it says, this statement is not altogether accurate; and in what it omits to say, it positively falsifies Shelley's whole philosophy. It is well enough to assert that "man had only to will . . ."; but the implications of that *only* have never been adequately dealt with. That Shelley's view is not so naïve as some critics seem to think, some of these same critics tacitly admit; for they assert, first, that he could not, because he would not, see that evil is deeply rootly in human life; and second, that he found the evil in that life unbearable, and so retreated to an ivory tower of dreams. The disingenuousness of mingling these two mutually exclusive views (neither of which, as a matter of fact, has more than a slight measure of truth) is characteristic of the poet's unfriendly critics: one is reminded of Newman's complaint against Kingsley for calling him "either a knave or a fool, and . . . he is not quite sure which, probably both."

It is a plain fact that, leaving aside for the time being Shelley's hopes for the future (which we shall see to be far different from the popular notion of them), the picture of actual human existence which we find in his poetry from *Queen Mab* to *The Triumph of Life* is one of the most painful to be found in English literature outside of Swift.[2] Even in his youth, he devotes two-thirds of his first long poem to picturing the complete corruption of human society, the degradation, the wrongs, the sufferings of men, before he turns to his vision of the millennium. In *Alastor* the poet dies still seeking vainly for an ideal which life cannot realize. *The Revolt of Islam,* like the French Revolution which partly inspired it, ends in the defeat of good and the triumph of oppression; Laon and Cythna are put to death and find happiness only in the eternal temple of the Spirit of Good, there to await (who knows how long?) the triumph of that Spirit. *Julian and Maddalo,* for all the hopeful arguments that Shelley opposes to Byron's cynicism,

---

[2] It is not at all strange that James Thomson, author of *The City of Dreadful Night,* should have been so passionate a worshipper of Shelley. (See his poem, *Shelley,* in which the poet is presented as the incarnation of an angelic Spirit, sent from Heaven to redeem the earth.) Thomson's pessimism is more profound than Shelley's, not with reference to the state of man on earth, but in its cosmic scope and fatalistic tendency.

is actually morbid in its revelation — through the words of the Maniac, who is, for the poet, more or less a type of all sensitive and magnanimous natures — of the mental agony that can be inflicted upon a man by his own sins or those of his fellows, or by some malignant principle. "What Power delights to torture us?" cries the sufferer;[3] and compares himself to the trodden worm:

> "Even the instinctive worm on which we tread
> Turns, though it wound not — then with prostrate head
> Sinks in the dust and writhes like me — and dies?
> No: wears a living death of agonies!
> As the slow shadows of the pointed grass
> Mark the eternal periods, his pangs pass
> Slow, ever-moving, — making moments be
> As mine seem — each an immortality!" [4]

and again, he exclaims,

> "*Me* — who am as a nerve o'er which do creep
> The else unfelt oppressions of this earth . . ." [5]

In *Prometheus Unbound*, indeed, good is represented as triumphant; but only after Prometheus has endured

> Three thousands years of sleep-unsheltered hours,
> And moments aye divided by keen pangs
> Till they seemed years, torture and solitude,
> Scorn and despair . . .[6]

Moreover, it is questionable whether the millennial pictures of Act III, which have been the target for so many critical arrows, are intended to be any more than symbolical of "a city not built with hands"; as Plato says that it is no matter whether his Republic

---

[3] L. 320.

[4] Ll. 412–19. Hutchinson and some more recent editors read "dusk" in l. 414, but the arguments in favor of this reading are to me unconvincing.

[5] Ll. 449–50. The tone and many of the sentiments of the Maniac have a general resemblance to Shelley's own; but to take his speech as a record of particular events in Shelley's life and of their effect upon him is entirely gratuitous. Cf. A. Koszul, *La Jeunesse de Shelley* (Paris, 1910), pp. 320–25. M. Koszul takes this as a *literal* account of Shelley's relations with Harriet. This opinion has been held by many critics and biographers, including Mr. Peck, but I cannot regard it as anything more than a wild fancy. Cf. R. D. Havens, *Studies in Philology*, 27: 648–53, for the absurdity of an autobiographical interpretation. Mr. Havens suggests that the character of the Maniac had for its original the poet Tasso, upon whose life Shelley had been planning to write a drama.

[6] I, ll. 12–15.

shall exist on earth or not.[7] And even if the poet is hoping for some actual regeneration of human nature (and *not* of human institutions, except incidentally), it is a "far goal of Time" indeed which shall have been reached before that consummation shall come to pass. And in the meantime

> those who do endure
> Deep wrongs for man, and scorn, and chains, but heap
> Thousandfold torments on themselves and him;[8]

and

> The good want power, but to weep barren tears.
> The powerful goodness want: worse need for them.
> The wise want love; and those who love want wisdom;
> And all best things are thus confused to ill;[9]

and man is subject to

> terror, madness, crime, remorse,
> Which from the links of the great chain of things,
> To every thought within the mind of man
> Sway and drag heavily, and each one reels
> Under the load towards the pit of death;
> Abandoned hope, and love that turns to hate;
> And self-contempt, bitterer to drink than blood;
> Pain, whose unheeded and familiar speech
> Is howling, and keen shrieks, day after day;[10]

and to

> Evil, the immedicable plague, which, while
> Man looks on his creation like a God
> And sees that it is glorious, drives him on,
> The wreck of his own will, the scorn of earth,
> The outcast, the abandoned, the alone.[11]

And what is declared by Demogorgon, in the last stanza of the poem, to be the noblest destiny of man on earth?

> To suffer woes which Hope thinks infinite;
> To forgive wrongs darker than death or night;
> To defy Power, which seems omnipotent;

---

[7] At the close of Book IX. "And the question of its present or future existence on earth is quite unimportant." Translated by Davies and Vaughan.
[8] I, ll. 594–96.   [9] I, ll. 625–28.
[10] II, iv, ll. 19–27.   [11] II, iv, ll. 101–05.

To love, and bear; to hope till Hope creates
From its own wreck the thing it contemplates;
   Neither to change, nor falter, nor repent;
This, like thy glory, Titan, is to be
Good, great and joyous, beautiful and free;
This is alone Life, Joy, Empire, and Victory.[12]

How many of the parlor pessimists, and the scholars in their snug libraries, who sneer at Shelley's "shallow optimism" would care to live up to *this* creed? For the plain implication is that the sufferings and trials of Prometheus are no more severe than those which every man must face and conquer who, in an unregenerate world, seeks to live a truly spiritual life.

On *The Cenci* I need not dwell. Shelley himself said of it: "It is written without any of the peculiar feelings and opinions which characterize my other compositions . . ."[13] This is not altogether accurate; but at any rate the play is hardly optimistic. Those who deplore the earthly Paradise in *Prometheus* will find an earthly Hell in *The Cenci*. As a matter of fact, Shelley often thought and spoke of the human world as a hell. Such is the underlying idea of *Peter Bell the Third*, a poem too much neglected by students of the poet's work. The Dedication contains a bitter jest, as Shelley's jests about society were apt to be (though there is never, as so often in Byron, any *personal* bitterness). "You will perceive that it is not necessary to consider Hell and the Devil as supernatural machinery. The whole scene of my epic is in 'this world which is' — so Peter informed us before his conversion to *White Obi* —

   'The world of all of us, *and where*
   We find our happiness or not at all.' "[14]

And in the poem itself the bitterness grows until in Part the Third, entitled *Hell*, it swells into one of the most sweeping and terrible indictments of English society that is to be found (again excepting Swift) in English literature. Byron's satire in *Don Juan*, although quite sincere and very effective, often seems mere trifling in com-

---

[12] IV, ll. 570–78.   [13] *Letters*, II, 698.
[14] These lines from Wordsworth's *The Prelude* evidently rankled in Shelley's mind, for he repeats them in a letter to John Gisborne a few months before his death (April 10, 1822) and condemns them in the strongest terms. See below, Chapter VI.

parison. There is still a glimmer of humor at the beginning, but
it is forgotten in three lines.

> Hell is a city much like London —
>   A populous and a smoky city;
> There are all sorts of people undone,
> And there is little or no fun done;
>   Small justice shown, and still less pity.[15]

Politics, economics, religion, manners, all are grist for the mill of
Shelley's indignation. No stanza is more effective than that in
which he hits off the parties of fashionable society which he had
always hated. Byron also delights to jibe at them, but how much
more mordant is Shelley's picture of fashionable fops:

> Things whose trade is, over ladies,
>   To lean, and flirt, and stare, and simper,
> Till all that is divine in woman
> Grows cruel, courteous, smooth, inhuman,
>   Crucified 'twixt a smile and whimper.[16]

And when the picture is finished, the poet comments on it:

> And this is Hell — and in this smother
>   All are damnable and damned;
> Each one damning, damns the other;
> They are damned by one another,
>   By none other are they damned.
>
>   .   .   .   .
>
> Statesmen damn themselves to be
>   Cursed; and lawyers damn their souls
> To the auction of a fee;
> Churchmen damn themselves to see
>   God's sweet love in burning coals.
>
> The rich are damned, beyond all cure,
>   To taunt, and starve, and trample on
> The weak and wretched; and the poor
> Damn their broken hearts to endure
>   Stripe on stripe, with groan on groan.
>
> Sometimes the poor are damned indeed,
>   To take, — not means for being blessed, —

---

[15] III, i.
[16] III, x. Note the Christian imagery — even in treating a subject like this.

But Cobbett's snuff, revenge; that weed
From which the worms that it doth feed
    Squeeze less than they before possessed.

. . . .

All are damned — they breathe an air,
    Thick, infected, joy-dispelling:
Each pursues what seems most fair,
Mining like moles, through mind, and there
Scoop palace-caverns vast, where Care
    In thronèd state is ever dwelling.[17]

This is the kind of thing that our optimist does when he sets out to write a pleasant little *jeu d'esprit* satirizing an absurd and stupid poem. This is the void to which our "ineffectual angel" flees from life's little unpleasantnesses, and where he weakly beats his luminous wings. "Shelley," says Clutton-Brock, with reference to *The Cenci*, "did not understand wickedness at all. Therefore he was not fit to write a play about it." [18] There are some critical judgments that pass *all* understanding, and this is one. The truth is that Shelley understood wickedness too well to be able to write about it indifferently or entertainingly. He understood that hypocrisy and avarice and sensuality and cruelty degrade men and women into beasts; and he had too deep a reverence for the true dignity of human nature, and too little selfish vanity, to derive pleasure from the contemplation of the vice and misery of his fellow beings. He did not have, says the same critic, like Shakespeare, "a joyful sense of the imperfection of this life"; that is, he had ideals; that is, he was not satisfied with himself and indifferent to others; that is, in a word, he was religious. He could not see, we are told again, as could Shakespeare, "promise and significance in the very follies and weaknesses of mankind";[19] that is, he would not, like the critic, sell his divine birthright for a mess of complacent claptrap. It seems that critics as well as poets write upon subjects they are not fit to write about. Anyone who can talk of "a joyful sense of the imperfection of this life" certainly did not understand the man who wrote:

[17] III, xv, xvii–xix, xxiii.
[18] Arthur Clutton-Brock, *Shelley: The Man and the Poet* (4th ed., London, 1929), p. 221.
[19] *Ibid.*, p. 259. I think that the critic does an injustice to Shakespeare.

> And some few, like we know who,
>   Damned — but God alone knows why —
> To believe their minds are given
> To make this ugly Hell a Heaven;
>   In which faith they live and die.[20]

But when did the world ever understand a voice crying in the wilderness?

All of Shelley's long poems express this deep dissatisfaction concerning earthly life — for the stanza just quoted does not say that men *can* make this ugly Hell a Heaven, but only that some few are strangely condemned to try. He writes a political satire, and the English public is pictured as a drove of starving swine.[21] He writes an airy phantasia about a mythical and mystical Witch of Atlas; and even in this bright day-dream, as Leigh Hunt long ago pointed out, he cannot escape from "a perpetual consciousness of his humanity; a clinging load of the miseries of his fellow creatures"; he "cannot indulge himself long in that airy region, without *dreaming* of mortal strife";[22] the Witch must at last descend from her serene heaven to make vain "all harsh and crooked purposes" of men, to "humanize and harmonize" their life. He writes a poem almost deliriously lovely in its praise of Love: and "this world of life Is as a garden ravaged," an "eternal Curse," a "cold common hell," which must be redeemed, if at all, only by a Love that is more than earthly.[23] He writes a great elegy, and contrasts the serene immortality of the dead with the restless suffering of the living:

> He hath awakened from the dream of life —
> 'Tis we, who lost in stormy visions, keep
> With phantoms an unprofitable strife,
> And in mad trance, strike with our spirit's knife
> Invulnerable nothings. — *We* decay
> Like corpses in a charnel; fear and grief
> Convulse us and consume us day by day,
> And cold hopes swarm like worms within our living clay,[24]

---

[20] *Peter Bell the Third*, III, xx.
[21] *Oedipus Tyrannus, or Swellfoot the Tyrant.*
[22] *Lord Byron and His Contemporaries*, p. 183.
[23] *Epipsychidion*, ll. 186–87, 25, 214.
[24] *Adonais*, xxxix.

and the ruling Spirit of Love and Beauty is glorified as the Power which even "the eclipsing Curse Of birth can quench not." He writes a lyrical drama on the occasion of Greece's attempt to regain her liberty; and while the issue is still in doubt, he represents the effort as a failure, the Turks victorious, and "the glory that was Greece" exiled from the earth, sure of a home only in the eternal world of the ideal; and in the last lines of the poem he cries,

> The world is weary of the past,
> Oh, might it die or rest at last.

But the deepest pessimism of all is to be found in *The Triumph of Life*, Shelley's last long poem. It is unfinished, and no doubt the conclusion would have been less despairing than the part of the poem that we have. But as it stands, it recalls the cry of hopelessness that Milton puts into the mouth of the blind Samson:

> Irrecoverably dark, total eclipse
> Without all hope of day.

Rossetti pointed out that the theme of the poem might be stated in a line from *Adonais:* "The contagion of the world's slow stain." In the *Essay on Christianity* Shelley had written: "according to the indisputable facts of the case, some evil spirit has dominion in this imperfect world." In the essay *On the Devil and Devils* he had declared that in man's universe "the most admirable tendencies to happiness and preservation are forever baffled by misery and decay." [25] According to Trelawny, he once said, "It is difficult to see why or for what purpose we are here, a perpetual torment to ourselves and to every living thing"; and again, "Wise men of all ages have declared everything that is, is wrong." [26] *The Triumph*

---

[25] *Complete Works*, VIII, 89.

[26] *Records*, pp. 70, 76. Cf. a sonnet written in 1818, in which he speaks of himself as one who
sought,
> For his lost heart was tender, things to love.
> But found them not, alas! nor was there aught
> The world contains, the which he could approve.
>   (Hutchinson, p. 569.)

In this discussion I have mentioned only Shelley's longer poems, since these are commonly supposed to be optimistic in tone. The acknowledged sadness of many of the lyrics is usually attributed to self-pity. Nevertheless, such pieces as *To Time* and *A Lament*, written in 1821, and *A Dirge*, written in 1822, seem to me to *of Life* is his final and most convincing illustration of this sad text. Through the vast mass of humanity the car of Life takes its remorseless way, maddening, deforming, destroying all. Ahead of it rushes a lust-intoxicated mob of human beings, and in the midst of their "fierce and obscene" dance "One falls and then another in the path Senseless"; and when the car has passed over them no other trace remains

> But as of foam after the ocean's wrath
> Is spent upon the desert shore . . .[27]

And behind the chariot is an even more dreadful sight.

> Old men and women foully disarrayed,
> Shake their grey hairs in the insulting wind,
>
> And follow in the dance, with limbs decayed,
> Seeking to reach the light which leaves them still
> Farther behind and deeper in the shade.
>
> But not the less with impotence of will
> They wheel, though ghastly shadows interpose
> Round them and round each other, and fulfil
>
> Their work, and in the dust from whence they rose
> Sink, and corruption veils them as they lie . . .[28]

Such is the fate of the masses. What of those great ones

> whose fame or infamy must grow
> Till the great winter lay the form and name
> Of this green earth with them forever low . . .
>
> ". . . the wise
> The great, the unforgotten, — they who wore
> Mitres and helms and crowns, or wreaths of light,
> Signs of thought's empire over thought"?[29]

-----

express unquestionably a despair in regard to earthly human existence that could scarcely have arisen merely from the contemplation of his personal misfortunes. Mr. Newman I. White, in his introduction to *The Best of Shelley* (page xxxi), says: "It is hard to see how Shelley can be so disillusioned as to personal life and continue to be radiantly optimistic as to the race. The difficulty vanishes only when we realize that such expressions as those just quoted are scarcely more than subconscious generalizations from Shelley's view of his own fate." The difficulty also vanishes if we simply look at the facts and see that Shelley's radiant optimism as to the race is largely a myth. The manufacture of theories to explain the existence of what is only imagined to exist has been a favorite occupation of Shelley's critics and biographers, beginning with Hogg and Peacock.

[27] Ll. 163–64.   [28] Ll. 165–74.   [29] Ll. 125–27, 208–11.

Of such the fate is no less hopeless; all are chained, helpless, to the blindly guided car — all except Socrates and Christ.[30] In the whole course of human history, these two alone have kept their souls pure and free from the contamination of life. What wonder that the poet cries,

> "Mine eyes are sick of this perpetual flow
> Of people, and my heart sick of one sad thought — "

or that "what was once Rousseau" should speak of

> "a Hell
> Like this harsh world in which I wake to weep" [31]

or that he should look back with bitter longing to the loveliness of the mystic place where his life began, a loveliness which were his companion to behold, he says,

> "Thou wouldst forget thus vainly to deplore
> "Ills, which if ills, can find no cure from thee,
>   The thought of which no other sleep will quell,
>   Nor other music blot from memory . . ." [32]

This is the poet whose philosophy is always "the voice of enthusiasm." This is the "divine child" on a celestial carouse, who wants the world for his plaything.[33] And what a pretty toy it is, to be sure! So let us hear no more of Shelley as an irresponsible optimist; and when a critic calls him such, let us recommend that critic to read *The Triumph of Life*.[34]

[30] They are not named, but the poet clearly has them in mind. Cf. l. 134.

[31] Ll. 298–99, 333–34.

[32] Ll. 327–30. A. C. Bradley thinks these lines refer to Shelley's personal misfortunes, e.g., the death of Harriet. *Modern Language Review*, 9: 452–53. But this seems extremely unlikely. What makes the picture so terrible is simply its universality. To obtrude a personal grief here would be a fault, both artistically and morally, of which Shelley at this time would have been incapable.

[33] Cf. Francis Thompson's *Shelley* (London, 1909). H. J. Massingham, in *The Friend of Shelley*, describes Thompson's essay as "one of the worst written and least discriminating essays of our literature" (p. 119). I heartily concur in this judgment. For Thompson, Shelley is merely a skeleton upon which to fling the glittering cloak of his stylistic virtuosity. It is a typical example of the disservice done to the poet's reputation by his professed admirers.

[34] Mr. White (*op. cit.*, p. xxxiv) comments that *The Triumph of Life* is "also the triumph of abstract beauty, 'pinnacled dim in the intense inane' " — whence this judgment, until it is explained or qualified, must be presumed to have come. Contrast A. C. Bradley on the subject of Shelley's supposed optimism. "But a view

To leave the picture as it is, however, would be unfair to Shelley, who, for all his strong strain of asceticism, his sense of the vanity of the things of this world, his clear-eyed condemnation of sensuality and selfishness, was no moody medieval monk, following the first commandment and forgetting the second. He was intensely human in every better sense of the word, and his dark broodings upon the destiny of man were lightened by love of the beauty of nature, by boyish delight in simple enjoyments such as boating, or in the more refined pleasure of intellectual conversation, and by his unwearied efforts for the welfare of his friends.[35] Even in politics he did not lose interest; the attempt of a downtrodden people to throw off the chains of tyranny always kindled the old enthusiasm into flame; and as late as 1820 he wrote *A Philosophical View of Reform*, expressing temperate and often practical views on the political problems of England. And at the darkest there was always hope. It was not in so pure and gentle a nature to despair. He could hardly have forgotten the words of Prometheus, "I said all hope was vain but love: thou lovest." He might have said with Cythna, "The Spirit whom I loved, in solitude Sustained his child." It is doubtless true, as Trelawny says, that "the Poet bore his burden of life" in a "careless, not to say impatient way";[36] and Jane Williams declared, "He is seeking after what we all avoid, death."[37] But it was not a weak and fretful longing to escape from the positive ills of life into a kind oblivion. It sprang rather from the feeling that beneath or behind or beyond the trammels of life's illusion there was some far richer and purer state of being.

No single point of view, indeed, can do justice to Shelley. The

of existing mankind as composed almost wholly of tyrants and slaves, deluders and deluded, is surely pessimistic enough, hardly less so than the view of professed pessimists, like Schopenhauer and Leopardi." A. C. Bradley, *A Miscellany* (London, 1929), p. 153. Bradley is even disturbed by Shelley's low opinion of the mass of mankind; and if one is to criticize adversely his general view of human nature, it ought certainly to be on this ground. See below.

[35] The happy, human side of Shelley's character is well, though briefly, described in Oliver Elton's *Survey of English Literature, 1780–1830* (New York, [1912]), II, 192. The *Letter to Maria Gisborne* also illustrates the point, although even these light-hearted verses are interrupted by touches of grim realism. Cf. ll. 265–71.

[36] *Records*, p. 69.   [37] *Ibid.*, p. 109.

great fault of most biographical and critical studies is the attempt
to achieve a specious unity or consistency. Procrustes and his bed
offer the type of all this class of writing. This trait or that trait is
seized upon by the author and confidently presented to the reader
as the "key" to the person's character. The process is natural, but
deplorable. There never was one key that would open all the
chambers of a human personality. No man's life, as far as it can be
observed by others, or even by himself, is at all unified or consistent; and the greater his genius the more difficult it is to find
an all-embracing formula. I will not indulge in any cant about
seeking the truth; but one gets sick of seeing a man's life and work
distorted by the persistent application of a single theory or point
of view. Who can explain the picture we get of Shelley during the
last months of his life: floating on the blue Mediterranean with the
blue Italian sky above, far off from the strife and turmoil of human
existence, free for the moment from all outward pressure of personal responsibilities or universal problems, idly dreaming dreams
— and of what? A ghastly march of tortured phantoms of humanity, driven or led by some unresisted inward force through a realm
of agonizing unreality, apparently to a merciful extinction; while
light and love and beauty are only dimly visible, like

> "The ghost of a forgotten form of sleep;
> A light of heaven, whose half-extinguished beam
>
> Through the sick day in which we wake to weep
> Glimmers, forever sought, forever lost . . ." [38]

II

It should be clear at this point that evil was for Shelley a reality
far too painful and all-pervading to be easily escaped, least of all by
any mere abolition of political institutions, religious dogmas, or
social conventions. It is, of course, possible to be pessimistic about
the past and present, and optimistic about the future. This seems to
have been the state of Godwin, who indulges in a vicious attack upon
optimistic fatalism of the "best-of-all-possible-worlds" type, partly on
the ground that it destroys all distinction between virtue and vice
(as if his Necessarianism did not!), but largely because it is not

[38] *The Triumph of Life*, ll. 428–31.

true to the facts. "Contemplate the physiognomy of the species. Observe the traces of stupidity, of low cunning, of rooted insolence, of withered hope, and narrow selfishness, where the characters of wisdom, independence and disinterestedness might have been inscribed." [39] And yet he holds that Reason is leading man irresistibly along the road of perfectibility. This also, says Leslie Stephen, is Shelley's position. "A fusion of the satirist's view, that all which is, is bad, with the enthusiast's view that all which will be will be perfect, just expresses Shelley's peculiar mixture of optimism and pessimism." [40] And the critic says, besides: "His conception of the millenium . . . always embodies the same thought, that man is to be made perfect by the complete dissolution of all the traditional ties by which the race is at present bound together." [41] This may apply to Godwin accurately enough. But when Sir Leslie tries with the rusty key of Godwinism to unlock the door of Shelley's thought, he is led only into a dusty storeroom filled with the worn-out furniture of the poet's mind. So it happens that even a critic so clear-headed, though unimaginative, falls into the paradox that I have mentioned: Shelley is described first as believing the material world to be a mere painful illusion; and then is criticized, on the one hand, because the ideal world which he is supposed to desire is altogether unconnected with the actual, and is therefore unreal; and on the other, because he thinks the actual world can be easily reformed on Godwinian lines.

But Shelley was not such a fool as to think that a world so completely corrupt could be purified overnight by a dose of Reason or a new suit of clothes. He saw, or at any rate soon came to see, as clearly as Teufelsdröckh, that human nature weaves the cloth and cuts the patterns of the garments which society wears. To say that in his mature life he believed that an earthly paradise could be established merely through the overthrow of institutions is simply — or rather, extravagantly, stupidly, and perversely — false.

In the first place, he did not believe in the natural goodness of

[39] *Political Justice* (3d ed., 1798), I, 457. All future references will be to this edition.
[40] *Hours in a Library* (New York), III, 387.   [41] *Ibid.*, p. 379.

human nature. His ideal humanity was a beautiful vision, but for men and women in the mass he had little sympathy. How could he have? He was no snob, but he was an aristocrat to his finger ends. He was willing to pay homage to intellectual and moral worth, no matter whence it sprung; but he was revolted by coarseness and sensuality wherever they appeared, and while he might be sickened by seeing the guests at Lord Byron's parties turning themselves into vats of claret,[42] he was no more blind than anyone else to the fact that the lives of the lower classes contain an even greater measure of ugliness and vice.[43] Medwin tells us: "I have seen him, after threading the carnival crowd in the Lung' Arno Corsos, throw himself half fainting into a chair, overpowered by the atmosphere of evil passions, as he used to say, in that sensual and unintellectual crowd." [44] He did not, like present-day social reformers, glorify the "average man." He would have had no difficulty in accepting Carlyle's hero-worship or Arnold's doctrine of "the remnant." He had no more sympathy than either of these men for "the populace," "the great unwashed."

This feeling is forever breaking forth in his poetry and letters. Early in 1812 he writes to Miss Hitchener, upon hearing of the malicious rumor that he desired her to be his mistress, and urges her not to sacrifice her principles to the opinion of the world: "To the *world!* to the swinish multitude, to the indiscriminating million, to such as burnt the House of Priestley, such as murdered Fitzgerald, such as erect Barracks in Marylebone, such as began and such as continue this liberticide war, such wretches as dragged Redfern to slavery, or (equal in unprincipled cowardice) the slaves who permit such things: for of these two classes is composed what may be called the *world.*" [45] Even allowing for the fact that

[42] *Letters,* II, 932.

[43] Cf. the interesting remark (startlingly similar to Newman's comments on the same subject) in *A Philosophical View of Reform,* edited by T. W. Rolleston (Oxford University Press, 1920), p. 45, concerning the aristocracy of "great land proprietors and wealthy merchants": "Connected with the members of it is a certain generosity and refinement of manners and opinion which, though neither a philosophy nor virtue, has been that acknowledged substitute for them which at least is a religion which makes respected those venerable names."

[44] Thomas Medwin, *The Life of Percy Bysshe Shelley* (London, 1913), p. 268.

[45] *Letters,* I, 305.

these are the words of a very angry young man, they would hardly be written by a person with a deep faith in the natural wisdom and virtue of the proletariat. Nine months later he writes in a calmer mood to Hogg, expressing the same sentiment: "Perhaps you will say that my Republicanism is proud; it certainly is far removed from pot-house democracy, and knows with what smile to hear the servile applauses of an inconsistent mob." [46] In *Queen Mab* he condemns the soldier, who, according to the poet, sells his better self

> "For the gross blessings of a patriot mob,
>   For the vile gratitude of heartless kings,
>   And for a cold world's good word, — viler still." [47]

Twice in the poem he speaks of "the insensate mob," [48] and in his note against Christianity [49] he refers to "the vulgar, ever in extremes," and demands: "When will the vulgar learn humility? When will the pride of ignorance blush at having believed before it could comprehend?" Again in his note on vegetarianism, he states: "The vulgar of all ranks are invariably sensual and indocile." [50] In the Preface to *Alastor* the poet contrasts his hero, though the victim of a delusion, with the mass of humanity, "selfish, blind, and torpid . . . those unforeseeing multitudes who constitute together with their own, the lasting misery and loneliness of the world." In the *Lines Written among the Euganean Hills*, he fears the intrusion into his dream-Paradise of "the polluting multitude." [51] And he writes in a fragment belonging to the year 1821:

> Methought I was a billow in the crowd
>   Of common men, that stream without a shore,
> That ocean which at once is deaf and loud. [52]

A similar sentiment had previously been expressed in *Marenghi*, in which the hero has been driven into exile because of

[46] *Ibid.*, p. 382.
[47] V, ll. 211–13.
[48] VII, ll. 10, 239.
[49] Hutchinson, pp. 820, 821; note on VII, ll. 135, 136.
[50] *Ibid.*, p. 831; note on VIII, ll. 211, 212.
[51] L. 356.
[52] Hutchinson, p. 659.

some high and holy deed, by glory
Pursued into forgetfulness, which won
From the blind crowd he made secure and free
The patriot's meed, toil, death, and infamy.[53]

In the same year he wrote to his wife with reference to the Hoppner scandal (a typical example of the base and baseless malice with which he was pursued all through his life, and long after): "A certain degree and a certain kind of infamy is to be borne, and, in fact, is the best compliment which an exalted nature can receive from the filthy world, of which it is its hell to be a part." [54] And finally, in a letter to Leigh Hunt, which the author intended for publication in *The Examiner*, may be found two short but illuminating sentences: "Tyrants, after all, are only a kind of demagogues. They must flatter the Great Beast." [55]

One or two utterances of this sort might be explained away as due to temper.[56] But anyone who really knows Shelley's writings will find such a statement as this of Mr. Paul Elmer More, however widespread may be the belief which it expresses, to be not less than ludicrous: "With a child-like credulity almost inconceivable he accepted the current doctrine that mankind is naturally and inherently virtuous, needing only the deliverance from some outwardly applied oppression to spring back to its essential perfection." [57] Nothing is more absurd than to accuse Shelley of indiscriminate humanitarianism.

Again, however, I have presented only one side of the picture. There is, after all, considerable truth in Mrs. Shelley's statement that "Shelley loved the People; and respected them as often more

[53] Ll. 60–63.
[54] *Letters*, II, 890.
[55] *Ibid.*, p. 743.
[56] Cf. the letter to Clare Clairmont, October 29, 1820, in which he says, after recounting some business troubles with the Gisbornes: "The Gisbornes are people totally without faith. — I think they are altogether the most filthy and odious animals with which I ever came in contact." Yet on the same day he wrote a brief note to John Gisborne, beginning "Dear Friend" and sending "kindest regards"! See *Letters*, II, 826, 827. Such an episode, although not unique in Shelley's life, is so uncharacteristic that it is perhaps not disingenuous to suggest that the first statement was written when he was suffering from one of those attacks of almost intolerable physical pain to which he was subject.
[57] *Op. cit.*, p. 7.

virtuous, as always more suffering, and therefore more deserving of sympathy, than the great." [58] He was abnormally sensitive to the sufferings of all living things; and most of all, of course, to those of men, whose capacity for suffering is greatest. One of the most attractive pictures of Shelley we have is that given, not only by Mrs. Shelley but also by Leigh Hunt, Horace Smith, and others, of his active and altogether practical charity among the poor of Marlow and London in 1817.[59] It is true also that he blamed the sufferings and degradation of the poorer classes partly on the selfishness and callousness of the rich, and on the existing social system. And no thinking person has ever done otherwise. Obviously, reforms would never come about if everyone believed that human institutions are the inevitable result of human nature, and that changes in the framework of society can only come when they are no longer needed. The result of such a view is fatalism; and fatalism was something that Shelley (despite the fact that he has been labeled a Necessarian [60] and a determinist) hated from the depths of his being. It was no doubt the fatalistic tendency of Malthus' work, for example, that aroused Shelley's extreme antipathy toward a man whose sad and compassionate nature was in many ways so like his own. Again, one of his chief reasons for hating orthodox Christianity was that fatalism seemed to him to be implicit in it. The Christian doctrine of original sin seemed to lead to the conclusion that it is useless for man to try to make himself and his world better; and the thought of such a doctrine naturally made Shelley angry, and led him into extravagant denunciation. So Queen Mab tells Ianthe:

> "This is no unconnected misery,
>   Nor stands uncaused, and irretrievable.
>   Man's evil nature, that apology

[58] "Note on Poems Written in 1819." This is characteristic of the way in which Mrs. Shelley (doubtless unconsciously) does to her husband's memory what she could never do to the man, that is, makes him conventional and respectable. The result, as a critic well says of Dowden's biography, is simply to "flatten him out."

[59] See Mrs. Shelley's note on *The Revolt of Islam*; Beavan, *James and Horace Smith*, p. 168; Leigh Hunt, *Autobiography*; also Charles and Mary Cowden Clarke, *Recollections of Writers* (London, 1878), pp. 151–52.

[60] I use this form of the word, of which the more common is "Necessitarian," because it is used by Shelley himself, and is also considerably less tongue-twisting.

Which kings who rule, and cowards who crouch, set up
For their unnumbered crimes, sheds not the blood
Which desolates the discord-wasted land.
From kings, and priests, and statesmen, war arose . . ." [61]

If everything has a cause, argued the young reformer, then it is possible by removing the causes of evil to get rid of evil entirely. He did not see (any more than Godwin before him and a multitude of reformers since) that those causes must themselves be caused, and that there is thus set up an endless chain of cause and effect which it is impossible to break at any one point.

III

But let us see how far Shelley is consistent in holding to the view which he has just expressed: that kings and priests and statesmen, and marriage laws, and similar things, are the sole source of human woes. He says in the *Address to the Irish People,* written at the beginning of 1812:

I think those people then are very silly, and cannot see one inch beyond the end of their noses, who say that human nature is depraved; when at the same time wealth and poverty, those two great sources of crime, fall to the lot of the great majority of people; and when they see that people in moderate circumstances are always most wise and good. . . .[62] To begin to reform the government is immediately necessary, however good or bad individuals may be; it is more necessary if they are eminently the latter, in some degree to palliate or do away the cause, as political institution has even [ever(?)] the greatest influence on the human character, and is that alone which differences the Turk from the Irishman.[63]

These passages lend some color to the common criticism of Shelley's views. But what of the following statements from the same *Address* (written, it is to be remembered, just before *Queen Mab,* in the full sweep of the poet's youthful enthusiasm)?

Government is an evil; it is only the thoughtlessness and vices of men that make it a necessary evil. When all men are good and wise, government will of itself decay. So long as men continue foolish and vicious,

[61] IV, ll. 74–80. The last line, if "dictators" were substituted for "kings" and "capitalists" for "priests," would have a distressingly modern ring.
[62] *Prose Works,* I, 246. The idea is straight out of *Political Justice,* Book I, Chapter 3.
[63] *Ibid.,* p. 250.

so long will government, even such a government as that of England, continue necessary in order to prevent the crimes of bad men. . . . Before the restraints of government are lessened, it is fit that we should lessen the necessity for them. Before government is done away with, we must reform ourselves . . . O Irishmen, REFORM YOURSELVES . . .[64]

And again, we are told that political reform "in its own nature must be gradual, however rapid, and rational, however warm. It is founded on the reform of private men, and without individual amendment it is vain and foolish to expect the amendment of a state or government."[65] Such passages as these are too often over-looked by Shelley's critics; and the presence, in the poet's early thought, of this contradiction, as well as the natural explanation of it, is too often ignored. It is perfectly obvious that from the first there was a conflict in Shelley's mind between the theories of Godwin and his own common sense — a conflict in which common sense, aided by experience, was ultimately to triumph — as far as it ever ought to!

The same contradiction appears over and over in *Queen Mab*. Carried away by a not unadmirable enthusiasm for human perfection, and an altogether admirable hatred of the brutal and senseless oppression to which the English people were subjected (a critic will judge Shelley's denunciations of tyranny to be extravagant in direct proportion to his own ignorance of the actual conditions of the time), the poet indulges in sweeping statements which a deeper insight leads him elsewhere to unsay. He will not have human ills blamed upon original sin, for then there would be no hope of alleviating them; nor, for the same reason, will he attribute them to the "Spirit of Nature," or Necessity. So he accepts (or thinks that he does so) the solution offered by Godwin and the Revolutionists, which would seem to make reform so simple a matter.

> "Hath Nature's soul,
> That formed this world so beautiful, that spread
> Earth's lap with plenty, and life's smallest chord
> Strung to unchanging unison, that gave
> The happy birds their dwelling in the grove . . .
> And filled the meanest worm that crawls in dust

[64] *Ibid.*, p. 244.   [65] *Ibid.*, p. 249.

With spirit, thought, and love; on Man alone,
Partial in causeless malice, wantonly
Heaped ruin, vice, and slavery; his soul
Blasted with withering curses . . . ?
            . . . Nature! — no!
Kings, priests, and statesmen, blast the human flower
Even in its tender bud; their influence darts
Like subtle poison through the bloodless veins
Of desolate society . . .
Let priest-led slaves cease to proclaim that man
Inherits vice and misery, when Force
And Falsehood hang even o'er the cradled babe,
Stifling with rudest grasp all natural good . . .
            . . . On its wretched frame,
Poisoned, perchance, by the disease and woe
Heaped on the wretched parent whence it sprung
By morals, law, and custom, the pure winds
Of Heaven, that renovate the insect tribes,
May breathe not. The untainting light of day
May visit not its longings. It is bound
Ere it has life: yea, all the chains are forged
Long ere its being: all liberty and love
And peace is torn from its defencelessness;
Cursed from its birth, even from its cradle doomed
To abjectness and bondage!" [66]

This utterance is nihilistic enough to satisfy the severest of Shelley's critics; but although it is often echoed in the poem, it is quite as often denied, implicitly if not explicitly.

[66] IV, ll. 89–138. This passage is quite irreconcilable with that quoted in the last chapter, in which good and evil were declared to be purely relative manifestations of a "Spirit of Nature" beyond good and evil — the logical outcome of the doctrine of Necessarianism. Shelley's insistence here on the goodness of Nature is doubtless due not only to his refusal to admit that man could not, if he would, remove the evil from human life, but also to his natural piety, which made him wish to worship the Spirit of Nature but made him also unwilling to worship a Power not wholly good. The other contradiction in the two passages, that between Necessarianism and a program for reforming the world by overthrowing institutions, is also present in Godwin. As Leslie Stephen says, "According to this view, 'kings, priests, and statesmen' are something outside of, and logically opposed to, Nature." *Op. cit.*, p. 378. The critic continues: "The crude incoherence of the whole system is too obvious to require exposition; and yet it is simply an explicit statement of Godwin's theories, put forth with an inconvenient excess of candour. The absurdities slurred over by the philosopher are thrown into brilliant relief by the poet." *Ibid.*, pp. 378–79. Shelley introduces added contradictions of his own, however, because of the conflict between his own intuitions and Godwin's rationalism.

One naturally asks, after reading the passage quoted, If kings, priests, and statesmen are responsible for human sufferings, who or what is responsible for *them?* Curiously enough, Shelley asks himself the same question; and his answer apparently contradicts what we have just heard him saying.

> "Whence, think'st thou, kings and parasites arose?
> Whence that unnatural line of drones, who heap
> Toil and unvanquishable penury
> On those who build their palaces, and bring
> Their daily bread? — From vice, black loathsome vice;
> From rapine, madness, treachery, and wrong;
> From all that 'genders misery, and makes
> Of earth this thorny wilderness; from lust,
> Revenge, and murder. . . ." [67]

But it may perhaps be argued that, according to Shelley, "vice" is merely the result of the unnatural usages of society; for the poet has just declared that kings, after all, are not to be blamed, because

> "the unconquered powers
> Of precedent and custom interpose
> Between a *king* and virtue," [68]

just as they produce the slavish and cowardly spirit that leads the people to submit to tyrants. And later in the same canto he returns to the thought, declaring,

> "Nature rejects the monarch, not the man;
> The subject, not the citizen . . .
> Power, like a desolating pestilence,
> Pollutes whate'er it touches; and obedience . . .
> Makes slaves of men . . ." [69]

It is still not clear, however, whether society is responsible for vice, or vice for society; and the question is still left open by the following passage, in which the poet, after saying that all of Nature's works express "peace, harmony, and love," goes on:

> "All but the outcast, Man. He fabricates
> The sword which stabs his piece; he cherisheth
> The snakes that gnaw his heart; he raiseth up
> The tyrant, whose delight is in his woe . . ." [70]

[67] III, ll. 118–26.   [68] III, ll. 97–99.
[69] III, ll. 170–79.   [70] III, ll. 199–202.

Saving the shrillness of tone, this sounds more like the voice of a Hebrew prophet than of the disciple of Godwin. But the case is complicated still further by the verses called *Falsehood and Vice, a Dialogue,* which Shelley inserts in the notes, and in which he makes Vice declare that "the bloated wretch on yonder throne," as well as his "ten thousand victims" who "dream that tryants goad them there With poisonous war to taint the air," are entirely deceived; for "I — I do all." Vice is also said to have brought her "daughter, RELIGION, on earth"; so that religion is apparently not the cause but the effect of vice.[71]

The difficulty in determining the import of these passages lies in the fact that the word "vice" is so general and inclusive a term. But when we find the poet devoting nearly all of the fifth canto to a denunciation of "suicidal selfishness," and saying that, although "every heart contains perfection's germ," yet

> "mean lust
> Has bound its chains so tight around the earth,
> That all within it but the virtuous man
> Is venal;" [72]

then the issue becomes clearer. No one will pretend, I think, that so fundamental a fault as selfishness can be the result of "precedent and custom"; rather it must be the cause of these and the other evils of society, as it is said specifically to be the source of commerce, which in turn gives rise to a large measure of social injustice.

This analysis shows that in *Queen Mab* Shelley is still altogether uncertain as to the origin of the miseries and sufferings of the human race: whether these are due to the conventions and institutions of society; or are the natural (although not inevitable) outgrowth of certain innate human traits, such as selfishness; or are merely a predestined part of the inscrutable workings of Necessity.[73]

[71] Note on IV, ll. 178–79. Shelley says: "I will here subjoin a little poem, so strongly expressive of my abhorrence of despotism and falsehood, that I fear lest it may never again be depictured so vividly. This opportunity is perhaps the only one that will ever occur of rescuing it from oblivion." In view of the extravagant doggerel which follows, even the writer's earnestness cannot prevent these words from being somewhat ludicrous.

[72] V, ll. 166–69.

[73] It is interesting to note that Godwin himself admits, at the end of the third edition of *Political Justice,* that human nature as well as the structure of society

To say that any one of these alternatives is dominant, even in *Queen Mab*, is false. To say, as is so often done, that the first of them dominates the whole course of Shelley's thought, is monstrous. Already in *The Revolt of Islam*, which critics usually brush aside as a feverish vision of unreal evils and fantastic hopes, the poet has moved far from his early extravagance. A statement in the Preface is significant: "In recommending also a great and important change in the spirit which animates the social institutions of mankind, I have avoided all flattery to those violent and malignant passions of our nature which are ever on the watch to mingle with and to alloy the most beneficial innovations. There is no quarter given to Revenge, or Envy, or Prejudice." The poet sees now that it is not the forms but the *spirit* of social institutions which require to be changed, and that the evils of society arise from the "malignant passions" which are deeply rooted in human nature.[74]

In *Prometheus Unbound* this new attitude finds unequivocal expression. One who comes to the poem with a mind free from critical superstition will find scarcely a shadow of evidence that the author considers evil to be the outgrowth of institutions. Yet somehow or other the work has been commonly interpreted as an illustration of this Godwinian dogma. Prometheus is usually said to represent the mass of humanity, chained and made to suffer by the force of customs, conventions, institutions, laws, superstitions, and so on, for which man is not responsible but which have been mysteriously imposed upon him from without — personified by Jupiter. Presently arises Demogorgon, who symbolizes Revolution — or Necessity, since there is no discernible motive for his appearance — and mysteriously drags Jupiter out of sight. Then, all the restraints of civilization being destroyed, man is free to follow his natural impulses;

needs to be changed. Speaking of the equalization of property, he says: "If by positive institution, the property of every man were equalized today, without a contemporary change in men's dispositions and sentiments, it would become unequal tomorrow." *Political Justice*, II, 438, Book VIII, Chapter 2. Godwin is almost as hard to bring under a single formula as Shelley. I have no doubt that by a judicious selection of passages from his work, one could "prove" that any nineteenth century English poet derived most of his important ideas from Godwin's work.

[74] I pass over the poem itself because something of the same confusion is evident here as in *Queen Mab*, and the poet's utterances are often so vague that it is extremely difficult to determine their implications.

and crime, disease, and all other human sufferings immediately disappear, and an everlasting heaven on earth is ushered in.[75]

It is extraordinary that such a misconception could ever have gained a foothold in the realm of respectable criticism. Until the last scene of the third act, there is nothing that by itself justifies this interpretation, which exists only because critics come to the poem with their minds made up to find in it a system which Shelley had never accepted unreservedly, and the extreme principles of which he had long since cast aside. What we really have in *Prometheus Unbound,* above all else, is a drama of the individual human soul, and its effort to free itself from the evil within and without.[76] Prometheus' punishment and suffering is that which every person must pass through who would gain self-mastery. He is tempted first to surrender his individuality, his own sense of right and wrong, in order to escape from pain; he is tempted to sell his soul by conforming to the way of the world — "the world" in exactly the Christian sense. He is then tempted from within — as a man,

[75] This statement of the theme of *Prometheus* will be so surprising to those who have formed a judgment of Shelley by reading his poetry instead of by reading what critics have written about it, that I hasten to subjoin references to a few of the many criticisms which agree in accepting this point of view. Dowden speaks of "the philosophical errors in the doctrine which lies behind the poetry of *Prometheus Unbound,* the false conception of evil, as residing in external powers rather than in man's heart and will, the false ideal of the human society of the future." See *Transcripts and Studies,* p. 99. This dictum has often been repeated, with slight variations. "For the wonder, the miracle of all this unnatural, incomprehensible evil in the world, he found a complete explanation in the doctrine that 'positive institutions' have poisoned and distorted the natural good in man." (H. N. Brailsford, *Shelley, Godwin, and Their Circle,* p. 222. This is in many ways a valuable study, but like so many, distorted by the assumption that Shelley got all his ideas from Godwin.) "Demogorgon, the most powerful and unsubstantial of shades, conquers the vicious God of *Prometheus Unbound* with an ease that leads one to wonder why it was not done much earlier . . . Tyranny always falls without a struggle. Indeed, it has no chance. It exists only because men are wicked and foolish; but men cease to be wicked and foolish, and return to their natural purity and intelligence, when they catch the spark flung off from the mind of their savior. It is salvation by sentiment." See Crane Brinton, *The Political Ideas of the English Romanticists* (Oxford University Press, 1926), p. 169. Cf. also Gingerich, *Essays in the Romantic Poets;* Clutton-Brock, *op. cit.,* Chapter X; More, *op. cit.;* etc., etc. Perhaps the most complete and concise statement of the popular misconception as to the meaning of the poem is to be found in Miss Scudder's edition, pp. xxxiii–xxxix.

[76] Cf. M. T. Solve, *Shelley: His Theory of Poetry,* p. 90: "*Prometheus Unbound* is truly a psychological, a metaphysical drama. We have there the struggle between the forces of good and evil in the mind of man."

rejecting the dull stagnation of common life, should become embittered, and either retire from the world or prey upon it, instead
of trying to make it better. So the Furies sent from Jupiter proclaim,

> We are the ministers of pain, and fear,
> And disappointment, and mistrust, and hate,
> And clinging crime . . .[77]

Prometheus' words bring home the horror of his trial:

> Whilst I behold such execrable shapes,
> Methinks I grow like what I contemplate,
> And laugh and stare in loathsome sympathy.[78]

And one of the Furies elaborates the same thought:

> Thou think'st we will live through thee, one by one,
> Like animal life, and though we can obscure not
> The soul which burns within, that we will dwell
> Beside it, like a vain loud multitude
> Vexing the self-content of wisest men:
> That we will be dread thought beneath thy brain,
> And foul desire round thine astonished heart,
> And blood within thy labyrinthine veins
> Crawling like agony?[79]

But Prometheus answers,

>   Why, ye are thus now;
> Yet am I king over myself, and rule
> The torturing and conflicting throngs within,
> As Jove rules you when Hell grows mutinous.[80]

Surely it is absurd for any critic, in the face of a passage like this,
to pretend that Shelley had a naïve belief in the "natural goodness"
of man, that he was ignorant of the nature of human weakness and
sin, or that he considered evil to be something external.[81] It is true
that Shelley rarely portrays such a scene as this; but the explana-

---

[77] I, ll. 452–54.   [78] I, ll. 449–51.
[79] I, ll. 483–91.   [80] I, ll. 491–94.
[81] Mrs. Campbell, whose treatment of this whole scene is very fine, declares
without exaggeration that the lines just quoted express "perhaps more vividly than
any poet ever did before the agony of man's struggle to save his soul, not from
priests and kings, but from himself — poor hybrid of Heaven and Earth." See
Shelley and the Unromantics, p. 210. Contrast Dowden's absurd comment that
Shelley considered vice to be no more than "an intellectual error, a mistaken calculation of consequences." *Transcripts and Studies*, p. 87.

tion is perhaps that, not being blessed with "a joyful sense of the imperfection" of human nature, he found the task too painful; he doubtless realized to himself too well the suffering and struggle of his hero.

But there is still one more temptation that Prometheus must undergo, the temptation of which Christianity makes so much — despair. He must behold a vision of Christ crucified and a vision of the French Revolution; and must face the apparent fact that these two great efforts of the Spirit of Good to overthrow the power of the Spirit of Evil have only made the reign of Jupiter more secure; just as his own efforts to aid man have only plunged the human race deeper into misery. This appalling mystery of evil that always triumphs, changing good to its own nature, as the professed followers of Christ have so often crucified his true followers, as the world always desires to crucify those who would be its saviors — this is the hardest trial of the initiate into the deepest mysteries of religious experience. In Prometheus' lament, "Ah woe! Ah woe! Alas! pain, pain ever, for ever!" we hear the immemorial cry of the human soul as it faces the mystery of evil. It is the same cry that came from the cross: "My God! My God! Why hast thou forsaken me?"

Yet this is only one side of the struggle. These victories prevent Jupiter from triumphing completely over his victim, but they do not set Prometheus free. That freedom must come from the final renunciation of self, the extinction of all personal emotions or desires: symbolized here by the recalling of the curse upon Jupiter, the wish that no living thing may suffer pain, the transformation of hate into pity. It is Prometheus' hate of Jupiter that has kept him so long in bondage. When, made wise by ages of suffering, he ceases to hate his torturer, Jupiter's power upon him ceases. Thus is the fall of the tyrant motivated.[82] Thus, Shelley would say, it is possible for a man to cast out the evil in his own nature and become truly free and truly human. He saw, as every great moralist has seen, that the salvation of humanity from its present degradation of misery and woe must begin and end with the regeneration of the

[82] Although this fact has often been pointed out, critics still persist in regarding Jupiter's fall as completely causeless, the result of blind fate. Cf. note 74 above.

individual human soul. That regeneration is typified in the story of Prometheus. The paradise which the poet pictures at the end of the third act will come when every individual human being has undergone the same struggle as Prometheus and like him has arrived at moral perfection. Then indeed there will be no need for laws, for government, for dogmatic religion.[83] But this will be the effect and not the cause of man's conquest of evil. So in the *Essay on Christianity*, commenting on the communism of the early Christians, Shelley declares: "The system of equality which they established necessarily fell to the ground, because it is a system that must result from, rather than precede, the moral improvement of human kind." [84] In *A Philosophical View of Reform* we find him stating again: "That equality of possessions which Jesus Christ so passionately taught is a moral rather than a political truth, and is such as social institutions cannot inflexibly secure . . . Equality in possessions must be the last result of the utmost refinements of civilization." [85] All that Shelley is saying in the closing scene of the third act of *Prometheus* is that when man shall have made himself perfect, institutions will cease to matter. Implicit in this as in every part of the poem is the simple command: "Be ye therefore perfect . . . "

Here perhaps I may pause to destroy the myth that Shelley advocated "a return to nature" after the manner of Rousseau. Sir Leslie Stephen says, with reference to the close of the third act of *Prometheus Unbound*, "To be 'unclassed, tribeless, and nationless,' and we may add, without marriage, is to be in the lowest depths of barbarism. It is so, at least, in the world of realities." [86] Shelley, however, specifically rejects such a solution of human woes. "Nothing is more obviously false than that the remedy for the inequality among men consists in their return to the condition of

---

[83] For another statement of this view, see H. Richter, *Englische Studien*, XXX, 400 ff. "Der aüssern Reform der Gesellschaft muss die innere Reform jedes einzelnen vorgehen." (P. 402.)

[84] Shawcross, p. 116.   [85] Page 70.

[86] *Op. cit.*, p. 380. The sneer about marriage is characteristic of Victorian criticism. Shelley's refusal to limit love within the bounds of a comfortable domesticity was what the Victorians found it hardest to comprehend. One can trace the influence of (what I will venture to call) this narrow and selfish ideal in the criticism of Dowden, Arnold, Kingsley, and others.

savages and beasts." [87] We know "that uncivilized man is the most pernicious and miserable of beings, and that the violence and injustice, which are the genuine indications of real inequality, obtain in the society of these beings without palliation." [88] And most striking of all is the following description of the "natural man": "The immediate emotions of his nature, *especially in its most inartificial state*, prompt him to inflict pain, and to arrogate dominion. He desires to heap superfluities to his own store, although others perish with famine. He is propelled to guard against the smallest invasion of his own liberty, though he reduces others to a condition of the most pitiful servitude. He is revengeful, proud and selfish." [89] These are strange words to come from the pen of a naïve believer in the natural goodness of man. Is it credible in the slightest degree that the writer of them believed the institutions of society to be the *cause* of all the evils by which men are afflicted? He saw (again I repeat) that the evil is in man's own nature. In the beginning: "Too mean-spirited and too feeble in resolve to attempt the conquest of *their own evil passions* and of the difficulties of the material world, men sought dominion over their fellow men, as an easy method to gain that apparent majesty and power which the instinct of their nature requires." [90] What can one add to this except to ask of Shelley's critics, "Do words mean anything, or do they not?"

One more piece of evidence I offer in the attempt to crush what seems to me an ignorant and perverse prejudice in regard to Shelley's view of evil. If evil is the result of institutions, how are we to account for that incarnation of evil, Count Cenci? It is true that the play is not intended to express the author's philosophy; but he would hardly have chosen a theme that seemed to contradict his view of the world. He speaks of the play, in the Dedication, as "a sad reality." It is only too obvious that the course of the action

[87] *Essay on Christianity*, in Shawcross, p. 111.
[88] *Ibid.*, p. 114. [89] *Ibid.*, p. 75. Italics mine.
[90] *Ibid.*, p. 106. Italics mine. Cf., in regard to Shelley's perpetual distrust of the masses, the following note in *A Philosophical View of Reform* (page 15): "For two conditions are necessary to a theoretically perfect government, and one of them alone is adequately filled by the most perfect of practical governments, The Republic of the United States: to represent the will of the people as it is. To provide that that will should be as wise and just as possible."

is a reflection of human life as Shelley saw it — good always suffering at the hands of evil. And now, who can think that Count Cenci is the product of custom, convention, law, or institution? It is true that the corruption of the society of which he is a member makes possible his monstrous acts, and drives his daughter to parricide — although Shelley tells us that she might and ought to have refrained. But does the corruption of society account for *him*, for his being what he is? It is absurd to ask the question. He represents the (in a measure inscrutable) principle of evil in human nature. Prometheus asks of the Furies, "Can aught exult in its deformity?" [91] Shelley's answer, apparently, is that it can; and in giving this answer he accepts the Christian view of evil and rejects that of Godwin. It is doubtless this very fact that Clutton-Brock has in mind when he says that Shelley did not understand wickedness. And from the modern point of view, he did not; since we are now (judging from contemporary literature) all good followers of Godwin and think that moral evil is merely the result of circumstance and can be "explained" by psychology or physiology. And most of the few persons who deplore this tendency seem somehow to have persuaded themselves that Shelley was its prophet!

It is true, of course, as I have already said, that Shelley considers most social institutions to be an evil, although not the cause of evil. His position is simply that they aggravate the baser tendencies of human nature out of which they sprang; and that thus is created a vicious circle. As he held organized Christianity to be in large part the outgrowth of superstition, fear, and selfishness, so he felt that it tends to perpetuate and strengthen these very traits of human nature. Monarchical or oligarchical government, which has arisen from an unprincipled lust for power in the few and a timid servility in the many, renders the few more ruthless, the many more slavish. The thing to do, then, is to attempt to reform the structure of society, and at the same time to undertake the regeneration of human nature. What is simpler, more sensible, more admirable, more practical than this? [92] Shelley may write to Leigh Hunt, "The system of

[91] I, l. 464.
[92] On this general topic, see the section of the *Essay on Christianity* headed "Equality of Mankind," in Shawcross, pp. 106–17.

society as it exists at present must be overthrown from its foundations with all its superstructure of maxims and of forms before we
shall find anything but disappointment in our intercourse with any
but a few select spirits." [93] But one is not bound to infer from this
statement (of which the sentiment is, besides, almost unique in his
later writings) that he was a soap-box anarchist, believing that all
evil is the result of social institutions, and that the millennium will
follow straightway upon their destruction. The words will be truly
understood with reference not to the declamatory outbursts of a
poem written eight years before, but to the sad reflections expressed
in another letter of about the same time. "As it is," he writes, "all
of us who are worth anything, spend our manhood in unlearning
the follies, or expiating the mistakes, of our youth. We are stuffed
full of prejudices; and our natural passions are so managed, that
if we restrain them we grow intolerant and precise, because we
restrain them not according to reason, but according to error; and
if we do not restrain them, we do all sorts of mischief to ourselves
and to others. Our imagination and understanding are alike subjected to rules the most absurd . . ." [94] What is this but the
eternal protest of the philosopher against the stupidities of mass-
morality?

Again, Shelley may stress, all through *A Philosophical View of
Reform*, the influence of the form of government upon the condition of the population. And such a critic as Dowden may see behind
this fact the ever-present specter of Godwin. [95] But the explanation
lies rather in Shelley's immediate purpose than in his ultimate
philosophical views. Presumably nobody ever advocated reform
without thinking and saying that the proposed change would be of
some benefit. But surely it is hard if to every person who has ever
hoped to elevate and purify human society must be attributed a

[93] *Letters*, II, 777 (May 1, 1820). He continues: "This remedy does not seem
to be one of the easiest. But the generous few are not the less held to tend with all
their efforts towards it. If faith is a virtue in any case, it is so in politics rather
than religion; as having a power of producing a belief in that which is at once a
prophecy, and a cause." Here he partially abandons his former position that belief is
independent of will.

[94] *Letters*, II, 748.

[95] See *Transcripts and Studies*.

fanatical hatred of institutions in general, and a childish faith in perfectibility.[96]

IV

But if evil does not originate from customs and institutions, whence, according to Shelley, does it arise? To this question we are given no final answer, because, as will appear, Shelley considered the problem to be insoluble. But a partial answer may be found, and one which, as far as it goes, is identical with the Christian teaching: that evil exists through man's perverted will. "Man had only to will that there should be no evil, and there would be none." But if evil can be removed by an act of will, it must have come into existence by a similar act. And this is Shelley's view.

At this point, however, it is necessary to make a distinction between evil and pain in general; that is, the suffering that man brings upon himself and the suffering that is inseparable from mortal existence. Godwin, of course, extraordinarily insensible to any refinement of feeling, refuses to make any distinction. He declares, "Nothing is evil in the fullest sense but pain"; and goes on to assert that "pain is always an evil. Pleasure and pain, happiness and misery, constitute the whole ultimate subject of moral inquiry. There is nothing desirable but the obtaining of the one and the avoiding of the other." [97] Shelley's view, however, is different.[98] He holds that the pain which is imposed upon man by the external world is not truly evil; it need not affect a man's character. What is really evil is the suffering that arises *within* from the yielding to "malignant passions"; and this is not evil because it is painful, but painful because it is evil, because it degrades and brutalizes man's

---

[96] I ought to quote, however, the testimony of Horace Smith that "he was persuaded that evil, an accident, and not an inherent part of our system, might be so materially diminished as to give an incalculable increase to the sum of human happiness. All the present evils of mankind he attributed to those erroneous views of religion in which had originated the countless wars, the national hatreds, the innumerable public and private miseries that make history a revolting record of suffering and crime." See *James and Horace Smith*, p. 173. This is part of the summary of an oral statement made by Shelley in 1817. It is to be noted that the important phrase "those erroneous views of religion" is ambiguous. It may mean "erroneous views" *dictated by existent* religions; or it may mean "erroneous views" *as to what constitutes* true religion.

[97] *Political Justice*, I, 201.   [98] Cf. H. Richter, *Englische Studien*, XXX, 389–98.

nature and enslaves or casts out the Divine Spirit of purity and
goodness which is the birthright of the human soul. Such is the
thought underlying the description in *The Revolt of Islam* of the
triumph upon earth of the Spirit of Evil.

> "The Fiend, whose name was Legion; Death, Decay,
>   Earthquake and Blight, and Want, and Madness pale,
> Wingèd and wan diseases, an array
>   Numerous as leaves that strew the autumnal gale;
>   Poison, a snake in flowers, beneath the veil
> Of food and mirth hiding his mortal head;
>   And, *without whom all these might nought avail,*
> Fear, Hatred, Faith, and Tyranny, who spread
> Those subtle nets which snare the living and the dead." [99]

Again, in *Prometheus Unbound,* the elements of evil named by
Asia are significant: "terror, madness, crime, remorse . . . Abandoned hope, and love that turns to hate; And self-contempt . . .
Pain . . ." [1] Pain is chiefly an evil, it would seem, when it is
accompanied by (that is, when it is the effect or the cause of) the
corruption of man's inner nature. In this sense Shelley speaks of
regenerate man as

> free from guilt or pain,
> Which were, for his will made or suffered them . . . [2]

Yet he is not free from physical, or even from some kinds of emotional suffering; he is not

> exempt, though ruling them like slaves,
> From chance, and death, and mutability . . . [3]

And "labour and pain and grief" will still be present; but, in a
world ruled by love, they will have no power upon the soul, and
therefore will not be evil. [4]

[99] I, xxix. Italics mine. The only synonym for "Faith," as used by Shelley, seems
to be Mr. Chesterton's name for Calvinism, i.e., "devil-worship." It is not even
equivalent to "superstition," for the latter may be "an innocent dream" (*Revolt of
Islam,* VIII, vi) or even admirable, for in the Preface to *Alastor,* the author pities
those who are capable of being "duped by no illustrious superstition." "Tyranny"
is more strictly the "desire to tyrannize." The words "nought avail" are vague. It
is uncertain whether the poet means that the relative evils of the first part of the
stanza would be actually extinguished by the complete conquest of moral evil
(Godwin looked forward to an indefinite extension of the term of human life), or
whether, as is more likely, they would simply cease to matter.
[1] II, iv, ll. 19–26. [2] III, iv, ll. 198–99. [3] III, iv, ll. 200–01. [4] IV, ll. 404–05.

The cardinal sin in Shelley's code is hatred. It is indeed the whole of evil:

> " 'that shapeless fiendly thing
> Of many names, all evil, some divine,
> Whom self-contempt arms with a mortal sting . . .' " [5]

It is evil because it degrades the soul that indulges it, and because it creates an answering hatred in those against whom it is directed. It was Shelley's quarrel with certain aspects of government and of religion that the former give rise to hate, and the latter sanction it; and that both combine to force upon men the worst kind of slavery. So he writes in describing the ideal community:

> None fawned, none trampled; hate, disdain, or fear,
> Self-love or self-contempt, on human brows
> No more inscribed, as o'er the gate of hell,
> "All hope abandon ye who enter here";
> None frowned, none trembled, none with eager fear
> Gazed on another's eye of cold command,
> Until the subject of a tyrant's will
> Became, worse fate, the abject of his own,
> Which spurred him, like an outspent horse, to death.[6]

Poverty and servitude are evils, just as are wealth and power, because they degrade the characters, and lower the aims and motives, of those who endure or possess them, and make men selfish, sensual, and brutal.

The lines quoted above have a Godwinian ring; and indeed, the root of the idea they express is to be found in *Political Justice*.[7] But Godwin's teaching, after all, aims principally at bringing about a comfortable earthly existence; he is through and through a Utili-

---

[5] *Revolt of Islam*, VIII, xxi.

[6] *Prometheus Unbound*, III, iv, ll. 133–41.

[7] I do not wish to give the impression that everything in Godwin's philosophy is false or absurd. The Victorian depreciation of his work is as unreasonable as the enthusiasm of his contemporaries. With all his extravagance and inconsistency, he does some sound thinking, and enunciates some admirable moral principles. He says, for example, concerning the topic just discussed: "To be free is a circumstance of little value, if we could suppose men in a state of external freedom, without the magnanimity, energy and firmness, that constitute almost all that is valuable in a state of freedom. On the other hand, if a man have these qualities, there is little left for him to desire." *Political Justice*, I, 258–59. The sentiment is admirable, but the general tenor of Godwin's life and writings make one feel that for him it is only a theory; for Shelley it was a practical creed.

tarian. Shelley's morality, on the other hand, is absolute, like that of Socrates, Plato, and Christ: the outward life is nothing, the inward life is all. The logical outcome of his position, whether he would have been willing to admit it or not — and I think he would, if it had not been presented to him as a "Christian" dogma — is that stated by Newman in his *Apologia:* "The Catholic Church holds it better for the sun and moon to drop from heaven, for the earth to fail, and for all the many millions on it to die of starvation in extremest agony, as far as temporal affliction goes, than that one soul, I will not say should be lost, but should commit one single venial sin, should tell one wilful untruth, or should steal one poor farthing without excuse."[8] The only possible evil is that which the soul inflicts upon itself; and this evil is absolute.

To those who are accustomed to think of Shelley as a sentimental humanitarian, the view here presented will seem startling and paradoxical; yet its presence in his poetry is perfectly evident; it is, in fact, the real theme of *Prometheus Unbound*. It is Prometheus' hate of Jupiter that subjects him to the Tyrant's tortures; defiance is still a kind of submission. When he gains complete self-realization, when he knows that no external force has power over his soul, when hatred of his oppressor turns to pity, then he is free. Physical pain is nothing to him, evil passions cannot move him, the dreadful vision of evil coming from good is not evil to him. Those who make him suffer are evil; but his suffering is not evil. It is no matter whether or not Hercules sets the Titan free — he is free already. It is of no consequence whether or not Jupiter is dethroned by Demogorgon — he has already fallen. Prometheus need not retire with Asia to their mystic cave — they are already one. Nothing in heaven or on earth has power upon the human soul, except the soul itself. The just man of Plato has created his own absolute world; mortal suffering means nothing to him. The martyr Saviour says, "Not as I would, but as thou wilt"; and his kingdom then is truly not of the world. The world may scourge and crucify him, but what of that? "They know not what they do"; they do evil only to themselves; how can they injure him?

How literally Shelley was ready to apply this principle may be

[8] *Kingsley vs. Newman: The Full Text* (Oxford, 1913), p. 339.

seen in his Preface to *The Cenci*. Here is a beautiful, sensitive, brave, unselfish, pure-minded girl, subjected by the fiendish hate of her father to an unspeakable outrage. In return, not out of any mean spirit of revenge but as an act of justice, and thinking more of her mother and younger brother than of herself, she plans and has carried out the murder of her father. Yet Shelley condemns her action. "Undoubtedly, no person can be truly dishonoured by the act of another; and the fit return to make to the most enormous injuries is kindness and forbearance, and a resolution to convert the injurer from his dark passions by peace and love. Revenge, retaliation, atonement, are pernicious mistakes. If Beatrice had thought in this manner, she would have been wiser and better . . ."

This is so extraordinary a statement that critics have refused to take it at its face value; they urge that Shelley is completely in sympathy with his heroine; and most of them, if they believed the poet, would doubtless condemn him as unfeeling and inhuman.[9] Yet there can be no doubt of Shelley's complete sincerity. He wrote to Leigh Hunt that the play was "written with a certain view to popularity, a view to which I sacrificed my own peculiar notions in a certain sort by treating of any subject, the basis of which is moral error";[10] and of course the "moral error" is the act of Beatrice, not that of her father. His previous poems had been full of tyrants like Count Cenci; but his heroes and heroines had always been perfect. Moreover, the action of the play clearly points the moral: it is only a few minutes after the murder that the papal legate arrives with a warrant for Cenci's arrest. Had Beatrice waited she would have been free — and innocent. Instead, her action forms another link in the chain of evil that binds humanity.

> Revenge and Wrong bring forth their kind,
>   The foul cubs like their parents are,
> Their den is in the guilty mind,
>   And Conscience feeds them with despair.[11]

Beatrice, it is true, thinks herself justified; but that is because her suffering has warped her moral sense, as she ought not to have let

<hr />

[9] Cf. E. S. Bates, *A Study of Shelley's Drama The Cenci* (New York, 1908), pp. 71 ff.; Kurtz, *op. cit.*, pp. 190 ff.; and others.
[10] *Letters*, II, 777.   [11] *Hellas*, ll. 729-32.

it. And doubtless her despondency at the end of the play is to be connected with this fact. It is in striking contrast to the endings of Shelley's other poems, in which the protagonists endure to the end, and are saved.[12] And this is the true meaning of the statement that Shelley believed that "man had only to will that there should be no evil, and there would be none." Necessity's "sightless strength forever" binds evil to evil; but the human soul has the power to break this endless chain — if it can truly realize itself, if it can learn that nothing external need have power upon it, and if it can repay good for evil and love for hate. This is hardly a new creed; but it is surely no ignoble one.

Nor is it necessarily optimistic. To say that evil exists through man's perverted will, is not this, in a sense, the most pessimistic view that it is possible to take? Is it not, indeed, the only view that admits moral evil to have any reality? If evil exists by the will of God or the course of nature, then it ceases to be evil. Shelley's severest critics, in fact, are those with naturalistic leanings.[13] Another quotation from Leslie Stephen will just bring out the point. He remarks with reference to *Prometheus Unbound*, "But it would seem . . . that the fitting catastrophe to the world's drama must be in some sense a reconciliation between Prometheus and Jupiter; or, in other words, between reason and the blind forces by which it is opposed. The ultimate good must be not the annihilation of all the conditions of life but the slow conquest of nature by the adaptation of life to its conditions. We learn to rule nature, as it is generally expressed, by learning to obey it." [14] Now, if it were at all true that Shelley considered the conflict in life to be between "reason" and "the blind forces by which it is opposed," the criticism would be to some extent just. But that is Sir Leslie's view and not Shelley's. It is the distinguished critic who is really the optimist and who does not believe in evil. Like many thinkers since the time of Darwin, he assumes that what man has to do is not to change his own nature, to conquer his own perverse will, but only to change his environ-

---

[12] The idea that Beatrice's doubts are Shelley's own (cf. A. A. Jack, *Shelley: An Essay*, London, 1904, p. 124) seems to me untenable.

[13] Or at least *ought* to be. Certain of the Humanists, of course, call Shelley a naturalist; but that can only be because they do not understand him.

[14] *Op. cit.*, p. 382.

ment, the world outside him — or, where that is impossible, adapt himself to it; and in the course of time his existence will probably become easier and more comfortable — not morally better.[15] But which is the harder task, for man to adapt himself to his natural environment or for him to change his own inner nature? No respectable philosopher before the rise of positive science ever gave but one answer. "He that ruleth himself is greater than he that taketh a city." Stoic, Epicurean, Platonist, and Christian, on this point all are agreed: man's most difficult and most pressing task is to triumph over himself.[16] And this view is likewise Shelley's.

It will be enlightening, also, to contrast Shelley with Malthus. The reason for the poet's dislike of the author of *An Essay on Population* is to be found in the very issue now under discussion. Malthus feels as deeply as Shelley the sufferings of the poor; but he insists that all material attempts at alleviation will only increase their suffering. And this certainly looks like pessimism. But what is the author's final view? That "there is no more evil in the world than is absolutely necessary." [17] For the purpose of the universe, he believes, is the development of mind or intelligence; and the only force capable of effecting this end is suffering. He believes literally that this is the best of all possible worlds. But it is also best that man should not believe so, for then he would have no incentive to try to improve himself, and all distinction between virtue and vice would be destroyed.[18] Now, is this pessimism or is it optimism? At any rate, it is fatalism; and as such, is apparently the inescapable logical consequence of belief in an omnipotent and benevolent God.

[15] Yet this critic has the effrontery to remark, regarding Shelley's protest against the evil in the world: "It is not the passionate war-cry of a combatant in a deadly grapple with the forces of evil, but the wail of a dreamer who has never troubled himself to translate the phrases into the language of fact." *Op. cit.*, p. 402. It is perhaps permissible to suggest that Shelley had much more real experience in grappling with evil than most of his critics have had.

[16] The naturalists, of course, will not admit that the distinction is valid; in their view, man is merely a part of nature. When some thinker obviously begins with other assumptions, however, these persons ought to criticize his premises and not his conclusions.

[17] *Essay on Population* (reprint of 1st ed., London, 1926), p. 391. The later editions lack the statement of the metaphysical and theological inferences.

[18] See the final chapter of the earlier *Essay*. This criticism of optimism is exactly repeated in the third edition of *Political Justice*, at the end of Volume I.

And this view Shelley was never willing to accept. It is all very well to say that, human nature being what it is, suffering is necessary to whatever measure of happiness and virtue is possible of attainment by man. But is not God also responsible for human nature? Malthus would have to say "Yes"; Shelley says, "No — neither God nor Nature is responsible, but — as far as we can see — man himself. Therefore, human nature *can* be changed, and suffering avoided." But he never said that this would be an easy task; and he saw at last that it could never be completely accomplished on this side of eternity.

v

It has been said, however, that Shelley did not believe in free will; that, following always the theories of Godwin, he held, to the end of his life, a necessarian, or deterministic, philosophy. Arguing at length for a view that has always been more or less prevalent, a recent critic asserts: "Godwin said that 'man is really a passive and not an active being,' and devoted one long chapter in *Political Justice* to prove that the mind is merely a mechanism and that even in volition it is altogether passive. *Shelley accepted without qualification the doctrine of his master.*" [19] "Shelley had no conception of the will as operative in making one's life 'daily self-surpassed' and thereby achieving character by slow growth; nor did he possess any adequate philosophic theory of Free-will." [20] Such statements as these seem to me so completely and obviously mistaken that I find it hard to take them seriously. Yet the view which they express is apparently a common one,[21] and it is perhaps worth while finally to dispose of it.[22]

It is true that Godwin is a Necessarian, and one so consistent in holding to the doctrine that he lets it carry him into the absurdest

[19] S. F. Gingerich, *Essays in the Romantic Poets*, p. 203. Italics mine.
[20] *Ibid.*, p. 230. One might infer that some one *does* possess an "adequate" theory or ever has possessed one! Mr. Gingerich refers to three passages in which Shelley speaks as if he believed in free will, but says "the exceptions here simply prove the rule" (p. 231n.). And the more exceptions, I suppose, the more secure the proof — in which case I shall add considerable proof to Mr. Gingerich's assertions.
[21] Cf. More, Clutton-Brock, Bagehot, Stephen, *et al.*
[22] Helene Richter, *Englische Studien*, XXX, pp. 258–65, has argued well, but briefly, for Shelley's belief in free will.

inconsistencies. He declares, "In the life of every human being there is a chain of events, generated in the lapse of ages which preceded his birth, and going on in regular procession through the whole period of his existence, in consequence of which it is impossible for him to act in any instance otherwise than he has acted." [23] Hence, "in a strict sense, there is no such thing as action. Man is in no case, strictly speaking, the beginner of any event or series of events that takes place in the universe, but only the vehicle through which certain antecedents operate." [24] And this is the man who hoped by his writings to bring about profound changes in society! The very name of his great work contradicts the theory it contains: for according to the doctrine of Necessity, *justice* is a word without a meaning. It is amazing that Godwin could not see the "abyss of nonsense" into which such a theory was bound to lead him. With a consistency almost sublimely ridiculous, he goes on to say that the Necessarian, in communicating ideas or spreading virtue, "would not exhort, for this is a term without a meaning. He would suggest motives to the mind, but he would not call upon it to comply, as if it had a power to comply or not to comply. His office would consist of two parts, the exhibition of motives to the pursuit of a certain end, and the delineation of the easiest and most effectual way of attaining that end." [25] As if his doctrine did not also deprive of meaning the words *suggest, pursuit, end, easiest, effectual,* and *attaining!*

This irresponsible intellectualism finds, in one section of *Queen Mab,* as uncompromising expression as in the work of Godwin. I quote some fragments of a long passage.

> "So that when waves on waves tumultuous heap
>   Confusion to the clouds, and fiercely driven
>   Heaven's lightnings scorch the uprooted ocean-fords,
>   Whilst, to the eye of shipwrecked mariner . . .
>   All seems unlinked contingency and chance;
>   No atom of this turbulence fulfils
>   A vague and unnecessitated task,
>   Or acts but as it must and ought to act.

[23] *Political Justice,* I, 384 (Book IV, Chapter 7).   [24] *Ibid.,* p. 385.
[25] *Ibid.,* p. 390. There must be something radically wrong with a person who talks like this!

> . . . not a thought, a will, an act,
> No working of the tyrant's moody mind,
> Nor one misgiving of the slaves who boast
> Their servitude, to hide the shame they feel,
> Nor the events enchaining every will,
> That from the depths of unrecorded time
> Have drawn all-influencing virtue, pass
> Unrecognized, or unforeseen by thee,
> Soul of the Universe!" [26]

That there may be no mistaking his position, Shelley adds a long
note, in the course of which he says, "Every human being is irresistibly impelled to act precisely as he does act: in the eternity
which preceded his birth a chain of causes was generated, which,
operating under the name of motives, make it impossible that any
thought of his mind, or any action of his life, should be otherwise
than it is." And he goes on to draw the conclusion "that there is
neither good nor evil in the universe, otherwise than as the events
to which we apply these epithets have relation to our own peculiar
mode of being."

These passages seem to prove that Shelley was, beyond all question, a Necessarian. As a matter of fact, they prove nothing except
that *Queen Mab* is sometimes in complete opposition to the poet's
mature and characteristic views. Even in this poem, however, he
not only assumes (even Godwin does that), but states explicitly,
that man is his own master.

> "Nature, impartial in munificence,
>   Has gifted man with all-subduing will.
>   Matter, with all its transitory shapes,
>   Lies subjected and plastic at his feet . . ." [27]

A few lines farther on he speaks of the ideal man as possessing
"elevated will"; [28] and toward the end of the same canto he declares that a man can purchase life's dearest possession, "the consciousness of good," only by "unalterable will." [29] Finally, near the
end of the poem, we find that the doctrine of Necessity and the
relativity of good and evil have been completely forgotten:

> ". . . but bravely bearing on, thy will
>   Is destined an eternal war to wage

[26] VI, ll. 165–73, 182–90.   [27] V, ll. 132–35.
[28] L. 155. The expression is repeated, IX, l. 73.   [29] L. 226.

With tyranny and falsehood, and uproot
The germs of misery from the human heart." [30]

Here, I will venture to suggest, we have "the real Shelley" throwing off the swaddling clothes of Godwinian theory.

In *The Revolt of Islam* Shelley speaks still more like himself. Cythna declares that by her words all persons shall be won to share her feelings and purposes:

"Hearts beat as mine now beats, with such intent
As renovates the world; a will omnipotent!" [31]

Later she declares:

"For to my will my fancies were as slaves
To do their sweet and subtile ministries . . ." [32]

And finally, speaking of the corrupt condition of society, she exclaims:

" 'This need not be; ye might arise, and will
That gold should lose its power, and thrones their glory;
That love, which none may bind, be free to fill
The world, like light . . .
Dungeons and palaces are transitory —
High temples fade like vapour — Man alone
Remains, whose will has power when all beside is gone.' " [33]

How unnecessary it is to read Necessarianism into *Prometheus Unbound*, the previous discussions ought to have shown. Prometheus' will is the force that dominates the whole play, that motivates the action, that gives the story moral significance. How can the great closing stanza be possibly reconciled with any theory of Necessity? The Titan himself declares that only his "all-enduring

---

[30] IX, ll. 189–92. I think that "destined" is merely a poetical way of speaking. If anyone wishes to read into it the doctrine of Necessity, however, he may; my position requires the support of no questionable passages. The expression "eternal war" is worth noting; but of course, my opponents may call that a mere poetical expression. A similar inconsistency occurs in Shelley's early letters. On November 20, 1811, he exhorts Miss Hitchener: "Be yourself a living proof that human nature is a creation of its own, resolves its own determinations . . . " See *Letters*, I, 166. Six days later he writes to her: "Man is the creature of circumstances . . ." *Ibid.*, p. 176. In between — on November 24 — after advancing the theory that Nature is "but an organized mass of animation," he urges: "Free-will must give energy to this infinite mass of being, and thereby constitute Virtue." *Ibid.*, p. 174. Comment seems superfluous.
[31] II, xli.   [32] VII, xxxiv.
[33] VIII, xvi.

will" [34] has saved man from destruction; and his curse upon Jupiter contains the words

> O'er all things but thyself I gave thee power,
> And my own will.[35]

The human soul has allowed evil to gain power in the world; but it *cannot* give away its own freedom.[36] It can, however, fail to use that freedom; and then man becomes, in fact, a slave. So Shelley defines *slavery* in *The Mask of Anarchy:*

> " 'Tis to be a slave in soul
> And to hold no strong control
> Over your own wills, but be
> All that others make of ye." [37]

And the same thought finds a grander expression in the *Ode to Liberty:*

> He who taught man to vanquish whatsoever
> Can be between the cradle and the grave
> Crowned him the King of Life. Oh, vain endeavour!
> If on his own high will, a willing slave,
> He has enthroned the oppression and the oppressor.[38]

On the other hand, all that is great and good rests upon the human will. So the poet says that the splendor and the glory of Athens were "on the will Of man, as on a mount of diamond, set"; [39] and repeats the thought in *A Defence of Poetry:* "never was blind strength and stubborn form so disciplined and rendered subject to the will of man, or that will less repugnant to the dictates of the beautiful and the true, as during the century which preceded the death of Socrates." [40]

[34] I, l. 114.   [35] I, ll. 273–74.

[36] There is one passage which might be wrenched into support of the doctrine of Necessity. Prometheus says (I, ll. 815–16) "I would fain Be what it is my destiny to be." But this means, I take it, only that he is determined to be what he *may* be (or may fail to be): "the saviour and the strength of suffering man."

[37] Stanza xlvi.

[38] Ll. 241–45. On the whole, I am inclined to regard this as the most exceptional of the exceptions which "prove the rule" of Shelley's Necessarianism. The "He" of the first line of the quotation looks like an allusion to some particular person, although I have found no editorial comment on it. A year or two later (this was written early in 1820) the reference would almost certainly have been to Christ. Here it is perhaps to Prometheus, who "taught" men, first, by his gift of knowledge and the arts, and, second, by his example.

[39] *Ode to Liberty*, ll. 70–71.   [40] Shawcross, p. 132.

These illustrations should be convincing; but Shelley's most explicit statements have not yet been touched upon. These are to be found in *Julian and Maddalo*, written in 1818. In the Preface the poet describes himself "as passionately attached to those philosophical notions which assert the power of man over his own mind." [41] In the poem itself he argues against Byron's cynicism and despair:

> "if man be
> The passive thing you say, I should not see
> Much harm in the religions and old saws
> (Tho' I may never own such leaden laws)
> Which break a teachless nature to the yoke:
> Mine is another faith . . ."[42]
>
> . . . .
>   "it is our will
> That thus enchains us to permitted ill—
> We might be otherwise — we might be all
> We dream of happy, high, majestical.
> Where is the love, beauty, and truth we seek
> But in our mind?[43] and if we were not weak
> Should we be less in deed than in desire?"[44]

To Byron's scornful objections, he replies,

>   "We are assured
> Much may be conquered, much may be endured,
> Of what degrades and crushes us. We know
> That we have power over ourselves to do
> And suffer — what, we know not till we try;
> But something nobler than to live and die —"[45]

Byron urges an instance of madness as offering a practical contradiction; but his companion persists

> "that a want of that true theory, still,
> Which seeks a 'soul of goodness' in things ill
> Or in himself or others, has thus bowed
> His being . . .

[41] This is another bit of evidence that Shelley did not consider mind to be the ultimate reality.

[42] Shelley here lays his finger exactly upon the chief paradox in Godwin's teaching—asserting an unqualified determinism while advocating changes in society.

[43] I do not think that this is necessarily incompatible with the belief, presented in the preceding chapter, in a universal Spirit of Good.

[44] Ll. 160–76.

[45] Ll. 182–87.

                                     . . . this is not destiny
          But man's own wilful ill." [46]

Very similar in spirit to these passages from *Julian and Maddalo*
is a statement in *A Philosophical View of Reform*, written two
years later. The first sentence has already been quoted.

Equality in possessions must be the last result of the utmost refinements
of civilization; it is one of the conditions of that system of society towards
which, with whatever hope of ultimate success, it is our duty to strive.
We may and ought to advert to it as to the elementary principle, as to
the goal, unattainable, perhaps, by us but which, as it were, we revive in
our posterity to pursue. We derive tranquillity and courage and grandeur
of soul from contemplating an object which is, because we will it, and
may be, because we hope and desire it, and must be if succeeding generations of the enlightened sincerely and earnestly seek it.[47]

Here again I might rest my case as proved. But there is still
another argument that must not be overlooked. Shelley is one of
the great English poets of liberty; it will be felt by many readers
that his passion for freedom is deeper and wider than that of Byron
or Swinburne. He champions it in prose as well as in poetry, in
act as well as in thought. This cannot be dismissed as an incon-

[46] Ll. 203–11. On the other hand, I must quote two passages in which Shelley
declares that a person's way of life is the result of circumstance. There are numerous
others in his early letters, written when he was under the influence of Godwin;
but those that follow belong to his last years. In a letter to Leigh Hunt concerning
the shortcomings of his publisher, Ollier, he writes: "It is less the character of the
individual than the situation in which he is placed which determines him to be
honest or dishonest, perhaps we ought to regard an honest bookseller, or an honest
seller of anything else in the present state of affairs as a kind of Jesus Christ." See
Letters, II, 777. There follows the passage already noted as exceptional in the later
writings, in which it is declared that the present system of society "must be overthrown from the foundations."—Again, in a note to *Hellas*, speaking of a former
servant of Byron's who had become a leader of the Greek revolutionists, he says: "It
appears that circumstances make men what they are, and that we all contain the
germ of a degree of degradation or of greatness whose connection with our character is determined by events." These statements undoubtedly contradict the absolute freedom of the will asserted in *Julian and Maddalo*. But if everyone who has
ever expressed a similar sentiment were to be classed among the upholders of the
doctrine of Necessity, a very numerous and varied company would be the result.
Moreover, it is a commonplace of Platonic philosophy, although not consistent with
some other elements in that philosophy.

[47] Pp. 70–71. The clause "which is, because we will it" is rather curious, since
the object must have an *ideal* existence *before* it can be willed, and it does not gain
an *actual* existence until long after. Perhaps Shelley means that the act of will is
already a step toward the realization of what is willed. At any rate, the practical
freedom of the will could hardly be more strongly asserted.

sistency or as "the exception which proves the rule" of his Necessarianism. It shows, on the contrary, that his seeming acceptance
of Necessarianism was a trifling and transient divergence from the
real principles of his thought and character. In one of his last essays
he declares that freedom is "the most sacred prerogative of man." [48]
The very universe could not come into being until God "unfurled
The flag of Freedom over Chaos." [49] Even Love itself could not
exist without freedom, as Shelley declares in this exquisite lyric,
one of numberless passages that prove his devotion to liberty:

> Life may change, but it may fly not;
> Hope may vanish, but can die not;
> Truth be veiled, but still it burneth;
> Love repulsed, — but it returneth!
> Yet were life a charnel where
> Hope lay coffined with Despair;
> Yet were truth a sacred lie,
> Love were lust — if Liberty
> Lent not life its soul of light,
> Hope its iris of delight,
> Truth its prophet's robe to wear,
> Love its power to give and bear.[50]

This one lyric alone would effectually contradict every pedantic
argument that Shelley was a Necessarian.[51]

There is, however, another side to the question. The confusion
in regard to Shelley's view of free will is not quite so inexcusable
as I have so far made it out to be. The real difficulty here lies in
the nature of the idea of freedom. Concerning this question, man's
conscience is ever in hopeless conflict with his reason. The moralist
cannot deny the freedom of the will; the rationalist cannot admit
it. No man can *live* according to a fatalistic philosophy; but none
can *think* according to any other. Logically, there is no middle
ground between absolute necessity and absolute freedom; but abso-

[48] *A Philosophical View of Reform*, p. 68. The context is a bitter attack on
militarism, and its effect on character. "From the moment that a man is a soldier, he
becomes a slave. He is taught obedience; his will is no longer, which is the most
sacred prerogative of man, guided by his own judgment."
[49] *Hellas*, ll. 47–48. Cf. also the *Ode to Liberty*, stanzas ii and iii, and the comment on them in Chapter VII, Section I, of the present study.
[50] *Hellas*, ll. 34–45.
[51] Godwin, of course, also pleads for liberty; but in him the plea is *really* inconsistent. In Shelley it is not.

lute freedom is identical with chance; and chance is the worst kind (if there *is* a worst kind) of fatalism. It is this notion, as much as the inability of reason to get away from cause and effect, that is behind the Necessarianism of *Queen Mab*. In the note already quoted [52] Shelley puts his finger on the difficulty. "Were the doctrine of Necessity false . . . we could not predict with any certainty that we might not meet as an enemy to-morrow him with whom we have parted in friendship to-night; the most probable inducements and the clearest reasonings would lose the invariable influence they possess. The contrary of this is demonstrably the fact." In other words, the very notion of character, or even of identity, involves that of continuity. Shelley says elsewhere, "The savage and the illiterate are but faintly aware of the distinction between the future and the past . . . they live only in the present, or in the past, as it is present. It is in this that the philosopher excels one of the many; it is this which distinguishes the doctrine of philosophic necessity from fatalism; and that determination of the will, by which it is the active source of future events, from that liberty or indifference, to which the abstract liability of irremediable actions is attached, according to the notions of the vulgar." [53]

"That liberty or indifference" — for liberty *is* indifference. If the will is absolutely free, the world of man is reduced to a chaos ruled by chance; a man of the most scrupulous honesty might at any time, without difficulty, without effort, without cause, become a thief; the most gentle and charitable person might, for no reason whatever, become the murderer of his dearest friend; and no one would be at all surprised. Such a supposition is an outrage upon human nature and common sense; yet it must be accepted by the advocate of the doctrine of free will. Once admit that a person's future life is in the slightest measure dependent on his past, or that his actions are in any degree the result of his character, or even that he *has* a character, and the implication of necessity is inevitable. [54]

Is it not evident, then, that Bradley's dictum concerning free will is entirely correct? "Considered either theoretically or practically,

---

[52] On VI, l. 198.   [53] Note to *On the Punishment of Death*, in Shawcross, p. 51.

[54] Godwin had argued also that "the idea correspondent to the term *character*, inevitably includes in it the assumption of necessity and system" (I, 370). For a very clear treatment of this subject — of which the very simplicity makes it at first difficult to grasp — see F. H. Bradley, *Ethical Studies*, Chapter I.

'Free Will' is, in short, a mere lingering chimera. Certainly no writer who respects himself, can be called on any longer to treat it seriously."[55] So Shelley assumes (logically contradicting the former assumption of freedom) the existence in the moral realm of a principle of continuity, by which that realm is redeemed from chaos. "Men must reap the things they sow" [56] — this is a constant element in Shelley's moral creed. It is this principle, which is the foundation of all morality, but is itself unmoral, that the poet doubtless means by "Necessity" in *The Revolt of Islam,* which forever binds evil with evil, and good with good. The same conception seems to explain, at least partially, the significance of Demogorgon in *Prometheus Unbound.* And it is also to be identified with the Destiny which one feels to be omnipresent in *Hellas,* and which decrees that the triumph of tyranny and darkness can never extinguish, even in the world of Time, the light of beauty and wisdom that Greece once kindled. And if this conception changes a little — as I feel that it does in Shelley's very last poems — it clearly passes over, not into blind fatalism or scientific determinism, but into the Christian conception of Providence — as when Christ pleads before the Almighty in the Prologue to *Hellas.*

> By Greece and all she cannot cease to be,
> Her quenchless words, sparks of immortal truth,
> Stars of all night — her harmonies and forms,
> Echoes and shadows of what Love adores
> In thee, I do compel thee, send forth Fate,
> Thy irrevocable child: let her descend,
> A seraph-wingèd Victory [arrayed]
> In tempest of the omnipotence of God
> Which sweeps through all things.[57]

Surely it is strange that the author of these lines should be condemned as a Necessarian.

[55] *Appearance and Reality* (2d ed., Oxford, 1930), p. 385 n. Bradley is not, of course, a determinist: he simply means that the whole problem is beyond the power of the mind to deal with. The same theme is developed at length in a very fine study by Charles Campbell, *Scepticism and Construction* (New York, 1931). The author argues that free will is incompatible with any conception of the universe as entirely rational. But, he says, free will is a *fact;* from our own experience we have more right to believe in freedom than in the reason's denial of freedom. Therefore, the world is essentially irrational — or rather supra-rational.

[56] *Lines Written among the Euganean Hills,* l. 231.

[57] Ll. 96–104. Does not this sound like *Political Justice?*

VI

There is, however, another basis for the criticism that Shelley had no adequate conception of will; namely, the apparent absence in him of the sense of Sin, according to the peculiarly Christian conception. It is said that his life and writings are quite devoid of evidence that he ever experienced in himself, or was capable of comprehending in others, that inward conflict between good and evil motives, between the higher and the lower natures, which is described with such painful intensity by Paul. "For I delight in the law of God after the inward man: But I see another law in my members, warring against the law of my mind, and bringing me into captivity to the law of sin which is in my members. O wretched man that I am! who shall deliver me from the body of this death?" [58] And this struggle comes into existence, according to Paul's own account, from a sense of duty to a stern Lawgiver, and the fear of being visited by God's anger. Now, it may be speciously argued that Shelley's love of liberty, upon which I have just been dwelling, is precisely the result of his refusal to recognize this inward conflict; that the freedom he really desired was merely *freedom from responsibility*, which he found in his theory of Necessarianism; that he had no desire for, even no conception of, the freedom that comes from a slow and arduous conquest over evil; and that therefore, from the ethical standpoint, his conception of will is still inadequate.[59] This belief, although not often clearly formulated, underlies a vast amount of adverse criticism of Shelley and his work.

For this, as for many mistaken views, there is a certain amount of justification. In a life beset with much trouble and suffering,[60]

---

[58] Romans 7: 22–24.

[59] Cf. Bagehot, *Estimations in Criticism*, I, 115: Shelley "could not imagine the struggling kind of character — either those which struggle with their own nature and conquer, or those which struggle and are vanquished . . ."; R. H. Hutton, *Literary Essays*, pp. 160–61: Shelley did not use the expression "awful Loveliness" "to refer to that bending of the humiliated spirit before a holy Power from which it craves much, from whom it can compel nothing, that expresses to most of us the essence of awe"; V. D. Scudder, *Prometheus Unbound*, p. xxxix: "The interpretation of evil is hopelessly superficial; not only does it ignore the scientific aspect of evil as imperfect development, but also the far deeper and truer aspect of evil as Sin . . . it is no wonder that man, as Shelley depicts him, is a creature of no personality, scarcely higher, except for his aesthetic instincts, than an amiable brute." The same idea animates many of the "Humanist" attacks on Shelley.

[60] It is usual to speak loosely of the sufferings which Shelley caused himself *and others*. As a matter of fact, the only person who really suffered because of him

there is hardly any evidence that Shelley felt any inner discord, any doubt as to what he ought to do, any difficulty in doing what he believed to be right, any remorse at anything he had ever done. The struggle seems almost always to have been against the outer world, his will against that of society. It apparently never occurred to him that there was even a remote possibility that he might be wrong in refusing to be reconciled to his father through the abandonment of his principles, in separating from Harriet when he was convinced that they had nothing in common,[61] in offering friendship and addressing verses to women other than his wife. The simple statement that he was *not* wrong in so doing (which I believe to be perfectly true)[62] still leaves something of a mystery; for it seems usually the case that those persons whose minds are purest and whose actions are most unselfish are the most critical of their own conduct, the most sensible of their own faults and weaknesses, the least confident of the rightness of their own judgments.[63]

was his first wife, and if any real blame can justly be attached to either him or her (which I doubt), no fair-minded person can deny that her share is as great as his. No doubt Timothy Shelley is to be pitied — because his son did not grow up to be a fool, a hyprocrite, and a political parasite! Who can help pitying Godwin with his lacerated feelings — at being obliged secretly to beg money from a man whom he had publicly condemned for practising what he himself had advocated a few years before? What middle-aged moralist can withhold from Mary a sad compassion (not unmixed with stern censure of her erring spouse) in recalling (the words are Mary's own) "Shelley's Italian Platonics"? How great the offence must have been to call forth from such an angelic nature so spiteful a phrase! How hard for her to be married to a man who would perversely see only pettiness, banality, and smug mediocrity in that fashionable society where she aspired to shine! It is rather hard to make out a respectable list of those who suffered from Shelley's alleged moral irresponsibility.

[61] There is one question that few people seem to have asked themselves. Why should Harriet have wanted to keep a husband who did not love her, whose enthusiasms she laughed at, whose ideals she did not share, whose judgment she had disregarded for that of her sister, whose pleas for sympathy she had refused, from whose company she had deliberately withdrawn for weeks at a time? She threw away his affection and respect — and then wanted to keep him!

[62] Mary Shelley's note (on *Alastor*) is again characteristic of her attempt to placate the world: "In all he did, he at the time of doing it believed himself justified to his own conscience." As far as I can see, he *was* justified; and if his wife had worshipped him as after his death she pretended, she would never have tacitly accepted (as in the above statement she does) the contemptible and unjust verdict passed by the scribes and Pharisees of the world of letters upon one the latchet of whose shoes they were not worthy to stoop down and unloose.

[63] Such generalizations as this are, of course, always dangerous. It may be questioned, also, whether such a connection is necessary — whether it is not often the result of a somewhat morbid temperament.

But Shelley is apparently an exception, as not only his life but his poetry seems to show. With the great exception of Prometheus, and possibly Rousseau in *The Triumph of Life,* there is no character in any of his poems who is ever aware of any conflict within his own nature. Even Beatrice, whom Shelley glorifies while insisting that she acted wrongly, undergoes no struggle, feels no doubts, suffers no remorse.[64]

This apparent difficulty in imagining "a will or conscience at odds with itself" is, as Oliver Elton has justly remarked, "an artistic disability." [65] How far it indicates a lack of ethical insight is a question the individual reader must answer for himself. That it entirely destroys Shelley's claim to be called a religious poet I can by no means admit.

What made it impossible for Shelley to accept the idea of Sin was that it seemed to him to be based upon fear. If fear of some external power is a necessary part of religion, then Shelley was certainly not religious. Fear of any kind — at least with reference to anything outside himself — seems to have been to an extraordinary degree foreign to his nature. Few powers of earth or heaven, few things on this side of the grave or the other, seem to have inspired him with dread. The Spirit of Good which he worshiped as God was not a judge, awarding human souls salvation or damnation; and the Spirit of Evil could have no power over the soul except what the soul itself allowed. Moreover, to Shelley's philosophy as to his temperament, the thought of fear was repugnant. In his eyes, fear was itself a sin against the true dignity of human nature; it de-

[64] Perhaps this is the place to clear up a misinterpretation of a passage in one of Shelley's letters to Mary. He writes (*Letters,* II, 906): "And good, far more than evil impulses, love, far more than hatred, has been to me, except as you have been its object, the source of all sorts of mischief." This is frequently taken as an admission that he himself had acted wrongly, though ignorantly, and had therefore been responsible for the troubles and sufferings connected with his life. It is obviously nothing of the sort; the implication is simply that good actions are usually misinterpreted by the malice and ignorance of the world, which is incapable of understanding pure and noble motives. The statement occurs in a passage where he is speaking about fleeing from society; he has just remarked, very characteristically, that "where two or three are gathered together, the devil is among them"! Far less can the passage be taken as indicating a view of evil as "essentially the result of good passions overshooting their mark." F. M. Stawell, *Essays and Studies,* V, 109.
[65] *A Survey of English Literature, 1780–1830,* II, 192. This is the best brief treatment of Shelley's work that I have met. In regard to this particular point, however, I think the critic goes too far.

graded man, it made him act cruelly and selfishly in the miserable hope of propitiating a jealous God, it was the mother of hate, the parent of countless woes. It must be expelled from man's nature.[66]

On the other hand, the statements previously made with reference to the apparent lack of any understanding on Shelley's part of a struggle within man's own nature (without reference to any external God) must be greatly qualified. A closer study of his writings will show that even so pure a nature as his, whose instinctive tendencies were almost always noble and right, was not always at one with itself. In the *Hymn to Intellectual Beauty*, which is nothing but an outpouring of his own inner experience, he asks "why man has such a scope For love and hate, despondency and hope"; and at the end he speaks of himself as one "Whom, Spirit fair, thy spells did bind *To fear himself*, and love all humankind." [67]

[66] It may be worth while at this point to make a few remarks on Shelley's views concerning the general problem of punishment, which are often misunderstood. It seems to be generally thought that his attitude is accurately expressed in the notes to *Queen Mab*, where punishment is deprecated on the ground that man is not responsible for his actions. Nothing could be farther from the truth. Shelley's real objections are two: first, that punishment does no good to the offender while it does harm to those who inflict it; and second, that evil is its own punishment. I do not think that anyone has done justice to the subtlety and depth of the latter conception. It has already been stated that Shelley believed in the absolute sovereignty of the soul and held that nothing can be truly evil except what the soul chooses to inflict upon itself, through indulgence in fear, anger, envy, hatred, and other evil passions. But the indulgence of these, according to the very nature of things, destroys the freedom of the soul, enslaves it to powers not properly its own, and condemns it *to continue to choose* evil instead of good. This is essentially the thought behind the vision of Er at the end of Plato's *Republic*. It is also, I should say, the true interpretation of Dante's *Inferno*. That is, the souls of sinners are not *sent* to Hell (and could not be)—they *go* there. Dante (or Dante's God) does not put his criminals in Hell to spite them or punish them; it is their native and chosen element. They would not leave it if they could; they cannot because they will not. Heaven to such as these would be infinitely more a hell than Hell itself. It is, humanly speaking, not the least of God's mercies that the wicked should be allowed to withdraw themselves as far as possible from the Goodness which they hate. But this is merely a metaphor, couched in the poor language of space and time. We are here in the presence of a Law which we cannot scan. It is not unnatural, however, that the mind should try to represent this Law in terms of personality, and that it should then mistake its own creation for the reality. This I take it, is Shelley's real objection to the Christian doctrine of punishment as commonly held. Even so great a poet as Milton seems only occasionally to rise to anything like an adequate conception of the nature of Satan's punishment (as in Book IV, ll. 32–113). The general impression given by Milton's treatment of the subject is that the Almighty is a vulgar tyrant, dealing out arbitrary penalties.

[67] Ll. 23–24, 83–84. Italics mine. Shelley wrote to Leigh Hunt that "the poem was composed under the influence of feelings which agitated me even to tears." *Letters*, II, 529.

One of his friends at Eton wrote long afterward that he "feared nothing, but what was base, and false, and low"; nothing, that is, but that tendency of his own nature which might lead him to be guilty of an unworthy act. There have been few men, perhaps, who needed less to fear themselves. Yet one can still find in his letters — although he was not one to make a parade of moral struggle — occasional references to some real or imagined weakness of will. In a letter to Leigh Hunt, written in 1819, after speaking at some length about his work, he adds, "So much for self — *self*, that burr that will stick to one. I can't get it off, yet." [68] Two years later he speaks of himself in a letter to Clare Clairmont as "your friend . . . who has enough to do in taming his own will . . ." [69] Not long after, writing to Hunt concerning Lord Byron, he says: "He has many generous and exalted qualities, but the canker of aristocracy wants to be cut out, and something, God knows, wants to be cut out of us all — except perhaps you!" [70] With this we may connect the following lines from *Peter Bell the Third*, where the poet says of Peter:

His virtue, like our own, was built
Too much on that indignant fuss
Hypocrite Pride stirs up in us
To bully one another's guilt.[71]

This observation is sound, if not startlingly original; and the expression of it rings true in a way that contradicts the common assertion that Shelley was naïvely and completely self-righteous. And to Hunt he writes again, but a few months before his death: "I did wrong in carrying this jealousy of my Lord Byron into his loan to you, or rather to me; and you in the superiority of wise and tranquil nature have well corrected and justly reproved me. And plan your account with finding much in me to correct and to reprove. Alas, how am I fallen from the boasted purity in which you knew me once exulting!" [72] Some allowance must be made, of course, for Shelley's innate modesty and for his habitual and unconscious self-depreciation. But these very traits are significant. It was only the *rightness* of the dictates of his conscience that he never distrusted;

[68] *Letters*, II, 706.   [69] *Ibid.*, p. 869.   [70] *Ibid.*, p. 910.
[71] IV, vi.   [72] *Letters*, II, 952.

as to whether his obedience to them was all it should have been, he sometimes had doubts.

But the circumstances of his own life are, after all, only incidental to the question. Shelley was a poet, with a poet's imagination, a "faculty of creative imagination," as a critic has written with just and deep insight, that seems "to exceed immeasurably his ability to execute conception" [73] — great as that ability was. And for the creations of such an imagination, actual experience need furnish but the barest suggestions. Whatever the course of his personal life, Shelley might have understood perfectly well the nature of moral conflict. And his poems are not without evidence that he did so. If my interpretation of *Prometheus Unbound* is at all correct, the hero of that play is an example of a nature which has certainly been "at odds with itself," and which still is so, despite the "three thousand years of sleep-unsheltered hours" of suffering by which it has been purified: for the furies that torture Prometheus are but objectifications of his own thoughts and passions, and the vision of human suffering would not weaken him were he not already weak. It is true that Prometheus is almost a unique instance. But for this fact, I think, some other explanation must be found than Shelley's supposed failure to recognize that all morality, "the great means and end of man," [74] rests finally upon a conflict within the individual. He speaks in *Prometheus* of man as being "the wreck of his own will" [75] and elsewhere declares that man's will "with all mean passions, bad delights, And selfish cares, its trembling satellites" is "a spirit ill to guide, but mighty to obey . . ." [76] In the *Lines Connected with Epipsychidion,* he declares that Socrates and Christ always urged

all living things to love each other,
And to forgive their mutual faults, and smother
The Devil of disunion in their souls.[77]

[73] Woodberry, *Poetical Works,* p. 636.
[74] *On the Revival of Literature,* in Shawcross, p. 119. Is Shelley, in this curious manner of speaking, hinting at the conception of morality as self-contradictory — that is, as striving to realize an ideal, with the realization of which morality itself, which is essentially a striving, would cease to exist — developed by Bradley in *Ethical Studies?*
[75] II, iv, l. 104.   [76] IV, ll. 406–08.
[77] Ll. 35–37. Italics mine.

With this passage may be compared the closing lines of *An Ode Written October, 1819, before the Spaniards Had Recovered Their Liberty,* where Shelley exhorts the Spaniards thus:

> Conquerors have conquered their foes alone,
> Whose revenge, pride, and power they have overthrown:
> Ride ye, more victorious, over your own.

Again, among the poems of 1821, we find a sonnet on *Political Greatness,* of which the close would satisfy the sternest moralist.

> Man who man would be,
> Must rule the empire of himself; in it
> Must be supreme, establishing his throne
> On vanquished will, quelling the anarchy
> Of hopes and fears, being himself alone.

This is not precisely the Christian conception of morality, it is true; it approaches, perhaps, rather to the ideal of Stoicism. But it is at any rate a far cry from Necessarianism. And it is not, as some critics will hasten to say, uncharacteristic of Shelley's work, for it reappears in *The Triumph of Life:* the great spirits chained to the car of Life had not been able to "rule the empire" of themselves,

> "their lore
> Taught them not this, to know themselves; their might
> Could not repress the mystery within . . ."; [78]

and such also was the fault without which

> "Corruption would not now thus much inherit
> Of what was once Rousseau, — nor this disguise
> Stain that which ought to have disdained to wear it." [79]

An honest and intelligent critic, one would think, might hesitate a bit before calling Shelley's ethical views "hopelessly superficial."

In these passages, *will* seems to be spoken of as something bad; but Shelley must really mean that in itself it is neither good nor evil, but only so according to the Power it serves. For, after all, the struggle within man's nature is only part of a cosmic conflict between the Spirit of Good and the Spirit of Evil. Neither the impulse to good nor the impulse to evil is properly his own. In the essay *On the Devil and Devils,* Shelley writes: "The Manichean

[78] Ll. 211–13.   [79] Ll. 203–05.

philosophy respecting the origin and government of the world, if
not true, is at least an hypothesis conformable to the experience of
actual facts. To suppose that the world was created and is super-
intended by two spirits of a balanced power and opposite dispositions, is simply a personification of the struggle which we experience
within ourselves, and which we perceive in the operations of external things as they affect us, between good and evil." [80] He goes
on to contrast the views of the Greeks. "They accounted for evil by
supposing that what is called matter is eternal, and that God in
making the world, made not the best that he, or even inferior intelligence could conceive; but that he moulded the reluctant and
stubborn materials ready to his hand, into the nearest arrangement
possible to the perfect archetype existing in his contemplation.
. . ." [81] On the whole, as was seen in the last chapter, Shelley inclines toward the former view; the other evidently attracted him,
but it is hardly compatible with the active and malignant nature
which he could not help attributing to the evil in the world.

In man the Evil Spirit and the Good meet and contend. In a
certain sense he is a passive instrument in their hands; they make
their presence known within him independently of his will or
desire.[82] But he has the power to distinguish between them, and he
can, and must, by an act of will ally himself to one or the other. In
a passage already quoted from the *Essay on Christianity*, Shelley
declares that "those who have seen God have . . . been harmonized *by their own will*" to a "consentaneity of power" with the
divine Spirit of Good; [83] and later he interprets, with the same
thought in mind, Christ's exhortation to "take no thought for the
morrow": "*Permit*, therefore, the Spirit of this benignant Principle
to visit your intellectual frame, or, in other words, *become* just and
pure. . . . The universal Harmony, or Reason, which makes your
passive frame of thought its dwelling, in proportion to the purity
and majesty of its nature will instruct you, *if ye are willing to
attain* that exalted condition, in what manner to possess all the ob-

[80] *Complete Works*, VII, 87.   [81] *Ibid.*, pp. 88–89.
[82] Shelley's emphasis upon the relative weakness of man in comparison to these
cosmic Powers, especially the Spirit of Good, has furnished critics another argument
for the mistaken view that the poet is a Necessarian.
[83] Shawcross, p. 91. Italics mine.

jects necessary for your material subsistence." [84] On the other hand:
"The nature of a narrow and malevolent spirit is so essentially
incompatible with happiness as to render it inaccessible even to the
influencings of the benignant God. All that his own perverse propensities will permit him to receive, that God abundantly pours
forth upon him." [85] And not only is the good repelled but the evil
is welcomed by a being of perverse will, as in *The Revolt of Islam*
Cythna declares in ringing words:

> "Look on your mind — it is the book of fate —
>   Ah! it is dark with many a blazoned name
>   Of misery — all are mirrors of the same;
> But the dark fiend who with his iron pen
>   Dipped in scorn's fiery poison, makes his fame
>   Enduring there, would o'er the heads of men
> Pass harmless, if they scorned to make their hearts his den." [86]

It is man's own weakness that subdues him to the power of Evil.
Thus Shelley describes the world of men as it seemed to him in his
youth, as well as later.

> For they all pined in bondage; body and soul,
>   Tyrant and slave, victim and torturer, bent
> Before one Power, to which supreme control
>   *Over their will by their own weakness lent,*
> Made all its many names omnipotent . . .[87]

In a certain sense, then, as some critics have remarked with disapprobation, good and evil both have their origin outside of human
nature. Yet I do not see that, so far, Shelley's view differs in the
slightest from that of Christianity. To say that he, any more than
any other moralist, regards evil as something "external," to which
man is arbitrarily subjected, is simply absurd. And finally, to those
who persist that Shelley had no conception of moral struggle, I offer
this quotation from the essay *On the Devil and Devils*. (Allowance
must be made, of course, for Shelley's habitual reversal of the
meaning of the names God and Devil — though it is rare at so
late a date.)

---

[84] *Ibid.*, p. 112. Italics mine. The second *its* in the second sentence I take to refer
to *frame*.
[85] *Ibid.*, p. 94. I have changed the text slightly according to the MS. reading as
printed by M. Koszul.
[86] VIII, xx.   [87] *Ibid.*, II, viii. Italics mine.

The Devil, it is said, before his fall, as an Angel of the highest rank and most splendid accomplishments placed his peculiar delight in doing good. But the inflexible grandeur of his spirit, mailed and nourished by the consciousness of the purest and loftiest designs, was so secure from the assault of any gross or common torments, that God was considerably puzzled to invent what he considered an adequate punishment for his rebellion; he exhausted all the varieties of smothering and burning and freezing and cruelly lacerating his external frame, and the Devil laughed at the impotent revenge of his conqueror. At last the benevolent and amiable disposition which distinguished his adversary, furnished God with a true method of executing an enduring and terrible vengeance. He turned his good into evil, and by virtue of his omnipotence, inspired him with such impulses, as, in spite of his better nature, irresistibly determined him to act what he most abhorred, and to be a minister of those designs and schemes of which he was himself the chief and original victim. He is forever tortured by passion and affection for those whom he betrays and ruins; he is racked by a vain abhorrence of the desolation of which he is the instrument; he is like a man compelled by a tyrant to set fire to his own possessions, and to appear as the witness against and the accuser of his dearest friends and most intimate connections; and then to be their executioner, and to inflict the most subtle and protracted torments upon them. As a man, were he deprived of all other refuge, he might hold his breath and die — but God is represented as omnipotent, and the Devil as eternal.[88]

If we substitute *Devil* for *God,* and *man* for *Devil* in this passage, we can hardly say without qualification that Shelley did not understand the Christian doctrine of sin, or that he could not have portrayed, had he chosen, a nature "at odds with itself." "For the good that I would I do not," cries Paul, "but the evil which I would not, that I do." [89] It is true that the element of fear is not present in Shelley's conception, and that the Devil is withheld from submission to his torturer, not by any dread of a greater suffering to be inflicted by some higher power but only by his own consciousness

[88] *Complete Works*, VII, 95–96. Shelley adds, "Milton has expressed this view of the subject with the sublimest pathos." There can be no doubt, I suppose, that it was not Milton's *intention* to present such a view; and I do not think that Shelley attributed to him such an intention, but rather considered him to have expressed it unconsciously, in spite of his theological views. I cannot, personally, agree with Shelley's interpretation of the poem; but certainly the above quotation presents his admiration for Milton's Satan as something quite other than (what it is so often said to be) the result of an irresponsible spirit of rebellion.

[89] Romans 7: 19.

of right, by his fear of being untrue to himself, which would be the one worse evil than that which he now suffers. It is also true that, according to Shelley's view, such an experience is impossible for a human soul to suffer, since it depends upon the existence of an omnipotent Demon; and Shelley holds that evil can have no power over man except through man's own will. But the quotation shows the extraordinary power which the poet possessed to realize in his own imagination experiences and points of view naturally foreign to his nature; and it shows, like many other utterances, that he possessed a measure of ethical insight apparently denied to many persons who have presumed to be his critics.

VII

So much for Shelley's view of evil as it exists in the world. What are his views as to its origin? For him only one position is possible: that evil is an inexplicable mystery, a problem quite beyond the power of the human mind to solve; something to be resisted, and, as far as possible, overcome, rather than something to be explained. He cannot accept the Manichean view because he will not grant to evil a real equality of power with good, whatever may be indicated by the actual conditions of the world. He does not accept the view we have just seen him attributing to the Greeks, because it fails to account for the activity of evil, and because it also makes evil really an inexplicable accident in the scheme of things, which renders man more or less the creature of circumstance instead of the master of his own soul.[90] Nor will he sacrifice feeling to reason, and say with

[90] On the same grounds he would have rejected, had he encountered it, the "scientific" or "naturalistic" view of our own times, which makes evil merely a part of "nature," as incompatible both with the actual facts of moral experience and with his belief in the dignity and freedom of the human soul. Mrs. Shelley, with her usual aptness in giving a handle for Shelley's detractors to take hold of, says that Shelley regarded evil as an "accident." It all depends upon the point of view. In the sense that he believed the universe to be ultimately on the side of good, he did consider evil an accident; but he also believed it to be due, in large part at least, to man's own will (as Mrs. Shelley herself implies in saying that he believed that it could be expelled by an act of will), and thus it would seem to be anything but an accident. From this standpoint, the theory which makes evil *really* accidental is that which represents it as an original and inevitable element in the nature of things, as does the view which Shelley attributes to the Greeks, or the naturalistic view of the present day; for in this case, there seems to be nothing that man can do about it.

the absolute idealist that evil is a mere illusion, and that he is living not merely in the best of all possible worlds but in the only and absolutely good world.[91] The Christian view, finally, he rejects as logically inconsistent and morally inadequate.

The only thing left is to confess one's ignorance; and this Shelley does. "The whole frame of human things is infected by an insidious poison. Hence it is that man is blind in his understanding, corrupt in his moral sense, and diseased in his physical functions." [92] But how this came to be he does not pretend to know. "Evil minds Change good to their own nature." [93] But why or how this should be possible remains a mystery. When Asia asks Demogorgon who made evil, the only answer is, "He reigns"; which is only to say that evil is dominant in the world. Then Asia tells what she herself knows:

> There was the Heaven and Earth at first,
> And Light and Love; then Saturn, from whose throne
> Time fell, an envious shadow: such the state
> Of the earth's primal spirits beneath his sway,
> As the calm joy of flowers and living leaves
> Before the wind or sun has withered them
> And semivital worms; but he refused
> The birthright of their being, knowledge, power,
> The skill which wields the elements, the thought
> Which pierces this dim universe like light,
> Self-empire, and the majesty of love;
> For thirst of which they fainted. Then Prometheus
> Gave wisdom, which is strength, to Jupiter,
> And with this law alone, "Let man be free,"
> Clothed him with the dominion of wide Heaven . . .
> And Jove now reigned; for on the race of man
> First famine, and then toil, and then disease,
> Strife, wounds, and ghastly death unseen before,
> Fell; and the unseasonable seasons drove

[91] Cf. the comment of A. C. Bradley, a follower of Hegel, that what he misses in Shelley is "the perception, or the faith, that evil is not here for nothing, that progress is made, not simply by resisting it, but no less by transmuting it, and even that the greatness of the mind is seen *most* in its power to win good out of evil." See *A Miscellany*, p. 155. In point of fact, the criticism is just; in Shelley's religion, as in Christianity, evil is absolute. Whether Hegelian optimism is preferable is perhaps a matter of individual temperament.

[92] *Essay on Christianity*, in Shawcross, p. 113.

[93] *Prometheus Unbound*, I, ll. 380–81.

With alternating shafts of frost and fire,
Their shelterless, pale tribes to mountain caves:
And in their desert hearts fierce wants he sent,
And mad disquietudes, and shadows idle
Of unreal good, which levied mutual war,
So ruining the lair wherein they raged.[94]

Now, all this is a description rather than an explanation. Why did Saturn withhold from the earth's inhabitants the birthright that would have made them men? And why, receiving it, are they made miserable under the reign of Jupiter? And why did Prometheus give Jupiter his power? The problem of evil still remains a mystery. One thing, however, the passage does make clear: that Jupiter does not represent, primarily, custom or government or religion. Even Shelley's most bitter critics would hardly accuse him of thinking that these could have been responsible for bringing

[94] II, iv, ll. 32–58. This is a very interesting passage, based, of course, on the myth of a lost golden age, or age of innocence, which occurs in varying forms among many races. Especially apposite (if one wishes to find a particular source) is the myth in Plato's dialogue *The Statesman* (§269–74). It need hardly be said, I suppose, that Shelley's account is intended to be symbolical and not literal. Some of the points of interest are the following: (1) What is meant by Time falling as an envious shadow from Saturn's throne? Does it perhaps mean that at this point time came into existence (with partial self-consciousness) as with the fall of Jupiter (with the coming of complete self-consciousness) it ceases to exist, giving way to Eternity? Cf. III, iii, l. 174; III, iv, ll. 108–09; IV, ll. 9–14; and see the following chapter. (2) The use of the expression "primal spirits" suggests the idea that *man*, properly speaking, only comes into being with self-knowledge and freedom. (3) How can these spirits "thirst" for things that they have never known? I would suggest that Shelley has in mind here some cosmic myth of the fall of spirit into matter, with the consequent birth of time and evil, according to certain occult traditions, such as those contained in the gnostic and cabalistic writings. This is the theme of many of Blake's prophetic books — with which Shelley seems not to have been familiar. Possibly the whole play is capable of a similar interpretation. The suffering of Prometheus would represent the discord consequent upon the Universal Spirit's manifesting itself in matter, and thereby limiting itself; the reunion with Asia and retirement to the cave would be the return of Spirit to complete self-consciousness, and withdrawal from manifestation. Jupiter would symbolize Time, dethroned by Eternity. This conception is also close to neo-Platonism. It is possible that Shelley was acquainted with Thomas Taylor, the neo-Platonist and translator of Plato. See Koszul, *La Jeunesse de Shelley*, Appendix III, p. 419. Moreover, Shelley's friend Newton, the vegetarian, was (according to Peacock, *Memoirs*, pp. 30–31) deeply read in zodiacal mythology, which leads straight into the same field of thought. For an elaborate study of the possible neo-Platonic sources of Shelley's ideas, see Grabo's *The Meaning of The Witch of Atlas*. I must say, however, that the truth of many of Mr. Grabo's conjectures seems to me extremely dubious.

death into the world or inaugurating the changes of the seasons. Jupiter simply represents the evil in the world,[95] and the origin of evil is inscrutable. Asia is sure that there is a Power above Jupiter who is responsible for his existence: she asks of Demogorgon, "Who is his master? Is he too a slave?" And the answer comes,

> All spirits are enslaved which serve things evil:
> Thou knowest if Jupiter be such or no; [96]

which "certainly means," as Rossetti says, that "he *is* a slave"; that Jupiter *does* serve an evil power greater than himself.[97] And the mystery is still unsolved. As Shelley says,

> a voice
> Is wanting, the deep truth is imageless;
> For what would it avail to bid thee gaze
> On the revolving world? What to bid speak
> Fate, Time, Occasion, Chance, and Change?[98]

And so Shelley's final solution of the problem of evil is that for man in his present state no solution is possible. More and more toward the end of his life he felt himself drawn in the direction of mysticism; more and more the life of sensation became a burden to him;[99] more and more he distrusted the powers of reason. From this state of mind it is an easy and natural step to the view that evil is an inevitable accompaniment of the world of space and time; and this view is not infrequent in Shelley's later poetry.

Even as early as *The Revolt of Islam,* he had spoken of

[95] Cf. III, iv, ll. 180–83.   [96] II, iv, ll. 110–11.

[97] *Shelley Society Papers,* Part I, p. 54. Mrs. Campbell (whose interpretation is usually good, although she seems unwilling to grant to anyone except herself the ability to understand and appreciate Shelley) comments strangely that Demogorgon's answer "makes it clear that evil is no essential principle of the universe and indeed no principle at all. She [Asia] understands that the real master of Jove is not an evil, but a good power . . ." *Shelley and the Unromantics,* p. 217. If she does, her mind acts in a very peculiar way!

[98] II, iv, ll. 115–19. Cf. Shelley's statement in the Preface to *The Cenci:* "But religion in Italy is not, as in Protestant countries, a cloak to be worn on particular days; or a passport which those who do not wish to be railed at carry with them to exhibit; or a gloomy passion for penetrating the *impenetrable mysteries of our being,* which terrifies its possessor at the darkness of the abyss to the brink of which it has conducted him." (Italics mine.)

[99] Cf. a passage in his letters: "the only relief I find springs from the composition of poetry, which necessitates contemplations that lift me above the stormy mist of sensations which are my habitual place of abode." *Letters,* II, 873.

> the chains which life for ever flings
> On the entangled soul's aspiring wings . . .[1]

Again, in Asia's speech, just quoted, the thought seems to be present that the power of Evil coincides with the rule of Time; and Demogorgon's answer seems to mean that in order to understand evil one must free himself from subjection not only to Time but also to Fate, Occasion, Chance, and Change.[2] In the opening stanza of *The Witch of Atlas* the poet lets his fancy dwell upon the same idea:

> Before those cruel Twins, whom at one birth
>   Incestuous Change bore to her father Time,
> Error and Truth, had hunted from the Earth
>   All those bright natures which adorned its prime . . .

Error and Truth, of course, are equivalent to Evil and Good, and the thought seems to be that the knowledge of good and evil, which makes the world no more a Paradise, is the inevitable offspring of Change and Time. Again in *Adonais* the whole burden of the poem is the contrast between the gloom and suffering that are felt to be inseparable from life and time and "the white radiance of Eternity" beyond. So also in the *Letter to Maria Gisborne* Shelley speaks of "The jarring and inexplicable frame Of this wrong world";[3] and in the same mood he refers, at the end of *The Sensitive Plant*, to

>   this life
> Of error, ignorance, and strife,
> Where nothing is, but all things seem,
> And we the shadows of the dream . . .

And finally, amid all the obscurity of *The Triumph of Life*, one thought seems clear: that in life itself there is present always, according to the inscrutable nature of things, some active principle of distortion and corruption, which veils from men's eyes the

---

[1] II, xxxiii.

[2] The use of the word "Chance" (cf. "Chance, and death, and mutability") seems to be another bit of evidence against Shelley's alleged Necessarianism. I take it to refer to the apparently causeless intrusion of the physical world into the moral world; something similar to the question in the Gospel concerning the man who was born blind, whether he or his parents had sinned. It shows again that Shelley's view of life was essentially moral, and not scientific.

[3] Ll. 159–60.

glory of Beauty and Love, and leads the soul astray through an unreal world of shadows — which is precisely the world which the mass of humanity believes to be real. This belief of Shelley's is perhaps to be connected with the theme of Wordsworth's *Ode on Intimations of Immortality:* that in childhood we feel a sense of the divinity of the world about us, and of our own kinship with it, which is gradually extinguished by the demands of practical worldly existence. Shelley develops the thought in the first three paragraphs of the essay *On Life,* where he says, for example, that the "mist of familiarity obscures from us the wonder of our being," and that "in living we lose the apprehension of life." [4] But Shelley's sense of the evil inherent in life in time is far more intense than Wordsworth's.

In the poet's letters, too, can be found occasional expressions of the same attitude. Referring in a letter to Mary to his relations with Byron, he remarks, "The demon of mistrust and pride lurks between two persons in our situation, poisoning the freedom of our intercourse. This is a tax, and a heavy one, which we must pay for being human. . . . I hope that in the next world these things will be better managed." [5] Later, expressing to John Gisborne his admiration of *Faust,* he declares his sympathy with "the scorn of the narrow good we can attain in our present state." [6] In a similar mood he speaks in *Hellas* of

> how man became
> The monarch and the slave of this low sphere,
> And all its narrow circles.[7]

In somewhat the same vein as these utterances is the statement attributed to Shelley by Trelawny: "With regard to the great question, the System of the Universe, I have no curiosity on the subject. . . . My mind is tranquil; I have no fears and some hopes. In our present gross material state our faculties are clouded; — when Death removes our clay coverings the mystery will be

---

[4] Shawcross, pp. 52, 53. Cf. also p. 56, and the *Lines Connected with Epipsychidion,* ll. 154–69; also, Rousseau's account of his childhood in *The Triumph of Life,* ll. 335 ff.; and the statement in *A Defence of Poetry* that poetry "purges from our inward sight the film of familiarity which obscures from us the wonder of our being." Shawcross, p. 156.

[5] *Letters,* II, 895.　　[6] *Ibid.,* p. 953.　　[7] Ll. 748–50.

solved." [8] The conditions of earthly existence simply preclude knowledge of ultimate things.

> Death is the veil which those who live call life:
> They sleep, and it is lifted . . . [9]

Occasionally Shelley allows himself to speculate upon whether there is not some one condition of life that, more than others, causes the delusion and woe by which man is surrounded. In the fragment called *The Coliseum* he writes: "The internal nature of each being is surrounded by a circle, not to be surmounted by its fellows; and it is this repulsion which constitutes the misfortune of the condition of life." [10] But this explains nothing; beyond every explanation there is another Why? and Shelley finally gives up the attempt. In a note upon some lines in *Hellas* which express the doctrine of reincarnation [11] he writes:

The concluding verses indicate a progressive state of more or less exalted existence, according to the degree of perfection which every distinct intelligence may have attained. Let it not be supposed that I mean to dogmatise upon a subject, concerning which all men are equally ignorant, or that I think the Gordian knot of the origin of evil can be disentangled by that or any similar assertions. The received hypothesis of a Being resembling men in the moral attributes of His nature, having called us out of non-existence, and after inflicting on us the misery of the commission of error, should superadd that of the punishment and the privations consequent upon it, still would remain inexplicable and incredible. *That there is a true solution of the riddle, and that in our present state that solution is unattainable by us, are propositions which may be regarded as equally certain:* meanwhile, as it is the province of the poet to attach himself to those ideas which exalt and ennoble humanity, let him be permitted to have conjectured the condition of that futurity towards which we are all impelled by an inextinguishable thirst for immortality. [12]

It is true that this belief seems to contradict the previous view that evil exists in man's life through his own perverted will; and it may seem, besides, to render vain and pointless all human effort

---

[8] *Records of Shelley, Byron, and the Author*, p. 80.
[9] *Prometheus Unbound*, III, iii, ll. 113–14.
[10] *Prose Works*, I, 399.
[11] Ll. 201–10. Doubtless the source of the idea is Plato.
[12] Italics mine.

toward good. But the same contradiction is found in Christianity and, indeed, in all religious thought; for religion apparently has its origin in the feeling of a discord between an ideal perfection and an imperfect actuality. And the aim of the religious life, and in fact of any life that can be truly called spiritual, is to achieve a practical reconciliation (for a rational reconciliation is, I think, impossible) between the claims, on the one hand, of what is seen to be mortal and earthly, and, on the other, of what is felt to be eternal and divine.

This is the view of all great minds and noble natures. A great Christian says, "We attain to Heaven by using this world well, though it is to pass away." [13] A great philosopher says, "Thus to the religious mind everything which is good is but the bringing to light of God's perfection and glory; and yet to the same religious mind nowhere is God more really present than in that will for good which in myself and others makes changes in the world." [14]

So Shelley. One aspect of his creed is expressed in the dedication of *The Cenci* to Leigh Hunt. "In that patient and irreconcilable enmity with domestic and political tyranny and imposture which the tenor of your life has illustrated, and which, had I health and talents, should illustrate mine, let us, comforting each other in our task, live and die." The other finds utterance in the speech of Christ to Satan near the close of the Prologue to *Hellas*.

> Boast not thine empire, dream not that thy worlds
> Are more than furnace-sparks or rainbow-drops
> Before the Power that wields and kindles them.
> True greatness asks not space, true excellence
> Lives in the Spirit of all things that live,
> Which lends it to the worlds thou callest thine.

[13] Newman, *The Idea of a University*, Discourse V, Section 10.

[14] F. H. Bradley, *Essays on Truth and Reality*, pp. 105–06. He continues: "This double nature and aspect of things will remain foolishness to the Personal Idealist, and it cannot be consistently held in human life; but the constant sense of it together with the endeavor to realize it in thought, may perhaps be said to make the life of philosophy."

CHAPTER V

A BRIGHTER HELLAS

I

"THAT THERE is a true solution of the riddle" of the existence of evil Shelley does not doubt. But he is equally convinced "that in our present state that solution is unattainable by us." If these statements express his real convictions — and they are in perfect harmony with the tenor of all his later writings — then clearly he believes that the true destiny of man can never find complete realization either in earthly life or in a personal immortality beyond the grave; for, I suppose, an immortality that can be properly called "personal" must be essentially a continuation of "our present state," even though amid new surroundings. Almost with the passion of an Indian mystic Shelley strove to free himself from the bonds of matter and time and space, of sensation and emotion and personality. Ever present in his later writings, this rebellion against the world of things finds most definite expression in *A Defence of Poetry;* and in this essay we have what will seem to most critics the anomaly of a poet glorifying poetry as the agent by which man may free himself from that natural world the simple representation of which is so often assumed to be the sole and sufficient purpose of the poet's art. Did one poet ever before pass upon another such a judgment as that of Shelley upon Lucretius, who is condemned for having "limed the wings of his swift spirit in the dregs of the sensible world"?[1] What other poet ever praised his muse as the power that "defeats the curse which binds us to be subjected to the accident of surrounding impressions"?[2] Like his master Plato, and like the Master whom he placed

[1] Shawcross, p. 147.
[2] *Ibid.,* p. 155.

above Plato, he felt that human life as it is, in the world that men call real, where Change and Time and Death and Chance and Mutability hold undisputed sway, is but a mirror that reflects partial and distorted images of a divine world beyond.

Yet his constant effort to rise above the realm of seeming into the realm of being was, of course, only partially successful. Whatever measure of success in such an attempt may be possible to men, the circumstances in which Shelley's life was involved were peculiarly unfavorable to the achievement of such an aim. But he succeeded so far, it seems, as to place his greatest works beyond the sympathies of the greater part of humanity. Even the small circle of friends who could not help loving the man were baffled by the poet. Mary was only expressing the wish of almost all his acquaintances in urging him to devote his poetic genius to "delineations of human passion." To the native incapacity of the European, and especially the English, mind to see beauty in any Tree of Life that does not have "blossoms as well as roots in the earth" may be attributed the antipathy of many of Shelley's unfriendly critics and the equivocal praise of numbers of his admirers. In this phenomenon, too, may perhaps be found the source of the common opinion that the world to which Shelley desires to escape is a lotos-eating realm of insubstantial daydream and languid reverie. But the mere retreat from "reality" to a subjective world of pleasant dreams and idle fancies, which so many critics profess to find in Shelley, is hardly so arduous an achievement that it results in men wearing out or neglecting their bodies as Shelley did. One wonders, sometimes, how many of those comfortable persons who patronize Shelley ever forgot their dinners in the pursuit of intellectual nourishment.[3] Yet to the poet, at last, the life of reason came to seem as inadequate as the life of sensation. Although the intellectual discipline which he imposed upon himself was probably more intense and persistent than that of any other English poet except Milton, he found it less and less satisfying as the years passed. "I read books, and, though I am ignorant enough, they seem to teach me noth-

---

[3] See Trelawny, *Records*, p. 63; also pp. 87–88. "The fact was that his excessive mental labour impeded, if it did not paralyze, his bodily functions."

ing." [4] The last ten years of his life show a steady conquest of rationalism by mysticism.[5]

His final position seems to be that to frame any conception of the meaning or the purpose of life which will satisfy men's most persistent desires and justify their deepest intuitions is simply beyond the power of the human mind. And this view obviously precludes the possibility of regarding either a perfected social order or a personal immortality (in the popular sense) as the final goal.

Yet such a conviction, even when it came to dominate the emotional and intellectual life of the poet, did not at all dissuade him from speculating both about the destiny of the human soul and about the improvement of human society. From first to last these two themes are present in Shelley's writings. In the early years they alternate or run parallel with each other, with society perhaps claiming the first place in his thoughts. But toward the end the situation is altered, and his passion for social reform is gradually absorbed (without being extinguished or even greatly weakened) in his preoccupation with the thought of a life beyond life, and with the problem of the relation between Ultimate Reality and the individual soul. *Queen Mab, The Revolt of Islam, Prometheus Unbound, The Mask of Anarchy, Hellas,* in all these poems one may read the fervent though slowly fading hope of a better social order and a greater measure of earthly happiness for men. But in *Alastor, Prince Athanase, Epipsychidion, Adonais,* and most of the shorter poems, the actual earthly life of humanity is either completely forgotten, or is felt as an obstacle that hinders the individual soul from attaining its appointed end. Even in Shelley's prose — leaving aside his metaphysical speculations and his diatribes against religious dogma — may be found the same divided interest. The Irish pamphlets, *A Proposal for Putting Reform to a Vote,* and *A Philosophical View of Reform,* these are intended to serve alto-

---

[4] *Letters,* II, 831.

[5] Something like this is the thesis of M. Koszul's study of *La Jeunesse de Shelley.* But the author depreciates far too strongly Shelley's rationalistic bent during his early years, which is, he thinks, to be attributed solely to outward circumstances; and his view seems to be that Shelley *fell back* from rationalism to mysticism because of his inability to cope with intellectual problems. I believe, however, that he *went through* rationalism to mysticism, and deliberately abandoned the former because he saw that it was quite inadequate to meet the demands of life.

gether practical ends. But the *Essay on Christianity* and *A Defence of Poetry*, although by no means indifferent to the claims of "real life," are inspired almost wholly by the contemplation of ideas and ideals having only an indirect bearing upon the problems of society. Shelley was both an Arthur and a Galahad,[6] and the vision of the Grail was constantly drawing him away from the struggle in which he had so early and so ardently engaged against the worshippers of heathen gods.

So it comes about that many people find in Shelley's poetry many things to offend them. Pious conservatives who cling instinctively to the old order deprecate the poet's social iconoclasm. Rough-and-ready reformers who have come to feel at home amid the dirt and dross of practical politics are contemptuous of his dreams of perfection. Persons of artistic temperament who are satisfied with the richness and abundance of life as it is, who quite sincerely agree with God that His work is good, are disturbed by Shelley's revolt against things as they are. Social theorists enamored of a scientifically planned society have no sympathy with his search for ideal beauty. And one and all are offended by his brooding sense of the unreality of earthly things.

For these and other reasons the great mass of readers and critics seem to have agreed that the most charitable attitude to take toward Shelley as a poet is to consider him only a "Voice in the Air, singing" beautiful songs about nothing of any consequence. I believe, however, that this attitude rests upon a radical misconception. It is the aim of this and the following chapter to show that Shelley's thoughts about the destiny of man are neither shallow nor fanciful.

II

And, first, what of Shelley's earthly paradise and that doctrine of "perfectibility" of which we have heard so much? For this, as for many other supposedly fantastic beliefs alleged to have been held by Shelley, Godwin is usually blamed. But since *Political Justice* is a work (one suspects) oftener condemned than read, it may be well to see what its author really means by "perfectibility."

---

[6] I forestall the inevitable sneer of a certain class of critics by adding that he was not a Lancelot — except in being brave, generous, and chivalrous.

"Man is perfectible, or in other words susceptible of perpetual improvement."[7] But "perpetual improvement" implies that there is no end to the process, and therefore *that perfection is not attainable!* Precisely. "The term perfectible . . . not only does not imply the capacity of being brought to perfection, but stands in express opposition to it. If we could arrive at perfection, there would be an end of our improvement."[8] This is both interesting and amusing; for it shows that the late Victorian critics who, by means of a naïve application of evolutionary theories, are enabled to look forward happily to "endless progress," and to look back pityingly upon the Utopian dreams of the revolutionary age, are, in their views about the future of humanity, very nearly in agreement with that arch-Utopian, William Godwin.[9]

The grounds upon which these views rest are doubtless somewhat different in the two cases. Godwin declares that "every perfection or excellence that human beings are competent to conceive, human beings, unless in cases that are palpably and unequivocally excluded by the structure of their frame, are competent to attain"; but the "idea of absolute perfection is scarcely within the grasp of human understanding."[10] Moreover, all human knowledge is derived from "impression" (presumably through the senses, although the point is not important), and since man must forever receive additional impressions, his knowledge must be forever increasing, and the goals he sets himself forever changing.[11] These are not the terms in which a student of Darwin and Spencer would be likely to think, but they at least show that Godwin is fundamentally an evolutionist and not a revolutionist. And with later

[7] *Political Justice*, I, 86 (Book I, Chapter 5).   [8] *Ibid.*, p. 93.

[9] Practically, however, Godwin does seem to expect (at least at the time when he is writing *Political Justice*) that a relatively perfect society lies "just around the corner." Victorian smugness was willing to put it off indefinitely.

[10] *Political Justice*, I, 93.

[11] *Ibid.*, pp. 94–95. It seems to me that Godwin here falls into a paradox, first asserting that mind has power over the physical world so far as to attain whatever end it is capable of conceiving, and then declaring that mind is altogether dependent on the physical world for the material out of which it forms those conceptions. This second principle also contradicts, I should say, the view that mind produces motion, and not motion mind. "It is far from certain, that the phenomenon of motion can any where exist, where there is not thought." *Ibid.*, I, 419. But there is practically no end to Godwin's inconsistencies.

evolutionists he has something else in common than the expectation of endless progress, namely, agnosticism. He resolutely refuses to have anything to do with any other world than that of common experience. However expansive he may become concerning the power of mind over matter, he keeps his feet solidly on the earth. His hopes, like Wordsworth's in the passage that so infuriated Shelley, were entirely bounded by the world which is

> the world of all of us, and where
> We find our happiness, or not at all.

It is "idle to talk of the absolute immortality of man. Eternity and immortality are phrases to which it is impossible for us to annex any distinct ideas, and the more we attempt to explain them, the more we shall find ourselves involved in contradiction." [12] But why trouble ourselves about such things when it is probable that on this very earth "the term of human life may be prolonged, and that by the immediate operation of intellect, beyond any limits which we are able to assign"? [13] Here, indeed, Godwin becomes Utopian: he looks forward to a society composed entirely of mature persons, who will not be bothered by the necessity of propagating the race or educating their offspring, and will therefore be able to devote all their energies to their own "perpetual improvement."

These views of Godwin are present to some extent in Shelley's early writings. But even here they are greatly modified, for the poet at twenty had in some respects a deeper insight into human nature and its needs than the philosopher at sixty: and long before the end of Shelley's brief career, the teachings of Godwin had given way almost completely to those of Plato and the New Testament.

Even in *Queen Mab* there is something a little mystical and unworldly in the fervor with which the poet pictures a regenerate earth. One is not quite sure whether it is a terrestrial or a celestial world which is here envisioned.

> "O happy Earth! reality of Heaven!
> To which those restless souls that ceaselessly
> Throng through the human universe, aspire;
> Thou consummation of all mortal hope!
> Thou glorious prize of blindly-working will!

[12] *Political Justice*, II, 527 (Book VIII, Chapter 9, Appendix).   [13] *Ibid.*

Whose rays, diffused throughout all space and time,
Verge to one point and blend for ever there:
Of purest spirits thou pure dwelling-place!
Where care and sorrow, impotence and crime,
Languor, disease, and ignorance dare not come:
O happy Earth, reality of Heaven!

"Genius has seen thee in her passionate dreams,
And dim forebodings of thy loveliness
Haunting the human heart, have there entwined
Those rooted hopes of some sweet place of bliss
Where friends and lovers meet to part no more.
Thou art the end of all desire and will,
The product of all action; and the souls
That by the paths of an aspiring change
Have reached thy haven of perpetual peace,
There rest from the eternity of toil
That framed the fabric of thy perfectness." [14]

The quality of the poetry in these lines, perhaps the finest in the whole work, shows what a truly passionate dream it is that the poet here attempts to fix in words. Very different is this, one would say, from the "perpetual improvement" of Godwin, and his hoped-for society of perfectly rational and unimpassioned human beings, moving about upon a very solid earth. Not "perpetual improvement" but "perpetual peace," this is the cry of the religious nature in every age. The Hebrew prophet looks forward to an age when, in the words that Shelley was so fond of quoting, "the lion shall lie down with the lamb"; the Greek philosopher dreams of a "real earth," radiant and eternal, hovering above the mist- and shadow-shrouded valleys of mortal existence; and the Christ proclaims a kingdom that is not of this world, which shall endure though heaven and earth shall pass away. And so Shelley is impelled to seek some final end of the great scheme of things, to which human souls may and do aspire, and though "an eternity of toil" may separate them from it, yet it is always *there*, at last.[15] He may try

[14] IX, ll. 1–22. In *The Daemon of the World* the last part of this passage is completely changed, so that "those rooted hopes" have for their object only the overthrow on earth of "the proud Power of Evil" (ll. 306 ff.).

[15] The critics who ascribe to Shelley the hope of a quickly coming millennium (which he certainly does express in some parts of *Queen Mab*) seem to overlook the

to justify the existence in the world of change and struggle, as when he says,

> "But, were it virtue's only meed, to dwell
> In a celestial palace, all resigned
> To pleasurable impulses, immured
> Within the prison of itself, the will
> Of changeless Nature would be unfulfilled." [16]

But it is clearly not in the struggle itself but in the contemplation of the end to which it is directed that Shelley finds his inspiration. The critic is right, so far, who judges Shelley to be lacking in "a joyful sense of the imperfection of this life"; for such a sense is, in the very nature of things, simply incompatible with the religious point of view.

It is rather curious that in *The Revolt of Islam,* a far more imaginative poem than *Queen Mab,* and one in which Shelley's innate tendency toward mysticism is much more evident, the poet should picture an earthly paradise that is really to exist upon the earth, and that is comparatively definite and human; although in spirit, at least, it is immeasurably removed from the conception set forth by Godwin. It appears most clearly in Cythna's hymn in Canto V.

> "My brethren, we are free! the plains and mountains,
> The gray sea-shore, the forests and the fountains,
> Are haunts of happiest dwellers; — man and woman,
> Their common bondage burst, may freely borrow
> From lawless love a solace for their sorrow;
> For oft we still must weep, since we are human.
> A stormy night's serenest morrow,
> Whose showers are pity's gentle tears,
> Whose clouds are smiles of those that die
> Like infants without hopes or fears,
> And whose beams are joys that lie
> In blended hearts, now holds dominion;

frequent statements of the poet that "an eternity of toil" is necessary to "frame the fabric" of the perfect world, that man's will "is destined an eternal war to wage With tyranny and falsehood" (IX, ll. 190–91), and so on. It may be argued, of course, that such utterances creep in by accident; but are they not then all the more significant, as showing Shelley's own intuitions and beliefs, temporarily obscured by the ideas of the Revolutionary writers?

[16] *Queen Mab,* II, ll. 59–63.

> The dawn of mind, which upwards on a pinion
> Borne, swift as sunrise, far illumines space,
> And clasps this barren world in its own bright embrace!" [17]

In the next stanza Cythna describes how in this happy society of the future, man will cease to prey upon his fellow creatures, and will be at peace with "the dwellers of the earth and air"; [18] and she concludes:

> "Our toil from thought all glorious forms shall cull,
> To make this Earth, our home, more beautiful,
> And Science, and her sister Poesy,
> Shall clothe in light the fields and cities of the free."

The conception here appears to be quite without metaphysical or mystical elements. The thought of immortality, also, is deliberately set aside, and men do not look beyond the present life, which, though calm and sweet, still has place for grief and pity, and is capable of being made yet better and more beautiful. For a moment Shelley has laid by his dreams of absolute perfection, and with serene optimism looks forward to a renovated society, the achievement of which seems adequate to the satisfaction of man's highest aspirations. The same comparatively sober hope animates some words of Shelley reported by Horace Smith, in the same year in which *The Revolt of Islam* was written.

Without asserting the absolute perfectibility of human nature, he had a confident belief in its almost limitless improvability; especially as he was persuaded that evil, an accident, and not an inherent part of our system, might be so materially diminished as to give an incalculable increase to

---

[17] Stanza 4. The hymn occurs after stanza li. The expression "lawless love," of course, does not mean "free love" in the ordinary sense, which Shelley as a matter of fact (notwithstanding the slanders of malicious or ignorant critics from his day to our own) condemned in the strongest terms. See his review of Hogg's *Memoirs of Prince Alexy Haimatoff* (Shawcross, pp. 12–13), and Chapter VII of the present study.

[18] I cannot bring myself to quote this passage on vegetarianism: certain lines are hopelessly unpoetic. But it is a mistake to treat Shelley's vegetarianism as an unimportant whim. (I consider Peacock's famous story about the mutton chops, as well as many other parts of his account, to be purely fictitious. Aside from the consideration that several of his statements in regard to very important matters of fact are known to be false, it should be remembered that he had caricatured Shelley as Scythrop in *Nightmare Abbey*; and in the course of forty years it is altogether likely that the man and the caricature became confused.) He firmly believed that all living creatures have their place in the cosmic scheme, and no less than man are entitled to "life, liberty, and the pursuit of happiness."

the sum of human happiness . . . Now, if mankind . . . could be brought universally to adopt that religion of Nature which, finding its heavenly revelation in man's own heart, teaches him that the best way to testify his love of the Creator is to love all that he has created, that religion, whose three-leaved Bible is the earth, and sea, and sky — eternal and immutable Scriptures, written by God himself,[19] which all may read and none can interpolate, there would be a total cessation of the *odium theologicum* which has been such a firebrand to the world; the human race, unchecked in its progress of improvement, would be gradually lifted into a higher state, and all created beings, living together in harmony as one family, would worship their common Father in the undivided faith of brotherly love and the gratitude of peaceful happiness.[20]

It is a little hard to see why such thoughts as these should call forth from critics the ridicule, contempt, or pity with which it has ever been the custom to regard Shelley's hopes for the future of humanity. But, passing by for the moment such criticism as this, it must be emphasized that those occasions are rare, especially toward the end of his life, when Shelley is satisfied with the thought of *any* state of existence, no matter how loftily conceived, that is subject to the limitations of matter, time, and space. Even in *The Revolt of Islam,* we have heard the despairing cry that

> "There is delusion in the world — and woe
> And fear, and pain — we know not whence we live,
> Or why, or how . . ."[21]

a cry, however, that is not without the echo of a hope that all is *not* vanity, as from the experience of reason and the senses we must conclude. In the *Essay on Christianity,* too, written in the same year, we find Shelley strongly attracted by the words of Christ concerning a future life.

This is Heaven, when pain and evil cease, and when the Benignant Principle, untrammelled and uncontrolled, visits in the fullness of its power the universal frame of things. Human life, with all its unreal ills and transitory hopes, is as a dream, which departs before the dawn, leaving no trace of its evanescent hues. . . . How delightful a picture, even if it be not true! How magnificent and illustrious is the conception

---

[19] Cf. *Lines Connected with Epipsychidion,* ll. 30–31: ". . . there is the God in heaven above, Who wrote a book called Nature."

[20] *James and Horace Smith,* pp. 173–74.

[21] IX, xxxiii.

which this bold theory suggests to the contemplation, even if it be no more than the imagination of some sublimest and most holy poet, who, impressed with the loveliness and majesty of his own nature, is impatient- and discontented with the narrow limits which this imperfect life and the dark grave have assigned forever as his melancholy portion.[22]

"This imperfect life and the dark grave" — this somber theme is never long absent from Shelley's poetry. His brightest dreams of peace on earth and good will among men fade away and vanish at the approach of this cold specter, as Lamia before the cruel gaze of Apollonius; and the poet is driven to direct his hopes to some eternal world.

Again, in the much-discussed scenes at the end of *Prometheus Unbound,* in which Shelley pictures a regenerate earth, appear the same two tendencies: toward humanitarianism on the one hand, and mysticism on the other; and although in the poet's thought they are never in conflict, yet in this poem they are still unrelated, and consequently are not fused, but confused. The first picture is given by Prometheus, who first tells Asia and her "fair sister nymphs" of the magical cave

> Where we will sit and talk of time and change,
> As the world ebbs and flows, ourselves unchanged.
> What can hide man from mutability? [23]

and then continues:

> And hither come . . .
> The echoes of the human world, which tell
> Of the low voice of love, almost unheard,
> And dove-eyed pity's murmured pain, and music,
> Itself the echo of the heart, and all
> That tempers or improves man's life, now free;
> And lovely apparitions, — dim at first,
> Then radiant, as the mind, arising bright
> From the embrace of beauty (whence the forms
> Of which these are the phantoms) casts on them
> The gathered rays which are reality —
> Shall visit us, the progeny immortal
> Of Painting, Sculpture, and rapt Poesy,

[22] Shawcross, pp. 96–97. As always in quoting from this essay, I follow Koszul's text.
[23] III, iii, ll. 23–25.

And arts, though unimagined, yet to be.
The wandering voices and the shadows these
Of all that man becomes, the mediators
Of that best worship love, by him and us
Given and returned; swift shapes and sounds, which grow
More fair and soft as man grows wise and kind,
And, veil by veil, evil and error fall:
Such virtue has the cave and place around.[24]

This vision is still of the earth, though scarcely earthly. The pain
of pity — and, by implication, objects of pity — still lingers. And
man, though free, is free only to *become,* and *becoming* implies conditions. And evil and error, though passing away, are not yet past.
Still, on the other hand, the vision is winged; its feet are on the
earth, but its eyes arc gazing, not forward, but upward. It is
scarcely strange, perhaps, for all the loveliness of the verse, that the
lines should have small appeal for those eager or idle lovers of
imperfection who constitute an overwhelming majority of humanity.

The next account of a regenerate society is that of the Spirit of
the Earth, which after telling its mother, Asia, how it had once
been made "sick at heart" by the sight of evil, and especially by the

[24] III, iii, ll. 40–63. The reader may be interested, and possibly enlightened, by
a few typical samples of the almost universal critical reprobation of which this
part of the play has been the object. Mr. G. R. Elliott indulges in the following
sneer: "The initial nobility of Prometheus is soon softened down by his rising pity
for all things, including the powers of evil; and finally this active striver for
mankind becomes a retired well-wisher, throbbing only with millennial reverie and
sympathy." *Op. cit.,* p. 18. Miss Scudder (who, it will be remembered, finds "man,
as Shelley depicts him . . . scarcely higher . . . than an amiable brute") de-
livers, from the critic's "awful throne of *im*patient power," this Jovian judgment: "Weak, sentimental, empty, — guilty of the worst of aesthetic sins, pretti-
ness, — is Shelley's description of the ideal state. After their titanic throes, their
radiant achievement, Prometheus and Asia are united. Surely the progressive rapture
of their life will at least in glorious hint form the conclusion of the drama. Not
so . . . For a regenerate humanity Shelley had no message. His ideal is radically
unprogressive, — the return to a Golden Age of pastoral innocence, rather than the
advance into new regions of material and spiritual conquest. 'Equal, unclassed,
tribeless and nationless, exempt from awe, worship, degree,' is the humanity of the
future; and the poetry is flat, the thought is even flatter, in which its life is
described." *Op. cit.,* p. xxxviii. Even Mrs. Campbell remarks (apparently on the
theory that much fine and discriminating praise will be more acceptable if seasoned
with an occasional dash of extravagant and irresponsible depreciation) that "in
the third and fourth scenes of Act III we see him [Prometheus] slowly asphyxiated
before our eyes in the vapours of a universal carouse." *Op. cit.,* p. 220.

foul masks, with which ill thoughts
Hide that fair being whom we spirits call man,[25]

describes the magic change which Prometheus' triumph has wrought
among earth's creatures.

> Well, my path lately lay through a great city
> Into the woody hills surrounding it:
> A sentinel was sleeping at the gate:
> When there was heard a sound, so loud, it shook
> The towers amid the moonlight . . .
> And all the inhabitants leaped suddenly
> Out of their rest, and gathered in the streets
> Looking in wonder up to Heaven . . .
>   . . . and soon
> Those ugly human shapes and visages
> Of which I spoke as having wrought me pain,
> Passed floating through the air, and fading still
> Into the winds that scattered them; and those
> From whom they passed seemed mild and lovely forms
> After some foul disguise had fallen, and all
> Were somewhat changed . . .
>   . . . and when the dawn
> Came, wouldst thou think that toads, and snakes, and efts,
> Could e'er be beautiful? Yet so they were,
> And that with little change of shape or hue:
> All things had put their evil nature off . . .[26]

Here again one must ask whether this passage is intended to represent at all literally any actual future state of human society. And
the answer, I think, must be in the negative. The sound of the
mystic shell, the sudden falling of the ugly masks from human
faces, the passing away from the whole animate world of all that
was unbeautiful, or cruel, or evil in any way, all these point to the
conclusion that the picture is only symbolic of the belief that human
life, and indeed all life, will or may achieve some more nearly
perfect state of existence. Shelley is not trying to tell us, as some
critics seem to think, *what* the *best* world is like, but only *that* a

[25] III, iv, ll. 44–45.
[26] III, iv, ll. 51–77. The magical sound (which comes from a "mystic shell"
breathed into by the Spirit of the Hour) is doubtless a remembrance on Shelley's
part of that haunting myth of the mysterious and mournful cry which announced
the passing of the pagan gods of nature and the triumph of Christianity. Cf. *Hellas*,
ll. 225–38.

better world is possible; and the passage is therefore the result of a perfectly legitimate poetic method, and all criticisms to the effect that the state described is impossible or unsatisfying become irrelevant. Shelley himself foresaw this type of criticism and attempted to forestall it. In the Preface to *The Revolt of Islam* he writes: "I have made no attempt to recommend the motives which I would substitute for those at present governing mankind, by methodical and systematic argument. I would only awaken the feelings, so that the reader should see the beauty of true virtue, and be incited to those inquiries which have led to my moral and political creed, and that of some of the sublimest intellects in the world." And again in the Preface to *Prometheus Unbound* he declares: "Should I live to accomplish what I purpose, that is, produce a systematical history of what appear to me to be the genuine elements of human society, let not the advocates of injustice and superstition flatter themselves that I should take Aeschylus rather than Plato as my model." It is scarcely necessary to point out where this statement leaves those critics who have sneered at Shelley's pictures of a future society as "Utopian." All that can be inferred from them is that the poet believed that a purer and more exalted existence than has yet been attained is possible to man on earth. Certainly he hoped that some of the conditions he describes would sometime be realized; but it does not follow that he would be satisfied (or that he fancies that he would be so) in this or any other earthly paradise.

These remarks may be applied also to the third and final description of the new order of things, which is given by the Spirit of the Hour.[27]

> And behold, thrones were kingless, and men walked
> One with the other, even as spirits do:
> None fawned, none trampled; hate, disdain, or fear,
> Self-love or self-contempt, on human brows
> No more inscribed, as o'er the gate of hell,
> "All hope abandon ye who enter here;"
>
> . . . .
>
> None, with firm sneer, trod out in his own heart

[27] Doubtless this persistence in dwelling on a single theme constitutes an artistic defect. Certainly it is a dramatic anticlimax. But Shelley was occupied with more important things than dramatic artifice.

The sparks of love and hope, till there remained
Those bitter ashes, a soul self-consumed,
And the wretch crept a vampire among men,
Infecting all with his own hideous ill . . .
And women, too, frank, beautiful, and kind
As the free heaven which rains fresh light and dew
On the wide earth, past; gentle radiant forms,
From Custom's evil taint exempt and pure . . .
Thrones, altars, judgment-seats, and prisons, — wherein,
And beside which, by wretched men were borne
Sceptres, tiaras, swords, and chains, and tomes
Of reasoned wrong, glozed on by ignorance . . .
Stand, not o'erthrown, but unregarded now.
And those foul shapes, abhorred by God and Man, —
Which, under many a name and many a form
Strange, savage, ghastly, dark and execrable,
Were Jupiter, the tyrant of the world . . .
Frown, mouldering fast o'er their abandoned shrines:
The painted veil, by those who were, called life,
Which mimicked, as with colours idly spread,
All men believed or hoped, is torn aside;
The loathesome mask has fallen, the Man remains, —
Sceptreless, free, uncircumscribed, — but man:
Equal, unclassed, tribeless and nationless,
Exempt from awe, worship, degree, the King
Over himself; just, gentle, wise, — but man:
Passionless? no: yet free from guilt or pain,
Which were, for his will made or suffered them,
Nor yet exempt, though ruling them like slaves,
From chance, and death, and mutability,
The clogs of that which else might oversoar
The loftiest star of unascended Heaven,
Pinnacled dim in the intense inane.[28]

[28] III, iv, ll. 131–204. In this passage I follow Locock's text in regard to punctuation and capitalization, which in turn follows, for the most part, the Bodleian
MS. Lines 194–98, especially, have caused much editorial difficulty; and since the
exact meaning is important to this discussion, I quote Locock's note. "His [Rossetti's]
interpretation is that man, in spite of the new era, 'is still man. He has not passed
from the human into any other condition; only his human condition is now an
exalted instead of a dejected one.' Since this antithesis provides something like an
anticlimax, it might be possible to find another — not between the divine and the
man, but between the mask and the man. In that case the sense would be — 'The
mask has fallen, — the real man becomes visible, free to follow his own true
nature. And this man is not the masked, cowering, vicious slave called man by
mankind, but "that fair being whom *we spirits* call Man": equal, virtuous, inde-

More definitely than either of the two passages quoted just before, these lines describe a future state of society upon earth. It is an existence, to be sure, that is too highly spiritualized to have much appeal either to "muscular Christians" of the Kingsley type or to those who embrace the frank naturalism of a generation that fancies itself to be "enlightened" and "scientific." But man is stated specifically to be still human and mortal. The painted veil of life that is here torn aside is not, like that in the previous scene,[29] the all-enfolding curtain of illusion that time and space inevitably draw between mortal sight and Ultimate Reality; but rather the illusion in which man is plunged by the fear and folly and falsity, the greed and coarseness and cruelty, which in society he has always imposed upon himself;[30] and it is these evil passions that have created the foul mask that now falls away, while Man remains.

Yet Shelley is not satisfied; at the end he is still haunted by those specters which he could never exorcize — "chance, and death, and mutability." They are no longer terrifying — true; but they are clogs to the unceasing aspiration of the human soul; and, besides, one wonders if even this ultimately unsatisfying life is not, after all, different in kind rather than in degree from the everyday existence with which all are familiar. "The loathesome mask has fallen"; but in *The Triumph of Life* one finds described the falling of other masks from human faces, which by each change become more deformed and repulsive.[31] And this dreadful alteration is

pendent,—"Whose nature is its own divine controul." ' 'But man' would then mean 'but really man, though hardly recognizable as such in his altered state.' " The last suggestion seems to me most satisfactory. — It is worth noting, in passing, that this very passage, which Shelley's critics always seize on to condemn, contains distinct evidence that Shelley did *not* believe that evil is solely, or even primarily, the result of custom, government, and religion, with the abolition of which it would entirely disappear. The evil man is described as "a soul *self-consumed*." "Thrones, altars," and so on, are "not o'erthrown," but merely neglected; that is, social reform must in general follow and not precede the regeneration of individual men. Finally, man is not exempt from *law*, but only from *compulsion*: he is "the King over himself," no longer in need of an *external* ruler. Of course, as I have said, Shelley recognized that institutions and customs often prevent man's progress toward self-conquest, and that outward and inward reform must go hand in hand.
[29] III, iii, ll. 113–14.
[30] This distinction between the two meanings which Shelley gives to the figure of life as a veil is discussed by Mr. Kurtz, *op. cit.*, pp. 182–83. It is also suggested by Mrs. Campbell, *op. cit.*, p. 221.
[31] Cf. ll. 535 ff.

unmistakably the result of some contaminating and corrosive principle that is apparently inseparable from life as we know it. Moreover, turning back to *Prometheus Unbound,* we find the poet, after Jupiter's fall, playing with the idea that Time has given way to Eternity. Eternity, it will be remembered, is the name which Demogorgon gives himself in addressing Jupiter. Elsewhere, the Earth praises Prometheus for having borne the "torch of hope" "most triumphantly To this far goal of Time," as if Time were at an end.[32] And at the beginning of the fourth act, the chorus of "dead Hours" sings, "We bear Time to his tomb in eternity." [33] So in the end, as always in Shelley's descriptions of the millennium, we are left wondering as to just what this new world is to which the poet looks forward. Unconsciously, it seems, he lets his vision of a regenerate earth take flight for heaven until it is in danger of being "lost in the white day." [34]

In *Hellas,* still, but a few months before Shelley's death, there is the same divided allegiance. In the Preface the poet declares himself contented "with having wrought upon the curtain of futurity, which falls upon the unfinished scene, such figures of indistinct and visionary delineation as suggest the final triumph of the Greek cause as a portion of the cause of civilization and social improvement." And a note on the final chorus shows his youthful faith in a future golden age of human happiness still unextinguished, though sadly chastened. "The final chorus is indistinct and obscure, as the event of the living drama whose arrival it foretells. Prophecies of wars, and rumours of wars, etc., may safely be made by poet or prophet in any age, but to anticipate however darkly a period of regeneration and happiness is a more hazardous exercise of the faculty which bards possess or feign. It will remind the reader 'magno *nec* proximus intervallo' of Isaiah and Virgil, whose ardent spirits overleaping the actual reign of evil which we endure and bewail, already saw the possible and perhaps approaching state of society in which the *'Lion shall lie down with the lamb,'* and

---

[32] III, iii, ll. 173–74.   [33] IV, l. 14.

[34] Cf. the comment on the end of Act III made by Marjorie Bald: "Wherever or whenever this consummation may take place, it will be in no atmosphere breathed by men. When earthly considerations intervene, the note of disillusion is sounded. 'Fear and self-contempt and barren hope' — this is the epitome of all earthly existence." *Essays and Studies by Members of the English Association,* XIII, p. 117.

'omnis feret omnia tellus.' Let these great names be my authority and my excuse." A regenerate society, he still thinks, is possible.

But from the poem itself one receives another impression. Above all in the series of magnificent choruses with which the play is concluded, and which some critics have judged to mark the absolute summit of English lyric poetry, Shelley's unconquerable moral idealism forces him to lift his gaze beyond a world and a life where ideals seem destined always to meet defeat. The words of Beatrice might have been his own:

> Many might doubt there were a god above
> Who sees and permits evil, and so die:
> That faith no agony shall obscure in me.[35]

Truth and justice, beauty and love, *shall* prevail, and if not here, then elsewhere.

> If Greece must be
> A wreck, yet shall its fragments reassemble,
> And build themselves again impregnably
> In a diviner clime,
> To Amphionic music on some Cape sublime,
> Which frowns above the idle foam of Time.[36]

The crucified ideal is *not* destroyed, though driven from the world of men.

> Darkness has dawned in the East
> On the noon of time:
> The death-birds descend to their feast
> From the hungry clime.
> Let Freedom and Peace flee far
> To a sunnier strand,
> And follow Love's folding-star
> To the Evening land![37]

> Through the sunset of hope,
> Like the shapes of a dream,
> What Paradise islands of glory gleam!

[35] *The Cenci*, III, i, ll. 100–02. The construction of the first two lines is extremely loose. I take the meaning to be: "Many might doubt that any God exists, since such evils are permitted."

[36] Ll. 1002–07.

[37] Ll. 1023–30. The "Evening land," of course, is America. But it is only an *ideal* America. Shelley had no extravagant illusions about the real one. Cf. ll. 993ff.

> Beneath Heaven's cope,
> Their shadows more clear float by —
> The sound of their oceans, the light of their sky,
> The music and fragrance their solitudes breathe
> Burst, like morning on dream, or like Heaven on death,
> Through the walls of our prison;
> And Greece, which was dead, is arisen! [38]

And then comes the last great chorus, in whose mingling of many voices we seem to hear the echoes of all the throbbings of the poet's heart and brain through all the stormy years since he had turned away from his childish interest in wild romance, and dedicated himself, in the name of that divine Spirit of Love and Beauty which is "seen nowhere" but "felt everywhere" by such a soul as his, to the service of suffering humanity. Hidden behind the veil of music, all the old ideas and emotions are still present: the dream of life, the riddle of death, the Heaven-sent beauties of nature and art and thought which may find on earth no more than an imperfect and fleeting existence, and the final prayer for peace — all these are pure Shelley; and all are the marks of a deeply religious nature.

> The world's great age begins anew,
> The golden years return,
> The earth doth like a snake renew
> Her winter weeds outworn:
> Heaven smiles, and faiths and empires gleam,
> Like wrecks of a dissolving dream.
>
> . . . .
>
> Oh, write no more the tale of Troy,
> If earth Death's scroll must be!
> Nor mix with Laian rage the joy
> Which dawns upon the free:
> Although a subtler Sphinx renew
> Riddles of death Thebes never knew.
>
> Another Athens shall arise,
> And to remoter time
> Bequeath, like sunset to the skies,
> The splendour of its prime;
> And leave, if nought so bright may live,
> All earth can take or Heaven can give.

[38] Ll. 1050–59.

. . . .
   Oh, cease! must hate and death return?
     Cease! must men kill and die?
   Cease! drain not to its dregs the urn
     Of bitter prophecy.
   The world is weary of the past,
   Oh, might it die or rest at last!

It is a far cry from *Political Justice* and *Queen Mab* to this last stanza. On the other hand, however, the lines are not to be taken as a confession of despair and a plea for extinction, but only as a prayer for peace. If one remembers how even Chaucer, at the end of *Troilus and Criseyde,* turns away with a profound feeling of revulsion from "this world that passeth soone as floures faire," and how Spenser at the close of the *Cantos of Mutabilitie* cries out in passionate longing for "that same time when no more change shall be," one need find no weakness or loss of faith in the words of Shelley, who more than any other English poet was consumed by a sense of the vanity and nothingness of all things earthly. Indeed, the very words *life* and *death* came to have for him a peculiar meaning. Like so many mystics of all ages, he came to feel that what most men call life is really death, and hence that death must be life.[39]

III

But before we advance to a consideration of Shelley's views upon immortality, there are certain general comments to be offered concerning both the pictures that Shelley offers of an earthly paradise and the almost universal critical dispraise that has been heaped upon them. This disapproval rests largely, as I have already suggested, upon the fact that the condition of life that Shelley describes is too spiritualized to appeal to most men. As Santayana says, "an earth really made perfect is hardly distinguishable from a posthumous heaven: so profoundly must everything in it be changed, and so angel-like must everyone in it become. Shelley's earthly paradise, as described in *Prometheus* and *Epipsychidion*, is too festival-like,

[39] This is a distinction rather to be felt than reasoned about, although I shall presently be under the unfortunate necessity of trying to make it intelligible in words. Something like this is the theme of Mr. Kurtz's study, *The Pursuit of Death*. But I do not feel that that work succeeds in making clear the essential features of Shelley's belief. It may be, of course, that in such an attempt success is unattainable.

too much of a mere culmination, not to be fugitive: it cries aloud to be translated into a changeless and metaphysical heaven. . . ." [40]

Now, most persons, of course, feel insulted and angry when it is suggested that they ought to become "angel-like." A scientifically "planned society" in which no person should lack the wherewithal to gratify his desires for sensuous pleasure, or those emotional satisfactions that have their origin solely in the external order, without the need of any attempt to purify and elevate his own nature, such an ideal appears desirable to many. But an ideal of *moral* perfection, to be achieved by triumphing over every base and sensual and selfish impulse, a life in which inward purity is the prerequisite of outer harmony, for this few men or women have any taste, and they hide their dislike by stigmatizing as "Utopian" any such ideal. And such an ideal is Shelley's. Not to adapt oneself to the external world but to become independent of it by enriching and elevating one's own inner life, this is the road to happiness. So the poet addresses Freedom in *The Mask of Anarchy:*

> "Science, Poetry, and Thought
> Are thy lamps; they make the lot
> Of the dwellers in a cot
> So serene, they curse it not." [41]

"The man who has fewest bodily wants approaches nearest to the Divine Nature." [42] "Your physical wants are few, while those of your mind and heart cannot be numbered or described, from their multitude and complication. To secure the gratification of the former, men have made themselves the bond-slaves of each other." [43] Shelley's earthly paradise is only accidentally upon the earth; its true place of existence is in the minds and hearts of men. It is in himself that Prometheus must find his freedom, and not by triumphing over physical suffering only but also, what is far harder, over despair and hatred. The teaching implied in the drama is that every man must do likewise; and in the final stanza the teaching is made explicit: "To suffer, to forgive, to love and bear, to hope," and through all to remain unchanged and inwardly at peace,

---

[40] *Op. cit.*, pp. 167–68. Santayana, of course, is not among those who condemn Shelley for his dreams of perfection.

[41] Stanza lxiii.

[42] *Essay on Christianity*, in Shawcross, p. 112.   [43] *Ibid.*, p. 109.

this is Shelley's heaven.[44] So also in *The Triumph of Life* it is *desire* — for physical pleasure, emotional satisfaction, wealth, fame, achievement, whatever *the world* can give — that makes life a veritable hell. Let man overcome this, and he will find within himself that kingdom of heaven whose coming is preached by so many great religious teachers.[45]

But the very nature of this paradise dooms to defeat the poet's attempt to picture it. Charity, compassion, selfless sympathy with suffering or joy — how make these experiences incarnate in words? How make them live, especially, for those whose actual lives are seldom visited by feelings such as these? No wonder Shelley, who had recognized the profound paradox that "truth cannot be communicated until it is perceived," [46] remarked that " 'Prometheus' was never intended for more than five or six persons." [47]

[44] I remarked above that Shelley declares this way of life to be an end in itself: "These *are* alone Life," etc. It would be more accurate to say that they are the *conditions* of a pure and noble life on earth: as Carlyle says that men can "do without Happiness, and in place thereof find Blessedness." The soul, in overcoming this world, realizes itself in an eternal world.

[45] Cf. Kurtz, *op. cit.*, p. 213. He says with reference to the ending of *Prometheus Unbound*, "Utopia is spiritualized. It becomes in effect a state of mind." I am quite aware that some critics will feel it to be little short of blasphemy to compare Shelley's ideal with Christ's. They believe that Shelley desired only unlimited and irresponsible self-indulgence, that he wished only to be a butterfly flitting eternally from one to another sweet flower of femininity, and diluting passion with "priggish theorizing." "Shelley's Paradise was a place in which passion would be always new and yet always perfectly satisfied, still an appetite, but not subject to the laws of appetite . . . an incongruous mixture of present pleasure of the flesh with imagined delights of the spirit." See Clutton-Brock, *op. cit.*, p. 277. Or again: "The heaven of Shelley's faith is not to be attained by subduing the flesh, not to be won by labor and sacrifice; it is entered simply by submitting to the impulse of the moment, by keeping this impulse free from external circumstances. For this heaven must be on earth." See Brinton, *op. cit.*, p. 178. (To substantiate this view, he quotes *Julian and Maddalo*, "It is our vice [!] That thus enchains us," etc.) I believe this to be the exact opposite of the truth. But I do not see that any argument is possible: the question must be one not of conclusions, but of premises, and the reader must decide for himself. Only, I beg him to read Shelley first.

[46] Shawcross, p. 105.

[47] *Letters*, II, 955. This is something of an exaggeration, but not much. He had written to Ollier while the poem was being printed: "I think, if I may judge by its merits, the 'Prometheus' cannot sell beyond twenty copies" (*ibid.*, p. 766), and he does not mean that there is anything wrong with the *poem!* Keenly as Shelley felt the public neglect of his work, he to the end refused to write according to other ideals than his own, despite the importunities of Mary and the advice of all his friends. *The Cenci* was his only attempt to win popularity, and of this work he never had a high opinion.

It should be said, too, that Shelley was not, as some of his critics imply, one of those idealists who are indifferent to actualities, and scorn all good that stops short of their particular ideal. He never became so absorbed in his dreams of perfection that he ceased to care for the present welfare of human beings. As the philosophers in Plato's *Republic* were at times to be compelled to descend from their rapt contemplation of the Idea of Good in order to serve their less fortunate fellow men, so Shelley always returned, but with unselfish ardor, from the worship of his ideal into the world of men, and there strove to bring about the realization of the visioned good. In *A Philosophical View of Reform*, after asserting the need for having ideals and believing in the possibility of making them real, he continues: "But our present object is with the difficult and unbending realities of actual life, and when we have drawn inspiration from the great object of our hopes it becomes us with patience and resolution to apply ourselves to accommodating our theories to immediate practice." [48] So in the *Hymn to Intellectual Beauty*, he would not be satisfied to live in the mere contemplation of the highest beauty, even if it were possible: he calls "the phantoms of a thousand hours" to bear witness

> that never joy illumed my brow
> Unlinked with hope that thou wouldst free
> This world from its dark slavery . . . [49]

Nor do I see any need for assuming, with some critics, that Shelley is not deeply sincere in pointing the moral of *Alastor* in the Preface to the poem, when he says: "The picture is not barren of instruction to actual men. The Poet's self-centered seclusion was avenged by

[48] Pp. 70–71.

[49] Ll. 68–70. The anecdote told by Leigh Hunt in his Preface to *The Mask of Anarchy* is too good to be omitted: "I remember his coming upon me when I had not seen him for a long time, and after grappling my hands with both his, in his usual fervent manner, sitting down and looking at me very earnestly, with a deep though not melancholy interest in his face. We were sitting in a cottage study, with our knees to the fire, to which we had been getting nearer and nearer in the comfort of finding ourselves together; the pleasure of seeing him was my only feeling at the moment; and the air of domesticity about us was so complete, that I thought he was going to speak of some family matter — either his or my own; when he asked me, at the close of an intensity of pause, what was 'the amount of the National Debt.' " R. Brimley Johnson, *Shelley — Leigh Hunt: How Friendship Made History* (2d ed., London, 1929), p. 79.

the furies of an irresistible passion pursuing him to speedy ruin."
Granting that the Poet is glorified in comparison with "the unforeseeing multitudes" of men, still, his life is clearly represented as a
failure from which springs no future good; and the unqualified
pessimism of the ending of the poem, here as in *The Cenci*, may
be taken to indicate Shelley's disapproval of the moral conduct of
the protagonist. With *Alastor*, moreover, should be compared
Cythna's imprisonment in the cavern after her violation by the
Tyrant. Shelley apparently means it to be a symbol of her selfish
absorption in her own woes, in forgetfulness of mankind. So she
describes her awakening from the trance.

> "My spirit felt again like one of those
>   Like thine, whose fate it is to make the woes
> Of humankind their prey — what was this cave?
>   Its deep foundation no firm purpose knows
> Immutable, resistless, strong to save . . ." [50]

I have already spoken of how the Witch of Atlas, although she
is said to be undisturbed by human ills, nevertheless finds her greatest pleasure in bringing peace and happiness to men. In his most
ethereal visions Shelley never passed beyond hearing of "the terrible cry of human crime for resistance and of human misery for
help," [51] and it never failed to call him back to earth, and to bring
forth a ringing protest. No poet of his age was so closely in touch
with political and social conditions.[52] Hogg's story (repeated by
Medwin) that he never read a newspaper is false on the face of
it, even if the biographer did not contradict himself.[53] The efforts
begun in 1812 with the Irish pamphlets and the *Letter to Lord
Ellenborough* were continued in 1817 with *A Proposal for Putting
Reform to the Vote* and the *Address on the Death of the Princess
Charlotte;* the first a very moderate suggestion as to how to begin
political reform; the second a protest against the legal murder of
three poor and ignorant men on trumped-up charges of treason.
In 1819 he wrote a long letter for the *Examiner* defending the

[50] *The Revolt of Islam*, VII, xxviii.
[51] This phrase is from one of Ruskin's letters.
[52] Leigh Hunt, of course, whose profession was journalism and for whom poetry
was only an avocation, is to be excepted.
[53] Cf. D. F. MacCarthy, *Shelley's Early Life* (London, 1872), pp. 51-52.

printer Carlile, imprisoned for publishing *The Age of Reason;* and
the following year he was working on *A Philosophical View of Reform.*[54] His letters from Italy to his friends in England are full
of comments and questions about political and social conditions in
England and in Europe. In his poetry, *The Mask of Anarchy,
Oedipus Tyrannus, Hellas,* the *Ode to Liberty,* the *Ode to Naples,*
and many shorter poems were directly inspired by current public
affairs. What other English poet has written so much and so well[55]
upon topics of the day, as the "ineffectual angel," the "eternal
child"? Nor is it true, as some would say, that political liberty and
social welfare were to him only fine-sounding phrases and subjects
for verses. His practical charity has already been mentioned, and
it finds an echo in *The Mask of Anarchy,* when the poet asks, "What
art thou, Freedom?" and answers:

> "For the labourer thou art bread,
>   And a comely table spread
>   From his daily labour come
>   In a neat and happy home.
>
> "Thou art clothes, and fire, and food
>   For the trampled multitude —
>   No — in countries that are free
>   Such starvation cannot be
>   As in England now we see." [56]

The same interest in practical things appears in Shelley's letters.
As late as the beginning of 1819, he writes to Peacock, "I consider
poetry very subordinate to moral and political science, and if I were
well, certainly I would aspire to the latter; for I can conceive a great
work, embodying the discoveries of all ages, and harmonizing the
contending creeds by which mankind have been ruled." [57] And if
this seems still a poet's dream, the following letter to Hunt is no
less characteristic. "I fear that in England things will be carried

[54] This was never completed and was not published until 1920. It is significant,
however, that many of the proposed reforms have now been achieved.

[55] *Oedipus Tyrannus; or, Swellfoot the Tyrant* must be admitted to be, for the
most part, rather unpleasant reading. There is no lack of power, but the humor is
so bitter that, for once, Shelley's poetry is not far from disgusting. Of course, it
was a disgusting theme.

[56] Stanzas liv–lv.

[57] *Letters,* II, 660.

violently by the rulers, and they will not have learned to yield in time to the spirit of the age. The great thing to do is to hold the balance between popular impatience and tyrannical obstinacy; to inculcate with fervour both the right of resistance and the duty of forbearance. You know my principles incite me to take all the good I can get in politics, for ever aspiring to something more. I am one of those whom nothing will fully satisfy, but who are ready to be partially satisfied in all that is practicable. We shall see." [58] The last thought is repeated in *A Philosophical View:* "But nothing is more idle than to reject a limited benefit because we cannot without great sacrifices obtain an unlimited one." [59] And a week before his death, he writes to Horace Smith: "England appears to be in a desperate condition, Ireland still worse; and no class of those who subsist on the public labour will be persuaded that *their* claims on it must be diminished. But the government must content itself with less in taxes, the landholder must submit to receive less rent, and the fundholder a diminished interest, or they will all get nothing. I once thought to study these affairs, and write or act in them. I am glad that my good genius said, *refrain* — I see little public virtue, and I foresee that the contest will be one of blood and gold . . ." [60] It can hardly be wished that his genius had commanded otherwise: but it may well be regretted that among the English political leaders of the time there should not have been a few as reasonable in their views and as charitable in their motives as the man whom respectability and reaction hounded out of England, and whom the critical magnanimity of a later generation condescends to recognize only as "the idle singer of an empty day." [61]

But this chapter must not close upon the note of despondency that is struck in the letter just quoted. Seeing clearly all the obstacles in the way of human advance toward virtue and happiness, recognizing that in man's present state the solution of the problem of evil is impossible, Shelley still refuses to abdicate the throne of prophecy which he conceives to be the poet's birthright; and, true

---

[58] *Ibid.*, p. 756 (November, 1819).   [59] Page 77.   [60] *Letters*, II, 983.
[61] For an admirable exposition and appraisal of Shelley's political thought, see H. Buxton Forman's essays in the *Shelley Society Papers:* "The Vicissitudes of *Queen Mab*," "Shelley, 'Peterloo,' and *The Mask of Anarchy*," and "The Hermit of Marlow."

to his ideal, regardless of whether or not it be attainable, does not cease his efforts to inspire mankind with his own passionately cherished vision of a better world. Conceiving of history as a series of cycles of "creation and decay," he sees each succeeding age of intellectual and moral progress advancing beyond the point attained by the preceding civilization, from whose ruins it took its birth.[62] The *Essay on Christianity* closes with this paragraph.

Meanwhile, some benefit has not failed to flow from the imperfect attempts which have been made to erect a system of equal rights to property and power upon the basis of arbitrary institutions. They have undoubtedly, in every case, from the instability of their formation, failed. Still, they constitute a record of those epochs at which a true sense of justice suggested itself to the understandings of men, so that they consented to forego all the cherished delights of luxury, all the habitual gratifications arising out of the possession or the expectation of power, all the superstitions with which the accumulated authority of ages had made them dear and venerable. They are so many trophies erected in the enemy's land, to mark the limits of the victorious progress of truth and justice.[63]

And in *A Defence of Poetry* he exclaims, after describing the fall of the Roman civilization, "But mark how beautiful an order has sprung from the dust and blood of this fierce chaos! how the world, as from a resurrection, balancing itself on the golden wings of knowledge and of hope, has reassumed its yet unwearied flight into the heaven of time." [64] So Cythna had declared her sacrifice and Laon's not to have been in vain:

> "And to long ages shall this hour be known;
> And slowly shall its memory, ever burning,
> Fill this dark night of things with an eternal morning." [65]

[62] The common belief that Shelley lacked any historical sense and, like Godwin, regarded the French Revolution as the real beginning of civilization, is only another of many myths, conceived in ignorance and dedicated to the proposition that all Romantic poets are fools, from which his fame has suffered. Three sentences from *A Defence of Poetry* offer sufficient refutation. "The true poetry of Rome lived in its institutions . . . They are the episodes of that cyclic poem written by Time upon the memories of men. The Past, like an inspired rhapsodist, fills the theater of everlasting generations with their harmonies." See Shawcross, pp. 140–41. Cf. also his statement that "it may be assumed as a maxim that no nation or religion can supersede any other without incorporating into itself a portion of that which it supersedes." *Ibid.*, p. 143.

[63] Shawcross, pp. 116–17.   [64] *Ibid.*, pp. 141–42.

[65] *The Revolt of Islam*, XII, xxix.

And even Rousseau in *The Triumph of Life* can forget his torment
in exclaiming,

> "If I have been extinguished, yet there rise
> A thousand beacons from the spark I bore." [66]

To his last breath, Shelley remained a rebel against the "evil spirit"
which "has dominion in this imperfect world."

* * *

Perhaps some further answer should be made here to those who
condemn Shelley's frequent attempts to picture a perfect existence.
Granted that this ideal of life cannot at present appeal to any
great part of humanity, granted even that it is quite impossible of
realization, who has the right to call it an empty and ignoble illusion? What shall we say to the traditional attitude of half-
contemptuous condescension so perfectly typified in the judgment of
Sir Leslie Stephen that Shelley's ideal world is "so hopelessly dis-
severed from the real, that it can give us no consolation," "existing
all by itself in a transcendental vacuum entirely unrelated to what
we call fact," "a fabric spun of empty phrases"? [67] What, indeed,
but that the critic possesses that "joyous sense of the imperfection
of this life" which is the antithesis of any truly religious attitude?
Shelley's imagined paradises were never near enough to perfection
to satisfy *him;* but they are much too nearly perfect to satisfy most
of his readers. It is not, as Stephen declares, that they have no connection with life: all the qualities and powers that Shelley feels
to be exalting and ennobling elements of human nature are still
present. But the trouble is that all things which he considers ignoble
and degrading, or even only dull and narrow and commonplace,
have been left behind; and among these are many things that many
people are unwilling to sacrifice. "What have we to do with thee?"
— this is always the world's reply to a poet's dream of perfection.
"How weary, stale, flat, and unprofitable" is that ideal life to which
the poet calls us, where everybody is kind and unselfish! What,
sell all we have and give the money to the poor? Trade all our
great possessions in this world, our physical comforts, our not too

[66] Ll. 206–07.
[67] *Op. cit.,* pp. 398, 403.

strenuous mental enjoyments, our pleasure in being patronized by our superiors and of patronizing our inferiors, trade these for an existence where men are equal, unclassed, exempt from awe and worship of the "Goddess of Getting-on"? The man must be mad! Let us tell him that his dream is impossible — as to be sure it is! — and turn away, not sorrowfully but in contempt.

"Now wait a minute!" says our critic. "Don't get so excited. That's the trouble with all you idealists. You want to get to heaven in one jump. Don't you realize that imperfection is a necessary condition of progress toward perfection? The evils of injustice and inequality, of selfishness and pride and all the rest, which you condemn so strongly, are really evils, no doubt, and ought to be condemned. But you must understand that they are not mere accidents, but are in large part, if not wholly, the necessary accompaniments of the present level of growth, or development, or evolution, of man and society; and hence are not to be got rid of so easily as you think. And besides, don't you realize that the real satisfaction of life comes not from achievement but from struggle? You admit yourself that you couldn't be satisfied with the ideal that you set up. So why not come down to earth and be satisfied with living a decent and respectable life, doing the best you can for yourself and the world, and not worrying because other people are doing their best in a different way? Your ideal is unrealizable, to begin with; and if it *could* be realized, you wouldn't be satisfied with it."

Now, this conception of progress, which, we are told, Shelley did not understand, calls for some consideration; as does the very closely related view that would make struggle and not attainment, the process of achieving and not the thing achieved, the real purpose of life — the view, that is, which holds that all values are *moral* values. And first with regard to the view that evil is a necessary part of progress. Clutton-Brock's comment is typical of many. "He always conceived of our imperfection, not as a process of growth, but as something imposed upon us by a malignant external power, upon the fall of which we should all at once become perfect." [68] Miss Scudder likewise says that one of the two main defects of *Prometheus Unbound* is "the entire absence of the modern

[68] *Op. cit.*, p. 85.

scientific conception of Law and Evolution." [69] Now, all such criticisms as these seem to me to depend upon the once (and perhaps
still) common but logically baseless and morally repugnant assumption that evolution and progress are identical, an assumption which,
besides being open to many other objections, leads inevitably to
blind fatalism. If evil is nothing more than the result of a necessary "process of growth" or "imperfect development," then it
neither can nor ought to be opposed. Are Shelley's critics ready to
accept the implications of this position? If not, why do they blame
him for believing that the at least partial removal of evil from
human life is both possible and desirable?

And now for the persons who glorify progress for progress' sake,
and become lyrical at the thought of man's "advance into new
regions of material and spiritual conquest," at the "idea of progressive development," "of continual advance through struggle,"
"of endless growth towards an infinite perfection." [70] The answer
is simply that the idea of mere *progress*, like that of *morality*, is
self-contradictory, and therefore ultimately meaningless; and that
to talk about "endless growth" or "endless development" or "endless progress" is to talk nonsense. For progress is not progress unless
it be toward an end; and moral struggle, likewise, only exists as
the effort to realize an end, with the realization of which the
struggle will necessarily cease. Either one must set up a definite
ideal which it is desirable to realize, or condemn himself (or the
race) to endless progress, which is no progress at all. For *higher*
and *lower*, or *better* and *worse*, with reference to moral values or
spiritual life, mean nothing except in relation to some end which is
(at least, for us at present, although it may, and in fact must, itself
be ultimately transcended in some way that is to us incomprehensible) absolute. The only alternative is endless, and therefore
meaningless, activity. Now, if any person is satisfied with mere
indiscriminate experience; if he is so much in love with this life
as to desire its eternal continuance; if he would desire nothing more

[69] *Op. cit.*, pp. xxxviii–xxxix. Cf. also the essays of Bagehot and Stephen.
[70] All from Miss Scudder, *loc. cit.* One must be grateful to her for stating with
such uncompromising fervor a view which many critics hold. — The last phrase
continues "in the hereafter"; but that is irrelevant, since the same principle must
hold either for the progress of society or of the individual soul.

than "an infinite number of days to live through, an infinite number of dinners to eat, with an infinity of fresh fights and new love affairs, and no end of last rides together" [71] — or, perhaps, an infinite number of books to read through, an infinite number of facts to digest, an infinity of scholarly controversies and theories, and no end of idealistic young poets to be weighed and found wanting in the balance of a worldly self-satisfaction — then certainly he will not care for Shelley's dreams of perfection. But let such a person remember that he thereby shows himself quite insensible to the whole side of human experience that finds expression in religion; and also that he deprives himself of any right whatever to speak of moral values (or, I presume, any other kind). It is one thing to say that Shelley's ideal is unsatisfying, and to try to set up one more adequate; it is another to condemn his ideal *because it is an ideal,* and to call him a fool for desiring to attain perfection. I need not say in which category the greater number of his adverse critics belong. It is quite comprehensible that many persons should have a love of imperfection, and should desire to dwell with it for all eternity. But while one may look with envy upon those who can hold so vigorous and virile a philosophy, one may also wish that they might be sufficiently magnanimous to make allowance for their weaker-minded brothers who are humble enough to desire nothing more than perfection.[72]

[71] As Santayana unkindly says of Browning (*Interpretations of Poetry and Religion,* p. 204).

[72] For a full discussion of the principle upon which the argument of this paragraph is based, see the last chapter of F. H. Bradley's *Ethical Studies,* and Chapter XXV of his *Appearance and Reality.*

CHAPTER VI

LIFE, DEATH, AND ETERNITY

I

YET, DESPITE the fact that his hopes of a happier life on earth never entirely vanished, it seems clear that Shelley could never have been satisfied with any "religion of humanity." If in *Peter Bell the Third* he classes himself among "some few" who are "damned"

> To believe their minds are given
> To make this ugly Hell a Heaven;
> In which faith they live and die. . . .[1]

yet in the Dedication of that poem he speaks with obvious bitterness of Wordsworth's declaration that man must find happiness on earth or not at all. And in a letter to John Gisborne written but a short time before his death he returns to the attack with a violence that is very rare in his later writings.

I have been reading over and over again "Faust," and always with sensations which no other composition excites. It deepens the gloom and augments the rapidity of ideas, and would therefore seem to me an unfit study for any person who is a prey to the reproaches of memory, and the delusions of an imagination not to be restrained. And yet the pleasure of sympathizing with emotions known only to few, although they derive their sole charm from despair, and the scorn of the narrow good we can attain in our present state, seems more than to ease the pain that belongs to them. Perhaps all discontent with the *less* (to use a Platonic sophism) supposes the sense of a just claim to the *greater*, and that we admirers of "Faust" are on the right road to Paradise. Such a supposition is not more absurd, and is certainly less demoniacal, than that of Wordsworth, where he says —

> "This earth,
> Which is the world of all of us, and where
> *We find our happiness, or not at all.*"

[1] III, xx.

As if, after sixty years' suffering here, we were to be roasted alive for sixty million more in hell, or charitably annihilated by a *coup de grace* of the bungler who brought us into existence at first![2]

These are strong words, yet they express an attitude that seems to' have been almost habitual during his last years: that life on earth, in and for itself, is not worth living. We meet in his writings precisely the mixture of despair and faith that finds expression in the cry of Paul: "If in this life only we have hope in Christ, we are of all men most miserable."[3] If there has never been a poet who strove more earnestly than Shelley to bring about a heaven on earth, there has likewise been none more constantly preoccupied with the problem of the immortality of the soul.

Let me say at once, however, that I can find little evidence that Shelley ever believed (at least, after the *Zastrozzi* and *St. Irvyne* days) in what I suppose to be commonly meant by the expression "personal immortality"; that is, that the individual soul will continue to exist after death, presumably in some hypostatic world and perhaps united to some sort of glorified body, in a state in which it will be conscious of its own identity, will remember its former existence on earth, and will think and feel in essentially the same manner as before, except that what was previously unpleasant in thought and feeling will be miraculously absent.[4] Such a belief would be completely out of harmony with his characteristic manner

[2] *Letters*, II, 953–54. The actual reading of the original of Shelley's quotation (from *The Prelude*, XI, ll. 140–44) is

Not in Utopia, — subterranean fields, —
Or some secreted island, Heaven knows where,
But in the very world, which is the world
Of all of us, — the place where, in the end,
We find our happiness or not at all.

Perhaps Shelley had forgotten the context, for these lines are part of a passage describing Wordsworth's early enthusiasm for the ideals of the French Revolution — exactly the same ideals that Shelley had been bent on glorifying in *Queen Mab*. On the other hand, he had by 1821 come to despise, almost as much as he had once admired, the materialistic philosophy which preceded and accompanied the Revolution.

[3] I Corinthians 15:19.

[4] This is rather a blunt statement of the matter. Yet if we try to form a definite conception of a "personal" future life, must it not be in similar terms? And, on the other hand, if we believe in a future life which cannot be adequately conceived by us at present, then it seems that the adjective *personal* can hardly apply to it without considerable qualification.

of thought and feeling. If life on earth is ultimately unsatisfying, and is so because of what *we are* (for this seems to be Shelley's belief), will a life in which we continue to be essentially as we are be any more satisfying, even though it be transplanted to some transcendental world? And if we become essentially other than we now are, have we a right to call such an existence personal? If in our present state the solution of the riddle of evil by which we are tormented is unattainable by us, will it be attainable by *us* in *any* state? And in the state in which such a solution is attainable (and Shelley asserts, it will be remembered, that a solution certainly is possible), shall not *we* necessarily have ceased to exist? That is, a "personal immortality" will still leave the self in a limited, and therefore imperfect, and therefore (to Shelley, at least) unsatisfying state, and it seems that with the attainment of perfection (which, as Godwin says, we cannot conceive), the existence of the self, as such, will cease.

So much by way of preface. And now, proceeding to an examination of Shelley's writings, we find, curiously enough, that it is precisely during the years when the youthful thinker seems to be inclining most strongly toward materialism that he believes most confidently in some sort of immortality of the soul. The first utterances are, to be sure, rather indefinite as to both these points. At the beginning of 1811 he writes to Hogg declaring his belief "that some vast intellect animates infinity," and he adds, "If we disbelieve *this*, the strongest argument in support of the existence of a future state instantly becomes annihilated." [5] The question arises again in a letter written to the same friend four months later, asking advice as to the proper attitude toward his "little friend Harriet Westbrook." "It is, perhaps, scarcely doing her a kindness — it is, perhaps, inducing positive unhappiness — to point out to her a road which leads to perfection, the attainment of which, perhaps, does not repay the difficulties of the progress. What do you think of this? If trains of thought, development of mental energies influence in any degree a future state; if this is *even* possible—if it stands on *at all* securer ground than mere hypothesis; then is it not

[5] *Letters*, I, 29.

a service?" [6] A little later, in an epistolary discussion of the problem with his strangely eager correspondent, Elizabeth Hitchener, he shows himself more confident of "the eternal existence of Intellect," and concludes a long argument thus: "How contrary then to all analogy to infer annihilation from Death, which you cannot prove suspends for a moment the force of mind. This is not hypothesis, this is not assumption, at least, I am not aware of the admission of either." [7] A few months later he declares himself to be quite convinced, despite the difficulties which reason would advance. "I have considered it in every possible light; and reason tells me that death is the boundary of the life of man, yet I feel, I believe the direct contrary. . . . The senses are the only inlets of knowledge, and there is an inward sense that has persuaded me of this." [8]

Toward the end of 1811, however, the question seems still to be unsettled; for, contrasting the world's conception of love with his own, he declares: "The one perishes with the body whence on earth it never dares to soar, the other lives with the soul which was the exclusive object of its homage. Oh if this last be but true. You talk of a future state: 'is not this imagination,' you ask, 'a proof of it?' To me it appears so: to me everything proves it. But what we earnestly desire we are very much prejudiced in favor of." [9] And he launches into another maze of argument and suggestion. Three weeks later his enthusiasm is still growing. "Every day makes me feel more keenly that our being is eternal. Every day brings the conviction how futile, how inadequate are all reasonings to demonstrate it. Yet are we — are these souls which measure in their circumscribed domain the distance of yon orbs — are we but bubbles which arise from the filth of a stagnant pool, merely to be again re-absorbed into the mass of its corruption? I think not: I feel not. Can *you prove* it? Yet the eternity of man has *ever* been believed.

[6] *Ibid.*, pp. 57–58. Here again pious critics may shake their heads and opine that Shelley's fears were only too well founded. But as a matter of fact, Shelley's teachings had not the slightest effect on Harriet. Otherwise, there might never have been any need of the unhappy separation that later came to pass. It was the fact that Harriet was *not* influenced by her husband, but remained a commonplace girl entirely uninterested in proposed roads to perfection, that made the separation inevitable.

[7] *Ibid.*, p. 107.   [8] *Ibid.*, p. 142.
[9] *Ibid.*, pp. 173–74 (November 24).

. . . all religions have taken it for their foundation." [10] At the beginning of 1812 the Irish expedition fills a larger and larger place in his thoughts, and immortality is relegated to postscripts such as the following: "I find you begin to doubt the eternity of the soul: I do not. — More of that hereafter." [11] "You have said no more of the immortality of the soul. Do you not believe it? I do; but I cannot tell you why in a letter — at least not clearly. You will want some feelings which are to me cogent and resistless arguments. Do not consider it a gloomy subject: do not think me prejudiced. We *will* reason and abide by the result. I shall get Godwin's opinion of this if I can." [12]

At this point the problem of immortality seems temporarily to have got lost in the press of Shelley's affairs. But if it vanished from his letters, it remained in his thoughts, and presently made its appearance in poetry. A blank verse poem dated 1812 and entitled *To Harriet* begins with the lines

> It is not blasphemy to hope that Heaven
> More perfectly will give those nameless joys
> Which throb within the pulses of the blood
> And sweeten all that bitterness which Earth
> Infuses in the heaven-born soul.

And later the youthful enthusiast exclaims with an ironic lack of prescience,

> Harriet! let death all mortal ties dissolve,
> But ours shall not be mortal! [13]

[10] *Ibid.*, pp. 191–92. This position is in some points similar to the more sober statement in the notes to *Hellas* ten years later. In the same letter we find this boy of nineteen referring to his plan to liberate the Irish! We also find what appears to be an allusion to *Queen Mab:* "I have now . . . in contemplation a poem. I intend it to be by anticipation a picture of the manners, simplicity, and delights of a perfect state of society, tho' still earthly. . . . After, I shall draw a picture of Heaven." As I have already suggested, the two purposes seem to have become confused.

[11] *Ibid.*, p. 217.

[12] *Ibid.*, p. 232. *Want* in the third sentence means, of course, "to be wanting in." The letter proper closes with "Yours beyond this being, *Most imperishably,* P. B. S."! A few months before (October 10, 1811) he seems to have been less confident, ending "With, I hope, eternal love, Your Percy Shelley"! — which suggests an epitaph which I once read in an old New England graveyard: "Our beloved brother. Our loss we hope is your gain."

[13] Ll. 24–25. This poem is usually printed among the Juvenilia.

At the end of *Queen Mab,* also, after his long attacks on social abuses, his fierce denunciation of religion, and his picture of a regenerate earth, he must look beyond "birth and life and death"; and Queen Mab tells Ianthe unequivocally:

> "Death is a gate of dreariness and gloom
> That leads to azure isles and beaming skies
> And happy regions of eternal hope." [14]

And she asks, as if there could be but one answer,

> "Are there not hopes within thee, which this scene
> Of linked and gradual being has confirmed?" [15]

II

Here the question seems settled. But the problem of immortality was like many another which Shelley in youth believed that he had solved, only to conclude, after years of thought, that it was insoluble. And in this instance his doubts, if they had ever entirely disappeared, were not long in returning. It is impossible, however, to trace the course of his changing views, since between 1812 and 1815 he did little formal writing. *A Refutation of Deism,* the most ambitious effort, contains nothing upon the subject of immortality. Nor are his letters more fruitful.

But by 1815, at least, the optimism of the close of *Queen Mab* has vanished utterly. Except for *The Cenci, Alastor* stands alone among the longer poems which Shelley completed, in that it ends on a note of unmingled sadness, without any sort of consoling hope for the future. The life of the hero has been only "a dream Of youth, which night and time have quenched forever," [16] and which remains to those behind only a mournful memory.

> It is a woe too "deep for tears," when all
> Is reft at once, when some surpassing Spirit,
> Whose light adorned the world around it, leaves
> Those who remain behind, not sobs or groans,
> The passionate tumult of a clinging hope;
> But pale despair and cold tranquillity,
> Nature's vast frame, the web of human things,
> Birth and the grave, that are not as they were. [17]

[14] IX, ll. 161–63.   [15] IX, ll. 180–81.
[16] Ll. 669–70.   [17] Ll. 713–20.

And previously he has suggested that we believe in immortality only because we desire it; that

> the human heart,
> Gazing in dreams over the gloomy grave,
> Sees its own treacherous likeness there.[18]

The somber and profound mystery of death broods over the whole poem, and inspires some of its finest passages.

> O stream!
> Whose source is inacessibly profound,
> Whither do thy mysterious waters tend?
> Thou imagest my life. Thy darksome stillness,
> Thy dazzling waves, thy loud and hollow gulfs,
> Thy searchless fountain, and invisible course
> Have each their type in me: and the wide sky,
> And measureless ocean may declare as soon
> What oozy cavern or what wandering cloud
> Contains thy waters, as the universe
> Tell where these living thoughts reside, when stretched
> Upon thy flowers my bloodless limbs shall waste
> I' the passing wind! [19]

A like mood animates the essay *On a Future State,* probably written in the same year, where Shelley gives poignant expression to what he declares to be the common feeling in the face of death: "When you can discover where the fresh colors of the faded flower abide, or the music of the broken lyre, seek life among the dead." [20] And philosophy, he contends, leads to the same conclusion. "All that we see or know perishes and is changed. Life and thought differ indeed from everything else. But that it survives that period, beyond which we have no experience of its existence, such distinction and dissimilarity affords no shadow of proof, and nothing but our own desires could have led us to conjecture or imagine." [21] Moreover, we know of no existence prior to our birth, and "if there are no reasons to suppose that we have existed before that period at which our existence apparently commences, then there are no grounds for supposition that we shall continue to exist after our existence has apparently ceased. So far as thought and life is concerned, the

[18] Ll. 472–74.   [19] Ll. 502–14.
[20] Shawcross, p. 60.   [21] *Ibid.,* p. 62.

same will take place with regard to us, individually considered, after death, as had taken place before our birth." [22]

This is a question, however, upon which Shelley never dogmatizes. If in the passage just quoted he argues from the fact of our ignorance, that a future existence is improbable, he recognizes, in the essay *On the Punishment of Death*, that the same fact, considered with reference to different premisses, may point to an opposite conclusion.[23] The whole problem, however — and this is his position to the end — lies, as Mrs. Shelley suggests, outside the limits of rational investigation. "The philosopher is unable to determine whether our existence in a previous state has affected our present condition, and abstains from deciding whether our present

[22] *Ibid.*, p. 63. Mrs. Shelley says of this essay that in it Shelley "gives us only that view of a future state which is to be derived from reasoning and analogy. It is not to be supposed that a mind so full of vast ideas concerning the universe, endowed with such subtle discrimination with regard to the various modes in which this does or may appear to our eyes, with a lively fancy and ardent and expansive feelings, should be content with a mere logical view of that which even in religion is a mystery and a wonder." Preface to *Essays, Letters from Abroad*, etc., in *Complete Works*, V, x. Notwithstanding Mrs. Shelley's obvious desire to conciliate the upholders of orthodoxy and propriety, one may readily admit the general truth of the contention which seems to underlie this statement: that the ideas presented in this essay do not adequately represent Shelley's mature opinion. On the other hand, it is not true that he takes "a mere logical view" of the question; and it seems clear, from passages of his poetry which I shall presently quote, that the doubts expressed in this essay were very deeply rooted in Shelley's thought. In the same place, Mrs. Shelley quotes from a journal of her husband "with regard to a danger we incurred together at sea [probably on the occasion of their elopement in July, 1814]: — 'I had time in that moment to reflect and even to reason on death; it was rather a thing of discomfort and disappointment than of terror to me. We should never be separated; but in death we might not know and feel our union as now. I hope — but my hopes are not unmixed with fear for what will befall this inestimable spirit when we appear to die.'"

[23] "That that within us which thinks and feels, continues to think and feel after the dissolution of the body, has been the almost universal opinion of mankind, and the accurate philosophy of what I may be permitted to term the modern Academy, by showing the prodigious depth and extent of our ignorance respecting the causes and nature of sensation, renders probable the affirmative of a proposition, the negative of which it is so difficult to conceive, and the popular arguments against which, derived from what is called the atomic system, are proved to be applicable only to the relation which one object bears to another, as apprehended by the mind, and not to existence itself, or the nature of that essence which is the medium and receptacle of objects." See Shawcross, p. 46. This sentence is rather obscure, but the general thought is clear: that it is presumptuous for reason to deny the probability of some sort of future existence. The "modern Academy" I take to refer chiefly to Locke, Berkeley, Hume, and Sir William Drummond. With this passage compare the stanza from *The Revolt of Islam* (IX, xxxiii) quoted in Chapter III above.

condition will affect us in that which may be future. That, if we continue to exist, the manner of our existence will be such as no inferences nor conjectures, afforded by a consideration of our earthly experience, can elucidate, is sufficiently obvious." [24] The same thought is the theme of the poem *On Death*, published in 1815.[25] The motto is from Ecclesiastes: "There is no work, nor device, nor knowledge, nor wisdom, in the grave, whither thou goest." But the poem itself is not so definite in its denial of hope; it is simply a great question mark. The "flame of life" is only the "meteor beam of a starless night." And "this world," however insubstantial, is "the nurse of all we know" and "the mother of all we feel"; and at death,

> all that we know, or feel, or see
> Shall pass like an unreal mystery.

There may be another existence; but

> Who telleth a tale of unspeaking death?
>   Who lifteth the veil of what is to come?
> Who painteth the shadows that are beneath
>   The wide-winding caves of the peopled tomb?
> Or uniteth the hopes of what shall be
> With the fears and the love for that which we see?

If the poet has hopes of a better life, they are only like the innocent imaginings of a child.

> Here could I hope, like some inquiring child
> Sporting on graves, that death did hide from human sight
> Sweet secrets, or beside its breathless sleep
> That loveliest dreams perpetual watch did keep.[26]

> Whether the dead find, oh, not sleep! but rest,
> And are the uncomplaining things they seem,
> Or live, or drop in the deep sea of Love; — [27]

he does not pretend to know.

[24] *Ibid.*, p. 47. The last sentence I take to mean, not that a future state will necessarily be altogether different from the present one, but simply that we can know nothing about it.

[25] "These stanzas occur in the Esdaile MS. along with others which Shelley intended to print with *Queen Mab* in 1813; but the text was revised before publication in 1816." (Hutchinson's note.)

[26] *A Summer Evening Churchyard* (composed in September, 1815), ll. 27–30.

[27] *The Sunset*, ll. 47–49.

Nor does this view of Shelley's ever really change: we can have
no *knowledge* of what lies on the other side of death, or at least
not the knowledge that is derived from reasoning and demonstration. And sometimes the poet doubts whether anything is there at
all. So Cythna, taking, as she thinks, a final leave of Laon, has
no hope of personal survival to offer in consolation.

> "We part to meet again — but yon blue waste,
>   Yon desert wide and deep holds no recess,
> Within whose happy silence, thus embraced
>   We might survive all ills in one caress:
>   Nor doth the grave — I fear 'tis passionless —
> Nor yon cold vacant Heaven: — we meet again
>   Within the minds of men . . ." [28]

Still, when Laon thinks her dead, he does not wholly despair,
although he can console himself only with a question.

> What then was I? She slumbered with the dead.
>   Glory and joy and peace, had come and gone.
> Doth the cloud perish, when the beams are fled
>   Which steeped its skirts in gold? or, dark and lone,
>   Doth it not through the paths of night unknown,
> On outspread wings of its own wind upborne
>   Pour rain upon the earth? [29]

But in the *Lines Written among the Euganean Hills*, the poet
returns to the darker side of the picture.

> What, if there no friends will greet;
> What, if there no heart will meet
> His with love's impatient beat;
> Wander wheresoe'er he may,
> Can he dream before that day
> To find refuge from distress
> In friendship's smile, in love's caress?
> Then 'twill wreak him little woe
> Whether such be there or no:
> Senseless is the breast, and cold,
> Which relenting love would fold;
> Bloodless are the veins and chill
> Which the pulse of pain did fill [30]

[28] *The Revolt of Islam*, II, xlviii.
[29] *Ibid.*, IV, xxxi.
[30] *Lines Written among the Euganean Hills*, ll. 27–39. (1818.)

But a mood so definitely pessimistic — if, indeed, it be pessimism to believe that death means extinction, when life is little else than pain — is not usual with Shelley. His view more often is simply that the lands that lie beyond the sea of life can never be explored by the human mind.

> We, the weak mariners of that wide lake
> Where'er its shores extend or billows roll,
>   Our course unpiloted and starless make
> O'er its wild surface to an unknown goal . . .[31]

And in the strange poem *A Vision of the Sea,* the woman cries,

> Alas! what is life, what is death, what are we,
> That when the ship sinks we no longer may be?[32]

In a sonnet written in 1820, his opinion is the same.

> Ye hasten to the grave! What seek ye there,
> Ye restless thoughts and busy purposes
> Of the idle brain, which the world's livery wear?
> O thou quick heart, which panteth to possess
> All that pale Expectation feigneth fair!
> Thou vainly curious mind which wouldest guess
> Whence thou didst come and whither thou must go,
> And all that never yet was known would know —
> Oh, whither hasten ye, that thus ye press
> With such swift feet life's green and pleasant path,
> Seeking, alike from happiness and woe,
> A refuge in the cavern of gray death?
> O heart, and mind, and thoughts! what thing do you
> Hope to inherit in the grave below?

This fits in perfectly with what he told Trelawny in answer to the question, "Do you believe in the immortality of the spirit?" "Certainly not; how can I? We know nothing; we have no evidence; we cannot express our inmost thoughts. They are incomprehensible even to ourselves."[33]

But such utterances as these, although they cannot be ignored,

---

[31] *The Witch of Atlas,* lxiii. (1820.)   [32] Ll. 82–83.

[33] *Records,* 62. Perhaps this is the place to quote, letting the reader attribute to it whatever measure of significance he may think fit, the following passage from a letter to Trelawny, dated June 18, 1822. "You, of course, enter into society at Leghorn: should you meet with any scientific person, capable of preparing the *Prussic acid, or essential oil of bitter almonds,* I should regard it as a great kindness if you could procure me a small quantity. . . . I would give any price for this medicine; you remember we talked of it the other night, and we both expressed a

must not be taken to express the whole of Shelley's thought and feeling in regard to immortality. The very fact that he expresses so often the opinion that "we know nothing" shows how difficult it was for him to be satisfied with that answer. The sonnet just quoted, indeed, seems to be addressed to himself — for whose "restless thoughts and busy purposes" so much inclined as his to "hasten to the grave"? — in recognition of his unconquerable longing to learn the meaning of death. Moreover, beside Trelawny's testimony we must put that of Medwin and Byron. Medwin, in relating his success in alleviating Shelley's physical sufferings by the use of mesmerism, records that the poet characteristically raised the question whether the phenomenon supported materialism or immaterialism. "Shelley thought the latter — 'that a separation from the mind and body took place — the one being most active and the other an inert mass of matter.' He deduced from this phenomenon an additional argument for the immortality of the soul, of which no man was more fully persuaded." [34] Byron's comment is briefer, but perhaps sounder, evidence. In a letter to Moore, referring to the latter's mention of Shelley as "an annihilating infidel," he writes, "Shelley believes in immortality, however — but this by the way." [35]

This apparent inconsistency, I think, can be easily removed. The philosopher, Shelley holds, can have little to say either as to whether there is a future existence or as to what the nature of that existence must be; but the poet is bound by no such restrictions. To reason about the matter is futile; but man has a right to hope and to imagine; to a certain extent he is justified in trusting his feelings, even though these defy the pronouncements of the rational faculty. Even in his most rationalistic years he had recognized the claims of other powers than reason. In 1811 we find him assuring Miss Hitchener, "But you do right to indulge feeling where it does not militate with reason: I wish I could too." [36] And later he writes

wish to possess it; my wish was serious, and sprung from the desire of avoiding needless suffering. I need not tell you I have no intention of suicide at present, but I confess it would be a comfort to me to hold in my possession that golden key to the chamber of perpetual rest." *Letters*, II, 980.

[34] *Life of Shelley*, p. 270.   [35] *Letters and Journals*, VI, 35.

[36] *Letters*, I, 122. One cannot help remarking, without any implied censure of Shelley, that this wish seems somewhat gratuitous.

to her in regard to the existence of God: "But it does not prove the non-existence of a thing that it is not discoverable by reason: *feeling* here affords us sufficient proof. I pity those who have not this demonstration, tho' I can scarcely believe that such exist. Those who *really feel* the being of a God, have the best right to believe it." [37]

This principle, as we have seen, he was willing at that time to apply to the problem of immortality. And if his doubts about a future existence soon became stronger, so also did his distrust of the claims of reason; and when, in 1821, he wrote *A Defence of Poetry*, he had become so sensible of the limitations of purely rational processes as to speak of them with definite contempt. Hence, he feels himself at liberty, while admitting that "Sense and Reason . . . would bid the heart That gazed beyond the wormy grave despair," [38] both to believe in some sort of immortality (as I think he certainly did) and to speculate concerning its nature. If man feels that there is some power or principle within him that is not doomed to extinction, there is no reason, Shelley would have said, why that feeling should be an object of distrust. And of such a feeling, or intuition, he himself is constantly aware. He declares in the essay *On Life* that "man is a being of high aspirations, 'looking both before and after,' whose 'thoughts wander through eternity,' disclaiming alliance with transience and decay; incapable of imagining to himself annihilation; existing but in the future and the past; being, not what he is, but what he has been and shall be. Whatever may be his true and final destination, there is a spirit within him at enmity wih nothingness and dissolution." [39] And the same sentiment, asserted less buoyantly, it is true, but with the serene assurance of self-mastery that sets the mark of a great mind and a noble nature on almost all his later letters,[40] is ex-

---

[37] *Ibid.*, p. 150. He continues, in seeming contradiction of the second sentence quoted: "They may, indeed, pity those who do not; they may pity *me*, but *until* I feel it I must be content with the substitute, Reason."

[38] *The Revolt of Islam*, IX, xxxii.   [39] Shawcross, p. 54.

[40] The contrast between the letters and the lyrics during the year and a half preceding the poet's death is startling. The former, despite an undercurrent of sadness, are remarkable for evenness of temper and constancy of purpose; the latter, with some exceptions, show an utter self-abandonment to despondency, and appear to be the record of continual and almost unendurable loneliness, disillusion, despair, and weariness of spirit. I can offer no complete explanation, and, indeed, there seems

pressed to Horace Smith a few days before his death. "Let us see the truth, whatever that may be. The destiny of man can scarcely be so degraded, that he was born only to die; and if such should be the case, delusions, especially the gross and preposterous ones of the existing religion, can scarcely be supposed to exalt it." [41]

But to clutch at delusions is not the same as to cherish hopes, or to imagine some purer and nobler state of being to which our present perception and adoration of what is good and beautiful may point the way. In this spirit Shelley lets himself dwell on the conception of immortality that is found in the teachings of Christ, while committing himself neither to its acceptance nor to its rejection.

It appears that we moulder to a heap of senseless dust; to a few worms, that arise and perish, like ourselves. Jesus Christ asserts that these appearances are fallacious, and that a gloomy and cold imagination alone suggests the conception that thought can cease to be. Another and a more extensive state of being, rather than the complete extinction of being, will follow from that mysterious change which we call Death. There shall be no misery, no pain, no fear. The empire of evil spirits extends not beyond the boundaries of the grave. The unobscured irradiations from the fountain-fire of all goodness shall reveal all that is mysterious and unintelligible, until the mutual communications of knowledge and of happiness throughout all thinking natures constitute a harmony of good that ever varies and never ends.[42]

---

to me something mysterious and unaccountable in the depth of his depression. But I insist that it is unfair to judge him by the lyrics alone. A comparison of these with his letters and, to some extent, his longer poems, must lead to the conclusion that the lyrics bear witness only to passing moments of weakness, and that in giving expression to the emotion of these moments, the poet is not yielding to it but triumphing over it. Cf. the comment of Thornton Hunt, who, seeing Shelley for the first time in four years, immediately before the poet's death, was impressed by "the air of strength and cheerfulness which I noticed in his voice and manner." *Shelley and Keats as They Struck Their Contemporaries*, edited by Edmund Blunden (London, 1925), p. 26. The article by Hunt, "Shelley as I Knew Him," appeared first in the *Atlantic Monthly*, February, 1863.

[41] *Letters*, II, 983.

[42] *Essay on Christianity*, in Shawcross, pp. 95–96. With this passage should be contrasted Shelley's statement, near the end of the fragment, of the reason for the downfall of the communistic social system established by the first Christians: that unscrupulous demagogues "silenced the voice of the moral sense among them by engaging them to attend, not so much to the cultivation of a virtuous and happy life in this mortal scene, as to the attainment of a fortunate condition after death; not so much to the consideration of those means by which the state of man is adorned and improved, as an inquiry into the secrets of the connection between God and the world — things which, they well knew, were not to be explained, or even to be conceived." *Ibid.*, p. 116. These apparently contradictory sentiments are only

In a note to *Hellas*, likewise, after presenting a theory of reincarnation, he defends himself, on the ground that "it is the province of the poet to attach himself to those ideas which exalt and ennoble humanity," for having "conjectured the condition of that futurity towards which we are all impelled by an inextinguishable thirst for immortality." And he adds, still unwilling either to dogmatize or to surrender his hope, "Until better arguments can be produced than sophisms which disgrace the cause, this desire itself must remain the strongest and the only presumption that eternity is the inheritance of every thinking being."

III

But Shelley is not content with speculating merely as to *whether* the soul is immortal; he is continually driven, as it seems, to try to imagine (although at times he pronounces such imaginings to be futile) *what* the nature of that immortality is to which man feels himself to be the heir. Nothing is more characteristic of Shelley's poetry than the constant recurrence of his dreams and hopes of another life than this.

He saw at once that the question of a future existence naturally suggests that of a past existence. He seems, indeed, to have been almost as much interested in the latter as in the former. Hogg tells of occasions during the Oxford days when Shelley "discoursed of souls . . . — of a future state — and especially of a former state — of pre-existence, obscured for a time through the suspension of consciousness — of personal identity, and also of ethical philosophy, in a deep and earnest tone of elevated morality."[43] It is easy to imagine, even without Hogg's testimony, with what enthusiasm he must have greeted the theories about such subjects which Plato sets forth in the *Meno*, the *Phaedo*, the *Phaedrus*, and the tenth book of *The Republic*; "he was vehemently excited by the striking doctrines which Socrates unfolds, especially that which teaches that all our knowledge comes from reminiscences of what we have learned in a former existence."[44] He even, if we may trust this wit-

another aspect of the difficulty mentioned at the end of Chapter IV, which is involved in all religious experience, of harmonizing the claims on the one hand of what is mortal and earthly, and on the other, of what is eternal and divine.

[43] *Life*, p. 51.   [44] *Ibid.*, p. 72.

ness, would sometimes go so far as to desert the doctrine of his idolized Locke, that all knowledge comes ultimately from sensations, for the Platonic theory of reminiscence, which he loved to uphold "in strenuous and protracted disputation." [45] There is also the familiar and delightful story of his earnest interrogation of the infant in the perambulator as to the conditions of its previous life, which, he maintained, it could scarcely be supposed to have forgotten, being but a few weeks old.

Shelley's poems and letters both bear witness to the interest which Hogg so vividly describes. Not only in the first but in the last two of his major poems he dwells upon the thought of some kind of pre-existence. As in *Queen Mab* he speaks of "that strange state Before the naked soul has found its home," [46] so in *Hellas* Ahasuerus instructs Mahmud how he may learn of his destiny by communing with

> That portion of thyself which was ere thou
> Didst start for this brief race whose crown is death . . . [47]

And Rousseau, also, in *The Triumph of Life*, telling of the sweet sleep from which he awoke to bitter earthly existence, adds:

> "And whether life had been before that sleep
> The Heaven which I imagine, or a Hell
>
> Like this harsh world in which I wake to weep,
> I know not." [48]

Exactly the same thought had appeared in *Prince Athanase* long before, where the poet recounts the wonder of the hero's friends at his mysterious sadness and tells how some believed

[45] *Ibid.*, p. 148.

[46] IX, ll. 149–50. In *The Daemon of the World* (ll. 533–34) this passage is changed to
> Before the naked powers that thro' the world
> Wander like winds have found a human home.

[47] Ll. 855–56. The world from which Mahmud calls the Phantom of himself is very strikingly described (ll. 879–88), and is apparently the same as that in *Prometheus Unbound* (I, ll. 195–209), which is pictured even more powerfully. But I am quite unable to connect this conception with any other of Shelley's speculations, or to fit it into either his metaphysical theories or his views on immortality. For an interesting discussion of possible sources and meanings of the passage in *Prometheus*, see Carl H. Grabo, *Prometheus Unbound : An Interpretation* (University of North Carolina Press, 1935), pp. 22–28.

[48] Ll. 332–35.

> That memories of an antenatal life
> Made this, where now he dwelt, a penal hell . . .[49]

In *Prometheus*, likewise, Shelley indulges the fancy (it is here probably no more, although it is always dangerous to call anything in Shelley a "mere fancy") that the Heaven of his hopes exists before birth rather than after death. Thus Asia sings of her mystic voyage with Panthea:

> We have passed Age's icy caves,
> And Manhood's dark and tossing waves,
> And Youth's smooth ocean, smiling to betray:
> Beyond the glassy gulfs we flee
> Of shadow-peopled Infancy,
> Through Death and Birth, to a diviner day . . .[50]

In Shelley's letters the most significant references to the idea of pre-existence have their origin, after the manner of the *Phaedrus*, in thoughts about the nature and powers of love. In a letter written to Miss Hitchener at the height of his admiration for the ideal being with which he had confused her, he asks, "Might there not have been a prior state of existence? might we not have been friends then? The creation of soul at birth is a thing I do not like. Where we have no premisses, we can therefore draw no conclusions. It *may* be all vanity; but I cannot think so." [51] Ten years later, his youthful enthusiasm gone, he remarks sadly in a letter to John Gisborne, "Some of us have, in a prior existence, been in love with

[49] Ll. 91–92.

[50] II, v, ll. 98–103. It is to be noted that no period of human life is regarded as happy. With regard to the sequence of Death and Birth, I take it that Shelley is simply being consistent in speaking of a backward course, in which the moment of what we call birth would really be death, and the moment of death for the soul passing forward from a previous life would be that of *birth* for the soul moving backward. Possibly the origin of this curious conception is the myth in Plato's dialogue *The Statesman* (§ 270, 271). Cf. E. M. W. Tillyard, "Shelley's *Prometheus Unbound* and Plato's *Statesman*," *Times Literary Supplement*, September 29, 1932, p. 691. To his statement that the passage is "meaningless without reference" to Plato's myth, however, Mr. George Sampson properly retorts "(1) that we are entitled to read an English poem as an English poem, and (2) that the extent to which an English poem is inexplicable save by reference to a recondite source in another language is the extent to which it fails as an English poem." He suggests that the thought is essentially the same as that in Wordsworth's *Intimations of Immortality*. *Ibid.*, October 20, 1932, p. 762.

[51] *Letters*, I, 178 (November 26, 1811).

an Antigone, and that makes us find no full content in any mortal tie." [52]

But we think of Shelley, and rightly, as the poet not of the past but of the future. And the doctrine of pre-existence, after all, offers only a possible poetic explanation of some of life's mysteries; the solution of the Great Mystery lies ahead. But if we suppose that we have lived before, we are naturally led to suppose also that we shall live again; and thus we arrive at the doctrine of reincarnation, which was so dear to the imagination of Plato, and which Shelley seriously presents in *Hellas* as a theory that may be reasonably supposed to approximate the necessarily unknown facts concerning the life of the soul. The doctrine had, however, been familiar to him from the days of his youth. It seems to be confusedly present in the following passage from a letter to Miss Hitchener, written in June, 1811.

Is then soul annihilable? Yet one of the properties of animal soul is consciousness of identity. If this is destroyed, in consequence the *soul* (whose essence this is) must perish. But as I conceive (and as is certainly capable of demonstration) that nothing can be annihilated, but that everything appertaining to nature, consisting of constituent parts infinitely divisible, is in a continual change, then do I suppose — and I think I have a right to draw this inference — that neither will soul perish; that in a future existence it will lose all consciousness of having formerly lived elsewhere, — will begin life anew, possibly under a shape of which we have no idea. [53]

A few months later he allows himself to play with the idea that "perhaps a future state is no other than a different mode of terrestrial existence to which we have fitted ourselves in this mode.

---

[52] *Ibid.*, II, 921. It is impossible not to feel the immeasurable difference of tone in these two passages, brief as they are — a difference which separates all the writings of his youth from those of his maturity. Yet with his deepening seriousness and growing sadness there went also a playfulness of fancy of which in his youthful writings he shows few signs. So in a letter to Peacock this theme of pre-existence becomes the subject of a gay jest: for, having described the menagerie connected with Byron's household, he adds the following postscript: "After I have sealed my letter, I find that my enumeration of the animals in this Circean Palace was defective, and that in a material point. I have just met on the grand staircase five peacocks, two guinea hens, and an Egyptian crane. I wonder who all these animals were before they were changed into these shapes." *Ibid.*, p. 898.

[53] *Ibid.*, I, 99. He adds: "But we have no right to make hypotheses — this is not one: at least I flatter myself that I have kept clear of supposition"!

Is there any probability in this supposition? On this plan, *congenial* souls must meet; because, having fitted themselves for nearly the same mode of being, they cannot fail to be *near* each other." [54] At the beginning of 1812 we find him putting forward a theory of cosmic evolution, apparently extending through infinite time. "I think reason and analogy seem to countenance the opinion that life is infinite; that, as the soul which now animates this frame was once the vivifying principle of the *infinitely* lowest link in the Chain of existence, so it is ultimately destined to attain the highest . . . that everything is animation . . . and in consequence being infinite we can never arrive at its termination." [55]

As we have seen, however, Shelley's early enthusiastic confidence in a future existence soon gave way to a more rationalistic and judicial attitude, which resulted either in pessimism or in a not too buoyant hope, according to his prevailing mood. But in his later years, as his pessimism in regard to earthly life, and his sense of its unreality, took deeper root in his intellectual and emotional nature, so the thought and hope of another existence came to fill an ever larger space in the poet's spiritual life.[56] And the doctrine of reincarnation again finds a place in his thoughts. It appears, I believe, in a much-discussed passage near the end of *Prometheus Unbound*, where Demogorgon addresses in turn the various spiritual powers of the universe, among them the spirits of the dead:

> Ye happy Dead, whom beams of brightest verse
> Are clouds to hide, not colours to portray,
> Whether your nature is that universe
> Which once ye saw and suffered —

to which "A Voice from beneath" replies

> Or as they
> Whom we have left, we change and pass away.[57]

[54] *Ibid.*, p. 174.   [55] *Ibid.*, p. 205.

[56] I must insist again that this changing attitude in Shelley is not to be considered as a retreat or an escape — unless the words are to be applied to every human aspiration toward a purer and richer and more satisfying existence. Persons are never wanting, of course, who are willing to make this application. It is commonly held, I believe, by students of the "psychology of religion" that the teachings of Christ himself in regard to immortality were the result of an "escape complex" consequent on the discovery that the "real" world was not amenable to his ideals.

[57] IV, ll. 534–38.

Upon these lines W. M. Rossetti comments: "The alternative presented appears to be this: The Dead are either reabsorbed into the universe of spirit, and, as a portion of that universe, they continue to be cognizable by mortal men — or else the state of physical change natural to men when alive is natural to them also when dead, and thus the Dead change, pass away, and qua men, absolutely cease to exist." [58] I believe the first alternative to be correctly stated. But, as Rossetti himself admits, with characteristic candor, there is something almost absurd in having the Dead state that they have ceased to exist. And the very fact that Demogorgon addresses them must mean that they certainly possess or participate in some kind of spiritual life. It seems to me much more probable that Shelley is here developing essentially the same thought that occupies his attention in the letters just quoted: that the souls of those who have died have only become incarnate in other forms, which in turn will give way to still others. The alternative would then be between *immediate* union with the "one Spirit" and a union to be achieved by a long process of evolution through ever higher forms. Perhaps even the "elemental Genii" are to become the "Kings of suns and stars, Daemons and Gods" before they pass out of Time into complete union with the One.[59]

But in *Hellas* the doctrine is stated unequivocally.

> Worlds on worlds are rolling ever
>   From creation to decay,
> Like the bubbles on a river
>   Sparkling, bursting, borne away.
>   But they are still immortal
>   Who, through birth's orient portal
> And death's dark chasm hurrying to and fro,
>   Clothe their unceasing flight

[58] "Shelley's *Prometheus Unbound*, Its Meaning and Personages," *Shelley Society Papers*, p. 171.

[59] For a fanciful treatment of the idea of reincarnation (though under Shelley's seemingly lightest fancies are apt to be hidden "Thoughts that do often lie too deep for tears"), see the first part of *With a Guitar, to Jane*. Shelley and Jane had been Ariel and Miranda, and "from life to life" he had sought her happiness.

> Now, in humbler, happier lot,
> This is all remembered not;
> And now, alas! the poor sprite is
> Imprisoned, for some fault of his,
> In a body like a grave . . .

> In the brief dust and light
> Gathered around their chariots as they go;
> New shapes they still may weave,
> New gods, new laws receive,
> Bright or dim are they as the robes they last
> On Death's bare ribs had cast.[60]

Upon these lines the best commentary is Shelley's own: "The first stanza contrasts the immortality of the living and thinking beings which inhabit the planets, and to use a common and inadequate phrase, *clothe themselves in matter*, with the transience of the noblest manifestations of the external world. The concluding verses indicate a progressive state of more or less exalted existence, according to the degree of perfection which every distinct intelligence may have attained." [61]

IV

But the doctrine of reincarnation in itself has no moral or spiritual significance, answers no questions about the meaning of life or the destiny of the soul, until we know what the end is toward which the soul thus moves, and by what Power it is drawn thither. And these questions, also, Shelley faces and attempts to answer.

Upon this topic Mary Shelley says: "I cannot pretend . . . to say what Shelley's views were — they were vague certainly; yet as certainly regarded the country beyond the grave as one by no means foreign to our interests and hopes. Considering his individual mind as a unit divided from a mighty whole, to which it was united by restless sympathies and an eager desire for knowledge, he assuredly believed that hereafter, as now, he would form a portion of that whole — and a portion less imperfect, less suffering, than the shackles inseparable from humanity impose on all who live be-

---

[60] Ll. 197–210. Shelley doubtless has in mind here the vision of Er at the close of Book X of Plato's *Republic;* but his imagination seems to me to have a vaster and more cosmic sweep. The "new gods, new laws" seem to imply an evolution of the race as well as of individual souls.

[61] I have quoted portions of the same note elsewhere. But it ought to be read entire. It has more significance for the student of Shelley's religious thought than any other single passage, prose or verse, in his writings. With the remark about "the transience . . . of the external world," cf. *The Witch of Atlas*, xxiii.

> The boundless ocean like a drop of dew
> Will be consumed — the stubborn center must
> Be scattered, like a cloud of summer dust.

neath the moon." [62] If I may venture to make more definite the statement of a person who surely ought to have known, as well as anyone, what Shelley believed, I should say that the belief which he holds most consistently and finds to be most nearly satisfying, is this: that the end of life is the union of every individual consciousness with the universal Spirit of Good which I have elsewhere spoken of as Shelley's God, conceived as both transcending the world of things and at the same time being immanent in whatever that world contains of beautiful and good. This I take to be the thought (as nearly as it can be expressed in cold and lifeless prose) of the great stanzas in *Adonais* where Shelley asserts the immortality of the soul of Keats.

> Nor let us weep that our delight is fled
> Far from these carrion kites that scream below;
> He wakes or sleeps with the enduring dead;
> Thou canst not soar where he is sitting now. —
> Dust to the dust! but the pure spirit shall flow
> Back to the burning fountain whence it came,
> A portion of the Eternal, which must glow
> Through time and change, unquenchably the same
> . . . .
>
> He is made one with Nature; there is heard
> His voice in all her music, from the moan
> Of thunder to the song of night's sweet bird;
> He is a presence to be felt and known
> In darkness and in light, from herb and stone,
> Spreading itself where'er that Power may move
> Which has withdrawn his being to its own;
> Which wields the world with never-wearied love,
> Sustains it from beneath, and kindles it above.
>
> He is a portion of the loveliness
> Which once he made more lovely: he doth bear
> His part, while the one Spirit's plastic stress
> Sweeps through the dull dense world, compelling there,
> All new successions to the forms they wear;
> Torturing th' unwilling dross that checks its flight
> To its own likeness, as each mass may bear;
> And bursting in its beauty and its might
> From trees and beasts and men into the Heaven's light. [63]

[62] *Complete Works*, V, x.   [63] Stanzas xxxviii, xlii, xliii.

Concerning the exact meaning of these lines there has been much controversy, which may for the present be passed by. What seems to be clear is Shelley's belief that the real self or soul, by virtue of which an individual being exists and is himself, is indestructible; and that as this real self must originally have come from the "burning fountain" of all life and form, all love and beauty; as while "clothed in matter" it is still a part of the "one Spirit" of Good, "the instrument to work [the] will divine" of the "Great Spirit, deepest Love! Which rulest and dost move," as far as the Spirit of Evil permits, the world of things; so, after what "those who live call life" shall have ceased, it remains a part of the divine Spirit in which alone, whether existing in the material world or elsewhere, it can live and move and have its being. That is, I think, Shelley had come to feel that life and death are in themselves rather unimportant accidents, necessary in the world of time and matter, but not disturbing or essentially altering the great scheme of things.[64]

It should be remembered, too, that the Spirit in which the soul continues to exist after death is not conceived by Shelley as a mechanical or blindly working impersonal force, but as an intelligent, benevolent, and purposive Power, including in its nature all that man calls good; so that complete union with it would involve not the extinction of being but the immeasurable expansion of it. Hence, the criticism of Francis Thompson (though frequently echoed) seems largely beside the point. He speaks of "Shelley's inexpressibly sad exposition of Pantheistic immortality," and continues: "What deepest depth of agony is it that finds consolation in this immortality; an immortality that thrusts you into death, the maw of Nature, that your dissolved elements may circulate through her veins?"[65] And Alfred Noyes is surely right in answer-

[64] If this sounds like one of Mary Shelley's notes, I must submit to be judged as I have judged. And if it be objected (what is much more serious, since it concerns Shelley and not me) that such a view renders irrational and inconsequent the poet's indignation against the reviewers and his sorrow for the death of Keats, I can only answer that we are here faced with the insoluble paradox that has been touched upon before, of the irreconcilability of a belief in the goodness of ultimate reality (which I take to be an essential element in religion) and the existence of evil as an experienced fact (in which religion apparently has its origin).

[65] *Shelley*, p. 63. Thompson seems not to realize that by "Nature" Shelley means not the sum of physical existence, but the *benevolent* principle which he believes to

ing that Shelley's conception is of "a perfected harmony, embracing, completing every individual note, and making it more, not less itself. . . . not a degradation of the individual, but an apotheosis." [66] So also Mr. E. E. Kellett comments that "the thoughts he [Keats] had given us were taken up into the thought of God, and lasted when the body died. But it was no *personal* survival; personality, to Shelley, as to Spinoza, was a sub-illusion of the great deception, Time." [67] On the other hand: "Absorption in the One . . . is not a mere suppression of the individual; it is its assumption into that after which it strives, and an attainment of, or a step towards, its ideal. For Adonais to become a portion of Loveliness is no annihilation; any more than for Goethe it was annihilation to find the light for which he longed." [68] Here, too, we may recall the lines of the *Hymn to Intellectual Beauty:*

> Man were immortal, and omnipotent,
> Didst thou, unknown and awful as thou art,
> Keep with thy glorious train firm state within his
> heart . . .
> Depart not, — lest the grave should be
> Like life and fear, a dark reality.[69]

Man's immortality must come from union with something greater than himself; and this union involves not the extinction of his true self but its complete and perfect realization.

Such an interpretation seems to be confirmed by certain passages in *Epipsychidion;* Shelley declares concerning his dreamed-of mystic "isle 'twixt Heaven, Air, Earth, and Sea" [70] that

> like a buried lamp, a Soul no less
> Burns in the heart of this delicious isle,
> An atom of th' Eternal . . .[71]

And to his beloved (who is not Emilia or any woman, but an "embodied Ray Of the great Brightness," the imagined incarnation in

---

be at work, although resisted, in the physical world; the power personified by Asia in *Prometheus Unbound.*

[66] *Some Aspects of Modern Poetry*, pp. 41–42.

[67] E. E. Kellett, *Suggestions: Literary Essays* (Cambridge University Press, 1923), p. 152.

[68] *Ibid.*, pp. 153–54.   [69] Ll. 39–41, 47–48.

[70] This seems clearly to indicate that the island is not in the material world at all.

[71] Ll. 477–79.

human form of the "Life of Life," the "Lamp of Earth") the poet
says:

> Be this our home in life, and when years heap
> Their withered hours, like leaves, on our decay,
> Let us become the overhanging day,
> The living soul of this Elysian isle,
> Conscious, inseparable, one.[72]

The souls of the lovers are united not only with each other but
with "the living soul" of their dwelling-place, which is "an atom
of th' Eternal"; yet they are still conscious — only, we may suppose, with a consciousness unspeakably heightened and intensified.

With Shelley's utterances in *Adonais* and *Epipsychidion* should
be compared a passage in his prose fragment *The Coliseum*, which
critics have too often overlooked.

The internal nature of each being is surrounded by a circle, not to be
surmounted by his fellows; and it is this repulsion which constitutes the
misfortune of the condition of life. But there is a circle which comprehends, as well as one which mutually excludes, all things which feel.
And, with respect to man, his public and his private happiness consists
in diminishing the circumference which includes those resembling himself, until they become one with him and he with them. It is because
we enter into the meditations, the designs and destinies of something
beyond ourselves, that the contemplation of the ruins of human power
excites an elevating sense of awfulness and beauty. It is therefore that the
ocean, the glacier, the cataract, the tempest, the volcano, have each a
spirit which animates the extremities of our frame with tingling joy . . .
O, Power! . . . thou which interpenetratest all things, and without
which this glorious world were a blind and formless chaos, Love, Author
of Good, God, King, Father! Friend of these thy worshippers! Two
solitary hearts invoke thee, may they be divided never! If the contentions
of mankind have been their misery; if to give and seek that happiness
which thou art, has been their choice and destiny; . . . if the justice, the
liberty, the loveliness, the truth, which are thy footsteps, have been sought
by them, divide them not! It is thine to unite, to eternize; to make
outlive the limits of the grave those who have left among the living,
memorials of thee.[73]

---

[72] Ll. 536–40.

[73] *Prose Works*, I, 399–400. These are the words of a character in a story, but it
seems to me quite evident that the ideas which are expressed or implied are Shelley's
own. The passage should be compared with the essay *On Love*. This fragment was
probably written in 1819.

The thought of the concluding sentence is echoed in the lovely lines at the end of *Epipsychidion,* in which the poet bids his verses sing:

> "Love's very pain is sweet,
> But its reward is in the world divine
> Which, if not here, it builds beyond the grave."

Love, that is to say, is the power which destroys that principle of separateness to which Shelley attributes much, if not all, of the evil in this world, and extends the circle by which the self is limited so that the selves of all other beings are at last included in it, and it becomes identical with the One Self, the Spirit of Good, or God. Such seems to be the nature of the immortality in which Shelley believes.[74]

v

And now I must admit that, after all, there is a certain justification for Francis Thompson's complaint; and that, as I stated at the beginning, there is little reason to say — indeed, there is every reason to deny — that Shelley believed in "personal" immortality. For, in the first place, there is to be found in none of his speculations about reincarnation or ultimate union with the "one Spirit" any assertion that the soul remains conscious of any past existence;[75] and if there is no consciousness of continuity, is it not mere mockery to talk about "immortality"? Many persons will say, not unreasonably, If in a future life I am not to remember this present life, then the being who exists in that life will not be I, but someone else, and neither the fact nor the conditions of his existence can be of the slightest importance to me. And to this objection I do not

[74] The philosophical or religious tradition that Shelley's conception most nearly approaches is, I believe, neo-Platonism. His general view differs from the neo-Platonic, however, in that he seems never to be willing to regard evil as a merely negative principle.

[75] The close of *The Revolt of Islam* is an exception, and I must regard it either (as Mr. Kurtz suggests, probably rightly) as part of the "fairy-machinery of the poem," or as symbolic of the poet's belief in some unknown state of future existence. In *Adonais,* although the survival of personality is in some places suggested (e.g., stanzas xlv, xlvi, and the last two lines of the poem), the question of memory is not touched upon. Of course, in the final union with the One, time is apparently to be transcended; and the question then ceases to be relevant. Cf. *Hellas,* ll. 766–67: "Sultan! talk no more Of thee and me, the Future and the Past." Cf. also the Buddhist belief that, although most men do not remember their previous incarnations, those souls which have progressed far toward Nirvana *do* remember.

see that any rational answer is possible. As far as I am aware, no philosophical or religious system involving the doctrine of reincarnation has ever succeeded in making clear exactly what the principle is which becomes incarnate in a succession of bodies and personalities. To the question, What is immortality without memory? it may indeed be answered, Something less unendurable, at any rate, than *with* memory. For perfect happiness (which is assumed, however illogically, to be a condition of personal immortality) seems hardly compatible with any clear recollection of the events of earthly life. Such at least would have been the view of Shelley, who in 1818, at a comparatively happy period of his life, writes to Peacock: "The curse of this life is, that whatever is once known, can never be unknown . . . Time flows on, places are changed; friends who were with us, are no longer with us; yet what has been seems yet to be, but barren and stripped of life." [76]

Moreover, if Shelley's conception of immortality is not thus deprived of all power to give consolation, it will perhaps be so by the fact (which seems to me clearly evident) that it denies the continued existence of what is commonly meant by "personality." If from one point of view the circle of the self is to be expanded to include all other selves, yet from another standpoint it is at the same time to be contracted, until finally it becomes a point and ceases to exist. And it is this second view that the great majority of persons are bound to take. For the self that Shelley hates and wishes to annihilate is precisely that which most human beings are accustomed to consider as the personal, or real, self. The very principle of separateness which the poet condemns as the source of evil and illusion must seem to most of his readers to be the *sine qua non* of their existence. Shelley is at one with the adherents of Buddhism, Brahmanism, and other Eastern faiths in regarding the human personality as something to be got rid of or transcended; and so is in direct opposition to the main tendency of European religious thought. We have already found him writing to Leigh Hunt: "So much for self — *self*, that burr that will stick to one. I can't get it off, yet." [77] And in one of his early letters to Hogg he exclaims in the same vein, "I am sick to death at the name of *self*. Oh, your

[76] *Letters*, II, 593.   [77] *Letters*, II, 706.

theory cost me much reflection . . . Is it not, however, founded
on that *hateful* principle? Is it *self* which you propose to raise to a
state of superiority by your system of eternal perfectibility in
love?" [78] Nor should this utterance be taken (as some critics will
think) for a piece of mere boyish affectation. It strikes a note that
echoes through all his poetry. The theme of *Alastor* and *Epipsychidion,* among his longer poems, is the desire to lose the self —
and *realize* a *higher* self — in perfect union with the "Spirit fair,"
the "unseen Power," the "awful Loveliness," which he addresses in
the *Hymn to Intellectual Beauty:*

> I vowed that I would dedicate my powers
> To thee and thine —

So in "Life of Life," in the sudden intense perception of the presence
of that divine Spirit, he cries:

> And all feel, yet see thee never,
> As I feel now, lost for ever!
>
> Lamp of Earth! where'er thou movest
> Its dim shapes are clad with brightness,
> And the souls of whom thou lovest
> Walk upon the winds with lightness,
> Till they fail, as I am failing,
> Dizzy, lost, yet unbewailing! [79]

And surely in *Adonais* it is not the *man* who remains. "Dust to the
dust"; only "the pure spirit" returns to "the burning fountain,"
by whose fire, likewise, Shelley prays that in himself "the last clouds
of cold mortality" may be consumed. For to what are due the
"stormy visions," the "mad trance," the "fear and grief," "the
shadow of our night," to what but that thing which the world calls
"personality"? Again in a letter to Byron belonging to the same
year as *Adonais,* the antagonism to *self* finds expression. "You say
that you feel indifferent to the stimuli of life. But this is a good
rather than an evil augury. Long after the *man* is dead, the immortal spirit may survive, and speak like one belonging to a higher
world." [80] So, too, in *A Defence of Poetry,* the pure emotions in-

---

[78] *Ibid.,* I, 28.   [79] *Prometheus Unbound,* II, v, ll. 64–71.
[80] *Lord Byron's Correspondence,* edited by John Murray (2 vols., London, 1922),
II, 179. This is characteristic of Shelley's unceasing efforts to urge his friend to
nobler aims and loftier achievements, more worthy of his genius and his better

spired by poetry are described as lifting men "out of the dull
vapours of the little world of self"; [81] and in another place the poet
declares that while such emotions last, "self appears as what it is,
an atom to a universe." [82] And in *Hellas* the wise Ahasuerus adjures
Mahmud to

> talk no more
> Of thee and me, the Future and the Past;
> But look on that which cannot change — the One,
> The unborn and the undying. [83]

These lines clearly express what is implicit in all the later poetry,
the denial of the real or permanent existence of human personality.
I will venture to suggest, also, that in *The Triumph of Life* the
error of those who are the victims of Life's destructive power lies
in centering all their purposes and desires in their own separate
personalities, that this is the source of the veil of illusion that hides
from men the vision of the true "Life of Life." And this is clearly
the same error that Shelley speaks of in the famous passage of his
letter to Gisborne when he says with reference to *Epipsychidion*,
"I think one is always in love with something or other; the error,
and I confess it is not easy for spirits cased in flesh and blood to
avoid it, consists in seeking in a mortal image the likeness of what
is perhaps eternal." [84] Critics quote these words with approval, and
remark with complacent superiority that Shelley finally learned
something about the facts of life. One wonders if they realize that
in a single sentence the poet here quietly dismisses to the limbo of
error and unreality everything that the world calls love — everything, indeed, that the world values. For to say, as he does, that
every "mortal image" is an illusion is to declare that personality
has no real existence; that the only enduring love is not the love
of persons as persons, but as the embodiment, though imperfect, of
the divine Spirit of Love; that all abiding values exist not in relation to this passing conjunction of flesh and spirit, enslaved by

---

nature. It is my personal conviction that most of what is finest and most beautiful
in Byron's poetry is due to his friendship with Shelley — the one man, apparently,
whom he ever looked up to and acknowledged to be his superior. The same conviction is expressed by Thornton Hunt, in the article already referred to, "Shelley As
I Knew Him."

[81] Shawcross, p. 144.   [82] *Ibid.*, p. 154.
[83] Ll. 766–69.   [84] *Letters*, II, 976.

"Sense and reason, those enchanters fair," preoccupied with petty wants and passions more shadowy and fleeting than itself, which is called personality, but in relation to the Power "which wields the world with never-wearied love," "whose influencings are distributed to all whose natures admit of a participation in them," and in whose being man, by the sacrifice of self, may find immortal life.

> I loved — oh, no, I mean not one of ye,
> Or any earthly one, though ye are dear
> As human heart to human heart may be; —
> I loved, I know not what — but this low sphere
> And all that it contains, contains not thee,
> Thou, whom, seen nowhere, I feel everywhere . . .
>
> By Heaven and Earth, from all whose shapes thou flowest,
> Neither to be contained, delayed, nor hidden;
> Making divine the loftiest and the lowest,
> When for a moment thou art not forbidden
> To live within the life which thou bestowest . . . [85]

The personality is nothing; the one Life is all.

To this quality of Shelley's thought and poetry, above all others, I attribute the traditional criticism that his work is marked by "unreality" and "lack of substance." Hazlitt in 1824 struck the

[85] *The Zucca*, stanzas iii and iv. Written in 1822. Mr. Kurtz calls this "a throwback to his purely Platonic days. To that philosophy of being, which makes all sensible experience a falling away from perfection, and so encourages an impatient love-longing for something unattainable save in ephemeral ecstasy, the poet who rose higher in *Adonais* has sunk backwards." *Op. cit.*, pp. 325–26. To me it seems perfectly in harmony with all Shelley's later poetry. In *Adonais* no less than here, the world of sense experience is declared to be an illusion, something to be transcended. And Shelley's longing is not for "something unattainable save in ephemeral ecstasy," but for something unattainable except in the serene depth of eternal being, in perfect union with the transcendent Spirit which is Deity. I must remind the reader again that all this does not imply that Shelley was lacking in capacity for giving and receiving human affection. The popular belief that he was fickle in his friendships, especially with women, is false. His life (and I say this deliberately, knowing, I believe, as much about the important "facts" as anyone now can) is remarkable for steadfast loyalty to every person who had a claim on his affections — to some far beyond their deserts. Cf. H. S. Salt, *Shelley: Poet and Pioneer*, p. 62n. But with his human affection there seems always to have been mingled the sense of the presence in the objects of his love of some transcendent, divine Spirit. I am not merely *saying* this: one comes to *feel* it, in both his letters and his personal poems. Cf. Bradley, *Essays on Truth and Reality*, p. 435: "The finite minds that in and for religion form one spiritual whole, have indeed in the end no visible embodiments, and yet, except as members in an invisible community, they are nothing real. For religion, in short, if the one indwelling Spirit is removed, there are no spirits left."

note that has chiefly prevailed from that day to this, in declaring that Shelley made his poetry "out of nothing," [86] and it is not unnatural that the majority of critics should have followed his lead. When it is an unquestioned dogma that the highest function of poetic art is to hold the mirror up to nature, when it is assumed that the supreme achievement in creative literature is the creation of "real" characters, when almost by definition literature is a representation of unregenerate human nature, it is remarkable that there have been so many critics who have acknowledged Shelley to be a prophet as well as a poet. It is remarkable, too, that as far as I know, none of the poet's defenders has ever questioned this dogma. It is more than high time, in the interests of a just estimation of Shelley and his poetry, that it should be resolutely challenged.

The indictment of Shelley on the ground just mentioned is perhaps best stated by Roden Noel. "Yet I think he had not grip enough, condensation and fusion enough, to make him grasp the idea of will, of personality, of individual identity, nor does he make us feel it." [87] "The raptures of *Epipsychidion* . . . seem presumptuously to overleap eternal boundaries, and violate those awful penetralia of individuality, aspiring to lose distinction in a unit, which would be neither unity, nor possession, nor knowledge through love and sympathy, but rather the blank chaos and non-being of an unorganized, inharmonious, and essentially unrealizable absorption." [88]

In the first place, I deny completely the truth of the assertion that Shelley could not, or did not, *understand* "personality." Such a view can have been held only by persons whose judgment has been confused by the beating wings of that beautiful and ineffectual (and "inflammable") angel which certainly never existed outside the realm of inanity; and who have therefore never taken the trouble to make an honest and thorough study of Shelley's life and work. I have already touched upon this mistake in the fourth chapter of the present study, and shall not dwell upon it here.

[86] *Edinburgh Review*, XL, 494.
[87] Roden Noel, *Essays on Poetry and Poets* (London, 1886), p. 125.
[88] *Ibid.*, p. 127. Cf. also the essays of Bagehot, Gingerich, and Elliott.

But *in the end,* according to Shelley, personality certainly *is* to be extinguished; for in his eyes it is a source of pain and error, a limitation to be transcended. And for this, it seems, he is to be censured. But why? By what right do critics set up this wayward, restless, strife-torn image of half-being, this self-absorbed slave of its material environment and its own caprice — in a word, *personality* — as the God whose decrees are to be the ultimate measure of all the values of life; and then stigmatize as morally and intellectually incompetent the poet who refuses to worship the object of their idolatry? What is this talk about "eternal boundaries" which it is presumptuous to overleap, and "awful penetralia" which it is blasphemous to violate? What indeed but the voice of that imperfection which loves itself and hates the perfection in which it would cease to exist, as darkness hates the light before whose coming it must vanish? The very conception of personality is irrational, unintelligible; every attempt to think it through lands us in self-contradiction. And yet we are told that whatever transcends it can be nothing else than "blank chaos and non-being." We are told also that personality is essential to love and sympathy as we know them; and doubtless that is true. But it is also true that it makes love and sympathy forever partial and forever unsatisfying. There is a half truth in those magnificent lines of Donne:

> So must pure lovers soules descend
> T' affections, and to faculties,
> Which sense may reach and apprehend,
> Else a great Prince in prison lies.[89]

But the other half of the truth is that these affections and faculties are themselves a prison confining love to endless and tormenting unfulfilment. And I do not know what kind of love it is by which the recognition of this fact is not too surely forced upon us.[90] It is not for nothing that certain religions which have claimed the alle-

---

[89] *The Extasie,* ll. 65–68.

[90] There is, of course, a paradox in assuming, as Shelley and others who share his view on this question do assume, that an experience (e.g., love) which is only known to us under finite conditions, within the limits of personality, will become perfect, and completely satisfying, when those conditions have been transcended. But this paradox seems to me inseparable from any belief in a transcendental reality.

giance of some millions of people through the course of some thousands of years have based their moral codes on the fundamental assumption that personality is an illusion. And according to this view, the persons who are *really* weak and presumptuous are those who fear the annihilation and desire the everlasting continuance of personality; for it is personality itself, and not a state transcending it, that must be truly characterized as *necessarily* "unorganized, inharmonious, and essentially unrealizable." I must think, I repeat, that the critical attitude which I have here brought in question can arise only from the love of imperfection which I have characterized as the antithesis of true religion, and the inability or the unwillingness to think through the problems that religion involves.

And what has just been said on the question of personality in general must also be applied to the question of the continued existence of personality after death. Doubtless this is a question concerning which none of us should be more hasty to dogmatize than was Shelley, and in regard to which everyone must respect the feelings of his neighbor. He would have little claim to the title of philosopher or critic who should affect contempt for the natural human hope that the bitterness and frustration which seem so often dominant in life upon the earth should not be somehow made right hereafter, or for the heart's instinctive rebellion against the sad thought that of all our experience of beauty and of love, death must be the end. No one, I believe, has felt these emotions more poignantly than Shelley, or desired less to disparage them. Yet the problem as it presents itself to subtle minds and sensitive natures involves many other elements; and it seems to me that careless thinking may cast undeserved imputations on Shelley and his belief. I have already spoken of the difficulty of framing any satisfying conception of personal immortality. And I must add, for my own part, that there seems to be something a trifle egotistical and ignoble in desiring that this limited and imperfect being which I call my self, and all those limitations and imperfections without which that self would cease to be what it is, should be guaranteed an eternal existence. Such a feeling Shelley himself appears to express in the *Ode to Heaven*. One spirit, addressing Heaven, declares:

Thou art . . .
But the portal of the grave
Where a world of new delights
Will make thy best glories seem
But a dim and noonday gleam
From the shadow of a dream!

But another spirit answers:

Peace! the abyss is wreathed with scorn
At your presumption, atom-born!
What is Heaven? and what are ye
Who its brief expanse inherit?
What are suns and spheres which flee
With the instinct of that Spirit
Of which ye are but a part?
Drops which Nature's mighty heart
Drives through thinnest veins! Depart![91]

And besides this, it is hard to see, as I have already emphasized, that "personality" is anything more than a synonym for "imperfection." As Bradley says, "Surely perfection and finitude are in principle not compatible. If you are to be perfect, then you, as such, must be resolved and cease; and endless progress sounds merely like an attempt indefinitely to put off perfection." [92] And I may add that endless life without either perfection or progress would seem a much more accurate description of Hell than of Heaven.

And here it is not out of place, perhaps, to recur to the conception of a "personal" God. I have contended that Shelley believed in a Deity which can as justly be called personal as the God of Christianity. Yet I do not see how, strictly speaking, the adjective can be applied to a perfect being. The very conception of personality involves limitation, separateness, exclusiveness; and the popular notion, at least, implies, besides, a nature at odds with itself and with other selves. An absolutely good or perfect Being can scarcely be thought of (so far as it can be thought of at all) as a person. It

[91] Ll. 28–45. Cf. Locock's note (*Poems*, II, 505): ". . . Heaven, with its suns and spheres, and the mind of man, are merely drops of Nature's blood . . . The Spirit of Nature is alone immortal." — If the "Spirit of Nature" is rightly conceived, the note may stand.

[92] *Appearance and Reality* (2d ed., Oxford, 1930), p. 450. A full understanding of the force and implications of this statement, of course, can come only from studying it in its context.

seems necessary, if we wish to believe in a personal God, and if
we are at the same time to be completely rational, to adopt some
such conception as that portrayed in the historical books of the
Old Testament: a God of revenge as well as pity, and of hate as
well as love; and many persons, like Shelley, would perhaps think
it less ignoble, were there no other alternative, to believe in no
Deity at all. I cannot think that such a capricious and wilful God
can be that in which the great Christians have found their inspiration.[93]

All this discussion may be clarified by the simple statement of
a fact upon which I have already dwelt at length: namely, that man
possesses a dual nature. The ultimate destiny of the human soul is
considered by Shelley to be the realization of the "higher" self —
by virtue of which man participates in the divine "soul of goodness" which is God — through the denial of the "lower" self which
binds him to the world of change and time, of error and evil; and

---

[93] The thought of this paragraph, and, indeed, this whole phase of my discussion,
is based upon Bradley's *Appearance and Reality*, Chapters XXV and XXVI, especially the closing portion of each, and *Essays on Truth and Reality*, Chapter XV.
I do not think that I am misstating Bradley's views, and I therefore feel at liberty
to suggest to the critic whom my opinions may move to adverse comment, that he
first read and answer Bradley. It may clarify my general position, however, to
remark that it is based on the fact (for I believe it is a fact) that life and the
universe are in the last analysis unintelligible, and that in dealing with such ultimate
problems as those concerned with God and immortality it is folly to suppose that
complete rationality is possible either in the formulation or criticism of any particular opinion or theory. That is, when I say that we cannot *think* of an absolutely
good Being as a person, I do not mean that we cannot *believe* in a Being which is
both perfect in itself and at the same time related to us and responsive to the conditions of our finite existence. In fact, such a belief seems to me to be implicit in
the highest form of religion. But still, it is irrational. And those persons who argue
that because Shelley does not *think* of the supreme Being as a person, he has no
right to assert the existence of any meaningful relation between that Being and
finite human selves, ignore the irrational element which always exists in religion.
Cf. Bradley, *Essays on Truth and Reality*, p. 436: "I cannot, for one thing, deny
the relation in religion between God and finite minds, and how to make this relation
external, or again to include it in God's personality, I do not know." And again
(p. 437): "Banish all that is meant by the indwelling Spirit of God, in its harmony
and discord with the finite soul, and what death and desolation has taken the place
of living religion. But how this Spirit can be held consistently with the external
individual Person, is a problem which has defied solution. To confine ourselves to
the latter is, in principle, to bring disaster on our religion, and in practice tends to
empty and narrow it by an attempt at consistent one-sidedness . . . For the reality
of God means his own actual presence within individual souls, and, apart from this
presence, both he and they are no more than abstractions."

which Shelley (as I think, rightly) identifies with all those attributes that are included in the common conception of personality. The recognition of this dualism I take to be the beginning of religion; and the resolution of it must therefore be the end toward which religion strives. And I conclude that Shelley's attitude toward the problem of immortality is the result of a nature and a way of thinking that are essentially religious.

VI

There is still to be considered one more of Shelley's manifold speculations concerning immortality, although the discussion of it is difficult. Heretofore the opinions presented have been more or less capable of rational exposition and appraisal. But now we must approach a realm of nearly pure mysticism. The scorn of reason which the one-time disciple of Godwin avows so openly in *A Defence of Poetry* does not remain unmanifested in his verse. The most notable instance is the closing stanzas of that enchanting and baffling poem *The Sensitive Plant*. The lovely Lady who tended the garden has died, the Sensitive Plant has perished, and all the beauty of the place has passed into ruin and decay. And here is the epilogue that Shelley adds:

> Whether the Sensitive Plant, or that
> Which within its boughs like a Spirit sat,
> Ere its outward form had known decay,
> Now felt this change, I cannot say.
>
> Whether that Lady's gentle mind,
> No longer with the form combined
> Which scattered love, as stars do light,
> Found sadness, where it left delight,
>
> I dare not guess; but in this life
> Of error, ignorance, and strife,
> Where nothing is, but all things seem,
> And we the shadows of the dream,
>
> It is a modest creed, and yet
> Pleasant if one considers it,
> To own that death itself must be,
> Like all the rest, a mockery.
>
> That garden sweet, that lady fair,
> And all sweet shapes and odours there,

In truth have never passed away:
'Tis we, 'tis ours, are changed; not they.

For love, and beauty, and delight,
There is no death nor change: their might
Exceeds our organs, which endure
No light, being themselves obscure.

These stanzas elaborate a thought which the poet had already expressed, in a more somber mood, in *The Revolt of Islam*.

"Ye seek for peace, and when ye die, to dream
    No evil dreams: all mortal things are cold
And senseless then; if ought survive, I deem
    It must be love and joy, for they immortal seem." [94]

And later in the same poem, with an apparent strengthening of faith, he tells how Laon and Cythna, after their death, come to understand

That virtue, though obscured on Earth, not less
Survives all mortal change in lasting loveliness.[95]

And with these lines may be compared a characteristic fragment belonging to the same year.

Wealth and dominion fade into the mass
Of the great sea of human right and wrong,
When once from our possession they must pass;
But love, though misdirected, is among
The things which are immortal, and surpass
All that frail stuff which will be — or which was.[96]

Here, for once, Mary Shelley's comment is excellent. Speaking of the poet's views on immortality, she says: "A mystic ideality tinged these speculations in Shelley's mind; certain stanzas in the poem of 'The Sensitive Plant' express, in some degree, the almost inexpressible idea, not that we die into another state, when this state is no longer, from some reason, unapparent as well as apparent, accordant with our being — but that those who rise above the ordinary nature of man, fade from before our imperfect organs; they remain, in their 'love, beauty, and delight,' in a world congenial to them — we, clogged by 'error, ignorance, and strife,' see them not, till we are fitted by purification and improvement for their higher state." [97] Shelley had written once: "When you can discover

[94] XI, xvii.   [95] XII, xxxvii.   [96] Hutchinson, p. 549.   [97] *Complete Works*, V, x.

where the fresh colors of the faded flower abide, or the music of
the broken lyre, seek life among the dead." And now he has come
to believe, apparently, that these seemingly so transient things do
somehow have enduring life in a world of their own, which is,
nevertheless, the same world as ours; and of which we should be
aware but for the limitations forced upon us by the accident of
physical existence.

> Death is the veil which those who live call life:
> They sleep, and it is lifted: [98]

lifted, that is, for those who by their love of beauty and goodness,
as these appear in this world, have purified their natures so that
they may enter that world where goodness and beauty are not
transient appearances but unchanging realities. So in the great stanza
in *Adonais:*

> The One remains, the many change and pass;
> Heaven's light forever shines, Earth's shadows fly;
> Life, like a dome of many-coloured glass,
> Stains the white radiance of Eternity,
> Until Death tramples it to fragments. — Die
> If thou wouldst be with that which thou dost seek! [99]

It is obvious from these lines that Shelley does not think of Death
as a mere negation of life, or as only the last event in earthly
existence. And, indeed, have we not heard him speaking already,
in the note to *Hellas,* of "that futurity towards which we are all
impelled by an inextinguishable thirst for immortality"? But it is
not immortality which he desires; it is eternity, escape from the
illusion of time. And that escape is Death, which, according to his
view, is not a single event but a process: an achievement, in this
life or some other, of that which is beyond life. And in *Una Favola*
appears the same mystical persuasion, in the words which Death
addresses to the lovers who have chosen to dwell with her sister
Life. " 'Ye mistrust me, but I forgive ye, and await ye where ye
needs must come, for I dwell with Love and Eternity, with whom
the souls whose love is everlasting must hold communion . . .' " [1]

---

[98] *Prometheus Unbound,* III, iii, ll. 113–14.   [99] Stanza lii.

[1] Shawcross, p. 22. This fragment, written by Shelley in Italian, apparently in
1820, is obviously autobiographical. But it is equally obvious that the poet feels
that he is describing a universal experience.

It would perhaps be futile to attempt to analyze too minutely what is apparently the expression of a mystical experience, and therefore by its very nature not subject to rational analysis. Yet it may be worth while to mention some of the elements that seem to be present in it, to have been the origin of it. In themselves, these may appear to be rather disconnected; yet each points toward the thought of the last stanzas of *The Sensitive Plant,* and will perhaps help to make that thought more clear. And first, there is the poet's ever-growing apprehension of the unreality of the world of the senses, which has been stressed so often already that I offer only one more example, from what is perhaps the most human (in the narrow sense) and realistic (Hazlitt called it "prosaic") of Shelley's poems. Even the conversational tone of the *Letter to Maria Gisborne* does not prevent the poet from speaking

> Of this familiar life, which seems to be
> But is not; — or is but quaint mockery
> Of all we would believe . . .[2]

With this belief, also, we may naturally connect the Platonic doctrine of a world of Ideas, where the moral virtues and beauty have their essential and eternal existence, unaffected by the transience and imperfection of their manifestations in the sensible world.[3]

Again, we may recall Shelley's belief that man's true heaven exists within himself and must be sought and found only there. In *Julian and Maddalo* he asks,

> "Where is the love, beauty, and truth we seek
> But in our mind?"[4]

And Prometheus both exemplifies the principle in triumphing over his sufferings, and expresses it in words when he declares "Most vain all hope but love."[5] With the same sentiment, in a moment of apparent defeat, Cythna consoles Laon.

[2] Ll. 156–58.
[3] Except for his general belief in a transcendental reality, however, there seems to be in Shelley's thought no really close approach to this particular theory of Plato.
[4] Ll. 174–75. *Mind,* I take it, is here used in Shelley's customary broad sense — "will, passion, reason, imagination." And love, beauty, and truth do not exist only in our mind (I should say, in opposition to some critics), but are only *known* to us *through* the mind, by which we participate in the divine Spirit of "Love, Beauty, and Truth."
[5] I, l. 808.

"O dearest love! we shall be dead and cold
   Before this morn may on the world arise;
   Wouldst thou the glory of its dawn behold?
   Alas! gaze not on me, but turn thine eyes
   On thine own heart — it is a paradise
   Which everlasting Spring has made its own,
   And while drear Winter fills the naked skies,
   Sweet streams of sunny thought, and flowers fresh-blown
Are there, and weave their sounds and odours into one." [6]

Further, there is the thought, so strongly emphasized in *Hellas*, that whatever of good and beautiful has once come into existence, even in the world of time, can never really die or change or pass away. That is, for example, in the series of struggles between the Spirit of Good and the Spirit of Evil which is described in the first canto of *The Revolt of Islam*, the efforts put forth by the former are cumulative, so that by virtue of each attempt the succeeding one is more nearly successful, and ultimate triumph is certain. The same theme is later developed by Cythna in one of the greatest passages in the poem, which expresses a depth of moral insight and an intensity of moral passion hardly surpassed by anything in the later writings.

"In their own hearts the earnest of the hope
   Which made them great, the good will ever find . . .

"Our many thoughts and deeds, our life and love,
   Our happiness, and all that we have been,
   Immortally must live, and burn and move,
   When we shall be no more . . ." [7]

And it is not merely — as might seem to be implied when the poet adds that "the world has seen A type of peace" — that these things exist in the memories of men; they become in the most literal sense a part of the very being, they have in very truth immortal life in the thoughts and feelings and actions of future

[6] IX, xxvi. The apparent denial of continued personal existence is not absolute or dogmatic, for it is followed presently by the stanza already referred to, beginning "These are blind fancies . . ."

[7] IX, xxvii, xxx. Cf. these lines in *The Daemon of the World*, not present in *Queen Mab*:
   "For what thou art shall perish utterly,
   But what is thine may never cease to be." (Ll. 562–63.)

generations of living men and women; like "The Cloud" they "change, but" they "cannot die," they mock the claims of Death, they are the "wingèd seeds" driven by the West Wind through all the world of Time, forever quickening a new and better birth; they are one with the "Power" "which wields the world with never-wearied love." [8] From a certain point of view, and to a certain kind of nature, this may seem a very real and satisfying immortality.

And finally may be mentioned the idea, which Shelley evidently liked to entertain, that in moments of intense experience, time ceases to exist: dying to the world of time around us, we enter a world that is eternal. This conception had its origin in a psychological theory of Godwin, that time is measured to the mind by ideas or

[8] This conception, of course, is not to be confused with the idea frequently advocated at present of living for the sake of an abstraction called "humanity" or "the race." One is based on spiritualistic, the other on naturalistic, premisses. The question may be raised, of course (as it is by Mr. Kurtz in regard to *Hellas*, which he contrasts — as I think, mistakenly — with *Adonais* and the *Ode to the West Wind*), why, if goodness and beauty are by their very nature indestructible and have their true existence in a world of their own, they need to come into the actual world at all; and what, if anything, is to be gained by the whole process. But this, I suppose, is essentially to ask why the world exists; and I do not know that anyone has ever answered that question — at least, to the satisfaction of anyone but himself. A more interesting question, which may already have occurred to the reader, is: what is the fate of evil? If there is no death or change for love and beauty and delight, what of hate and ugliness and pain? If the soul of Keats survives, what of the soul of Count Cenci? This is a question on which Shelley says little, but the absolute opposition in which he places good and evil, and the positive content which he assigns to each, indicate that if goodness carries in its own nature the principle of life, evil must contain within itself the principle of death. Evil as such can have no part in the life of "the one Spirit," nor can it possibly be transformed or redeemed. So far as the soul yields to evil, so far it gives itself up to death. Evil *is* death. It does indeed "bring forth its kind" in the world of Time, but having no being beyond, is destined to extinction. (The whole question is another stumbling-block in the way of a "personal" immortality, unless one is willing to accept the doctrine of eternal punishment.) Doubtless, most of this is either platitude or tautology; but the point is one which needs to be touched upon in any consideration of the problem of immortality. Moreover, some of Shelley's commentators (e.g., Hicks, Kurtz) apparently consider that in Shelley's millennium — whatever exactly that is conceived to be — evil *becomes* good. Cf. *The Place of Christianity in Shelley's Thought*, p. 187: "There is no separation of the sheep from the goats, but all creatures — evil and good alike — are drawn into the mighty diapason of harmony and love which sweeps over the universe." Cf. also *The Pursuit of Death*, pp. 113–14. Such a view may possibly form a part of a profounder and more exalted religion than Shelley's; but it does *not* form part of Shelley's. It will be remembered that Leslie Stephen objected to *Prometheus* on exactly this ground: that there is no reconciliation between Prometheus and Jupiter, but that the latter is swept to oblivion. Cf. also *The Revolt of Islam*, XI, xxi.

sensations. It seems to follow that, if the progression of sensations and thought through the mind can be infinitely speeded up, the door to eternity stands open to the human consciousness. Upon this notion Shelley seizes in *Queen Mab* and writes enthusiastically of how

> "the thoughts that rise
> In time-destroying infiniteness, gift
> With self-enriched eternity . . .
> And man . . . stands
> Immortal upon earth." [9]

In a note he elaborates the theory. "Time is our consciousness of the succession of ideas in our mind. Vivid sensation, of either pain or pleasure, makes the time seem long, as the common phrase is, because it renders us more acutely conscious of our ideas. . . . If, therefore, the human mind, by any future improvement of its sensibility, should become conscious of an infinite number of ideas in a minute, that minute would be eternity." [10]

This conception appears in *The Revolt of Islam,* in one of the most daring and splendid expressions in English poetry of the raptures of physical love. Yet it is much more than that; for Shelley, as we have seen, had already come to regard the world of sensation as a delusion, and it is no sophistry but the simple truth to say that sensation here is only the beginning of an experience that is described as leading beyond the realm of sense and reason into a world absolutely distinct from that of matter, space, and time — into the very depth of divine Being.

> To the pure all things are pure! Oblivion wrapped
>   Our spirits, and the fearful overthrow
> Of public hope was from our being snapped,
>   Though linkèd years had bound it there; for now
>   A power, a thirst, a knowledge, which below
> All thoughts, like light beyond the atmosphere,
>   Clothing its clouds with grace, doth ever flow,
> Came on us . . .

[9] VIII, ll. 205–11.
[10] Hutchinson, p. 825. Cf. ll. 58–69 of the poem *To Harriet* (1812), which are included in this note. Shelley refers in this note to Godwin (*Political Justice*, I, 411 — apparently the third edition) and to Condorcet, but I cannot discover that either of them draws the inference which Shelley states in the passages just quoted.

Was it one moment that confounded thus
   All thought, all sense, all feeling, into one
Unutterable power, which shielded us
   Even from our own cold looks when we had gone
   Into a wide and wild oblivion
Of tumult and of tenderness? or now
   Had ages, such as make the moon and sun,
The seasons, and mankind their changes know,
Left fear and time unfelt by us alone below?

I know not. What are kisses whose fire clasps
   The failing heart in languishment, or limb
Twined within limb? or the quick dying gasps
   Of the life meeting, when the faint eyes swim
   Through tears of a wide mist boundless and dim,
In one caress? What is the strong control
   Which leads the heart that dizzy steep to climb,
Where far over the world those vapours roll,
Which blend two restless frames in one reposing soul?

It is the shadow that doth float unseen
   But not unfelt, o'er blind mortality . . .[11]

Godwin, with all his phlegmatic disdain for the pleasure of sense, nevertheless clung to the realm of sensation as the necessary basis of reason. Shelley, abnormally susceptible to sense impressions, strove to transcend not only sensation but also reason and emotion, and mingle his being with the eternal life of that Spirit of Good which he so worshipped. The stanzas just quoted seem to me to express a frank acceptance of mysticism, without even the pretense of rationalism which Godwin had flung over his original theory. And the mystical consummation which the experience here described seems to foreshadow can be nothing less than the death of personality and of life in the actual world.

It is true that there is an inconsistency here [12] in making physical love the starting point of an experience by which it is transcended; and that a safer and more logical way to overcome the limitations of personality would seem to be asceticism. And, indeed, Shelley's later attitude, as will appear in the following chapter, definitely inclines toward the ascetic ideal; and passionate love becomes, not a step toward the end which he seeks but only (where it is ap-

[11] VI, xxx, xxxv–xxxvii.   [12] Cf. note 90 above.

parently glorified) a symbol. The passage quoted here, however, is significant as showing that Shelley was not incapable of genuine passion; and as showing, also, that if (as I believe) he later came to the point of renouncing such passion, it was not through any innate coldness of temper, or any weak desire for release, but because of a stronger passion for what he believed to be a higher and deeper and richer state of being. This belief may have been a delusion; but there was nothing casual or impulsive in his acceptance of it. Few commentators seem to realize that Shelley *thought* about such subjects — thought about them earnestly and constantly.

The result of his early thinking upon the present topic is expressed again in *Rosalind and Helen*.

> "Heardst thou not, that those who die
> Awake in a world of ecstasy?
> That love, when limbs are interwoven,
> And sleep, when the night of life is cloven,
> And thought, to the world's dim boundaries clinging,
> And music, when one beloved is singing,
> Is death?" [13]

So, in a calmer mood, but pursuing the same theme, he describes the island paradise in *Epipsychidion*.

> I have sent books and music there, and all
> Those instruments with which high Spirits call
> The future from its cradle, and the past
> Out of its grave, and make the present last
> In thoughts and joys which sleep, but cannot die,
> Folded within their own eternity. [14]

[13] Ll. 1123–29.

[14] Ll. 519–24. An interesting question may be raised here. If joy and love lead to (or rather *are*) a kind of immortality, why not pain and hate? Shelley says in the note to *Queen Mab* that pain as well as pleasure prolongs time: and he develops the idea in the speech of the Maniac in *Julian and Maddalo*, who compares his own sufferings to those of the trodden worm, which

> "wears a living death of agonies!
> As the slow shadows of the pointed grass
> Mark the eternal periods, his pangs pass
> Slow, ever-moving, — making moments be
> As mine seem — each an immortality!" (Ll. 415–19.)

Prometheus, also, speaks of "moments aye divided by keen pangs Till they seemed years" (I, ll. 13–14). On such a basis, Shelley might — and logically, perhaps, ought to — have established a theory of eternal punishment for evil, which, as we have seen, is essentially the pain of hatred; and if this were intense enough, it

But it is in love, above all, that the limits of "blind mortality" may be transcended. For Love, the poet declares, is

> like Heaven's free breath,
> Which he who grasps can hold not; liker Death
> Who rides upon a thought, and makes his way
> Through temple, tower, and palace, and the array
> Of arms: more strength has Love than he or they;
> For it can burst his charnel, and make free
> The limbs in chains, the heart in agony,
> The soul in dust and chaos.[15]

And the grand climax of the poem is a development of the same theme, that Love belongs by its very nature to an eternal world, and that human love is a symbol figured upon life's "dome of many-coloured glass" — pointing beyond, to "the white radiance of Eternity." [16]

> We shall become the same, we shall be one
> Spirit within two frames, oh! wherefore two?
> One passion in twin-hearts, which grows and grew,
> Till like two meteors of expanding flame,
> Those spheres instinct with it become the same,
> Touch, mingle, are transfigured; ever still
> Burning, yet ever inconsumable:
> In one another's substance finding food,
> Like flames too pure and light and unimbued
> To nourish their bright lives with baser prey,

might become eternal suffering. This seems to be something like the conception by which Newman (confessedly) tries to make the doctrine of eternal punishment less painful to his imagination. But I do not find that Shelley ever suggests such a theory. The end of evil is apparently extinction. Love and beauty and delight have a real transcendental existence (if the adjectives do not contradict each other) in the being of the Spirit of Good. But hatred and pain, apparently, can have no existence except in earthly life.

[15] *Ibid.*, ll. 400–07.

[16] I cannot admit, as is often held, that this passage is a glorification of merely human passion, or that it is inspired to any great degree by Shelley's feeling toward Emilia Viviani. And indeed, some of the poet's detractors (e.g., those who deprecate Shelley's desire to transcend personality) find fault with the poem precisely on this account. The following lines — completely characteristic of Shelley — ought to settle the question definitely.

> To whatso'er of dull mortality
> Is mine, remain a vestal sister still;
> To the intense, the deep, the imperishable,
> Not mine but me, henceforth be thou united . . . (Ll. 389–92.)

And cf. the following chapter.

Which point to Heaven and cannot pass away:
One hope within two wills, one will beneath
Two overshadowing minds, one life, one death,
One Heaven, one Hell, one immortality,
And one annihilation.[17]

In that world to which Love leads us, where it and beauty and
delight suffer no death or change, there is neither life nor death as
we know them, and there are both immortality and annihilation.
Life as we know it implies death: where death is not, neither can life
be. And our "obscure organs," which bind us to the world of time
and space and matter, to "the dream of life" and its "stormy visions," and which, above all, condemn us to the separateness of personality, with all its hopeless loneliness and imperfection, its bitterness of unsatisfied desires directed, on the one hand, toward objects
that are illusory and, on the other, toward objects that *because* they
are real, are beyond our reach — these must be annihilated before
"the intense, the deep, the imperishable" soul can fulfil its ultimate
destiny of union with God.

*   *   *

There are many persons, no doubt, to whom such a view of
immortality will offer small consolation, and to whom it will seem
as much a mockery as the life of which they desire the eternal continuance seemed to Shelley. But here, as always, he lived up to his
principles. "Let us see the truth, whatever that may be," and the
truth as he saw it seems to have no place for "personal immortality."
On the other hand, it makes secure our faith in the absolute value
of love, beauty, and goodness; and assures us that no effort toward
the realization of these ideals can be vain or fruitless, and that the
divine economy will permit the destruction of nothing that is
worthy to be saved.

[17] Ll. 573–87.

CHAPTER VII

HEAVEN'S LIGHT ON EARTH

I

BUT WHATEVER uncertainty Shelley may have felt concerning the ultimate destiny of human life, he was not doubtful as to the means by which that destiny may be attained; for, it will be remembered, Shelley holds that man must achieve his own salvation: the only "Necessity" which he recognizes is that which, leaving man free to determine for himself the direction of his efforts, assures him of reaping as he has sown.

It will be remembered, too, that man's progress toward good is not primarily a matter of altering the forms of society — laws, customs, institutions — but of changing the moral character of individual human beings. And here I will dwell for a moment on the falsity of the common belief that Shelley was always in rebellion against law *as such*. Nothing could be farther from the truth. He revolted only against those laws of men that seemed to him to contradict the laws of God.[1] Like Carlyle, he believed of "the law of the universe," the *moral* law, that "there is written in the heart of every man an authentic copy of it direct from Heaven itself." And he would have agreed perfectly with the remark of the grim Scotch moralist concerning "the laws of God": "All men obey these, and have no freedom at all except in obeying them." On the other hand, he would have said with St. Augustine that "no man doth well against his will, even though what he doth, be well."

[1] Adverse critics have taken unfair advantage of the fact that Shelley usually speaks of these as laws of *Nature,* to falsify his moral teachings. Except in parts of *Queen Mab*, he means by "Nature" the Spirit of Good *in* nature, which is a moral force. I may add that if Shelley *had* considered the natural world to be entirely benevolent, he would perhaps have been nearer the truth than those moralists who look on nature as altogether "red in tooth and claw." This is merely the "pathetic fallacy" turned upside down. To talk as if "nature" and "evil" were synonymous is mere cant. Cf. James Thomson, *Biographical and Critical Studies,* pp. 284–85.

The liberty he demanded for men and women was simply the liberty to be truthful and charitable.

What were the laws against which Shelley rebelled? The law that made it a crime to speak one's belief in regard to religion; the law that made it treason to protest against the tyranny of a brutal government; the law that taxed the starving poor in order to give millions of pounds to a royal blackguard; the law that made woman the property of man, and chained together the bodies of those in whose hearts affection had long been dead. This is the kind of rebellion that once made the world call Shelley a monster, as it makes the world now call him a fool. It was only the enactments of narrow, selfish, and fearful human beings which he desired to abolish.[2] The position he states in the *Address to the Irish People* is characteristic: "The laws of his [man's] moral as of his physical nature are immutable, as is everything of nature; nor can the ephemeral institutions of human society take away those rights, annihilate or strengthen the duties that have for their basis the imperishable relations of his constitution . . . Any law is bad which attempts to make it criminal to do what the plain dictates within the breast of every man tell him that he ought to do." [3] So in *The Witch of Atlas* he speaks of "Custom's lawless law," [4] as in *The Revolt of Islam* he had spoken of "the Anarch Custom's reign";[5] and in *Prometheus Unbound* he describes Jupiter in these bitter words:

> To know nor faith, nor love, *nor law;* to be
> Omnipotent but friendless is to reign.[6]

Jupiter does not, as some critics have said, represent law: he represents (among other things) the denial of *law* by what men have agreed to call laws, which are in truth the offspring of the lust and passion they pretend to curb.

Shelley is often ignorantly called an anarchist. But *he* applied the

---

[2] Cf. Shawcross, Introduction, p. xviii: "It is against defective institutions that his attack on society is aimed — defective, because they fail to reflect outwardly the inner moral law."

[3] *Prose Works*, I, 276.

[4] Stanza lxii.

[5] Dedication, x.

[6] II, iv, ll. 47–48. Italics mine.

term, much more accurately, to "those ringleaders of the privileged gangs of murderers and swindlers, called Sovereigns"; [7] — because they desecrated and trampled under foot the laws of that spiritual world to which man's higher self aspires: justice and mercy, the love of God and the love of man. So in the *Ode to Naples* he pictures the monarchs of Europe hastening to crush the city's newly proclaimed liberty.

> Hear ye the march as of the Earth-born Forms
> Arrayed against the ever-living Gods? . . .
> The Anarchs of the North lead forth their legions
> Like Chaos o'er creation, uncreating . . .[8]

In *The Triumph of Life* he speaks of

> "Frederick, and Paul, Catherine, and Leopold,
> And hoary anarchs . . ."[9]

and of the Roman emperors as the "anarch chiefs." [10] And in the *Ode to Liberty* he addresses Napoleon as "The Anarch of thine own bewildered powers." [11] The whole of *The Mask of Anarchy* is a development of the same theme: that what is called law by those who rule and by their slaves is simply the antithesis of genuine law — an irresponsible and arbitrary power, like the Jehovah of the Old Testament. The companions of Anarchy are Murder, Fraud, and Hypocrisy; it is altogether an evil and destructive force; yet it calls itself "God, and King, and Law." And the Liberty by which it is opposed is simply obedience to the true, divine law: it is Justice, Wisdom, Peace, Love, Patience, Gentleness. It is incomprehensible that any critic with a care for truth should declare

---

[7] Preface to *Hellas*. This has been quoted against Shelley; but it is a simple statement of fact in regard to the Europe of his time. It is worth while to add here, perhaps, that as Shelley did not object to laws *as* laws, neither did he hate kings *because* they were kings, but because they were usually bad men. The sympathy with which he portrays the character of Charles I in the fragmentary drama of that name offers a remarkable contrast to the virulence of Shelley's idol, Milton, in regard to the same person. Had Shelley been a contemporary of Charles, however, no doubt his tone would have been different. Incidentally, a comparison of *A Philosophical View of Reform* with *A Ready and Easy Way to Establish a Free Commonwealth* would make an interesting study.

[8] Ll. 127–28, 137–38.

[9] Ll. 236–37.

[10] L. 285.

[11] L. 175.

the Liberty that Shelley glorified to be a mere yielding to instinct
and impulse, or should identify it with lawlessness and anarchy.[12]
Shelley understood as well as anyone that men have base passions
which must be held in check, and which, when loosed, result in
chaos. Thus Satan, in the Prologue to *Hellas*, prophesying his
triumph upon the earth, speaks of

> Three vials of the tears which daemons weep
> When virtuous spirits through the gate of Death
> Pass triumphing over the thorns of life,
> Sceptres and crowns, mitres and swords and snares,
> Trampling in scorn, like Him and Socrates.
> The first is Anarchy; when Power and Pleasure,
> Glory and science and security,
> On Freedom hang like fruit on the green tree,
> Then pour it forth, and men shall gather ashes.[13]

The victory of Prometheus and the defeat of Rousseau in *The
Triumph of Life* alike testify to Shelley's recognition of the need
of discipline, self-restraint, the subjection of the desires of the lower
nature to the ideals of the higher. Moreover, there is in the Preface
to *The Cenci* an implicit condemnation in the account that Shelley
gives of Roman Catholicism, in practice, as being "adoration, faith,
submission, penitence, blind admiration; not a rule for moral conduct . . . a passion, a persuasion, an excuse, a refuge; never a
check." It is as absurd to say that Shelley's theory of morality is
based on Rousseau's surrender to impulse as to identify it with
Godwin's reasoned calculation of consequences. Instead, it aims at
self-discipline in the service of ideals — ideals partly rational and
partly intuitive.

Further light is thrown on the subject by the second and third
stanzas of the *Ode to Liberty*, in which Shelley describes the chaos

[12] Leslie Stephen will again furnish an example of critical obliquity: "The absolute destruction of all law, and of law not merely in the sense of human law, but
of the laws in virtue of which the stars run their course and the frame of the
universe is bound together, is the end to which we are to look forward." *Op. cit.*,
p. 383. It suffices to quote in reply a few lines from *The Witch of Atlas*, telling
how the Witch's cave is "stored with scrolls of strange device," whose teaching

> might quench the Earth-consuming rage
> Of gold and blood — till men should live and move
> Harmonious as the sacred stars above. (St. xviii.)

[13] Ll. 151–59.

that existed during the early stages of life upon the earth, and declares that it was due to the absence of liberty. All living creatures, that is, were the slaves of aimless impulse and blind passion and selfish desire.

> But this divinest universe
> Was yet a chaos and a curse,
> For thou wert not; but, power from worst producing worse,
> The spirit of the beasts was kindled there,
> And of the birds, and of the watery forms,
> And there was war among them, and despair
> Within them, raging without truce or terms:
> The bosom of their violated nurse
> Groaned, for beasts warred on beasts, and worms on worms,
> And men on men; each heart was as a hell of storms.[14]

And the strife and suffering that still exist in human life, the cruelty and injustice that result from organized religion and monarchical government, are represented by the poet not as the later outgrowths of a civilized society but as the yet unconquered survivals of primeval chaos and anarchy.

> Man, the imperial shape, then multiplied
> His generations under the pavilion
> Of the Sun's throne: palace and pyramid,
> Temple and prison, to many a swarming million
> Were, as to mountain-wolves their ragged caves.
> This human living multitude
> Was savage, cunning, blind, and rude,
> For thou wert not; but o'er the populous solitude,
> Like one fierce cloud over a waste of waves,
> Hung Tyranny; beneath, sate deified
> The sister-pest, congregator of slaves;
> Into the shadow of her pinions wide
> Anarchs and priests, who feed on gold and blood
> Till with the stain their inmost souls are dyed,
> Drove the astonished herds of men from every side.[15]

This stanza offers an illuminating comparison with *Queen Mab*. Shelley has lost none of his hatred of the evils that spring from tyranny and superstition. But he no longer (as in some parts, at

[14] Ll. 21–30.
[15] Ll. 31–45. The "sister-pest" is religion in its early forms.

least, of the early poem) considers these to have come into existence miraculously and illogically, in despite of an omnipotent and benevolent Nature, or Necessity. Rather he regards them as the result of an original, elemental tendency *in* nature;[16] and man's freedom is here denied by a "necessity" that is a lawless, evil power.[17] According to Shelley's view, all moral law must be preceded by liberty; and "laws" that *force* "obedience," and make slaves of men, are not moral, but anarchic. Moreover, liberty is here described as involving self-consciousness, the knowledge of good and evil; as Milton declares that "reason also is choice."[18] Whence this knowledge comes, the *Ode to Liberty* does not tell us; but it does tell us that man now has such knowledge, and may, by an act of will, free himself from his ancient slavery to the lawless decrees of passion and selfishness, which are the real source of many human "laws."

But not all such laws are evil, even in Shelley's view. In his last years he came to see that even man-made law might be a vital power working for good. Toward the close of *The Mask of Anarchy* he exhorts the down-trodden population of England to

> "Let the laws of your own land,
> Good or ill, between ye stand
> Hand to hand, and foot to foot,
> Arbiters of the dispute,

> "The old laws of England — they
> Whose reverend heads with age are gray,
> Children of a wiser day;

[16] This passage should, once for all, show the falsity of the common belief that when Shelley speaks of "Nature" as a benevolent power, he means the *whole* of what is usually called the natural world. These stanzas should be compared with *The Triumph of Life*, especially the lines describing the effect of "that fierce Spirit, whose unholy leisure Was soothed by mischief since the world begun." Ll. 145–46.

[17] In regard to this general subject, no doubt confusion often arises from the failure to distinguish between *physical* law — "the statement of a process in nature not known to vary" — and *moral* law, which is a statement, not of what is, but of what *ought* to be. We may, of course, speak of the Necessity which "evil with evil, good with good must wind" as a moral law; but it is more properly the foundation of moral law, since in regard to it the idea of *obedience* becomes simply meaningless. By definition, a moral "law" is an ideal rule of conduct, which may be obeyed or not.

[18] Cf. John Todhunter, *A Study of Shelley* (London, 1880), p. 191.

And whose solemn voice must be
Thine own echo — Liberty!" [19]

Such a passage as this reminds one irresistibly of the utterances of
Edmund Burke. But Burke let his hatred of the violence and terrorism that accompanied the French Revolution drive him into the
acceptance of a virtual determinism which asserted bad laws as well
as good to be a necessary part of social progress; and thus he became the prophet of reaction and tyranny. Shelley, on the other
hand, distinguished between the arbitrary legislation of a small
number of men, "as frail and as ignorant as the multitude whom
they rule," [20] and the laws and institutions framed in accordance
with the imaginative apprehension of the universal Spirit of Good.
This second conception is expressed in the following passage from
A Defence of Poetry.

The true poetry of Rome lived in its institutions; for whatever of beautiful, true, and majestic, they contained, could have sprung only from
the faculty which creates the order in which they consist. The life of
Camillus, the death of Regulus; the expectation of the senators, in their
godlike state, of the victorious Gauls: the refusal of the republic to make
peace with Hannibal, after the battle of Cannae, were not the consequences of a refined calculation of the probable personal advantage to
result from such a rhythm and order in the shows of life, to those who
were at once the poets and actors in these immortal dramas. The imagination beholding the beauty of this order, created it out of itself according
to its own idea; the consequence was empire, and the reward everliving
fame. [21]

Once more, then, and for the last time: it was not law itself, or
restraint, or discipline, that Shelley hated; it was not anarchy, or
irresponsibility, or aimless self-indulgence, that he desired. It was
only evil that he fought against, and good that he wished to serve;
and nothing was sacred merely because of its name, or because of
its long existence. It was in no mood of rash rebellion, inspired only
by personal injuries, that he persisted, as he says, "in the task which
I had undertaken in early life, of opposing myself in these evil

[19] Stanzas lxxxi, lxxxii.
[20] *Essay on Christianity*, in Shawcross, p. 113.
[21] *A Defence of Poetry*, in Shawcross, p. 140. This passage will doubtless be
obscure to those to whom Shelley's peculiar views concerning imagination are un-
familiar. They will be discussed below.

times and among these evil tongues, to what I esteem misery and vice." [22] His motive was simply the desire to bring virtue and happiness into the lives of men. Like Milton and Dante before him, even like Christ himself (for he was a rebel, too), Shelley appealed from the laws of corrupt human society to what he believed to be everlasting divine decrees.

II

But before a man can perfectly know and obey these laws not made by men, he must experience an inward regeneration, like that experienced by Prometheus in the course (and apparently by the agency) [23] of his "Three thousand years of sleep-unsheltered hours" of suffering. And it seems to me that this need of a spiritual rebirth is what Shelley intends to symbolize by the suddenness with which the millennium arrives in *Prometheus Unbound*. He does not mean, of course, that evil will or ever can be quickly and miraculously removed from the world; he means simply that *when* all men shall become "pure in heart," their worst sufferings will cease. But he does not say when that time will be, nor does he ever say (except in one or two passages in *Queen Mab*, which are contradicted by the Irish pamphlets of about the same date) that it is to be looked for in the near future. It is true that in *The Revolt of Islam* he shows a whole nation made pure and good by the very sound of Cythna's voice. But elsewhere Laon addresses the victorious tyrants thus:

"O, that I whom ye have made
Your foe, could set my dearest enemy free
From pain and fear! but evil casts a shade,
Which cannot pass so soon, and Hate must be
The nurse and parent still of an ill progeny." [24]

And what does Shelley say in the Preface with reference to the excesses of the French Revolution? "Can he who the day before was a trampled slave suddenly become liberal-minded, forbearing, and independent? This is the consequence of a state of society to be produced by resolute perserverance and indefatigable hope, and

[22] *Letters*, II, 530 (December 8, 1816).
[23] Cf. I, ll. 57–58: "for I hate no more, As then ere misery made me wise."
[24] XI, xv.

long-suffering and long-believing courage, and the systematic efforts of generations of men of intellect and virtue." [25] Such words need no comment.

It is significant, too, and completely characteristic of Shelley's general attitude and way of thinking, that he rejected the notion, so popular in his and in our own time, that human ills can be removed or greatly alleviated by a mere increase in knowledge, the mere progress of "science." The fundamental doctrine of Godwinian ethics, that men automatically pursue what seems to them to be good, and only err through ignorance and the failure to follow a correct train of reasoning, although it certainly appealed to Shelley in his youth, was in his manhood cast aside. According to his mature view, the great problem of "political justice" and human happiness is not primarily to give men knowledge of what is right and good, but to arouse in them the will to do that right and act that good which they already know. Here Shelley parts company even with Plato, and practically aligns himself with Christianity, holding that evil exists not through man's ignorance but through his perversity. In *A Defence of Poetry* we find the poet saying, "nor is it for want of admirable doctrines that men hate, and despise, and censure, and deceive, and subjugate one another." [26] And later he elaborates the opinion with almost passionate fervor.

We have more moral, political and historical wisdom, than we know how to reduce into practice; we have more scientific and economical knowledge than can be accommodated to the just distribution of the produce which it multiplies. The poetry in these systems of thought, is concealed by the accumulation of facts and calculating processes. There is no want of knowledge respecting what is wisest and best in morals, government, and political economy, or at least, what is wiser and better than what men now practise and endure. But we let *"I dare not* wait upon *I would,* like the poor cat in the adage." We want the creative faculty to imagine that which we know; we want the generous impulse to act that which we imagine; we want the poetry of life; our calculations have outrun conception; we have eaten more than we can digest. The cultivation of those sciences which have enlarged the limits of the

[25] I have confessed to being a partisan of Shelley, but it seems to me that almost anyone must admit that this utterance (the whole paragraph should be read) contrasts rather favorably with some parts of Burke's *Reflections* or the later pronouncements of Wordsworth and Southey.

[26] Shawcross, p. 131.

empire of man over the external world, has, for want of the poetical faculty, proportionally circumscribed those of the internal world; and man, having enslaved the elements, remains himself a slave.[27]

Such is the final position, concerning what is perhaps the central problem of ethics, of this irresponsible child of rationalism and the Revolution; that men do *not* naturally do what they know to be good, but that they must be inspired to do it, must be inwardly regenerated, by what is practically (as will be seen) a "supernatural" power. Shelley's moral theory differs from that of certain Christian apologists (for example, Paley) chiefly in making the motive to right action not the fear of personal suffering but the unselfish love of universal good. It may be argued that in *A Defence of Poetry* Shelley is trying to prove a thesis; that is, to defend poetry against the charges of Peacock, by showing it to have a moral value. And this is true. But it is also true that the thesis is not a new one. In 1817 Shelley declares in the Preface to *The Revolt of Islam* that the poem was written with the purpose of "kindling within the bosoms of my readers a virtuous enthusiasm for those doctrines of liberty and justice, that faith and hope in something good, which neither violence nor misrepresentation nor prejudice can ever totally extinguish among mankind." Certainly there must be in human nature some latent element of good that can be appealed to, else man's future were dark indeed. But the appeal *must* be made, before that good can be brought to realization. So Shelley states in the Preface to *Prometheus Unbound:* "My purpose has hitherto been simply to familiarize the highly refined imagination of the more select classes of poetical readers with beautiful idealisms of moral excellence; aware that until the mind can love, and admire, and trust, and hope, and endure, reasoned principles of moral conduct are seeds cast upon the highway of life which the unconscious passenger tramples into dust, although they would bear the harvest of his happiness." No better statement of Shelley's creed as a poet and moralist can be made. At the age of twenty-seven, he knew exactly where he stood in ethical as well as esthetic theory [28] — and why. He had considered the doctrines of

---

[27] *Ibid.,* pp. 151–52.
[28] If there is a confusion of thought in *A Defence of Poetry*, it arises from his attempt partially to justify a realistic theory of art, which is incompatible with his

Godwin and the rationalists, and had concluded that they were empty and futile. His faith in the natural goodness of human nature had long since gone into the discard. He had come to believe that men must be born anew, and baptized not with the water of reason but with the fire of Imagination — which is in the most literal sense the gift of God to men to redeem them from their slavery to the powers of evil.

III

And here, for the last time, I shall dwell upon the completeness of Shelley's recantation of rationalism, and the absolute antithesis between what is most fundamental in his mature thought and what is most characteristic of the philosophy of William Godwin.

We have found Shelley already, in his youthful letters to Elizabeth Hitchener, insisting upon the claims of that "feeling" which Godwin ignored or deprecated: urging that "it does not prove the non-existence of a thing that it is not discoverable by reason: *feeling* here affords us sufficient proof";[29] and declaring his inability to tell her why he believes in immortality, because she lacks "some feelings" that are to him "cogent and resistless arguments."[30] Again, he writes to Hogg, early in 1813: "Now do not tell me that Reason is a cold and insensible arbiter. Reason is only an assemblage of our better feelings — passion considered under a peculiar mode of its operation."[31] Similarly, in 1817, he writes of a certain person that his "keen and subtle mind, deficient in those elementary feelings which are the *principles* of all moral reasoning, is better fitted for the detection of error than the establishment of truth."[32]

But the most definite pronouncements on the subject are in *A Defence of Poetry*. The essay begins, in fact, by contrasting reason with imagination — altogether to the disadvantage of the former.

According to one mode of regarding those two classes of mental action, which are called reason and imagination, the former may be considered as mind contemplating the relations borne by one thought to another,

---

ethical idealism. Cf. Melvin T. Solve, *Shelley: His Theory of Poetry*. And see below.

[29] *Letters*, I, 150.   [30] *Ibid.*, p. 232.   [31] *Ibid.*, p. 382.

[32] *Ibid.*, II, 581. The man referred to is David Booth, whose young wife had been a close friend of Mary's before her elopement with Shelley. Mr. Booth insisted that the friendship should cease, and this situation furnished the suggestion for *Rosalind and Helen*.

however produced; and the latter, as mind acting upon those thoughts so as to colour them with its own light, and composing from them, as from elements, other thoughts, each containing within itself the principle of its own integrity . . . Reason is the enumeration of quantities already known; imagination is the perception of the value of those quantities, both separately and as a whole. Reason respects the differences, and imagination the similitudes of things. Reason is to the imagination as the instrument to the agent, as the body to the spirit, as the shadow to the substance.[33]

Reason merely serves the purposes of "utility" in a narrow sense, the same "utility" which to Godwin was all in all: "that which banishes the importunity of the wants of our animal nature, the surrounding men with security of life, the dispersing the grosser delusions of superstition, and the conciliating such a degree of mutual forbearance among men as may consist with the motives of personal advantage." [34] And so far as reason achieves these ends, it is admitted by Shelley to be desirable.

Undoubtedly the promoters of utility, in this limited sense, have their appointed office in society . . . But whilst the sceptic destroys gross superstitions, let him spare to deface, as some of the French writers have defaced, the eternal truths charactered upon the imaginations of men. Whilst the mechanist abridges, and the political economist combines labour, let them beware that their speculations, for want of correspondence with those first principles which belong to the imagination, do not tend, as they have in modern England, to exasperate at once the extremes of luxury and want.[35]

No longer, with Godwin, does Shelley think of reason as sufficient unto itself: now it is a mere "calculating faculty," requiring the guidance of some higher power, if its results are not to be more harmful than beneficent. And, after all, what has reason ever *really* accomplished?

The exertions of Locke, Hume, Gibbon, Voltaire, Rousseau, and their disciples, in favour of oppressed and deluded humanity, are entitled to the gratitude of mankind. Yet it is easy to calculate the degree of moral and intellectual improvement which the world would have exhibited, had they never lived. A little more nonsense would have been talked for

[33] Shawcross, p. 120.
[34] *Ibid.*, p. 149. It would be hard to find a better statement of the ends which Godwin had in view.
[35] *Ibid.* Another characteristic instance of Shelley's flight to his ivory tower!

a century or two;[36] and perhaps a few more men, women, and children, burnt as heretics. We might not have been at this moment congratulating ourselves on the abolition of the Inquisition in Spain. But it exceeds all imagination to conceive what would have been the moral condition of the world if neither Dante, Petrarch, Boccaccio, Chaucer, Shakespeare, Calderon, Lord Bacon, nor Milton, had ever existed . . .[37]

And in a note on the first list of names, the author adds: "Although Rousseau has been thus classed, he was essentially a poet. The others, even Voltaire, were mere reasoners." "Mere reasoners"! Is this the man who remained all his life the disciple of the author of *Political Justice?* whose weak and wavering intellect was fatally warped by the Revolutionary writers? who "never got his head above the eighteenth-century thinkers, from Locke to Godwin"?[38] "Mere reasoners"! The once-idolized Locke, who, with Hume, had stood godfather to that unlucky brain-child of the young revolutionist, *The Necessity of Atheism!* Gibbon and Voltaire, the irreconcilable enemies of that Christian orthodoxy which he himself never ceased to oppose! It is strange that Shelley's detractors, in their eager search for evidence of his fickleness and ingratitude, have not brought forward this passage. And, on the other hand, his admirers might well be disturbed by this indifference to those who had been the heroes of his youth, and had first kindled the flame of his devotion to the service of truth and of humanity; save that other passages make it clear that he never weakened in his rebellion against the evils which they had also opposed, and that his reverence for them and for their principles yielded only to a reverence for those higher and deeper values for which, he felt, the religion of reason had no place. "What were virtue, love, patriotism, friendship — what were the scenery of this beautiful universe which we inhabit; what were our consolations on this side of the grave — and what were our aspirations beyond it, if poetry did not ascend to bring light and fire from those eternal regions where the owl-winged faculty of calculation dare not ever soar?"[39]

[36] The writer of this sentence is supposed to have believed that the millennium was "just around the corner."

[37] Shawcross, pp. 150–51.

[38] G. R. Elliott, *The Cycle of Modern Poetry*, p. 4.

[39] Shawcross, p. 153. Cf. the fragments of a proposed letter to Ollier on the same subject, referring specifically to Peacock and his essay on *The Four Ages of Poetry*,

Such passages as these lend a good deal of probability to the suggestion that the dominant theme of *The Triumph of Life,* or at least of Rousseau's story, is the evil consequences of the "abandonment of Imagination for Reason." [40] But, at any rate, there is one line in the poem that will bring to a fitting conclusion this discussion of Shelley's ultimate attitude toward rationalism. In the final scene of the poem, Shelley describes the ghastly swarms of phantoms which go forth from those who follow the car of Life; and among these various shadow-forms are those which

> like small gnats and flies, as thick as mist
> On evening marshes, thronged about the brow
> Of lawyers, statesmen, priest and theorist . . .[41]

So now the "theorist" takes his place with kings and priests and others who delude mankind and are themselves deluded. And the most eminent theorist of Shelley's time was certainly William Godwin. If the poet when he wrote this line did not have Godwin in mind, then he *ought* to have had; for it seems clear that the general reference is to that class of "mere reasoners" of whom he speaks so slightingly in *A Defence of Poetry.*[42] With these Godwin certainly belonged, as Shelley could hardly have helped recognizing. "And thus the whirligig of time brings in his revenges."

Here we may bid a last farewell to Godwin and his fellow rationalists. And I see no need of affecting to lament Shelley's having been unfortunately exposed, through his early enthusiasm for their work, "to the most insidious poison of the age." [43] To regret that Shelley should for a time have fallen under the influence of Revolutionary rationalism is as nonsensical as it is pharisaical. It is simply

to which *A Defence* was an answer: "He would extinguish Imagination, which is the Sun of life, and grope his way by the cold and uncertain and borrowed light of that moon which he calls Reason, stumbling over the interlunar chasm of time where she deserts us, and an owl, rather than an eagle, stare with dazzled eyes on the watery orb which is the Queen of his pale Heaven." *Letters,* II, 1000.

[40] Peck, *Life of Shelley,* II, 267. I should say rather that the poem implies that an unqualified acceptance of rationalism is only a part of the general surrender to the claims of Life (i.e., "the world" in the Scriptural sense), which results in disaster.

[41] Ll. 508–10.

[42] Perhaps Shelley here is thinking of Malthus, as well as the French sceptics. His objection is essentially the same in regard to both: that their speculations lack "correspondence with those first principles which belong to the imagination."

[43] P. E. More, *op. cit.,* p. 9.

to regret that Shelley was Shelley. But what *is* to be regretted is
that critics should have so long persisted in attributing to him a
permanent acceptance of the weakest and most extravagant elements
in that uneven school of thought, in defiance not only of the spirit,
but of the very letter, of all his latest work.

IV

And now, what *is* this Imagination which is, like Prometheus,
"the saviour and the strength of suffering man"? In the Preface to
The Cenci, Shelley says: "Imagination is as the immortal God
which should assume flesh for the redemption of mortal passion."
This, of course, is only a figure of speech, since the writer is here
defending a more or less realistic theory of poetic art, according to
which it should be a representation of "reality." [44] But his genuine
belief seems to be that Imagination literally *is* "the immortal God":
the Deity, the divine Spirit of Good, as it makes itself known within
the nature of man. The account of Imagination (or, as he sometimes calls it, "poetry") in *A Defence of Poetry* suggests inevitably
the attributes ascribed to God in the *Essay on Christianity.* In the
former Shelley declares, "Poetry ever communicates all the pleasure which men are capable of receiving: it is ever still the light
of life; the source of whatever of beautiful or generous or true can
have place in an evil time." [45] In the latter he speaks of "the Omnipotent God — that merciful and benignant Power who scatters
equally upon the beautiful earth all the elements of security and
happiness — whose influencings are distributed to all whose natures
admit of a participation in them . . . " [46] In the *Essay,* again, the
poet tells us:

[44] This, as I have suggested, is in opposition to Shelley's real belief, that art
should present a world better than that of reality. Doubtless he was here influenced
by the criticisms of his friends, and especially of his wife, who, for instance, implies
in one of her notes that *The Triumph of Life* is "divested from human interest"!
He was perhaps also led astray (I use the expression deliberately) by the universal
admiration of Shakespeare, although even here he would not altogether betray his
own genius, and, in *A Defence,* praises Calderón for having "attempted to fulfil
some of the high conditions of dramatic representation neglected by Shakespeare;
such as the establishing a relation between the drama and religion . . ." Shawcross, p. 134. He admits that Calderón is not altogether successful.

[45] Shawcross, p. 139.

[46] *Ibid.,* p. 92. The use of "Omnipotent" here must be a slip, as, indeed, the last
clause indicates. Or perhaps the term is loosely used as meaning simply "powerful";
cf. "more omnipresent" in the following quotation.

There is a Power by which we are surrounded, like the atmosphere in which some motionless lyre is suspended, which visits with its breath our silent chords at will.

Our most imperial and stupendous qualities — those on which the majesty and the power of humanity is erected — are, relatively to the inferior portion of its mechanism, active and imperial; but they are the passive slaves of some higher and more omnipresent Power. This Power is God; and those who have seen God have, in the period of their purer and more perfect nature, been harmonized by their own will to so exquisite [a] consentaneity of power as to give forth divinest melody, when the breath of universal being sweeps over their frame.[47]

So in *A Defence:* "Man is an instrument over which a series of external and internal impressions are driven, like the alternations of an ever-changing wind over an Aeolian lyre, which move it by their motion to ever-changing melody."[48] But man is not altogether passive: there is within him some divine element which responds to the external influence: "there is a principle within the human being, and perhaps within all sentient beings, which acts otherwise than in the lyre, and produces not melody alone, but harmony, by an internal adjustment of the sounds or motions thus excited to the impressions which excite them."[49] But still, Imagination is not subject to the government of the personality, of what man calls his *self:* "it acts in a divine and unapprehended manner, beyond and above consciousness."[50] "Poetry is not like reasoning, a power to be exerted according to the determination of the will. A man cannot say, 'I will compose poetry.' The greatest poet even cannot say it; for the mind in creation is as a fading coal, which some invisible

[47] *Ibid.*, pp. 90–91.
[48] *Ibid.*, p. 121. These parallels offer further evidence for a later date for the *Essay* than has usually been assigned it — perhaps even later than 1817.
[49] *Ibid.*
[50] *Ibid.*, p. 129. This is a little puzzling, since in *Prometheus Unbound* and *Hellas* Imagination is said to be one of the elements of "Thought," or consciousness, or mind. But mind, I have suggested, is not for Shelley the ultimate reality, and, before it can be centered in a self-conscious being, must be acted upon by some "higher" power, which may be called "Spirit" or "God." Imagination, then, is the element in finite mind which brings it into relation with the divine mind; for Shelley's God, although usually spoken of as a "Spirit" (cf. the Gospel of John), is evidently spirit plus mind; that is, the forms or patterns or ideas of what is good and beautiful, together with the active principle by which these are to be realized. In relation to the other elements of mind — Will, Passion, Reason — Imagination evidently supplies the ends toward which Will is directed, and also, by arousing Passion, impels the realization of those ends. Reason is a mere instrument.

influence, like an inconstant wind, awakens to transitory brightness; this power arises from within, like the colour of a flower which fades and changes as it is developed, and the conscious portions of our natures are unprophetic either of its approach or its departure." [51] "It is as it were the interpenetration of a diviner nature through our own . . . " [52] "Poetry redeems from decay the visitations of the divinity in man." [53]

Moreover, Imagination, or the spirit of poetry, as it is described in *A Defence*, is clearly identical with the Spirit of Intellectual Beauty, whose

> light alone — like mist o'er mountains driven,
> Or music by the night-wind sent
> Through strings of some still instrument,
> Or moonlight on a midnight stream,
> Gives grace and truth to life's unquiet dream.[54]

The same conception finds expression in the *Lines Connected with Epipsychidion*; and again we are irresistibly reminded of the nature of that "poetry" which Shelley defends.

> There is a Power, a Love, a Joy, a God
> Which makes in mortal hearts its brief abode,
> A Pythian exhalation, which inspires
> Love, only love — a wind which o'er the wires
> Of the soul's giant harp
> There is a mood which language faints beneath;
> You feel it striding, as Almighty Death
> His bloodless steed. . . .
>
> . . . .
>
> And what is that most brief and bright delight
> Which rushes through the touch and through the sight,
> And stands before the spirit's inmost throne,
> A naked Seraph? None hath ever known.
> Its birth is darkness, and its growth desire;
> Untameable and fleet and fierce as fire,

[51] *Ibid.*, p. 153. Mr. Gingerich (*op. cit.*, p. 223) quotes this passage as evidence of Shelley's acceptance of the doctrine of Necessity. But he omits the first sentence, in which it is asserted that, although *poetry* is not subject to will, *reason is*. It is true that he suggests that the passage should be read in its context; but he does not suggest that the context contains a flat contradiction of his thesis.

[52] *Ibid.*, p. 154.

[53] *Ibid.*, p. 155.

[54] Ll. 32–36.

> Not to be touched but to be felt alone
> It fills the world with glory — and is gone.[55]

Such is the nature of "the poetic principle."

Moreover, the Power that Shelley invokes in his own poetry is repeatedly identified with the universal Spirit of Good. In the *Ode to the West Wind*, in which the West Wind is in a sense a symbol of the Deity, he implores,

> Be thou, Spirit fierce,
> My spirit! Be thou me, impetuous one! . . .
> Be through my lips to unawakened earth
> The trumpet of a prophecy![56]

As he waits for inspiration, at the beginning of the *Ode to Naples*, he says that the sculptured forms about him

> Seemed only not to move and grow
> Because the crystal silence of the air
> Weighed on their life; even as the Power divine
> Which then lulled all things, brooded upon mine.[57]

And in the sentence which opens the last stanza of *Adonais*,

> The breath whose might I have invoked in song
> Descends on me . . .

we surely feel a rapture and awe that can have come only from the poet's faith in a divine source of inspiration.

And, further, we find that Imagination is a *creative* power, like "the one Spirit's plastic stress," which compels "All new successions to the forms they wear"; and like "the Power which models, as they pass, all the elements of this mixed universe to the purest and most perfect shape which it belongs to their nature to assume." [58] "No one deserves the name of Creator," writes Shelley, quoting Tasso, "save God and the Poet." [59] We have already heard him asserting that "whatever of beautiful, true, and majestic" was contained in the institutions of Rome had been created by Imagina-

[55] Ll. 134–49. Some of the lines were left by Shelley in a defective and fragmentary state.

[56] Cf. the closing sentence of *A Defence*.   [57] Ll. 19–22.

[58] *Essay on Christianity*, in Shawcross, pp. 94–95.

[59] "Non merita nome di creatore, se non Iddio ed il Poeta" (Shawcross, p. 156). The quotation also occurs in the essay *On Life*. In a letter to Peacock in 1818 Shelley gives the passage as: "Non C'e in mondo chi merita nome di creatore, che Dio ed il Poeta." *Letters*, II, 615.

tion. "The imagination beholding the beauty of this order, created it out of itself according to its own idea." [60] And when this creative principle ceased to act, the Roman empire fell, and the dark ages ensued.

It is an error to impute the ignorance of the dark ages to the Christian doctrines or the predominance of the Celtic nations. Whatever of evil their agencies may have contained sprang from the extinction of the poetical principle, connected with the progress of despotism and super-stition. Men, from causes too intricate to be here discussed, had become insensible and selfish: their own will had become feeble, and yet they were its slaves, and thence the slaves of the will of others: lust, fear, avarice, cruelty, and fraud characterized a race amongst whom no one was to be found capable of *creating*, in form, language, or institution.[61]

As in *The Revolt of Islam* the periods of advance and retrogression of civilization are attributed to a cosmic conflict between the Spirit of Good and the Spirit of Evil, so now it is Imagination that inspires an age of advancement, as it is the extinction of this power that brings an age of decay. Imagination *is* the Spirit of Good as it exists in man. And like that Spirit, as it is described in *Adonais*, it contains within itself both the forms or the ideas that man aspires to realize, and the power by which that realization is to be brought about. "The functions of the poetical faculty are two-fold; by one it creates new materials of knowledge and power and pleasure; by the other it engenders in the mind a desire to reproduce and arrange them ac-cording to a certain rhythm and order which may be called the beautiful and the good." [62] Thus Imagination is a moral principle — is, indeed, *the* moral principle: for it at the same time gives men knowledge of the good and kindles in them the desire to bring that good to realization, to be not "less in deed than in desire."

The consideration of the first of these two aspects of poetry touches upon the whole problem of the nature of art, as that of the second upon the question of its function. In neither of these do I wish to become involved; but it needs to be pointed out that here, as elsewhere, Shelley is a transcendentalist. Imagination does not bring forth its creations out of nothing (as Hazlitt charged

[60] *A Defence of Poetry*, in Shawcross, p. 140.
[61] *Ibid.*, p. 142. I trust the reader will not fail to notice the significance of this passage in relation to some topics that I have already discussed.
[62] *Ibid.*, p. 152.

that Shelley's imagination did), nor does it create merely by imitating the existing order. Rather it gives to man the power to look through the shows of things by which he is surrounded in the world of time, into the eternal world of goodness and beauty which lies beyond: "to be a poet is to apprehend the true and the beautiful, in a word, the good which exists in the relation, subsisting, first between existence and perception, and secondly between perception and expression." [63] And Shelley does not mean by "existence" what most men mean by it. "A poem is the very image of life" — but it is that image

expressed in its eternal truth. There is this difference between a story and a poem, that a story is a catalogue of detached facts, which have no other connexion than time, place, circumstance, cause and effect; the other is the creation of actions according to the unchangeable forms of human nature, as existing in the mind of the creator, which is itself the image of all other minds.[64]

And again he declares that

poetry defeats the curse which binds us to be subjected to the accident of surrounding impressions. And whether it spreads its own figured curtain, or withdraws life's dark veil from before the scene of things, it equally creates for us a being within our being. It makes us the inhabitants of a world to which the familiar world is a chaos. It reproduces the common world of which we are portions and percipients, and it purges from our inward sight the film of familiarity which obscures from us the wonder of our being.[65]

In the last sentence of this quotation, as in the preceding paragraph, where he says that poetry "adds beauty to what is deformed" and "marries exultation and horror," Shelley seems, as Mr. Shawcross says, "to approach a more modern conception of the true nature of poetic idealization, as consisting in an interpretation of life which suppresses nothing essential, but which by emphasizing the significant traits and omitting the irrelevant in its subject-matter (be this, morally speaking, good or bad), attains a vivid-

---

[63] *Ibid.*, p. 123. There is a good deal of similarity between Shelley's theory of poetry and that of Carlyle, as expressed in *The Hero As Poet.*

[64] *Ibid.*, p. 128. Italics mine. How completely Shelley has abandoned rationalism is again evident from the way in which he casually speaks of "*no other connexion than time, place, circumstance, cause and effect*"!

[65] *Ibid.*, pp. 155–56.

ness of portraiture which actual experience rarely or never affords." [66] So, likewise, Shelley declares in the Preface to *The Cenci:* "The highest moral purpose aimed at in the highest species of the drama, is the teaching of the human heart, through its sympathies and antipathies, the knowledge of itself; in proportion to the possession of which knowledge, every human being is wise, just, sincere, tolerant and kind." But this is not Shelley's characteristic position.[67] We have found him repeating more than once in *A Defence of Poetry* itself, that it is not *knowledge* which man lacks, but the *will* to put that knowledge into practice — "the generous impulse to act that which we imagine"; and it is hard to see how a mere representation of the world as it is will arouse that impulse, or how "teaching the human heart . . . the knowledge of itself" will give that heart either the desire or the power to become other than it is. We can only conclude that in such passages as those quoted, Shelley is for once confused as to the issue, and temporarily accepts the Socratic (and Godwinian) doctrine of the identity of knowledge and virtue, without recognizing that it is incompatible with his own fundamental belief that the existence of evil and its possible conquest by good both depend directly upon the human will; as well as with his "aspiring temper which would elevate all reality to the level of a prefigured excellence." [68] Shelley's real position comes out unmistakably in the Preface to *Prometheus Unbound,* which is much more characteristic of the writer than that to *The Cenci.* "Prometheus is, in my judgement, a more poetical character than Satan, because, in addition to courage, and majesty, and firm and patient opposition to omnipotent force, he is susceptible of being described as exempt from the taints of ambition, envy, revenge, and a desire for personal aggrandisement, which, in the Hero of *Paradise Lost,* interfere with the interest." [69]

[66] Introduction, p. xxxii.

[67] Cf., however, the *Speculations on Morals:* "The only distinction between the selfish man and the virtuous man is, that the imagination of the former is confined within a narrow limit, whilst that of the latter embraces a comprehensive circumference. . . . Virtue is thus entirely a refinement of civilized life. . . ." Shawcross, pp. 77–78.

[68] Shawcross, Introduction, p. xxxviii.

[69] A. C. Bradley regards this as a "strange notion," which exemplifies "Shelley's

Moreover, how are we to reconcile the view that poetry merely removes from "the common universe" its "veil of familiarity" with the view expressed a page previously that "it arrests the vanishing apparitions of the interlunations of life" and "redeems from decay the visitations of the divinity in man"? The former presupposes that the world and human nature are, in themselves and as they appear in the finite world, *always* the dwelling place of "divinity" and beauty and goodness; and such an assumption is entirely out of harmony with the general tenor of Shelley's work. Perhaps the most characteristic note of all his later poetry is the constant presence of a sense of the unreality of the temporal and material world, including personality; and why should a poetically hypostasized cross-section of it be any less unreal or any more desirable? Would the picture we find in *The Triumph of Life*, however beautiful the words and imagery and music with which it is painted, be more endurable than the "reality" it represents, did there not breathe in every line the overwhelming conviction that the life here portrayed seems to us so terrible, because, being able to conceive a better, *we know that this ought not to be*? [70] Or would any of the mass of men who in the vision which the poet saw, "Pursued their serious folly as of old," [71] blind to all good and beauty, be tempted merely by the sight of such a picture to turn aside from their pursuit of vanity? Nay, if the most of human life is nothing more than "serious folly," nothing more than painful persistence in the fatal quest of "shadows idle Of unreal

tendency to abstract idealism or spurious Platonism," which regards the actual world as illusory and is "the source of that thinness and shallowness of which his view of the world and of history is justly accused, a view in which all imperfect being is apt to figure as entirely gratuitous . . ." *Oxford Lectures on Poetry* (2d ed., London, 1909), pp. 166–67. That is, Shelley's view is Christian, and not Hegelian.

[70] This, I believe, is very close to A. C. Bradley's view that the ideal good may supply the subject-matter of poetry, without being presented directly; that is, for example, Shelley's sad lyrics may be said to present such an ideal *indirectly*, inasmuch as they are inspired by sorrow at its absence. This is an ingenious theory, and I think that in the given instance it is sound. But Bradley carries the application of it to a point to which I am by no means willing to do. In regard to Shelley's dislike of comedy, the critic says that "he did not see that to show the absurdity of the imperfect is to glorify the perfect." *Oxford Lectures*, p. 166. I believe that there is little comedy that can be so described. Certainly the principle does not apply to Shakespeare's famous comic characters, in which the dramatist's aim seems to be simply to glorify the imperfect.

[71] L. 73.

good," can there be less folly in making the representation of it, however "idealized," the chief end of poetry? [72]

And, after all, there are other passages which show that it really is another world to which the poet is lifted by Imagination, and which his work reflects: the eternal world of the good and the beautiful, from which life divides us.

The tragedies of the Athenian poets are as mirrors in which the spectator beholds himself . . . stript of all but that ideal perfection and energy which every one feels to be the eternal type of all that he loves, admires, and would become . . . The drama, so long as it continues to express poetry, is as a prismatic and many-sided mirror, which collects the brightest rays of human nature and divides and reproduces them from the simplicity of these elementary forms, and touches them with majesty and beauty, and multiplies all that it reflects, and endows it with the power of propagating its like wherever it may fall.[73]

With this passage may be compared the famous lines on the poet, from *Prometheus Unbound.*

> He will watch from dawn to gloom
> The lake-reflected sun illume
> The yellow bees in the ivy-bloom,
> Nor heed nor see, what things they be;
> But from these create he can
> Forms more real than living man,
> Nurslings of immortality![74]

And these forms are more real than living man, I take it, because they contain more beauty and goodness, which are to Shelley, as we have seen, the only ultimate reality of which man knows. Thus, in the Prologue to *Hellas,* Christ, pleading before the Almighty for the liberty of Greece, speaks of

> her harmonies and forms,
> Echoes and shadows of what Love adores
> In thee . . .[75]

So it becomes clear that Shelley's kingdom of the Imagination is not of this world. Imagination is the principle within us that responds to "the visitations of the divinity"; it is the gift of God

[72] I am not here attacking (although I have little sympathy with it) the realistic theory of poetic art. I am simply saying that when and so far as Shelley accepts it, he is inconsistent and untrue to his ideals.

[73] *A Defence,* in Shawcross, pp. 135-36.   [74] I, ll. 743-49.   [75] Ll. 98-100.

to man for his redemption from the temporal to the eternal world. The teaching concerning the divine nature of poetry which Shelley attributes to Coleridge is really Shelley's own.

> He spoke of poetry, and how
>   "Divine it was — a light — a love —
> A spirit which like wind doth blow
> As it listeth, to and fro;
>   A dew rained down from God above;
>
> "A power which comes and goes like dream,
>   And which none can ever trace —
> Heaven's light on earth — Truth's brightest beam."
> And when he ceased there lay the gleam
>   Of those words upon his face.[76]

In Shelley's religion, Imagination corresponds to the Christian doctrine of Grace.[77]

V

Such a statement may seem to be intended as a startling paradox; but, as a matter of fact, this belief is, in Shelley, perfectly natural. Always oppressed by the mystery of evil, of the world's "dark slavery," and of man's "scope For love and hate, despondency and hope"; seeing in the mass of human beings no apparent tendency or desire to elevate and purify their lives; yet feeling in himself and in the world the presence, however rare and fleeting, of "some unseen Power," some "awful Loveliness"; he is driven at last to place his faith in what amounts to a supernatural salvation — not, however, as some of his critics have said, a salvation to be granted completely and simultaneously to all living beings, but only a partial one, to be offered now and then to individuals, perhaps to every individual, at some time or other, in greater or less degree.

It will doubtless seem strange that Shelley, a rebel almost from

[76] *Peter Bell the Third*, V, iv, v.
[77] Cf. F. C. Prescott, *Poetry and Myth* (New York, 1927), p. 185. ". . . Shelley, drawing upon a vigorous imagination implanted in a highly gifted, noble, and aspiring nature, gives us what amounts to a new and independent revelation of religious truth, embodying this in a series of surprisingly beautiful mythical or fictional creations. Shelley's religion was the product of a fresh imaginative apprehension of man's relation to the world of spirit . . . The Holy Ghost, which, like revelation, I fear many religious persons will think of as visiting mankind only in a remote past, was to Shelley a vivid present reality."

his cradle, to the end of his life a passionate crusader in the cause
of liberty, and a preacher of the doctrine that, except for hatred of
others, self-contempt is perhaps the greatest sin,[78] should not have
felt that man's salvation lies wholly with himself. But here again
it must be remembered that according to Shelley's view there are
in every human being two selves; and that what most men call
the self — that is, the personality — is an illusion that stands between the higher self and the divine Spirit to which that higher
self is akin, and with which it strives to be united.[79] And the business
of poetry, Shelley believes, is not with the personal self, but with
the "self" that is common to all men.[80] "A poet participates in the

[78] See *Prometheus Unbound*, II, iv, l. 25; III, iv, l. 134; *The Revolt of Islam*,
VIII, xxi–xxii.

[79] Doubtless this distinction between a lower and a higher "self" is often an easy
refuge for careless thinkers. But for me it signifies a real fact of experience, which
I do not know how to express in any other way. By the "higher self" I mean what
(I believe) Bradley means by the "Good Will"; by the "lower self," or "personality," I mean the "individual by himself," together with those attributes of his
finite nature which make him an individual whose "internal nature . . . is surrounded by a circle not to be surmounted by its fellows" (*The Coliseum*). Cf.
Bradley, *Essays on Truth and Reality*, p. 435: "For me, if the individual by himself anywhere is a fact, the whole Universe is wrecked, while, from the other side,
if anywhere the community is real, the reality of God in religion seems a matter
of course. The Supreme Will for good which is experienced within finite minds
is obviously a fact . . . If you turn this indwelling will into a mere relation between yourself and another individual, religion has perished and the world is so
far destroyed."

[80] In the second section of Chapter II of the *Speculations on Morals* (Shawcross,
pp. 83–86), Shelley propounds the theory that "moral science consists in considering
the difference, not the resemblance of persons"; since the resemblances between
individuals, which are merely the result of a common social environment, are
superficial and unimportant; while the really significant and permanent qualities
of character are determined from within by a power peculiar to each individual.
The same idea is hinted at in the *Essay on Christianity*. "Every mind has what
Bacon calls its '*idola specus*' — peculiar images which reside in the inner cave of
thought. These constitute the essential and distinctive character of every human
being . . ." See Shawcross, p. 103. I confess that I do not see just how this idea
fits into the general trend of Shelley's thought; since in neither passage does there
seem to be any implication that this singularity is something which ought to be
overcome. (Contrast *The Coliseum*.) Of course, in one sense, Shelley is always an
extreme individualist, hating the thought of a mechanized society and having no
desire to legislate for other people (cf. *The Revolt of Islam*, V, xlix), his moral
ideals being by their very nature such as cannot be forced upon the world but must
be freely accepted by each individual; and in the *Speculations on Morals*, he is
perhaps thinking in merely practical terms, with regard to immediate rather than
ultimate ends. It may be noted that the theory is exactly the opposite of Godwin's
view that character is almost entirely determined by external circumstances.

eternal, the infinite, and the one; as far as relates to his conceptions, time and place and number are not. The grammatical forms which express the moods of time, and the difference of persons, and the distinction of place, are convertible with respect to the highest poetry without injuring it as poetry . . . " [81]

It is this implicit transcending of personality which makes poetry, in Shelley's view, a force for good. It will be remembered that he asserts in *The Coliseum* that the source of all evil is the principle of separateness, which makes living beings the centers of mutually exclusive circles. In his mind, *self* is always associated with *selfishness;* and poetry is always the enemy of self. "Poetry, and the principle of Self, of which money is the visible incarnation, are the God and Mammon of the world." [82]

The great secret of morals is love; or the going out of our own nature, and an identification of ourselves with the beautiful which exists in thought, action, or person, not our own. A man to be greatly good, must imagine intensely and comprehensively; he must put himself in the place of another and of many others; the pains and pleasures of his species must become his own. *The great instrument of moral good is the imagination;* and poetry ministers to the effect by acting upon the cause. Poetry enlarges the circumference of the imagination by replenishing it with thoughts of ever new delight, which have the power of attracting and assimilating to their nature all other thoughts, and which form new intervals and interstices whose void forever craves fresh food.[83]

Nor does Shelley here have in mind a mere purging of the emotions through vicarious experience, such as is generally held to be the essential element in Aristotle's doctrine of *catharsis;* but the kindling of a desire to become the good which we behold. "The mind becomes that which it contemplates" [84] — this is the principle according to which poetry becomes a power for good; and this principle precludes any realistic theory of poetry. What Shelley's attitude actually was in regard to the moral purpose of poetry and of art in general is perhaps best expressed in the famous exhortation of Paul: "Finally, brethren, whatsoever things are true, whatsoever things are honest, whatsoever things are just, whatsoever

---

[81] *A Defence,* in Shawcross, pp. 124–25. The examples that Shelley gives are "the choruses of Aeschylus, and the book of *Job,* and Dante's *Paradise.*"

[82] *Ibid.,* p. 152.   [83] *Ibid.,* p. 131. Italics mine.

[84] *Prince Athanase,* l. 139. Cf. *Prometheus Unbound,* I, l. 450.

things are pure, whatsoever things are lovely, whatsoever things
are of good report; if there be any virtue and if there be any
praise, think on these things." [85] In this spirit Prometheus proph-
esies that man, now freed from the tyranny of Jupiter, shall find
in art the way to freedom from himself.

> And lovely apparitions, — dim at first,
> Then radiant, as the mind, arising bright
> From the embrace of beauty (whence the forms
> Of which these are the phantoms) casts on them
> The gathered rays which are reality —
> Shall visit us, the progeny immortal
> Of Painting, Sculpture, and rapt Poesy,
> And arts, though unimagined, yet to be.
> The wandering voices and the shadows these
> Of all that man becomes, the mediators
> Of that best worship, love, by him and us
> Given and returned; swift shapes and sounds, which grow
> More fair and soft as man grows wise and kind,
> And veil by veil, evil and error fall . . .[86]

Not what man is, but what he is *to become,* as he moves nearer and
nearer to divine perfection, such is the proper subject matter of art.

Thus Shelley says of the early love poets of Italy that their
"verses are as spells, which unseal the inmost enchanted fountains
of the delight which is in the grief of love. It is impossible to feel
them without becoming a portion of that beauty which we contemplate: it were superfluous to explain how the gentleness and the
elevation of mind connected with these sacred emotions can render
men more amiable, more generous and wise, and lift them out of

---

[85] Philippians 4: 8. Inasmuch as Shelley's constant aim in poetry is to glorify the
ideal, he may be said to be primarily a religious poet, in the broad sense of the
adjective. And it is precisely because he is religious, in this sense, that many persons
find his poetry "thin" and unsatisfying. For most persons are not religious.

[86] *Prometheus Unbound,* III, iii, ll. 49–62. Cf. the following passage from a
letter to Peacock, in which, after lamenting the impermanence of paintings, he continues: "There is one refuge from the despondency of this contemplation. The
material part, indeed, of their works must perish, but they survive in the mind of
man, and the remembrances connected with them are transmitted from generation
to generation. The poet embodies them in his creations; the systems of philosophers
are modelled to gentleness by their contemplation; opinion, that legislator, is infected with their influence; men become better and wiser; and the unseen seeds
are perhaps thus sown which shall produce a plant more excellent even than that
from which they fell." *Letters,* II, 642. This was written near the end of 1818. I
do not think that Shelley ever modified the view which is here expressed.

the dull vapours of the little world of self." [87] So also of the readers of Homer: their "sentiments" "must have been refined and enlarged by a sympathy with such great and lovely impersonations, until from admiring they imitated, and from imitation they identified themselves with the objects of their admiration." [88] And the poet himself is even more affected than his readers. Of the feelings that accompany poetic inspiration, Shelley declares that "the state of mind produced by them is at war with every base desire. The enthusiasm of virtue, love, patriotism, and friendship, is essentially linked with such emotions; and whilst they last, self appears as what it is, an atom to a universe." [89] Precisely the same conception finds expression in the third stanza of the *Hymn of Apollo*, in which Apollo is a symbol of Imagination.

> The sunbeams are my shafts, with which I kill
> Deceit, that loves the night and fears the day;
> All men who do or even imagine ill
> Fly me, and from the glory of my ray
> Good minds and open actions take new might,
> Until diminished by the reign of Night.

And not from the sphere of self, certainly, do "Good minds and open actions take new might," but from that which transcends self.

This conception of Imagination as the enemy of self, or personality, is the source of much that is characteristic in Shelley's poetry. It explains his willingness, even his eagerness, to surrender himself to his inspiration, to become merely the instrument of that "Great Spirit! Deepest Love!" whose voice is poetry, and whose presence in man's nature is Imagination. For such a surrender and such a union bring with them a state of being incomparably richer, more intense, more vital, than can ever be achieved within the limits of personality. Hence arises that peculiar ecstasy which, as in "Life of Life," the *Ode to the West Wind*, *Epipsychidion*, and the latter

---

[87] *A Defence*, in Shawcross, p. 144.

[88] *Ibid.*, p. 130. Shelley admits that these characters are not morally perfect, but says that "a poet considers the vices of his contemporaries as a temporary dress in which his creations must be arrayed, and which cover without concealing the eternal proportions of their beauty."

[89] *Ibid.*, p. 154.

part of *Adonais*, distinguishes Shelley from all other poets; and which, by its very purity and intensity, baffles or repels those readers who desire a more personal, or more "human," happiness. Hence comes, also, the despairing protest with which, so often, the poet descends into "the dull vapours of the little world of self." "Woe is me!" he cries at the close of *Epipsychidion*, as the vision of "Love's rare universe" fades away, and he awakens in the dull, cold world of things.[90]

I have already urged that the desire to transcend personality is not weakness but wisdom. And it should here be emphasized that Imagination does not so much deny explicitly the real existence of personality as it irradiates the world with so intense a light that personality appears the unreal shadow which it is. Thus Shelley describes his mystical Witch of Atlas, the daughter of Apollo, who is Imagination personified.[91]

[90] Mr. Solve, whose criticism is often penetrating and just, comments: " 'Woe is me!' says Shelley in the concluding verses, not because the dream union with the feminine ideal cannot be consummated; not because an earthly flight to a happy island is impracticable; but because he cannot get away from his mundane symbols — himself and Emilia — into a mystical union with the infinite. He never achieves the last and highest mystical state." *Shelley: His Theory of Poetry*, p. 169. It appears to me that it is rather perilous, in the nature of things, to talk about "the last and highest mystical state," and decide whether some person has or has not attained it. And I suppose that if a person did attain it, he would scarcely be able to express it in poetry — mysticism being by definition an incommunicable experience. It is often alleged, indeed, as a sign of weakness, that Shelley is never able to rest in the vision to which he has attained. But here again, perhaps, it is not impertinent to ask, "Who ever has been able to, or can be — at least as long as he remains human and mortal, 'Imprisoned . . . In a body like a grave'?" (*With a Guitar, to Jane*, l. 39.) Galahad never returns from his quest. I do not say that Shelley did reach "the last and highest mystical state," because I do not myself know what that is. But I cannot help wondering whether most of Shelley's critics are, in this respect, qualified to sit in judgment upon him.

[91] Cf. E. E. Kellett, *Suggestions*. Mr. Kellett has a long essay tending to show that the poem is an allegory illustrating the nature and workings of the Creative Imagination; and, I think, demonstrates beyond question the general truth of his view. I cannot believe, however, that Shelley worked with such a deliberate allegorical purpose as Mr. Kellett's essay implies; and many details of his interpretation seem questionable. I will, nevertheless, offer one suggestion of my own: that the meaning of the surpassingly beautiful but obscure stanzas lxix and lxxi is that Imagination is both the power which inspires men to high and noble deeds and that which enshrines them and their achievements in the memory of the race, "beyond the rage Of life or death." For a different and even more explicit interpretation of the poem see Carl H. Grabo, *The Meaning of the Witch of Atlas* (University of North Carolina Press, 1935). Mr. Grabo argues that Shelley is deliberately expounding esoteric neo-Platonic doctrines, as well as theories of contemporary

> For she was beautiful — her beauty made
>   The bright world dim, and everything beside
> Seemed like the fleeting image of a shade:
>   No thought of living spirit could abide,
> Which to her looks had ever been betrayed,
>   On any object in the world so wide,
> Or any hope within the circling skies,
> But on her form, and in her inmost eyes.[92]

All the beauty of art, of poetry, even of the whole world of sense, is but

> A shadow for the splendour of her love.[93]

Always Shelley insists that particular things are in themselves illusory, that the "one Spirit" which lives in them, and in which they live — so far as they have life — is the only reality. And this Spirit, and our kinship with it, are made known to us by Imagination. Nothing else but this is the meaning of the famous and often misunderstood passage in *Epipsychidion*, which here, for once, I bring into its proper context.

> True Love in this differs from gold and clay,
> That to divide is not to take away.
> Love is like understanding, that grows bright,
> Gazing on many truths; 'tis like thy light,
> Imagination! which from earth and sky,
> And from the depths of human fantasy,
> As from a thousand prisms and mirrors, fills
> The Universe with glorious beams, and kills
> Error, the worm, with many a sun-like arrow
> Of its reverberated lightning. Narrow
> The heart that loves, the brain that contemplates,
> The life that wears, the spirit that creates
> One object, and one form, and builds thereby
> A sepulchre for its eternity.[94]

Imagination is the enemy of self. But it is so because it awakens in us the consciousness of a higher Self. It is, indeed, nothing else

physical science. His arguments seem to me, however, to be unconvincing. What I am convinced of is that the prevalent tendency to read hard and fast allegorical meaning into imaginative poetry is both perilous and pointless.

[92] Stanza xii.   [93] Stanza xiii.

[94] Ll. 160–73. The real parallel here is not with Godwin's theory of free love, but with Bradley's philosophy of religion. Cf. note 79 above. With ll. 166–69 cf. the passage from the *Hymn of Apollo* quoted above.

than self-consciousness, in the fullest sense of the word. It is the
essence of divinity, as Apollo proclaims in the last stanza of his
splendid *Hymn*.

> I am the eye with which the Universe
>   Beholds itself and knows itself divine;
> All harmony of instrument or verse,
>   All prophecy, all medicine is mine,
> All light of art or nature . . .[95]

And again:

> Whatever lamps on Earth or Heaven may shine
> Are portions of one power, which is mine.

Imagination, for Shelley, is the lamp lighted by God in the soul
of man, by which it "beholds itself and knows itself divine," and
is guided toward the perfect realization of that divinity.[96]

But if Shelley's conception of Imagination, as being divine in
its origin and inscrutable in its workings, resembles very closely
the Christian doctrine of Grace, it is not the "irresistible Grace" of
Calvinism. Shelley was too resolute in his hatred of fatalism, and
too steadfast in his faith in the power of will, to accept such a
belief. He does indeed declare in *A Defence of Poetry* that poets
are often the passive instruments of a power greater than they,
and that "even whilst they deny and abjure, they are yet compelled

---

[95] Cf. the *Ode to Heaven*, ll. 19–22.

> Even thy name is as a god,
> Heaven! for thou art the abode
> Of that Power which is the glass
> Wherein man his nature sees.

[96] It is to be noted, also, that Shelley treats Imagination as *always* a power for
good. If it were a merely human attribute, there would be no reason why it might
not work for evil. Certainly, in actual experience, what is commonly called imagination may be a strong factor in leading persons to commit immoral acts. And,
as certainly (I should say, although I should hesitate to give examples), a work
of literature may be the result of a very powerful imagination and yet be extremely immoral both in aim and in effect. Shelley ought logically, perhaps (cf.
what was said in the last chapter in regard to eternal punishment), to have taken
these facts into consideration, and to have attributed them to the supernatural Spirit
of Evil of *The Revolt of Islam*. Possibly there is a suggestion of such a notion in
the reference in *Prometheus Unbound* to "the all-miscreative brain of Jove" (I,
l. 448). But Shelley chooses to define Imagination as the power by which man
"participates in the eternal, the infinite, and the one" — that is, in the Good; while
Evil is conceived by him as necessarily connected with Time, limitation, and
separateness.

to serve, the power which is seated on the throne of their own soul." [97] But such utterances as this may be taken merely as extreme statements of what no intelligent person denies, the inexplicability of poetic genius.[98] In the *Essay on Christianity*, which so closely resembles *A Defence*, it is explicitly stated that the harmonizing of man's nature with the Spirit of Good by which he is visited depends upon his own will.[99] A similar thought is elaborated in the Preface to *Alastor*.

The Poet's self-centered seclusion was avenged by the furies of an irresistible passion pursuing him to speedy ruin. But that Power which strikes the luminaries of the world with sudden darkness and extinction, by awakening them to too exquisite a perception of its influences, dooms to a slow and poisonous decay those meaner spirits that dare to abjure its dominion. Their destiny is more abject and inglorious as their delinquency is more contemptible and pernicious. They who, deluded by no generous error, instigated by no sacred thirst of doubtful knowledge, duped by no illustrious superstition, loving nothing on this earth, and cherishing no hopes beyond, yet keep aloof from sympathies with their kind, rejoicing neither in human joy nor mourning with human grief; these, and such as they, have their apportioned curse. They languish, because none feel with them their common nature. They are morally dead. . . . Among those who attempt to exist without human sympathy, the pure and tender-hearted perish through the intensity and passion of their search after its communities, when the vacancy of their spirit suddenly makes itself felt. All else, selfish, blind, and torpid, are those unforeseeing multitudes who constitute, together with their own, the lasting misery and loneliness of the world. Those who love not their fellow-beings live unfruitful lives, and prepare for their old age a miserable grave.[1]

In a similar mood Shelley declares in a note to *Hellas* that "it is the province of the poet to attach himself to those ideas which exalt and ennoble humanity." So it appears that it is not enough

[97] Shawcross, p. 159.

[98] Shelley was hard put to it, in defending his theory that poetry is always connected with good, to reconcile his great admiration for the writings of Wordsworth and Byron with his rather low opinion of their moral characters. In one of his letters he exclaims characteristically, at meeting fresh evidence of what he regarded as Wordsworth's apostasy from the cause of Liberty: "That such a man should be such a poet!" *Letters*, II, 607.

[99] See Shawcross, pp. 91, 112.

[1] I cannot refrain from asking the reader, once more, to consider whether this passage sounds like Godwin.

that a man should wait passively for the visitations of the divinity. "Poetry is the record of the best and happiest moments of the happiest and best minds." [2] And this statement clearly implies not only that men are good and happy because of the influence of a higher Power, but that they become subject to such influence because they have made themselves happy and good. "The mind becomes that which it contemplates"; and men may certainly choose the objects of their contemplation, and in the intervals between the moments of inspired existence, struggle toward the realization of the ideals which those moments have revealed to them.

In this struggle the impelling force is Love. The power that makes us conscious of the presence in the world and in ourselves of the divine Spirit of Good whose nature is the source of all our moral ideals, is Imagination. The desire which is aroused thereby for complete union with that Spirit, is Love. Imagination and Love are, indeed, only two different elements in the one Divine Nature; but in that Nature's wielding of the world they work in different ways: the first "kindles it above," the second "sustains it from beneath."

It is with Shelley's conception of Love that we have now to deal. No other part of his philosophy, perhaps, has been the object of such diversity of judgment, of such sharp censure and, occasionally, such passionate defense. In neither case has the critic usually attempted really to understand Shelley's views, by placing them in relation to his life and writings as a whole. Such is the aim of the present discussion.

VI

In the first place, *love*, according to Shelley, is not primarily sexual love, which is in itself relatively unimportant. In this, as in so many other respects, a number of factors have conspired to place Shelley in a false light before the world: his unfortunate union with Harriet, the jealousy of Mary, the fierce attacks on marriage and chastity in *Queen Mab*, the slanderous assaults of the reviews, the prudery of the Victorians, and the sheer stupidity or misapplied ingenuity which in every age manages to pass itself off as literary

[2] *A Defence*, in Shawcross, p. 154.

criticism. The result has been that even most of Shelley's professed
admirers have regarded him as (in Arnold's phrase) "extremely
inflammable." As a matter of fact, there is no real evidence that he
was ever in love with any woman except Mary Godwin, unless we
except his youthful romance with Harriet Grove. In regard to
Harriet Westbrook, we find him, in a letter to Hogg written three
months after he had made her acquaintance and three months before
she asked him to run off with her, declaiming against Intolerance
as follows: "Yes! The fiend, the wretch, shall fall! Harriet will
do for one of the crushers . . ." [3] To the same friend the young
Quixote writes after rescuing Harriet from her supposed sufferings:
"Gratitude and admiration all demand that I should love her *for
ever*." [4] And a few months later he asks Miss Hitchener to help
him "to mould a really noble soul [i.e., Harriet] into all that can
make its nobleness useful and lovely." [5] Surely this is strange
language for a lover! As for Miss Hitchener herself, Shelley's
letters to her, however extravagent and effusive they may appear,
are in a sense entirely impersonal. It would be hard to distinguish
them, either in tone or in content, from the letters to Hogg, except
that the latter contain more human affection. [6] In the same way,
the later letters to Clare Clairmont, of which so much has sometimes been made, are in tone very little different, except for an
occasional curt reproof, from his letters to Leigh Hunt. In the case
of Emilia Viviani, the following passage from a letter to Clare
written shortly after the composition of *Epipsychidion* will provide
the necessary handful of salt to be taken with most of the critical
comment on that poem. "My conception of Emilia's talents augments every day. Her moral nature is fine — but not above circumstances . . ." [7] Likewise, all that Shelley seems to have sought

[3] *Letters*, I, 63. He adds that Eliza, "with some taming, will do, too." As the
sequel shows, however, he underestimated Eliza.

[4] *Ibid.*, p. 130.   [5] *Ibid.*, p. 150.

[6] I do not know that any biographer, in recounting Shelley's alleged ill treatment
of Miss Hitchener, has noted the fact that, after being dismissed from the Shelley
household, she wrote a malicious and angry letter trying to injure Shelley with his
friend Williams of Tremadoc, and also, after returning to her home, tried to
blacken the reputation of Shelley and Harriet by publishing false charges against
them. (*Letters*, I, 396–97.)

[7] *Letters*, II, 844 (January 16, 1821). There seems to be some confusion as to
the date of composition of *Epipsychidion*. Hutchinson and Locock, in their respec-

from Jane Williams was the comradeship that he had ceased to receive from Mary.[8]

So much for the facts of Shelley's life in regard to his love for women. And now, what of his theories? Even in *Queen Mab* it will be apparent to the careful reader that Shelley's furious attacks on marriage and chastity (which is characterized as a "monkish and evangelical superstition," almost in the tone of most modern writers on sex problems) are not at all a plea for self-indulgence, but, on the contrary, a denunciation of selfishness and sensuality.[9] Further light is thrown on his attitude by his review of Hogg's novel, *Memoirs of Prince Alexy Haimatoff*, in which, speaking of the character of Alexy's tutor, he declares: "But we cannot regard his recommendation to his pupil to indulge in promiscuous concubinage without horror and detestation. The author appears to deem the loveless intercourse of brutal appetite a venial offense against delicacy and virtue! he asserts that a transient connexion with a cultivated female may contribute to form the heart without essentially vitiating the sensibilities. It is our duty to protest against so pernicious and disgusting an opinion." [10] And later he protests even more feelingly against "the fashionable superstitions of gallantry . . . the sordid feelings which with blind idolatry worship the image and blaspheme the deity, reverence the type, and degrade the reality of which it is an emblem."[11] Love seems always to have

tive editions of Shelley's poems, and Peck, in his *Life*, assign it to the first weeks of 1821. But Ingpen says in a note (*Letters*, I, 849–50): "Shelley had completed the poem before the end of the preceding year, for Mary Shelley in writing to Leigh Hunt on December 29, 1820, says: 'He [Shelley] has written a long poem [*Epipsychidion*] which no one has ever read, and like the illustrious Sotheby, gives the law to a few distinguished Blues of Pisa.'" Shelley had first seen Emilia early in December (Dowden, II, 370). It is probable, as Woodberry suggests (*Poetical Works*, p. 436), "that a poem, substantially *Epipsychidion*, was in Shelley's mind before his meeting with Emilia Viviani, and that she was less the inspiration of it than the occasion of the form it took." The MS. was sent to Ollier on February 16, 1821.

[8] At least, so we must conclude until we can examine the "unpublished letter to Byron" already referred to, which is mentioned by Mr. Peck.

[9] See the note on V, l. 189 (Hutchinson, pp. 806–08). For his later attitude toward marriage, see his comment on *Queen Mab* in a letter to Gisborne, June 16, 1821 (*Letters*, II, 878); and *The Witch of Atlas*, stanza lxxvii, where the Witch helps a pair of lovers to find "happiness in marriage warm and kind."

[10] Shawcross, pp. 12–13. Written in 1814. This is exactly the Victorian attitude toward Shelley — of which the injustice here becomes evident.

[11] *Ibid.*, p. 17.

meant, for Shelley, not so much a fulfilment of passion as a communion of intellectual interests and moral ideals, and the selfless sympathy to which such a community gives birth. So, when Harriet ceased to share his interests and care for his ideals, he felt that there was nothing left. Shelley states his position very clearly in his *Essay on the Literature and Arts of the Athenians*, written in 1818. In discussing the origin of love, he says:

Man is in his wildest state a social being: a certain degree of civilization and refinement ever produces the want of sympathies still more intimate and complete; and the gratification of the senses is no longer all that is sought in sexual connection. It soon becomes a very small part of that profound and complicated sentiment, which we call love, which is rather the universal thirst for a communion not only of the senses, but of our whole nature, intellectual, imaginative and sensitive, and which, when individualized, becomes an imperious necessity, only to be satisfied by the complete or partial, actual or supposed fulfillment of its claims. . . . The sexual impulse, which is only one, and often a small part of those claims, serves, from its obvious and external nature, as a kind of type or expression of the rest, a common basis, an acknowledged and visible link.[12]

This is perhaps the strain in Shelley which the critic objects to as "priggish theorizing." But it will at any rate go far toward discountenancing the popular belief that Shelley was constantly preoccupied with emotions arising directly from sex. Moreover, in the essay *On Love*, there is not only no mention of sex but it seems scarcely to be in the writer's mind. Here, as elsewhere in his later work, he records the struggle to transcend the limitations of personality; and not only difference of sex, but distinction of persons, is to be lost in the mystic ecstasy. It is worth noting, also, that Shelley in the first part of the essay clearly implies that he is speaking a language which few men will understand, and that, therefore, the meaning he attaches to the word *love* is widely different from that which it expresses in common speech.

What is love? Ask him who lives, what is life? ask him who adores, what is God?

I know not the internal constitution of other men, nor even thine, whom I now address. I see that in some external attributes they resemble

---

[12] Shawcross, pp. 39–40. He continues: "Still it is a claim which even derives a strength not its own from the accessory circumstances which surround it, and one which our nature thirsts to satisfy."

me, but when, misled by that appearance, I have thought to appeal to something common, and unburthen my inmost soul to them, I have found my language misunderstood, like one in a distant and savage land. . . .

Thou demandest what is love? It is that powerful attraction towards all that we conceive, or fear, or hope beyond ourselves, when we find within our own thoughts the chasm of an insufficient void, and seek to awaken in all things that are, a community with what we experience within ourselves. If we reason, we would be understood; if we imagine, we would that the airy children of our brain were born anew within another's; if we feel, we would that another's nerves should vibrate to our own, that the beams of their eyes should kindle at once and mix and melt into our own, that lips of motionless ice should not reply to lips quivering and burning with the heart's best blood. This is Love. This is the bond and the sanction which connects not only man with man, but with everything that exists. We are born into the world, and there is something within us which, from the instant that we live, more and more thirsts after its own likeness. . . . We dimly see within our intellectual nature a miniature as it were of our entire self, yet deprived of all that we condemn or despise, the ideal prototype of everything excellent or lovely that we are capable of conceiving as belonging to the nature of man. Not only the portrait of our external being, but an assemblage of the minutest particles of which our nature is composed;[13] a mirror whose surface reflects only the forms of purity and brightness; a soul within our soul that describes a circle around its proper paradise, which pain, and sorrow, and evil dare not overleap. To this we eagerly refer all sensations, thirsting that they should resemble or correspond with it. The discovery of its antitype; the meeting with an understanding capable of clearly estimating our own; an imagination which should enter into and seize upon the subtle and delicate peculiarities which we have delighted to cherish and unfold in secret; with a frame whose nerves, like the chords of two exquisite lyres, strung to the accompaniment of one delighted voice, vibrate with the vibrations of our own; and of a combination of all these in such proportion as the type within demands; this is the invisible and unattainable point to which Love tends; and to attain which, it urges forth the powers of man to arrest the faintest shadow of that, without the possession of which there is no rest nor respite to the heart over which it rules. Hence in solitude, or in that deserted state when we are surrounded by human beings, and yet they sympathize not with us, we love the flowers, the grass, and the waters, and the sky.[14]

[13] "These words are ineffectual and metaphorical. Most words are so — No help!" (Shelley's note.)

[14] Shawcross, pp. 43–45. Nobody seems to know when this essay was written. Mr. White says (*The Best of Shelley*, p. 511): "Mrs. Shelley in publishing it in

To a certain class of minds, as Shelley himself declares in the "Advertisement" to *Epipsychidion,* such an utterance as this "must ever remain incomprehensible, from a defect of a common organ of perception for the ideas of which it treats." And I do not myself understand the exact meaning of all that Shelley says in this essay; but it ought to be clear to the most prosaic mind that sexual love can be only an incidental part of the experience of which Shelley is here speaking.

There is evidence, too, that the poet's early condemnation of

> dull and selfish chastity,
> That virtue of the cheaply virtuous
> Who pride themselves in senselessness and frost,[15]

was later retracted, and that his attitude on this subject underwent a vast change. In a note to *Hellas* he writes, comparing the Greek gods to Christ, that it "cannot be said, that as far as temperance and chastity are concerned, they gave so edifying an example as their successor." Such a statement shows that Shelley was not oblivious to the implied disparagement of the love of the sexes which is present in so much of the Gospel teaching, and that he was not now repelled by it. And in this connection may perhaps be mentioned, for what it is worth, Trelawny's story of how, attempting to twit Shelley for his pretended non-recognition of his infant son by saying, "You are not the wise man that knows his own child," he received the terse answer: "The wise men have none." [16] No doubt this is a hard saying, and some may think it rather a bitter one for a man still in his twenties. But it shows the direction in which Shelley was moving. I do not say, of course, that he reached the

---

Essays, Letters, etc., 1840 seems to suppose it to have been written about 1820 or 1821, but Rossetti's and Forman's date of 1815 is generally accepted as more probable." I do not know why, except that it has been the usual practice of editors to lump all Shelley's short prose essays together, and assign them to 1815. In the apparent absence of any external evidence, however, I should assign it to 1818 (the year of *Prince Athanase*) at the very earliest; and I have no doubt that Mrs. Shelley had good reasons for placing it in 1820 or 1821.

[15] *Queen Mab,* IX, ll. 84–86.

[16] *Records,* p. 74. I do not think that even Trelawny's imagination was equal to the invention of this story. Just previously, upon the child's crying, the poet remarked:

> "When we are born, we cry that we are come
> To this great stage of fools."

point of advocating an ideal of celibacy.[17] But certainly *The Triumph of Life,* in its picture of the sufferings of Rousseau, and of
the destruction wrought by the "fierce Spirit" of passionate love,
or desire, as well as in its whole tone and feeling, points uncom-
promisingly in the direction of asceticism. And such is the natural,
perhaps the inevitable, outcome of Shelley's denial of the real
existence of personality.[18]

From this analysis of Shelley's views on sexual love, we may now
return to *Epipsychidion;* for as long as this poem continues to be
regarded as a record of personal passion and a defense of "free
love," Shelley will not be understood. And let us consider first
the passage which has already been quoted, beginning

> True Love in this differs from gold and clay,
> That to divide is not to take away,

and continuing with a comparison of Love and Imagination to the
conclusion:
> Narrow
> The heart that loves, the brain that contemplates,
> The life that wears, the spirit that creates
> One object, and one form, and builds thereby
> A sepulchre for its eternity.

The interpretation commonly given to this part of the poem is
accepted by the author of one of the latest and most pretentious
studies of Shelley. Mr. Peck declares that the poet is here [19] offering

---

[17] *A Philosophical View of Reform* (written early in 1820) contains a bitter
attack on Malthus for what Shelley calls his "insulting advice" to the poor "to
conquer, with minds undisciplined in the habits of higher gratification, a propensity
which persons of the most consummate wisdom have been unable to resist, and
which it is difficult to admire any one for having resisted" (page 52). Even this,
however, is a far cry from *Queen Mab;* and the chief reason for his objection is
that the hardship will fall mainly upon the poor, "whose igorance leads them to
exaggerate the advantages of sensual enjoyment" (page 53).

[18] For some interesting speculations concerning Shelley's attitude toward sex, see
Carpenter and Barnefield, *The Psychology of the Poet Shelley.* Mr. Carpenter's
essay is both sympathetic and suggestive. Mr. Barnefield bases fantastic theories
upon very superficial knowledge. If anything could convince an unbiased observer
of the truth of the contentions of the Freudians, it would be their own mental
processes, and the way in which they seem to become obsessed by the one idea of sex.

[19] Mr. Peck quotes only the lines preceding the passage that I have quoted:
> I never was attached to that great sect,
> Whose doctrine is, that each one should select,
> Out of the crowd a mistress or a friend,

a "defence of all those males who are not the home-makers, but, except as they are confined by law and custom, free lovers, ever seeking fresh inspiration in new acquaintanceships and new affections." [20] I do not know what sort of mind it can be that is able to perpetrate such a judgment. Timothy Shelley himself never showed a grosser ignorance of his son's character and ways of thinking, or betrayed a more Calibanic incompetence to understand the Ariel who inexplicably happened to be his son, than the biographer here manifests toward the pure spirit who had the ill fortune to come under his heavy hand. When we remember Shelley's despair of ever finding happiness within the limits of personality, and his constant reference to life in the physical world as "death" or "a mockery," and to his body as "a grave"; [21] when

(Note 19 cont.)   And all the rest, though fair and wise, commend
                   To cold oblivion, though it is in the code
                   Of modern morals, and the beaten road
                   Which those poor slaves with weary footsteps tread
                   Who travel to their home among the dead
                   By the broad highway of the world, and so
                   With one chained friend, perhaps a jealous foe,
                   The dreariest and the longest journey go. (Ll. 149–59.)

But he has no right to separate it from what follows, in the light of which it appears only as a protest against the mean jealousy and crude possessiveness which law and custom sanction in the marriage relation.

[20] *Life*, II, 190. Mr. Peck thinks that the poem *Ginevra* also refers to Shelley's love for Emilia (although the subject was taken from an Italian source; it is a pity that a person so addicted to source-hunting should, when he comes upon a source which really is of some slight significance, fail to make any use of it; of course, his theory would be absurd even if there were not a source); and that in it "we can feel Shelley's passion for the girl and his desire that she should embark with him on an adventure comparable to that which Mary had taken with him in 1814; though all this is concealed under a thin veil of dramatic narrative." (*Ibid.*, p. 207.) He also suggests that the *Epithalamium* written in 1821 celebrates the imagined consummation of Shelley's passion for Emilia, and that the sad lyrics of that year reflect the poet's grief that the consummation was *only* imaginary. To this sort of thing must be applied the words of W. M. Rossetti: "I am not aware that even

'A scandal-monger beyond all belief'

has ever said or insinuated that Shelley's love for Emilia (for love, in a certain sense, it may clearly be called) was other than 'Platonic': if anybody *has* said so, the statement is presumably as unworthy of attention as it is incapable of mathematical disproof." ("Memoir of Shelley," in *Poetical Works*, 1878, Vol. I, p. 103.) I do not understand how Mr. Peck can at times present Shelley as patient, practical, self-sacrificing, and high-minded, and at other times make him appear completely selfish, as well as passionate and capricious. I do not believe that such a contradiction can exist in a human being.

[21] *With a Guitar, to Jane*, l. 39; *Remembrance*, l. 21.

we recall the close relation which exists for him between Imagination and Love, as different manifestations of that transcendent Spirit in which man desires to lose his *self;* when we see how relatively slight an allowance, in his theorizing about love, is made for the claims of sex; when we find him regarding love as the bond which connects "not only man with man" (to say nothing of merely connecting man with *woman*) "but with everything which exists"; and when in the poem itself we find Shelley saying to Emilia, in two of the few passages where she can be felt to have any existence as a human being: "Would we two had been twins of the same mother!" and

> To whatsoe'er of dull mortality
> Is mine, remain a vestal sister still [22]

then we may — and must, unless we choose to be blind — see the folly of regarding the poem as a glorification of sexual passion. The critic is very near the truth who remarks that Shelley "hated the flesh and he was hardly of the flesh." [23]

It is true that there are a few lines near the end of the poem which seem at first glance to express an altogether earthly passion.

> Our breath shall intermix, our bosoms bound,
> And our veins beat together; and our lips
> With other eloquence than words, eclipse
> The soul that burns between them . . . [24]

As far as these lines give the impression of being a literal description, and thereby fail to harmonize with the pure mysticism — "too deep For the brief fathom-line of thought or sense" [25] — which informs almost the whole poem, so far they constitute an artistic defect. Still, it ought to be clear to the genuine student of Shelley that the poet here is only doing what all mystical poets have done: that is, using the experience of sexual love to symbolize that by which such experience is completely transcended. And critics who cannot understand such a procedure are in the situation of Adam inquiring of Raphael concerning love among the angels. To Shelley,

[22] Ll. 45, 389–90.
[23] J. de Gruyter, *English Studies*, IV, 131, "Shelley and Dostoievsky."
[24] Ll. 565–68.
[25] Ll. 90–91.

indeed, it is sometimes a mere poetic device; and we find him addressing such lines as

> Clasp me till our hearts be grown
> Like two shadows into one —— [26]

to a woman? no, to a mere abstraction — and *Misery* at that! A loftier example is Panthea's description of her dream of Prometheus:

> I saw not, heard not, moved not, only felt
> His presence flow and mingle through my blood
> Till it became his life, and his grew mine . . . [27]

where there can be no question of sexual love, except as a symbol of a purely spiritual and mystical experience. How altogether spiritual is Shelley's attitude toward love between the sexes is evident from his almost unbounded admiration of the *Paradise* of Dante's *Divine Comedy*. "His apotheosis of Beatrice in Paradise, and the gradations of his own love and her loveliness, by which as by steps he feigns himself to have ascended to the throne of the Supreme Cause, is the most glorious imagination of modern poetry." [28] *Epipsychidion* was avowedly written with Dante's work in mind, and it is inconceivable, however faulty may be the artistry, that the poem was intended to celebrate the pleasures of sexual love.

And now, returning to the passage with which this discussion began, it may be said without apology that nothing could make more bitterly clear the intellectual incompetence and spiritual insensibility that degrade so much of what passes for literary criticism than the fact that the majority of critics have held that by "True Love" Shelley means "free love" in the vulgar sense. For the essence of such "love" is that it is centered in personality, that principle of separateness, or self, which Shelley here, as elsewhere, condemns as the parent of error; that it is inspired not by worship of the ideal but by a mere craving for variety of emotional stimuli; and that it makes the gratification of personal desire, which Shelley

---

[26] *Invocation to Misery*, ll. 46–47. I must protest once more against the "fatal facility" with which most critics read into Shelley's poetry the record of an actual, personal experience.

[27] *Prometheus Unbound*, II, i, ll. 79–81.

[28] *A Defence of Poetry*, in Shawcross, p. 144.

from first to last condemned in others and strove to conquer in himself, the sole criterion of value.

Moreover (for, since Shelley's detractors raise this question, let us see it through to the end), must not much the same statement be made of that ideal of domestic love which was so dear to the Victorians, and which has impelled so many of the critical stones launched in Shelley's direction by those who have fancied themselves to be without sin? For that love, likewise, is in its very nature bounded by the narrow limits of personality, seeks only a personal satisfaction, and is after all essentially selfish in its aim. It no doubt conduces, human nature being what it is, to giving the greatest number of persons the greatest amount of what they call happiness; and it probably makes for social stability. And, moreover, it usually demands a measure — and often a large measure — of self-sacrifice, which always leads toward a purer and better state of being. But still, the ideal which it attempts to realize is a narrow one; and one which, when realized, does not lead beyond itself, or arouse any desire for more than the personal satisfaction of those involved; so that it rather quenches than kindles the aspiration, the constant presence of which I take to be the mark of the religious life, toward an ever more nearly perfect union with the supreme Good Will. I do not say, of course, that such is always the result. Even in marriage, one supposes, life may be lived well. But if so, it must be by a common devotion to an ideal of which the realization demands the transcending of every personal desire. "The preliminary moral act" is declared by Shelley, as by Carlyle, to be "annihilation of self"; and most of his adverse critics only betray their inability to rise to the height of his ideal of renunciation. Thus Sir Leslie Stephen asserts, in criticizing Shelley, that the highest human love is that which is directed toward a single person: "Human love, one would say, becomes a fitting type of a loftier emotion, in so far as it implies exclusive devotion to its object." [29] Does it? Is it better to love one object, *merely* as an object, than to love many objects, merely as objects? And if one loves an object because it is the partial embodiment of an ideal, must one be indifferent to every other object that embodies the same ideal? Such was not

[29] *Op. cit.*, p. 388.

the teaching of Plato, and it was not the teaching of a greater than Plato. "If any man come to me, and hate not his father, and mother, and wife, and children, and brethren, and sisters, yea, and his own life also, he cannot be my disciple." [30] The ideal Good which is the object of worship of every true religion permits to its worshippers no divided allegiance; it claims their love and service and sacrifice whenever and wherever it appears; and the love of any particular object or person for its own sake becomes idolatry. And this, I believe, is the doctrine which Shelley's poetry is intended to teach, as it is the doctrine which his life does in fact exemplify.

VII

Here I may perhaps add a few words to the many that have been written about Shelley and "Platonic love." And first I wish to offer a protest (to which Plato's master, at least, would not have objected) against regarding the phrase as a sort of magic talisman, or considering as the ultimate attainable truth any idea it may suggest. It seems to be a convention among literary critics to assume, when they think that they have shown that a writer did or did not hold certain beliefs which they think were held by Plato, that the writer is therefore necessarily deserving of praise or censure. Now, it is precisely such conventions as this that Socrates, at least in the early dialogues, takes most pleasure in assailing. Why should Shelley's views about love be condemned out of hand because they are thought not to be the same as those of Plato? Or why should they receive extravagant praise because they *are* thought to be the same? "Platonic love," as I understand it, is indeed a high and beautiful ideal. But I do not think that it is a higher or a better ideal than the love that is preached by Christ or the love that is taught by Buddha.

The theory of love most often associated with the name of Plato, which is put into the mouth of Diotima in the *Symposium,* and which appears again in Book VII of *The Republic,* represents the soul as gradually ascending, by a series of more or less definite steps, from the preoccupation with things to the contemplation of Ideas. Those who love after this manner "ascend through the

[30] Luke 14: 26.

contemplation of these transitory objects which are beautiful, towards that which is beauty itself, proceeding as on steps from the love of one form to that of two, and from that of two to that of all forms which are beautiful; and from beautiful forms to beautiful habits and institutions, and from institutions to beautiful doctrines; until, from the meditation of many doctrines, they arrive at that which is nothing else than the doctrine of the supreme beauty itself, in the knowledge and contemplation of which at length they repose." [31] If we neglect the almost mathematical precision of the process as it is here described, we may perhaps accept the definition or description which is given by Santayana: "the transformation of the appreciation of beautiful things into the worship of an ideal beauty, and the transformation of the love of particular persons into the love of God." [32] Now, the obvious and easy comment is that in Shelley we find no emphasis upon a gradual ascent, by means of an intellectual discipline, to the contemplation of the Idea of Beauty, or to that which Plato usually places still higher, the Idea of Good; but instead, an intuition (a "mere feeling") of the transient presence in all beautiful things of some transcendental Spirit of Beauty,[33] with which he desires immediate and complete union. This distinction seems to me to be in large measure just: the rationalistic element in Plato has no counterpart in Shelley. The worship of reason and the interest in logic which are so often present in the *Dialogues* seem to have had for Shelley small appeal.

But the matter must not be left at this point. Those who have been interested in comparing Shelley with Plato for the sake of disparaging the former have, I think, sometimes done an injustice to the latter. The course of love as described in the *Symposium* is far from being a hard and fast process, directed toward a definite and completely comprehensible end. It must in the last analysis be called a mystical experience. And, besides, against the *Symposium* may be placed the *Phaedrus*, in which love is described as depending

[31] *Symposium*, § 211 (Shelley's translation).
[32] *Interpretations of Poetry and Religion*, p. 120.
[33] And not, I think, an *Idea* of Beauty. But cf. Solve, *op. cit.*, p. 174. Mr. Solve elsewhere (pages 159–63) makes some excellent comments on Shelley and Platonic love.

upon divine inspiration, as being a "madness" (not in any disparaging sense) which has little to do with reason; and this view of love, so far as I can judge, agrees very nearly with Shelley's. And I do not see that this conception is inferior morally (for I take it that the common criticism of Shelley's theory of love is essentially moral in its bias) to that of the *Symposium*. I will even venture to suggest that in the latter dialogue Plato lets his intellectualism lead him into a neglect of the nature of love as it is in fact experienced. I do not believe that progress toward a more pure and intense and exalted love proceeds, as is implied in the *Symposium*, like the demonstration of a geometrical proposition. What, after all, has love to do with reason? How can it be a process of merely intellectual discipline? So far as I understand the subject, the highest and purest love is the result not at all of a rational, but primarily of a *moral*, development. It is not a matter of climbing some logical ladder, but of checking the struggles toward selfishness and sensuality of the dark steed of passionate desire, and compelling it to the service of the Ideal Beauty or Good.[34]

Moreover, as Plato in the *Meno* raises the question of whether we learn what we know or what we do not know, and is forced to accept the former alternative, so it may be asserted, likewise, that only that which we know can be the object of love.[35] And how, then, can it be possible to proceed from love of things to love of Ideas, unless the Ideas are already in some way known? "Perhaps all discontent with the *less* (to use a Platonic sophism), supposes the sense of a just claim to the *greater*, and that we admirers of *Faust* are on the right road to Paradise." [36] Must not even the love described by Diotima begin with an immediate intuition of

---

[34] Cf. *The Triumph of Life*, where Plato himself is represented as having been conquered by Life — through Love. Shelley doubtless had in mind the probably apocryphal story of Plato's love for the boy named Aster: cf. ll. 256 ff.: "The star that ruled his doom," etc.; see A. C. Bradley, *Modern Language Review*, IX, 449–50.

[35] The similar question, whether we love what we possess or what we do not possess, is raised by Plato in the *Symposium*; and his answer is echoed by Shelley in *The Sensitive Plant*:

> It loves, even like Love, its deep heart is full,
> It desires what it has not, the Beautiful.
>
> (i. ll. 76–77.)

[36] *Letters*, II, 953.

the real existence of the Idea of Beauty? What else can be the source of that desire for "birth in beauty" which is said in the *Symposium* to be the essence of love? And hence it becomes clear that Shelley's swift passage from the perception of beautiful things to the faith in an Ideal Beauty, or rather in a Spirit of Beauty which gives life to all beautiful forms, is not necessarily un-Platonic, or illogical, or weak, or indicative of a lack of insight or of a false inspiration. It shows merely that Shelley does not share Plato's rationalistic bent.

This difference, to be sure, is significant. Because of it, Plato regards the highest good as Idea, Shelley as Spirit;[37] and, as a result, Plato's doctrines appear at times to possess a certain firmness and fixity, whereas Shelley's have often an appearance of fluidity. It is not Intellectual Beauty but Spiritual Beauty to which Shelley's *Hymn* is dedicated, as are "Life of Life" and *Epipsychidion;* and this, unlike the world of archetypal Ideas, which, as Plato seems to say, the light of reason can reveal, is by its very nature capable of being "seen nowhere," although "felt everywhere." But in making such a distinction, I am by no means willing to admit that of itself it shows Shelley's view to be the result of a less deep or less clear insight into the nature of ultimate reality than was possessed by Plato, or that it is a conception any less adequate than Plato's to the actual needs of men in their struggle toward a higher state of existence than they have yet attained.

It is doubtless true that such a sentiment as that expressed in the following stanza from *The Zucca* is foreign to Plato's thought: but this is no disparagement of Shelley.

> In winds, and trees, and streams, and all things common,
>   In music and the sweet unconscious tone
> Of animals, and voices which are human,
>   Meant to express some feelings of their own;
> In the soft motions and rare smile of woman,
>   In flowers and leaves, and in the grass fresh-shown,
> Or dying in the autumn, I the most
> Adore thee present or lament thee lost.[38]

[37] This distinction, of course, is intended to be only suggestive, and not dogmatic. If it is not always folly to dogmatize on such subjects, it is certainly so in regard to their treatment by Plato.

[38] Stanza v.

Nothing that Shelley ever wrote is more characteristic than this stanza; and nothing, I suppose, would better exemplify what his detractors would doubtless speak of contemptuously as "Romantic Platonism." But the reason for such contempt is not obvious. If the stanza seems vague and emotional in comparison with the words of Diotima, yet, on the other hand, the experience it expresses is far less narrow in scope and far less rigid in outline, less intellectualistic and tending less toward esthetic self-absorption, than that described in the *Symposium*. Shelley's goal is no less transcendent than Plato's and the world of sense is for its own sake quite as worthless to the poet as to the philosopher; but the end sought is not the contemplation of the Idea of Beauty, but the complete union with the living Spirit of Beauty which animates all beautiful things, with the God who made and dwells in the whole of "the living world." And who shall judge that the end is in one case possible and desirable, and in the other not?

It is to be remarked, also, that Shelley's doctrine of love is not only less rationalistic than Plato's but far more inclusive. Shelley, after all, is the child of the Romantic Age, and he has a sense of divinity in the world of nature, of the sacredness of all life, and of the right of the meanest creature to participate in the being of its Creator, that seems to have been quite foreign to the Greek mind.[39] He feels that there is woven through all "the web of being" the same "sustaining Love." "I know," he cries in *Epipsychidion*,

> That Love makes all things equal: I have heard
> By mine own heart this joyous truth averred:
> The spirit of the worm beneath the sod
> In love and worship, blends itself with God.[40]

With Love there is no respect of persons. The humblest creature has its part in the divine scheme; and as it shares the burden of suffering that is borne by all living things in the world of Time, so it is not deprived of the presence of the redeeming power of Love. So Asia, herself the incarnation of Love, tells Panthea:

[39] Although Plato suggests (*Symposium*, § 207) that the lower animals participate, to some degree, in the same experience as that which man calls love.

[40] Ll. 126–29. F. H. Bradley quotes this couplet in his *Essays on Truth and Reality* (p. 244) and adds: "And not only in love and worship does such union hold, but in will also and in the knowledge and enjoyment of beauty and truth."

> all love is sweet,
> Given or returned. Common as light is love,
> And its familiar voice wearies not ever,
> Like the wide heaven, the all-sustaining air,
> It makes the reptile equal to the God . . .[41]

And this universality results not in the degradation but in the exaltation of love. As love becomes wider, it becomes deeper; as it becomes more inclusive, it becomes more pure and more intense: "to divide is not to take away," and this statement is true in the most literal sense.

> Mind from its object differs most in this:
> Evil from good; misery from happiness;
> The baser from the nobler; the impure
> And frail, from what is clear and must endure.
> If you divide suffering and dross, you may
> Diminish till it is consumed away;
> If you divide pleasure and love and thought,
> Each part exceeds the whole; and we know not
> How much, while any yet remains unshared,
> Of pleasure may be gained, of sorrow spared:
> This truth is that deep well, whence sages draw
> The unenvied light of hope; the eternal law
> By which those live, to whom this world of life
> Is as a garden ravaged, and whose strife
> Tills for the promise of a later birth
> The wilderness of this Elysian earth.[42]

VIII

This truth is also the deep well whence we must draw our understanding of Shelley's doctrine of love. But it is a truth not to be reasoned about, but to be felt; it must be known intuitively and immediately, or not at all. And if one does not feel it, and therefore chooses to say that it is not a truth, then, although he has a right to offer adverse criticism, yet this criticism will necessarily be point-

[41] *Prometheus Unbound*, II, v, ll. 39–43.
[42] *Epipsychidion*, ll. 174–89. These lines are also a part of the passage which Mr. Peck characterizes as a "defence of all those males who are not the homemakers." I offer no comment on the metaphysics of the first line. The words "evil from good," however, are significant as showing, again, Shelley's belief that evil does not participate in the eternal life which belongs to the nature of good, from which all true creation must proceed.

less to one whose feeling is the same as Shelley's. Here, as else-where, I can only say what seems to me to be true.

And, first, something should be said concerning the bearing of this doctrine of Shelley's upon our conception of the quality of love, as it is directed toward nature, man, and God. It is the humor of a certain school of critics and moralists to draw, as it seems to me unreasonably and presumptuously, "a resolute distinction between man and nature and between man and the divine." [43] The conclusion about Shelley that must be drawn from such an assumption is obvious: that in his desire to love everything, he in fact loves nothing, and therefore lives in that "void" to which men are always ready to dismiss whatever they have no sympathy with. But it is difficult to understand why a love of what is beautiful in nature should exclude a love of what is good in man, or that either love is incompatible with the love of the divine Spirit of Beauty and Goodness which is the source of the good and the beautiful, wherever these may appear. Rather it would seem that as the love of one of these portions of being becomes more pure and more intense, it should lend purity and intensity to the love of the others. So Shelley feels, in the realm of nature and of human life, the presence of that Deity which he also feels to be present in himself as "a soul within the soul," and in whose being he desires to lose his own; and a particular object is loved not for its own sake but as a manifestation of the divine.[44]

Such a love, as I have suggested, refuses to be confined within the limits of personality; and therefore it will seem to many persons to be vague, and empty, and unsatisfying, and less than human. But there are others to whom it opens what they know beyond the shadow of a doubt to be ever richer and fairer vistas of being, leading toward the final awakening from "the dream of life."

> I can give not what men call love,
>   But wilt thou accept not
>   The worship the heart lifts above

[43] Norman Foerster, *Humanism and America*, p. vii.

[44] Cf. *Symposium*, § 203: "The divine nature cannot immediately communicate with what is human, but all that intercourse and converse which is conceded by the Gods to men, both whilst they sleep and when they wake, subsists through the intervention of Love." (Shelley's translation.)

> And the Heavens reject not, —
> The desire of the moth for the star,
> Of the night for the morrow,
> The devotion to something afar
> From the sphere of our sorrow?

"The desire of the moth for the star" — this indeed is not "what men call love." But is it therefore something less, even though at times "a mortal image" may be mistaken for what can only be eternal? Is one who is satisfied with human love necessarily wiser than one who is like the

> silver moth fresh from the grave

> Which is its cradle — ever from below
> Aspiring like one who loves too fair, too far,
> To be consumed within the purest glow

> Of one serene and unapproachèd star,
> As if it were a lamp of earthly light,
> Unconscious, as some human lovers are,

> Itself how low, how high beyond all height
> The heaven where it would perish! [45]

The soul that seeks only human and personal love "builds thereby," as Shelley truly says, "a sepulchre for its eternity"; for such love never leads beyond itself. Only as its object is felt to participate in the divine perfection does love become the "Star above the Storm" of life, which

> Beacons from the abode where the Eternal are;

from that Heaven whence the Heaven which is beheld by human eyes is seen as only

> a globe of dew,
> Filling in the morning new
> Some eyed flower whose young leaves waken
> On an unimagined world:
> Constellated suns unshaken,
> Orbits measureless, are furled
> In that frail and fading sphere,
> With ten millions gathered there,
> To tremble, gleam, and disappear; [46]

---

[45] *The Woodman and the Nightingale*, ll. 24–32.   [46] *Ode to Heaven*, ll. 46–54.

where

> all things seem only one
> In the universal sun [47]

and where, in the ocean of Being, the soul becomes

> The wave that died the death which lovers love,
> Living in what it sought . . . [48]

It should be said, finally, that Shelley's love, although it seeks to transcend personality, is not indifferent to persons. One loves the object not less, but more, through loving the ideal. One cannot be the disciple of Christ who listens to the claims of the love of persons as persons; but through the love of Christ (the love, that is, of the ideal, the perfect, the absolute Good) one comes to love persons for the Christ within them; and this is the only love that is worthy of the name. "Inasmuch as ye have done it unto one of the least of these my brethren, ye have done it unto me." [49] And it may be added that this love, according to the Christian teaching, does not come through reason or intellectual discipline, but through immediate inspiration; and is not reserved for philosophers and scholars and men of letters. Christianity teaches that "the real Good . . . is open to all; and the more a man has of it, the more he gives to others. That Good is the love of God, and through the love of God the love of man. These are old phrases, but their sense is not old; rather it is always new, for it is eternal. Now, as of old, in the midst of science, of business, of invention, of the multifarious din and hurry and confusion of the world, God may be directly perceived and known. But to know Him is to love Him, and to love Him is to love his creatures, and most of all our fellow-men, to whom we are nearest and most akin, and with and by whom we needs must live." [50]

It has been charged against Shelley as a weakness that he never attained "the last and highest mystical state," that he was not able

---

[47] *To Jane: The Invitation*, ll. 68–69.

[48] *The Boat on the Serchio*, ll. 108–09. Cf. the last line of *The Light of Asia*: "The dewdrop slips into the shining sea."

[49] Matthew 25:40.

[50] G. Lowes Dickinson, *A Modern Symposium*, p. 147. The passage from which these sentences are quoted is not altogether a statement of the writer's own creed, but of his conception of Christianity. It is perhaps worth noting that Dickinson was a passionate admirer of Shelley.

to rest in the contemplation of the Beatific Vision. Rather it should be said that he could never rest while the cry of human suffering and sin was ringing in his ears; that in no heaven of Ideas would he ever have been able happily to forget the miseries of men. From the time of *Queen Mab* to that of *The Triumph of Life,* the wrong and pain and evil of human existence weighed always more heavily upon his spirit. It is characteristic that in the *Essay on Christianity* he chooses for comment these words of Christ: "The spirit of the Lord is upon me, because he hath chosen me to preach the gospel to the poor: He hath sent me to heal the broken-hearted, to preach delivery to the captives and recovery of sight to the blind, and to set at liberty them that are bruised." [51] On this text Shelley speaks in part as follows:

The only perfect and genuine republic is that which comprehends every living being. . . . I love my country; I love the city in which I was born, my parents, my wife, and the children of my care; and to this city, this woman, and this nation, it is incumbent upon me to do all the benefit in my power. To what do these distinctions point, but to an indirect denial of the duty which humanity imposes on you, of doing every possible good to every individual, under whatever denomination he may be comprehended, to whom you have the power of doing it? You ought to love all mankind; nay, every individual of mankind. You ought not to love the individuals of your domestic circle less, but to love those who exist beyond it more. [52]

But his idealism will not permit him to fall into an indiscriminate humanitarianism. Commenting on the text "Blessed are the pure in heart, for they shall see God," he declares: "Whosoever is no deceiver or destroyer of his fellow men — no liar, no flatterer, no murderer — may walk among his species, deriving, from the communion with all which they contain of beautiful or majestic, some intercourse with the Universal God." [53] Not for men merely as men, nor for women merely as women — as sentient lumps of protoplasm

<hr/>

[51] Shawcross, p. 106. The quotation is from Luke 4:18.

[52] *Ibid.,* p. 108. This sounds something like Godwin; but aside from the fact that Godwin "will not exhort" people to do anything, he never speaks of the *duty* of loving humanity, nor of loving anything; men simply *do* (when they are not prevented) what reason tells them will give the most pleasure to the race. It is interesting to remember also, the fierce assertion in *Queen Mab* that love is not subject to will, any more than is belief. Yet now Shelley says, "You *ought* to love all mankind."

[53] *Ibid.,* p. 90.

having for a certain time certain animal appetites to be satisfied, according to the prevalent conception of social reformers of our own time — is the love to be felt which Shelley preached; but for men and women as they are able to apprehend and to direct their lives toward the realization of ideals of goodness and beauty for which "there is no death nor change"; as there dwells within them "a portion of the Eternal" drawn from "the burning fountain" at the heart of "the living world"; as their "high hope and unextinct desire" may be "the instrument to work" the "will divine." Not sense nor reason nor "any earthly thing" but the "awful Loveliness" of the Supreme Good bound Shelley "To fear himself, and love all humankind." And this I take to be the essential quality of that love which was preached by One whom Shelley reverenced above all men.

And such a love lies at the heart of the ideal of sacrifice, which is perhaps the essential article in the ethical creed of Christianity. And this ideal is also Shelley's. Gilbert Murray has rightly said that "almost the only great English poet who was really inspired by the ideals commonly called Christian, and built his poetry largely out of them, was Shelley." [54] As hate and selfishness are in his eyes the deadliest of sins and the greatest source of evil in human life, so love and sacrifice are the noblest virtues, and offer the surest salvation. The faith in the supreme efficacy of sacrifice for the sake of an ideal is the power, above all others, that animates *The Revolt of Islam* and makes it, with all its faults, a great and noble poem. And nowhere in English poetry has this faith been given such consummate expression as in *Prometheus Unbound*. That mysterious paradox of self-realization through self-sacrifice which is the core of Christianity, if not of all religion, is the dominant theme of Shelley's greatest poem, as it is the central principle of his whole ethical code.

> To suffer woes which Hope thinks infinite;
> To forgive wrongs darker than death or night;
> To defy Power, which seems omnipotent;
> To love, and bear; to hope till Hope creates
> From its own wreck the thing it contemplates;

[54] Gilbert Murray, *The Classical Tradition in Poetry* (Harvard University Press, 1927), p. 198.

> Neither to change, nor falter, nor repent;
> This, like thy glory, Titan, is to be
> Good, great and joyous, beautiful and free;
> This is alone Life, Joy, Empire, and Victory.[55]

But this is also the death of the personal self, the absolute surrender of all that most men live for, in the service of the highest Good. Here is no spirit of rebellion or self-assertion, save as the worship of the ideal commands rebellion against the tyranny of the actual, as the service of God demands defiance of the decrees of Mammon, of the evil Power which seems omnipotent in this world. This is the teaching with which the Christ always sends forth his disciples to bring light into the darkness of human life. And it is the teaching with which Shelley's spirit went forth in a "flaming robe of verse" to attempt the salvation of a suffering humanity.

"Most vain all hope but love" [56] — this is the first and the last of Shelley's religion. This is his creed as a poet and as a man. This is the source of his worship not only of Christ, but of Plato and of Dante —

> Of him who from the lowest depths of hell,
> Through every paradise and through all glory,
> Love led serene, and who returned to tell
>
> The words of hate and awe; the wondrous story
> How all things are transfigured except Love;[57]

this is

> that best philosophy, whose taste
> Makes this cold common hell, our life, a doom
> As glorious as a fiery martyrdom;[58]

this is that Liberty which is to regenerate human society:

> Thou art Love — the rich have kissed
> Thy feet, and like him following Christ,
> Give their substance to the free,
> And through the rough world follow thee;[59]

this is the inspiration of all true heroism, like that

> Of one who gave his enemy
> His plank, then plunged aside to die.[60]

[55] *Prometheus Unbound*, IV, ll. 570–78.   [56] *Ibid.*, I, l. 808.
[57] *The Triumph of Life*, ll. 472–76.   [58] *Epipsychidion*, ll. 213–15.
[59] *The Mask of Anarchy*, lxi.   [60] *Prometheus Unbound*, I, ll. 721–22.

This is that divine mystery that impels God to sacrifice himself for men, to tread "the thorns of death and shame," to endure the utmost of human suffering — "Torture and solitude, Scorn and despair," [61] and, worst of all, the experience of that apparent fact, which partial love only makes known, and which only perfect Love makes known to be illusion, that such a sacrifice is always for the most part vain, or worse, and that

> those who do endure
> Deep wrongs for man, and scorn, and chains, but heap
> Thousandfold torment on themselves and him —[62]

and through that suffering, according to the Ultimate Law, to compel the world to an ever greater measure of perfection.

And from this Love, burning in Shelley's "heart of hearts," comes forth the poetry which, like Love itself,

> from its awful throne of patient power
> In the wise heart, from the last giddy hour
> Of dread endurance, from the slippery, steep,
> And narrow verge of crag-like agony, springs
> And folds over the world its healing wings.[63]

[61] *Ibid.*, I, ll. 14–15.   [62] *Ibid.*, I, ll. 594–96.   [63] *Ibid.*, IV, ll. 557–61.

EPILOGUE

AT THE beginning of this study I asked the reader to grant, for the time being, the assumption that Shelley possessed a brilliant mind and a noble character. Concerning his mental ability, I have nothing more to say. If the preceding discussions have not demonstrated his capacity for subtle and profound, if not systematic, thinking, then any further statement is futile. But of his character something still needs to be said; and I now propose to show that the admiration, verging on idolatry, which I myself feel for Shelley, and which I have been at no pains to conceal, was also felt by most of those persons who knew him most intimately.

Nor, otherwise, would the study be complete. When a man sets himself up as a teacher of moral truth, we not only may but ought to demand, making due allowance for human fallibility, that his life shall exemplify his teachings and his actions accord with his principles. And when this demand has been satisfied, we must still ask whether his character and actions have been such as to permit us to infer that those principles have a beneficent effect upon human life. If a man, in attempting to live up to the ideals he urges upon other men, and to act upon the beliefs he professes to hold, lives a useful and brave and unselfish life, he thereby claims from the world, in the strongest possible manner, serious consideration in regard to the value of those ideals and the truth of those beliefs.

It is a singular fact, in view of the conception of Shelley's character which seems generally to prevail, that the feeling with which the poet was regarded by almost all those who knew him most intimately was one of admiration and affection; and that it remained for the malice of the "literary prostitutes" [1] who wrote for the reviews, the self-righteousness of the Victorians, [2] and the ignorance

[1] As Shelley justly called them in the Preface to *Adonais*.
[2] H. S. Salt in *Percy Bysshe Shelley : Poet and Pioneer* (New York, 1896), p. 150, quotes Pecksniff in comparison with Arnold's essay. The identity of tone is startling.

and conceit of twentieth-century men of letters to picture him as
a prig, a pedant, and a blackguard, shallow, selfish, fickle, heartless,
and contemptibly prone to self-pity. Even Hogg and Peacock, with
whatever young enthusiasms they may once have possessed forty
years behind them, and with respectable reputations to uphold,
never venture to sit in judgment on Shelley, however much they
may patronize him. Is it the part of justice or wisdom to accept
the casual disparagement of armchair critics of later generations,
while rejecting the testimony of those who knew him and lived
with him from day to day?

And before presenting that testimony I will offer one more
comment. In the *Essay on Christianity* Shelley writes concerning the
character of Christ: "The rule of criticism to be adopted in judging
of the life, actions, and words of a man who has acted any con-
spicuous part in the revolutions of the world, should not be narrow.
We ought to form a general image of his character and of his doctrines, and refer to this whole the distinct portions of actions and
speech by which they are diversified." [3] In Shelley's own case,
unfortunately, the "general image" which has somehow got itself
impressed on the minds of most critics is, I believe, altogether inac-
curate. We are still haunted by that ghostly vision of an ineffectual
angel which Arnold conjured up so long ago. We shall never
understand the poet and his work until we lay aside the "poor, poor
Shelley" conception. The popular view, apparently held by ninety-
nine out of every hundred presumably educated persons, that Shelley remained all his life a weak, morbid, introspective, hypersensi-
tive, persecuted, defense-mechanized, and escape-complexed child,
I do not hesitate to characterize as pure humbug. [4]

[3] Shawcross, p. 102. The whole passage is worth reading.
[4] The most extreme statement of this view which I have yet encountered is *Percy
Bysshe Shelley : An Introduction to the Study of Character*, by T. V. Moore.
According to this person, the "dominant drive" of Shelley's life was his "father-
complex." All his actions and writings — or most of them, at any rate — were
inspired by hatred of his father, and were "compensations" for imagined wrongs
and sufferings. Thus the Tyrant of *The Revolt of Islam*, Jupiter, and Count Cenci,
are all pictures of Timothy Shelley as his son saw him; while Shelley himself
appears as Laon, Prometheus, and Giacomo, as well as Lionel *and* Rosalind! In
The Revolt of Islam, "Shelley pictures how he would have suffered and deserved
sympathy had he fallen into his father's hands" (page 26); in *Prometheus Unbound*
"Shelley pictures his final triumph over his own father who drove him from home
and was unmerciful and unrelenting to the end" (page 28); "*The Cenci* shows

From the records we have of Shelley's life between the days at Eton and his estrangement from Harriet four years later, at the age of twenty-two, there is only one picture that can be legitimately drawn: the picture of a youth of extraordinary high spirits, gaiety, confidence, and unbounded energy. Mr. Gribble thinks that at Oxford he was "one of the rowdiest men in a rather rowdy college" [5] (the adjective, I suppose, implying a tendency to get into trouble, institute rebellion, and make life generally miserable for his immediate superiors); and it is altogether probable. Life was a mess, to be sure, full of stupidity, injustice, and thoroughly unpleasant things and people; and the obvious duty of every decent person was to aid in sweeping these from the face of the earth. But one might get a good deal of fun out of the sweeping. Picture him writing two Gothic romances before he was eighteen; publishing a small volume of poems soon after, entitled, with reference to "the mad washerwoman who had attempted to stab King George III with a carving knife," *The Posthumous Fragments of Margaret Nicholson,* concerning one of which (written by "a friend's mistress") he writes that "the *Epithalamium* will make it sell like wildfire";[6] entrapping innocent clergymen into correspondence, and

that unconsciously Shelley would have liked to kill his father" (pages 28–29); he "paid a visit to Ireland and took up the cause of Catholic emancipation because Ireland, down-trodden by existing authority, appealed to the mechanisms of his character" (page 35); and so forth. His pessimism must have been due to his cultivation of the same complex and to his seeking compensations for his troubles instead of overcoming the faults in himself which were of course responsible, since nine hundred out of a thousand married women in New York City declared themselves, in answer to a questionnaire, to be perfectly happy — and: "It would seem from this analysis that there is no warrant for the pessimistic view that happiness is not attainable" (page 60). Such stuff, of course, could only be written by a person whose intellect has been corrupted by the study of modern psychology — that parasite upon the Tree of Life, the "dismal science" of these days — and who is "compensating" for his own deficiencies by "analyzing" the characters of those who *lived* and were *men.* But only the prevalence of the "poor, poor Shelley" myth makes such unmitigated drivel possible at all.

[5] *The Romantic Life of Shelley,* p. 50.

[6] The poem is entitled *Fragment Supposed to Be an Epithalamium of Francis Ravaillac and Charlotte Corday.* Francis begins the closing symphony thus:

> Soft, my dearest angel, stay,
> Oh! you suck my soul away;
> Suck on, suck on, I glow, I glow!

and so on. In the same letter Shelley writes that the ending was omitted from some copies. "That which I sent to my Mother of course did not contain it." Later he

then falling upon them with fiercely skeptical arguments; writing *The Necessity of Atheism* and sending copies to bishops and heads of colleges with the signature "Jeremiah Stukeley"; defying the threats of his father, whom he calls (in letters to Hogg) "the Old Boy" and "the Honourable Member" (of Parliament); planning to use Harriet Westbrook "for one of the crushers" of Intolerance, and to "tame" Eliza for the same purpose; yielding to a school-girl's plea to run off with her and marry her; going to Ireland to free the inhabitants, making speeches, writing long pamphlets, trying to establish associations of philanthropists; joining an undertaking to reclaim land on the coast of Wales; publishing tracts in defense of the freedom of the press; starting subscriptions to help the victims of governmental tyranny; publishing, at the age of twenty-one, a 2300-line poem, with notes "long, philosophical, and anti-Christian" to "catch the aristocrats," who "will not read it, but their sons and daughters may;" [7] all the while reading and studying incessantly — politics, philosophy, natural science, general litera-ture; talking of these things when he had an opportunity and writing letters about them when he did not; — picture all this, and then bid farewell forever to that Rousseauistic wraith which, not only in the popular mind but in the minds of many men of letters as well, from Dowden and Arnold onward, has for half a century concealed "the real Shelley."

If there is one point of view that will remove most of the apparent contradictions in Shelley's life and character, and make him a living, credible human being, it is this. To take but one example, the letters to Elizabeth Hitchener, if judged from what may be called the traditional point of view, make the writer appear self-centered, if not morbid, and affected, if not priggish. But in view of the facts I have just presented, they appear simply as the bubblings-over of Shelley's intellectual energy. He had discovered, not long since, that he possessed a mind; and these letters reveal an altogether healthy, if uncommon, curiosity as to its workings. Watching his mental wheels go around was almost as much fun

adds: "Of course to my Father, Peg is a profound secret." See *Letters*, I, 15–16. This is a side of Shelley which has been usually overlooked.

[7] *Letters*, I, 394.

as sailing paper boats. He wanted to take his mind apart, and see what made it go. The letters to Miss Hitchener are the record of his attempts. And the same principle can be applied to much of his early poetry.

I do not mean to admit for a moment that Shelley during these years was not sensitive, serious, and high-minded, or that his general course of action was governed by other than altruistic motives. He was fighting for great causes, and he knew it. It is not for mere amusement that people write poems like *Queen Mab,* which, for all its intellectual and artistic shortcomings, is an astonishing achievement for a boy of twenty.[8] But still, he was a "happy warrior"; and I believe that the depression of his last years was chiefly due to the feeling that he had been rejected by those whom he had aspired to serve, that he no longer had anything to fight for, that the splendid powers which even *his* modesty could not keep him in ignorance of, had been deprived of their legitimate end, and causelessly condemned to "rust unburnished, not to shine in use." For such powers he certainly possessed. He need have felt no inferiority to Byron, although *power* is usually held to be one of Byron's great merits. The very quantity of his work bears witness to the volcanic energy of his genius. He wrote the five thousand lines of *The Revolt of Islam* in six months. He wrote the twenty-four hundred lines of *The Cenci* in two. He wrote the seventy-eight *ottava rima* stanzas of *The Witch of Atlas* in three days — surely one of the most extraordinary displays of creative power in the history of English poetry. Besides his writing, he read the masterpieces of seven languages. Besides his literary labors, he managed to a great extent the financial affairs of Godwin and Leigh Hunt (and if they had taken his advice as readily as they took his money, they would have been the better for it), and, what was still more difficult, the personal affairs of Clare Clairmont. He was also the one person who was ever able to manage Byron; and we even find him arranging (on request) various mat-

[8] It was not an empty achievement, either; for during the troubled decades following the poet's death, it went through edition after edition, despite a series of government prosecutions. It did not "catch the aristocrats"; but it caught the attention of many a poor laborer, who was not bothered by logical contradictions, and felt only the flaming hatred of cruelty and oppression.

ters between his noble friend and the Countess Guiccioli. In the rare moments when his slender shoulders were not overburdened by the troubles of his friends, he was likely to engage in such projects as the building of what would have been the first steamboat on the Mediterranean; and he was bitterly disappointed when his partners abandoned the enterprise. And all this, while he was in constant poor health, subject to frequent attacks of severe physical pain!

He certainly experienced periods of profound depression, as is often the case with sensitive and noble natures.[9] But he did himself an injustice in speaking of himself as "a tired child," a "frail form," "a phantom among men." Such passages, it is true, indicate a measure of weakness. But he was weak only in thinking himself weak when, as his own actions and the testimony of his acquaintances make clear beyond a doubt, he possessed remarkable courage, vigor, and strength of will. Even in the poems themselves, his confessions of weakness are often followed by magnificent outbursts of confidence in himself and his high calling. He cries in the *Ode to the West Wind*, "I fall upon the thorns of life! I bleed!" But he rises in the next stanza to his own Promethean heights, with a prayer so passionate in its faith that the Power he serves will not fail him, that it is almost a command:

> Scatter, as from an unextinguished hearth
> Ashes and sparks, my words among mankind!

And in *Adonais* he turns away from picturing his own weakness to hurl a searing rebuke at the reviewer whom he mistakenly believed to be responsible for the death of Keats,[10] and then passes at once to

[9] Cf. Newman, *Oxford Sermons*, p. 322: "Moreover, it is a question whether that strange and painful feeling of unreality, which religious men experience from time to time, when nothing seems true, or good, or right, or profitable, when Faith seems a name, and duty a mockery, and all endeavors to do right, absurd and hopeless, and all things forlorn and dreary, as if religion were wiped out from the world, may not be the direct effect of the temporary obscuration of some master vision, which unconsciously supplies the mind with spiritual life and peace."

[10] Some of Keats's admirers, sharing the common but unfortunate inability to praise one writer without aspersing another, speak as if they thought that Shelley invented this story. He received it, of course, from Keats's own friends and associates; and it is definitely implied in the inscription which was put on Keats's gravestone. Perhaps, even so, Shelley ought to have known Keats better than to accept such an account. But it is to be remembered that Keats deliberately avoided the

the most sublime expression that English poetry has yet to offer of an unquenchable "faith and hope in something good," an unwavering trust that beyond "the shadow of our night," "Heaven's light forever shines."

But enough of my own words: only, the reader is not to think that the purity and goodness so strongly emphasized in the following statements by a few of Shelley's friends imply any lack of strength or manliness. Trelawny himself says of Shelley that "his softness of expression and mild bearing were deceptive, as you soon found out he was a resolute, self-sustaining man." [11] "He was thoroughly masculine in act, prompt in reply, and bold in his opinions." [12] Indeed, had there been in his character any weakness of that kind which the world has been in the habit of ascribing to him, he would hardly have won the admiration of Trelawny, the rugged, untamed adventurer, in whose tempestuous life of nearly ninety years the few months of his friendship with Shelley remained in his own eyes the one supreme and hallowing experience, and who provided that his own ashes should be buried beside those of his friend. A few of many passages from the *Records* will suffice.

His young face looked as innocent of all guile as a cherub, and so he was. Simple, frank, and confiding, any one would trust him at sight. His mild earnest manners won all hearts, gentle and simple. There was no limit to his generosity and self-negation to serve a friend, and he considered all the poor and oppressed as his friends. [13]

When attacked, he neither fled, nor stood at bay, nor altered his course, but calmly went on with heart and mind intent on elevating his species. Whilst men tried to force him down to their level, he toiled to draw their minds upwards. [14]

To form a just idea of his poetry, you should have witnessed his daily life: his words and actions best illustrated his writings. If his glorious conception of Gods and men constituted an atheist, I am afraid all that listened were little better . . . The cynic Byron acknowledged him to be the best and ablest man he had ever known. The truth was, Shelley loved everything better than himself. Self-preservation is, they say, the first law of nature, with him it was the last; and the only pain he ever

intimacy which Shelley desired, because he feared Shelley's influence upon his poetry. See his letter to Benjamin Bailey, October 8, 1817.

[11] *Records*, p. 149.   [12] *Ibid.*, p. 150.
[13] *Ibid.*, p. 109.   [14] *Ibid.*, p. 67.

gave his friends arose from the utter indifference with which he treated everything concerning himself.[15]

Trelawny records, also, some of the praise given to Shelley by Byron, which is repeated in Byron's letters — such praise, it is safe to say, as he gave to no other man whom he had ever known. Every biographer who saw the two men together has commented on the respect and deference that Byron invariably showed his friend. In part, no doubt, he sympathized with Shelley for being an outcast like himself, and a rebel against political tyranny and social cant. On one occasion he told Trelawny: "Today I had another letter warning me against the Snake (Shelley). He, alone, in this age of humbug, dares stem the current, as he did today the flooded Arno in his skiff, although I could not see that he made any progress." [16] But Byron admired other qualities in Shelley besides his courage and independence. A few months before Shelley's death he wrote to Moore: "As to poor Shelley, who is another bugbear to you and the world, he is, to my knowledge, the *least* selfish and mildest of men — a man who has made more sacrifices of his fortunes and feelings for others than any I ever heard of." [17] To the same correspondent he wrote after Shelley's death: "There is thus another man gone, about whom the world was ill-naturedly, and ignorantly, and brutally mistaken. It will perhaps do him justice *now*, when he can be no better for it." [18] And to Murray he declared: "You were all brutally mistaken about Shelley, who was, without exception, the *best* and least selfish man I ever knew. I never knew one who was not a beast in comparison." [19] And elsewhere he offers the same unmeasured tribute: "He was the most gentle, most amiable, and least worldly-minded person I ever met; full of delicacy, disinterested beyond all other men, and possessing a degree of genius, joined to simplicity, as rare as it is admirable. He had formed to himself a *beau ideal* of all that is fine, high-minded,

[15] *Ibid.*, p. 60.
[16] *Ibid.*, p. 28. "The Snake" was one of Byron's nicknames for Shelley. It had its origin in the reference of Mephistopheles, in Goethe's *Faust*, to "my aunt, the renowned Snake," i.e., the serpent who tempted Eve.
[17] *Letters and Journals*, VI, 32–33 (March 4, 1822).
[18] *Ibid.*, p. 99 (August 8, 1822).
[19] *Ibid.*, (August 3, 1822).

and noble; and he acted up to this ideal, even to the very letter." [20]
It is hard to see how praise could go much farther; and, whatever
may be thought of Byron's truthfulness in general, in this case,
certainly, he could have had no other motive than to do justice
to a man whom he had been proud to know.

Nor can any charge of self-interest or prejudice impeach the evidence of Horace Smith, the London banker and man of letters, a
man as different from Byron as possible, yet quite as unrestrained
in his admiration of Shelley. Smith was a man of the world; he
moved in the best society; but Shelley remained for him to the end
a unique and radiant figure. Here is his first impression of the poet.
"Manifest as it was that his preoccupied mind had no thought to
spare for the modish adjustment of his fashionably made clothes, it
was impossible to doubt, even for a moment, that you were gazing
upon a *gentleman*; a first impression which subsequent observation
never failed to confirm, even in the most exalted acceptation of
the term, as indicating all that is gentle, generous, accomplished,
brave." [21] And this is Smith's account of Shelley's way of life.

Denying himself all luxuries, and scarcely ever tasting any other food
than bread, vegetables, and water, this good samaritan wandered to the
various prisons for debtors, and to the obscure haunts of poverty, to seek
deserving objects for the exercise of his unwearied and lavish charity.
. . . I can speak with certainty of his having bestowed upwards of five
thousand pounds on eminent and deserving men of letters, gracing his
munificence by the delicacy and tact with which he conferred it. And
this large sum was exclusive of smaller donations to less distinguished
writers, and of his regular alms to miscellaneous claimants and established pensioners. . . . No wonder that among such a nation of Mam-
monites as the English, a man so utterly self-denying and unworldly
should be viewed as a sort of *lusus naturae*. No wonder that rich cur-
mudgeons maligned him, for there was a daily beauty in his life which
made theirs ugly. No wonder that the writer of this record, educated in
the sordid school of mercantile life, could hardly trust the evidence of
his senses when he saw this extraordinary being living like the austerest
anchorite, denying himself all the luxuries appropriate to his birth and
station, that he might appropriate his savings to the relief of his fellow-

[20] I do not know the original source of this quotation. It is given by Horace
Smith in his recollections of Shelley (A. H. Beavan, *James and Horace Smith*, p.
177), and by Rossetti in his *Memoir*, p. 61.

[21] *James and Horace Smith*, p. 137.

creatures; and silently showing, for he never made a proclamation of his bounties, that despising riches on his own account, he only valued them so far as they enabled him to minister to the relief of others.[22]

And of his final meeting with the poet, Smith speaks thus:

when I recalled his exquisite genius, his intellectual illumination, his exuberant philanthropy, his total renunciation of self, the courage and grandeur of his soul, combined with a feminine delicacy and purity, and an almost angelic amenity and sweetness, I could almost fancy that I had been listening to a spirit from some higher sphere, who had descended upon earth to inculcate a self-realizing confidence in the lofty destinies of mankind . . .[23]

To Leigh Hunt must go the honor of saying the last word for Shelley. It seems the fashion in the literary world to speak of Hunt patronizingly and disparagingly. Why, I do not know. It is true that he was not a great poet, that he was sometimes guilty of lack of taste, and that he was hopelessly incompetent in worldly affairs. But he was an able critic, he was a fearless defender of civil liberty, and he possessed a measure of sincerity and charity and reverence for true greatness and nobility which perhaps some of those who affect to sit in judgment on him might well seek to imitate. It has been suggested that his praise of Shelley was largely due to the fact that Shelley gave him so much money. But this suggestion can only be the result either of ignorance or of a meanness of spirit so contemptible as to be unworthy of notice. What Leigh Hunt did for Shelley is not the kind of thing that money buys or pays for. Gratitude? Of course he was moved by gratitude — and it is a pity that the world contains so little of gratitude like his! so little willingness to do honor to those to whom it owes a debt! so little readiness to defend, when men despitefully use them and persecute them, those in whom it recognizes a "greatness of mind and nobleness" worthy of reverence and love! There is something not less than heroic in Hunt's devotion to Shelley and to Shelley's memory; a devotion that led him not only to defy the mighty *Quarterly*, not only to court the censure of the public (he had long been in the habit of doing these things), but to offer to break with intimate and admired friends if they ventured to speak in dispraise

[22] *Ibid.*, pp. 169–70.
[23] *Ibid.*, pp. 174–75.

of the friend most dearly beloved.²⁴ After Shelley's death he wrote: "His name is ever a talisman to reconcile me to all men, even his enemies." ²⁵ The statement is not quite true, of course; but it does honor to both Hunt and Shelley.

Hunt's most notable defense of Shelley appeared in the *Examiner*, in response to the vicious and slanderous review of *The Revolt of Islam* in the *Quarterly*,²⁶ in which, "failing in the attempt to refute Mr. Shelley's philosophy, the Reviewers attack his private life." ²⁷

The Reviewer asserts that "he is shamefully dissolute in his conduct." We heard of similar assertions, when we resided in the same house with Mr. Shelley for nearly three months; and how was he living all that time? As much like Plato himself as any of his theories resemble Plato, — or rather still more like a Pythagorean. This was the round of his daily life: — He was up early; breakfasted sparingly; wrote this *Revolt of Islam* all the morning; went out in his boat or into the woods with some Greek author or the *Bible* in his hands; came home to a dinner of vegetables (for he took neither meat nor wine); visited (if necessary) "*The sick and the fatherless*," whom others gave Bibles to and no help; wrote or studied again, or read to his wife and friends the whole evening; took a crust of bread or a glass of whey for supper; and went early to bed . . . We forbear, out of regard for the very bloom of their beauty, to touch upon numberless other charities and generosities which we have known him exercise; but this we must say in general, that we never lived with a man who gave so complete an idea of an ardent and principled aspirant in philosophy as Percy Shelley; and that we believe him, from the bottom of our hearts, to be one of the noblest hearts as well as heads which the world has seen in a long time. We never met in short with a being who came nearer, perhaps so near, to that height

²⁴ In a letter to Shelley dated August 28, 1821, Hunt says of Hazlitt: "if he attacks you again, I have told him in so many words that he must expect me to be his public antagonist." See Thornton Hunt, ed., *The Correspondence of Leigh Hunt* (2 vols., London, 1862), I, 169. On the subject of Hazlitt's dislike for Shelley, Hunt elsewhere asks: "Did Shelley ever cut him up at Godwin's table? Somebody says so, and that this is the reason of Hazlitt's attack. I know that Hazlitt does *pocket* up wrongs in this way, to draw them out again some day or other. He says it is the only pleasure which the friends of his own cause leave him." *Ibid.*, p. 166.

²⁵ *Shelley — Leigh Hunt : How Friendship Made History* (edited by R. Brimley Johnson), p. 346.

²⁶ As a matter of fact, the review was of *Laon and Cythna* (more than a year after it had been withdrawn), and the reviewer made the most of the passages that had been suppressed.

²⁷ *Shelley — Leigh Hunt*, p. 35.

of humanity mentioned in the conclusion of an essay of Lord Bacon's, where he speaks of excess of Charity and of its not being in the power of "man or angel to come in danger by it." [28]

Thirteen years later, in his Preface to *The Mask of Anarchy*, Hunt has not changed his tone.

His patience is the deposit of many impatiences, acting upon an equal measure of understanding and moral taste. His wisdom is the wisdom of a heart overcharged with sensibility, acquiring the profoundest notions of justice from the completest sympathy, and at once taking refuge from its pain, and working out its extremest purposes, in the adoption of a stubborn and loving fortitude which neutralizes resistance. [29]

For if there was ever a man upon earth, of a more spiritual nature than ordinary, partaking of the errors and perturbations of his species, but seeing and working through them with a seraphical purpose of good, such an one was Percy Bysshe Shelley. [30]

What need to quote further, though further quotation would be easy? Here is the testimony of four men who knew Shelley intimately; to three of whom, at least, not the most suspicious person can, and to the fourth of whom only the meanest person will, assign any ulterior motive for telling more than the truth; and who, differing as far as possible in character, were united in the faith that Shelley was the best man they had ever known. I submit that there is no other evidence that can alter in any essential detail the picture that is here given of Shelley's life and character; that this picture is in perfect harmony with the letter and the spirit of his religion as I have presented it; and that his life and work are an enduring challenge to men and women of succeeding generations to make their lives in thought and act as pure and noble as his own.

[28] *Ibid.*, pp. 37–38.   [29] *Ibid.*, pp. 77–78.   [30] *Ibid.*, p. 83.

SELECT BIBLIOGRAPHY

The following bibliography is only a selection from the works consulted in the course of this study. In general, only those items are listed that have a direct and definite bearing on the question of Shelley's religious views. Where I have quoted from works that have only an incidental relation to the subject and are consequently not listed here, I have specified in the note, where there is any possibility of confusion, the edition from which the quotation is made.

I. EDITIONS OF SHELLEY'S WORKS

The Complete Works of Percy Bysshe Shelley, edited by Roger Ingpen and Walter E. Peck. Julian Edition. 10 vols. London, 1926–30.

Shelley's Lost Letters to Harriet, edited by Leslie Hotson. London, 1930.

Shelley : Poems Published in 1820, edited by Arthur M. D. Hughes. Oxford: Clarendon Press, 1910.

The Complete Poetical Works of Percy Bysshe Shelley, edited by Thomas Hutchinson, with an introduction and notes by Benjamin P. Kurtz. Oxford University Press, 1933.

The Letters of Percy Bysshe Shelley, edited by Roger Ingpen. 2 vols. London, 1914.

Shelley's Prose in the Bodleian Manuscript, edited by André H. Koszul. London, 1910.

The Poems of Percy Bysshe Shelley, edited by Charles D. Locock, with an introduction by Arthur Clutton-Brock. 2 vols. London, 1911.

A Philosophical View of Reform, edited by Thomas W. Rolleston. Oxford University Press, 1920.

Adonais, edited by William Michael Rossetti. Oxford: Clarendon Press, 1891.

Prometheus Unbound, edited by Vida D. Scudder. Boston, 1892.

Shelley's Literary and Philosophical Criticism, edited by John Shawcross. London, 1909.

The Prose Works of Percy Bysshe Shelley, edited by Richard Herne Shepherd. 2 vols. London, 1888.

The Best of Shelley, edited by Newman I. White. New York, 1932.

The Complete Poetical Works of Percy Bysshe Shelley, edited by George Edward Woodberry. Cambridge Edition. Boston and New York, 1901.

II. WORKS CHIEFLY BIOGRAPHICAL

HELEN ROSSETTI ANGELI, *Shelley and His Friends in Italy*. London, 1911.

EDWARD DOWDEN, *The Life of Percy Bysshe Shelley*. 2 vols. London, 1886.

FRANCIS GRIBBLE, *The Romantic Life of Shelley and the Sequel*. London, 1911.

THOMAS JEFFERSON HOGG, *The Life of Percy Bysshe Shelley*, edited by Edward Dowden. London and New York, 1906.

J. H. LEIGH HUNT, *Lord Byron and Some of His Contemporaries*. Philadelphia, 1828. (The substance of the section on Shelley was later included in the *Autobiography*.)

ROGER INGPEN, *Shelley in England*. London, 1917.

J. CORDY JEAFFRESON, *The Real Shelley*. 2 vols. London, 1885.

DENIS F. MACCARTHY, *Shelley's Early Life*. London, [1872].

HAROLD J. MASSINGHAM, *The Friend of Shelley*. London, 1930. (A biography of Edward John Trelawny.)

THOMAS MEDWIN, *The Life of Percy Bysshe Shelley*, edited by H. Buxton Forman. Oxford University Press, 1913.

THOMAS LOVE PEACOCK, *Memoirs of Shelley*, edited by F. H. B. Brett-Smith. London, 1909.

WALTER E. PECK, *Shelley : His Life and Work*. 2 vols. New York, 1927.

JANE, LADY SHELLEY, ed., *Shelley Memorials*. 3d edition. London, 1875.

EDWARD JOHN TRELAWNY, *Records of Shelley, Byron, and the Author*. London, 1887.

III. WORKS CHIEFLY CRITICAL OR EXPOSITORY

(Some of these contain much biographical material, notably the studies by Mrs. Campbell, Koszul, Kurtz, and Stovall, and the *Memoir* by Rossetti.)

MATTHEW ARNOLD, *Essays in Criticism*. Second Series. London, 1888.

WALTER BAGEHOT, *Estimations in Criticism*, Vol. I. London, 1908.

MARJORY A. BALD, "The Psychology of Shelley," *Contemporary Review*, CXXI (March, 1927), 359 ff.

——— "Shelley's Mental Progress," *Essays and Studies by Members of the English Association*, XIII (1927), 112 ff.

GEORGE BARNEFIELD, see CARPENTER.

ERNEST SUTHERLAND BATES, *A Study of Shelley's Drama The Cenci*. New York, 1908.

JOSEPH WARREN BEACH, "Latter-Day Critics of Shelley," *Yale Review*, XI, N. S. (1922), 718 ff.

SOPHIE BERNTHSEN, *Der Spinozismus in Shelley's Weltanschauung*. Heidelberg, 1900.

G. S. BOWER, "The Philosophical Element in Shelley," *Journal of Speculative Philosophy*, XIV (1880), 421 ff.

ANDREW C. BRADLEY, *A Miscellany*. London, 1929.

——— *Oxford Lectures on Poetry*. 2d edition. London, 1909.

——— "Notes on Shelley's 'Triumph of Life,' " *Modern Language Review*, IX (1914), 441 ff.

HENRY N. BRAILSFORD, *Shelley, Godwin, and Their Circle*. New York [1913].

GEORGE SIDNEY BRETT, "Shelley's Relation to Berkeley and Drummond," *Studies in English by Members of the University College, Toronto*. University of Toronto Press, 1931.

CLARENCE CRANE BRINTON, *The Political Ideas of the English Romanticists*. Oxford University Press, 1926.

STOPFORD BROOKE, *Naturalism in English Poetry*. New York, 1920.

——— *Studies in Poetry*. New York, 1907.

ROBERT BROWNING, *An Essay on Shelley*, in *Complete Poetical and Dramatic Works*. Cambridge Edition. Boston and New York, 1895.

OLWEN WARD CAMPBELL, *Shelley and the Unromantics*. London, 1924.

EDWARD CARPENTER and GEORGE BARNEFIELD, *The Psychology of the Poet Shelley*. London, 1925.

ANDRÉ CHEVRILLON, *Études anglaises*. Paris, 1901.

ARTHUR CLUTTON-BROCK, *Shelley : The Man and the Poet*. 4th edition. London, 1929.

EDWARD DOWDEN, *Transcripts and Studies*. London, 1888.

ARNOLD EILOART, "Shelley's *The Question*," *Notes and Queries*, CLV (1928), 165 ff.

GEORGE R. ELLIOTT, *The Cycle of Modern Poetry*. Princeton University Press, 1929.

OLIVER ELTON, *A Survey of English Literature, 1780–1830*, Vol. II. New York, [1912].

EDMUND G. GARDNER, "The Mysticism of Shelley," *Catholic World*, LXXXVIII (1908), 145 ff.

RICHARD GARNETT, *Essays of an Ex-Librarian*. London, 1901.

ROBERT S. GARNETT, ed., *Letters about Shelley Interchanged by Three Friends — Edward Dowden, Richard Garnett, and William Michael Rossetti*. New York, 1917.

SOLOMON F. GINGERICH, "The Conception of Beauty in the Works of Shelley, Keats, and Poe," *Essays and Studies in English and Comparative Literature by Members of the English Department of the University of Michigan* (University of Michigan Publications: Language and Literature, Vol. VIII). University of Michigan Press, 1932.

———— *Essays in the Romantic Poets*. New York, 1929.

CARL H. GRABO, *A Newton among Poets*. University of North Carolina Press, 1930.

———— *The Meaning of the Witch of Atlas*. University of North Carolina Press, 1935.

———— *Prometheus Unbound : An Interpretation*. University of North Carolina Press, 1935.

J. DE GRUYTER, "Shelley and Dostoievsky," *English Studies*, IV (1922), 129 ff.

JOHANNA F. C. GUTTELING, *Hellenic Influence on the English Poetry of the Nineteenth Century*. Amsterdam, n. d.

RAYMOND D. HAVENS, "Shelley's Alastor," *Publications of the Modern Language Association*, XLV (1930), 1098 ff.

ARTHUR C. HICKS, "The Place of Christianity in Shelley's Thought." Unpublished Ph. D. thesis, Stanford University, 1932.

ARTHUR M. D. HUGHES, "The Witch of Atlas," *Modern Language Review*, VII (1912), 508 ff.

J. H. LEIGH HUNT, see JOHNSON.

RICHARD H. HUTTON, *Literary Essays*. 3d edition. London, 1908.

ADOLPHUS A. JACK, *Shelley : An Essay*. London, 1904.

R. BRIMLEY JOHNSON, ed., *Shelley — Leigh Hunt : How Friendship Made History*. 2d edition. London, 1929.

ERNEST E. KELLETT, *Suggestions : Literary Essays*. Cambridge University Press, 1923.

CHARLES KINGSLEY, *Literary and General Essays*. London, 1890.

ANDRÉ H. KOSZUL, *La Jeunesse de Shelley*. Paris, 1910.

BENJAMIN P. KURTZ, *The Pursuit of Death*. Oxford University Press, 1933.

DANIEL J. MACDONALD, *The Radicalism of Shelley and Its Sources*. Ph. D. thesis, Catholic University, Washington, D. C., 1912.

SALVADOR DE MADARIAGA, *Shelley and Calderón and Other Essays on English and Spanish Poetry*. London, 1920.

GEORGE L. MARSH, "The Early Reviews of Shelley," *Modern Philology*, XXVII (1929–30), 73 ff.

DAVID MASSON, *Wordsworth, Shelley, Keats*. London, 1874.

THOMAS VERNER MOORE, *Percy Bysshe Shelley, an Introduction to the Study of Character* (Psychological Review Publications. Psychological Monographs, Vol. XXXI, No. 2). Princeton, New Jersey, 1922.

PAUL ELMER MORE, *Shelburne Essays, Seventh Series*. New York, 1910.

GILBERT MURRAY, *The Classical Tradition in Poetry*. Harvard University Press, 1927.

RODEN NOEL, *Essays on Poetry and Poets*. London, 1886.

ALFRED NOYES, *Some Aspects of Modern Poetry*. New York, 1924.

FREDERICK C. PRESCOTT, *Poetry and Myth*. New York, 1927.

ARTHUR QUILLER-COUCH, *Studies in Literature*, Vol. II. New York, 1922.

HELENE RICHTER, "Zu Shelley's philosophischer Weltanschauung," *Englische Studien*, XXX (1901), 224 ff., 383 ff.

JOHN M. ROBERTSON, *New Essays towards a Critical Method*. New York, 1897.

WILLIAM MICHAEL ROSSETTI, "Memoir of Shelley," *The Complete Poetical Works of Percy Bysshe Shelley*, Vol. I. London, 1878.

HENRY S. SALT, *Percy Bysshe Shelley : Poet and Pioneer*. New York, 1896.

GEORGE SANTAYANA, *Winds of Doctrine*. London, 1913.

The Shelley Society's Papers, Part I. London, 1888. The more important of these, with regard to the present study, are the following (the "Inaugural Address" of Stopford Brooke is reprinted in his *Studies in Poetry*, listed above):

Edward Aveling and Eleanor Marx Aveling, "Shelley and Socialism."

Mathilde Blind, "Shelley's View of Nature Contrasted with Darwin's."

H. Buxton Forman, "The Vicissitudes of *Queen Mab*."

——— "Shelley, 'Peterloo,' and *The Mask of Anarchy*."

——— "The Hermit of Marlow, a Chapter in the History of Reform."

——— "*Rosalind and Helen*."

Kineton Parks, "Shelley's Faith."

William Michael Rossetti, "A Study of Shelley's *Prometheus Unbound*, Its Meaning and Personages."

——— "Shelley's *Prometheus Unbound* Considered as a Poem."

Henry Sweet, "Shelley's Nature-Poetry."

John Todhunter, "Notes on *The Triumph of Life*."

GERTRUDE SLAUGHTER, "Percy Bysshe Shelley," *North American Review*, CCXVI (1922), 67 ff.

MELVIN T. SOLVE, *Shelley : His Theory of Poetry*. University of Chicago Press, 1927.

THEODOR SPIRA, *Shelley's geistesgeschichtliche Bedeutung*. Giessen, 1923.

F. MELIAN STAWELL, "Shelley's *Triumph of Life*," *Essays and Studies by Members of the English Association*, V (1914), 104 ff.

LESLIE STEPHEN, *Hours in a Library*, Vol. III. New York, n. d.

FLOYD STOVALL, *Desire and Restraint in Shelley*. Duke University Press, 1931.

ARCHIBALD T. STRONG, *Three Studies in Shelley*. Oxford University Press, 1927.

JOHN ADDINGTON SYMONDS, *Shelley* (English Men of Letters). London, 1884.

ARTHUR SYMONS, *The Romantic Movement in English Poetry*. New York, 1909.

FRANCIS THOMPSON, *Shelley*. London, 1909.

JAMES THOMSON, *Biographical and Critical Studies*. London, 1896.

JOHN TODHUNTER, *A Study of Shelley*. London, 1880.

BENNETT WEAVER, *Toward the Understanding of Shelley* (University of Michigan Publications: Language and Literature, Vol. IX). University of Michigan Press, 1932.

NEWMAN I. WHITE, "Shelley's *Prometheus Unbound*, or Every Man His Own Allegorist," *Publications of the Modern Language Association*, XL (1925), 172 ff.

LILLIAN WINSTANLEY, "Platonism in Shelley," *Essays and Studies by Members of the English Association*, IV (1913), 72 ff.

GEORGE EDWARD WOODBERRY, *Literary Essays*. New York, 1920.

——— *Literary Memoirs of the Nineteenth Century*. New York, 1921.

George Edward Woodberry, *Studies of a Litterateur*. New York, 1921.
———— *The Torch, and Other Lectures and Addresses*. New York, 1920.
William Butler Yeats, *Essays*. London, 1924.

IV. MISCELLANEOUS WORKS

Arthur H. Beaven, *James and Horace Smith*. London, 1909.
Edmund Blunden, *Leigh Hunt and His Circle*. New York, 1930.
Edmund Blunden, ed., *Shelley and Keats as They Struck Their Contemporaries*. London, 1925. (The most important item is Thornton Hunt's "Shelley as I Knew Him," first printed in the *Atlantic Monthly*, February, 1863.)
Lord Byron's Correspondence, edited by John Murray. 2 vols. New York, 1922.
Byron's *Letters and Journals*, edited by Rowland E. Prothero (*The Works of Lord Byron*). 6 vols. New York, 1898–1901.
William Godwin, *Enquiry Concerning Political Justice*. 3d edition. 2 vols. London, 1798.
The Correspondence of Leigh Hunt, edited by Thornton Hunt. 2 vols. London, 1862.
Letters of Edward John Trelawny, edited by H. Buxton Forman. Oxford University Press, 1910.

INDEX